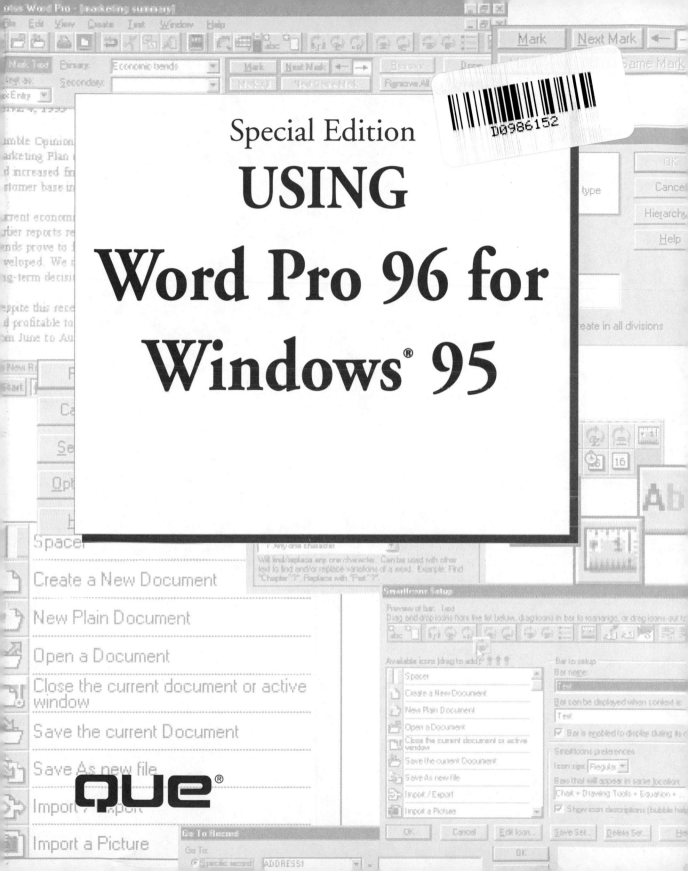

Special Edition

USING

Word Pro 96 for

Windows® 95

que®

Special Edition

USING
Word Pro 96 for
Windows® 95

Written by

Sue Plumley

with

Elaine Marmel and Lisa Bucki

que®

Special Edition Using Word Pro 96 for Windows 95

Library of Congress Catalog Number: 95-71437

ISBN: 0-7897-0149-9

97 96 95   6 5 4 3 2 1

Interpretation of the printing code: The rightmost double-digit number is the year of the book's printing; the rightmost single-digit number, the number of the book's printing. For example, a printing code of 95-1 shows that the first printing of the book occurred in 1995.

Screen reproductions in this book were created using Collage Plus from Inner Media, Inc., Hollis, NH.

Composed in *Stone Serif* and *MCPdigital* by Que Corporation

Credits

President
Roland Elgey

Vice President and Publisher
Marie Butler-Knight

Associate Publisher
Don Roche, Jr.

Editorial Services Director
Elizabeth Keaffaber

Director of Marketing
Lynn E. Zingraf

Managing Editor
Michael Cunningham

Senior Series Editor
Chris Nelson

Acquisitions Editors
Elizabeth South
Nancy Stevenson
Jenny Watson

Product Directors
Lorna Gentry
Dick Rhoades
Rob Tidrow

Production Editor
Lynn Northrup

Copy Editors
Geneil Breeze
Rebecca Mounts
Silvette Pope
Christine Prakel
Paige Widder

Assistant Product Marketing Manager
Kim Margolius

Technical Editors
Brian Ellison
Tish Nye
Lisa A. Warner

Acquisitions Assistant
Tracy M. Williams

Editorial Assistant
Carmen Krikorian

Book Designer
Ruth Harvey

Cover Designer
Dan Armstrong

Production Team
Mary Ann Abramson
Carol Bowers
Georgiana Briggs
Mona Brown
Charlotte Clapp
Terrie Deemer
Louisa Klucznik
Ayanna Lacey
Kevin Laseau
Paula Lowell
Steph Mineart
Brian-Kent Proffitt
SA Springer
Andrew Stone
Jill Tompkins
Susan Van Ness
Mark Walchle
Colleen Williams
Paul Wilson

Indexer
Carol Sheehan

Writing is often an exhausting task, and not only for those of us who write. We'd like to dedicate this book to our families, for the patience and support they provide us.

About the Authors

Sue Plumley owns and operates Humble Opinions, a consulting firm that offers training in popular software programs and network installation and maintenance. Sue's husband Carlos joined her company two years ago as a CNE. Sue is the author of numerous Que books, including *Crystal Clear DOS*, *Crystal Clear Word 6*, and *Microsoft Office Quick Reference*; and co-author of many additional books, including *Using WordPerfect 6 for DOS*, *Using OS/2 2.1*, and *Using Microsoft Office*.

Elaine Marmel is President of Marmel Enterprises, Inc., an organization which specializes in assisting small- to medium-sized businesses computerize their accounting systems. Elaine is the author of *Word for Windows 2 QuickStart* (also translated into Portuguese and Thai), *Quicken 1.0 for Windows Quick Reference*, *Quicken 6 for DOS Quick Reference*, *Using Quicken 2.0 for Windows*, *The PC User's Mac/The Mac User's PC*, *Word for Windows 6 Solutions*, *Word for the Mac Solutions*, and *1-2-3 Release 4 for Windows Solutions*. In addition, Elaine is a contributing editor to the monthly magazines *Inside Timeslips* and *Inside Peachtree for Windows*.

Lisa Bucki has been involved in the computer book business for more than five years. In addition to *Que's Guide to WordPerfect Presentations 3.0 for Windows*, she wrote the *10 Minute Guide to Harvard Graphics*, the *10 Minute Guide to Harvard Graphics for Windows*, and the *One Minute Reference to Windows 3.1*. She co-authored Que's *The Big Basics Book of PCs* and *The Big Basics Book of Excel for Windows 95*. She has contributed chapters dealing with presentation graphics and multimedia for other books, as well as spearheading or developing more than 100 titles during her association with Macmillan.

Acknowledgments

Many, many people had a hand in completing this project over the last year and I'd like to thank them all. Thanks to those first involved with the project: Nancy Stevenson, Chuck Stewart, and Steve Schafer, for their insight, advice, and support. Also, I want to offer my gratitude to my co-authors, Elaine Marmel and Lisa Bucki, for their patience and commitment through the project, with a special thanks to Elaine for her friendship. Also, I appreciate the efforts of Jenny Watson, Rob Tidrow, Elizabeth South, Lynn Northrup, Dick Rhoades, and the efficient and talented editors who contributed to this book. Finally, this book would not be possible without the dedicated people at Lotus; thanks to Eliza Hibbon and Cheryl Fields for their hard work and hospitality.

—Sue Plumley

Thanks to my family and friends for their support and understanding during this project. I'd like to offer a special thanks to Sue Plumley, who did a fine job as lead author on this book—a pleasure working with you, Sue. Production Editor Lynn Northrup also deserves recognition for her help during the production process—she did a great job!

—Elaine Marmel

I want to extend my appreciation to Jenny Watson of Que, who initially invited me to be a part of this project, as well as Elizabeth South, who aptly picked up the thread in Jenny's stead. The co-authors for this project deserve kudos, as well—Elaine Marmel, for providing free and constructive reality checks, and Sue Plumley, for having laid excellent groundwork in shaping the content for this book and making the job easier for the rest of us.

—Lisa Bucki

We'd like to hear from you!

As part of our continuing effort to produce books of the highest possible quality, Que would like to hear your comments. To stay competitive, we *really* want you, as a computer book reader and user, to let us know what you like or dislike most about this book or other Que products.

You can mail comments, ideas, or suggestions for improving future editions to the address below, or send us a fax at (317) 581-4663. For the on-line inclined, Macmillan Computer Publishing has a forum on CompuServe (type **GO QUEBOOKS** at any prompt) through which our staff and authors are available for questions and comments. The address of our Internet site is **http://www.mcp.com** (World Wide Web).

In addition to exploring our forum, please feel free to contact me personally to discuss your opinions of this book: on CompuServe, I'm at 75703,3251 and on the Internet, I'm **lgentry@que.mcp.com**.

Thanks in advance—your comments will help us to continue publishing the best books available on computer topics in today's market.

Lorna Gentry
Product Development Specialist
Que Corporation
201 W. 103rd Street
Indianapolis, Indiana 46290
USA

Contents at a Glance

Getting to Know Word Pro

Accelerating Your WP

Professional Output

Appendixes

Contents

3 Creating and Editing a Document   57

4 Formatting Text   79

5 Formatting the Page   105

6 Exploring Advanced Page Formatting Features   125

7 Using Views and Display Modes   139

II Accelerating Your Word Processing   239

12 Working with SmartMasters   241

13 Using Advanced SmartMasters   253

14 Outlining a Document   267

17 Working with Tables and Charts   325

18 Merging Data   351

III Producing Professional Output with Word Pro   381

19 Using Frames   383

20 Using Advanced Frame Techniques   397

21 Using Draw   423

22 Desktop Publishing with Word Pro   441

23 Understanding Typography 463

24 Making Document Revisions 479

Introduction

by Sue Plumley

Word Pro is a full-featured *WYSIWYG* (what you see is what you get) word processing program that closely rivals any desktop publishing application. Word Pro is a friendly, easy-to-use program that produces high-quality, professional-looking output.

Word Pro enables you to create various documents, from simple letters and memos to complicated reports and newsletters. Easy-to-use features enable you to enter your text, edit it, check the spelling, and print the document quickly and effortlessly. Using some of the more advanced features, you can create tables, borders, headers, indexes, and more. Word Pro has new features that enable you to easily create, manage, and organize long documents.

Word Pro's WYSIWYG feature shows you the page on-screen exactly as it will print. Format a large, bold heading, and it automatically appears; place a clip art picture in a column of text and immediately see how the text flows around the figure. Word Pro's new, improved WYSIWYG feature makes editing and formatting changes even faster and more accurate than before; you can produce a professional-looking document you can be proud of.

Word Pro is more than a word processor; it's also as close to a desktop publishing program as you can get without actually buying one. Many of Word Pro's features support professional output and desktop publishing tasks. One highlight in particular is the Word Pro frame feature. You can create, edit, and format frames that hold text, graphics, or even another frame. Size and move frames, group several together so you can perform one action on the group instead of individually, or add borders, shading, columns, tabs, or margins to the frame. You can even control how the text around the frame flows with the frame.

Another useful feature—SmartMasters—provides preformatted style sheets you can use in your documents. Suppose that you want to create a fax cover sheet, a calendar, or a letterhead for your company. You can use one of Word Pro's SmartMaster style sheets to complete the job quickly. Each SmartMaster contains text formatting, borders or shading, columns, clip art, or other items particular to the document you want to create. All you do is add your own text.

Additionally, Word Pro enables you to modify its SmartMasters and built-in styles to suit your specific needs. You can change fonts and text alignment, create headers, edit graphics, and change any formatting in a SmartMaster to personalize the styles and make your work easier.

Other handy innovations include toolbar buttons that perform common commands at the click of the mouse: spelling and grammar checkers, simple table and column creation, and more. With Word Pro's features, you can become as involved with the application as you want to be; you can use the program to easily create simple letters and memos, or you can produce professional, high-quality newsletters, reports, and more.

Discover What's New in Word Pro

One of the biggest changes in this word processing program is the name—Ami Pro is now Word Pro. Lotus renamed the program to emphasize more of a "team" word processor. Word Pro enables users to better collaborate on and share documents through new features and processes.

 Chapter 1, "What's New in Word Pro?" describes many of the new features in Word Pro. Additionally, new features are described throughout the book and are indicated by the icon shown next to this paragraph.

Some of the exciting changes in Word Pro include:

- *Properties InfoBox*. A new type of dialog box remains on-screen while you work, and offers many options for formatting the page, text, frames, tables, and table cells.

- *Object orientation*. You can control and manipulate objects because of nesting capabilities—inserting one object within another within another—and other new features.

- *Long documents*. Word Pro provides new methods of working in long documents: divisions and sections. You can easily separate long documents into divisions, then divide divisions into individually formatted sections.

- *Importing and exporting power*. Word Pro provides new features that enable you to quickly and easily import or export files for use in your documents.

■ *Modeless bars.* New user-interactive bars for grammar and spell checking, finding and replacing, and so on, make performing these tasks a breeze.

Who Should Use This Book?

Special Edition Using Word Pro 96 for Windows 95 is designed for everyday users: home-office workers, corporate personnel, students, teachers, consultants, and computer-support staff. The small business owner can use Word Pro to produce marketing documents such as flyers, business cards, invoices, and so on; a student can create research reports and personal journals. This book shows you how to use the program in a business context, but the same instructions apply to personal users. Simple guidelines and explanations keep you steadily on course and help you get the most out of Word Pro in the least amount of time.

This book assumes that you know Microsoft Windows 95 but are not familiar with all the Word Pro features.

This book is geared for the beginning, intermediate, and advanced Word Pro user. You can learn how to enter and edit text, mark and review revisions, or program script and use power fields. Whether you're a beginning user who starts with Chapter 1 or an advanced user who references only the topics you need, you can gain not only information but also tips and cautions that can save you enormous time and effort.

Special Edition Using Word Pro 96 for Windows 95 is a comprehensive guide to Word Pro, but no single book can fill all your personal computing needs. Que's *Using Windows 95* is an excellent, user-friendly guide and reference for the Windows environment. If you prefer an introductory text, try Que's *Easy Windows 95* as a basic guide to Windows, using step-by-step instructions and figures.

How This Book Is Organized

Like Word Pro itself, *Special Edition Using Word Pro 96 for Windows 95* attempts to be both amiable and professional. Several authors, skilled in various aspects of the program, have collaborated to bring you a comprehensive learning text.

This book is designed to complement the documentation that comes with the Word Pro program. It includes step-by-step information for beginners, as well as comprehensive coverage and expert advice for intermediate and experienced users. After you become proficient with Word Pro, you can use this book as a desktop reference.

Special Edition Using Word Pro 96 for Windows 95 is divided into the following four parts:

Part I introduces you to Word Pro and to the basics of working with the program. In Chapter 1 you learn what's new in this version of Word Pro. In Chapters 2 and 3 you learn about the Word Pro screen, tools, and basic techniques for entering and editing text. Chapters 4 through 6 explain how to format the text and the page. Chapter 7 describes the various views and modes you can use while working. The final four chapters of Part I explain such features of the program as marking and searching for text, proofreading and printing documents, and customizing the program for your personal use.

Part II shows you how to advance your word processing skills. You learn to use SmartMaster style sheets and paragraph styles in Chapters 12 and 13. Chapter 14 explains the outlining feature. Reference tools are discussed in Chapter 15. You also learn to manage long documents, work with tables, and merge data in Chapters 16 through 18.

Part III introduces you to advanced techniques you can use to create professional output with Word Pro. Chapters 19 and 20 discuss creating and modifying frames for use with text and graphics. Chapter 21 covers Word Pro's drawing program that enables you to enhance your documents for a more expert look. Chapters 22 and 23 cover desktop publishing with Word Pro, describing design and typographical elements to consider when working in Word Pro. Chapter 24 shows you how to use the document revision features to accelerate your work. Chapter 25 shows you how to import to and export from other programs and how to link data to other applications.

Part IV is the reference part of this book and contains the three appendixes. Appendix A discusses custom installations, and Appendix B lists an index of common problems and their solutions. Appendix C is a helpful glossary of Windows 95 terms and computer terminology in general.

Conventions Used in This Book

Certain conventions are used in *Special Edition Using Word Pro 96 for Windows 95* to help you understand the techniques and features described in the text. With Word Pro, you can use both the keyboard and the mouse to choose menu and dialog box items: you can press a letter or you can select an item by clicking it with the mouse. An underline indicates the letter you press (along with the Alt key) to activate menus, choose commands in menus, and choose options in dialog boxes: for example, choose File, Open.

Names of dialog boxes, InfoBoxes, and options within those boxes are written with initial capital letters. All-uppercase letters are used to distinguish file and folder names.

Words or phrases defined for the first time appear in *italics*. Characters you are to type appear in **boldface**. Words and prompts appearing on-screen and text quoted from a figure are printed in special typeface.

Word Pro includes SmartIcons for your convenience. By clicking a SmartIcon, you can execute a command or access a dialog box. Chapters in this book often contain button icons in the margins, indicating which button you can choose to perform a task.

> **Caution**
>
> This paragraph format alerts the reader to hazardous procedures (such as activities that delete files).

> **Tip**
>
> This format suggests easier or alternate methods of executing a procedure, or shortcuts to simplify or speed up processes described in the text.

> **Note**
>
> This format indicates additional information that may help you avoid problems or that you should consider in using the described features.

> ## Troubleshooting
>
> *This poses a common problem in question format...*
>
> ...and then provides guidance on how to find solutions to that problem.

▶ See "Later
Section Title,"
p. xx

Special Edition Using Word Pro 96 for Windows 95 has cross-references in the margin, similar to the one you see here, to help you access related information in other parts of the book.

Right-facing bullets point you to related information in later chapters. Left-facing bullets point you to information in previous chapters.

◀ See "Earlier
Section Title,"
p. xx

Now you're ready to begin your adventure with Word Pro 96 for Windows 95. Good luck!

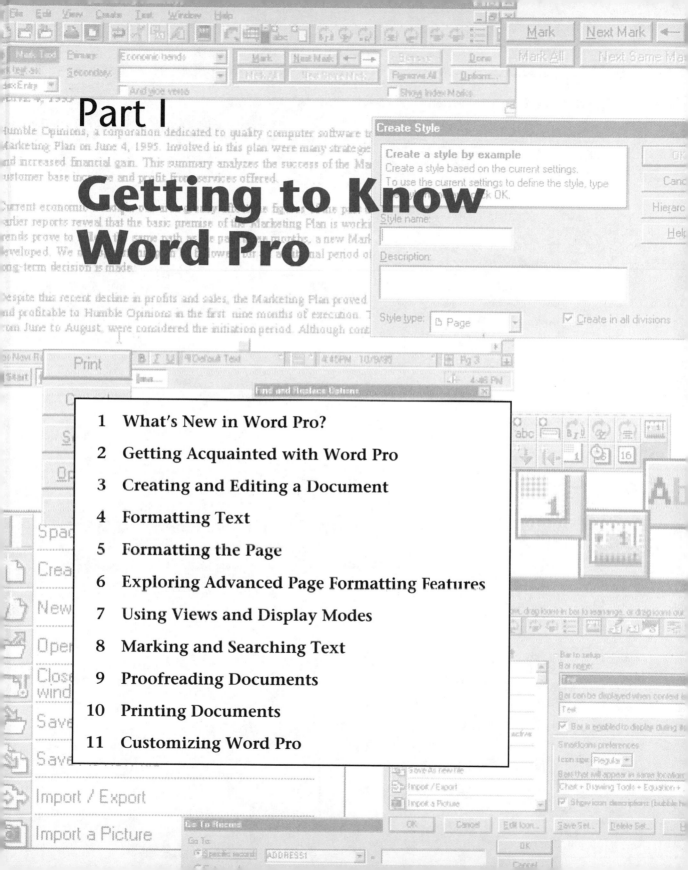

Part I

Getting to Know Word Pro

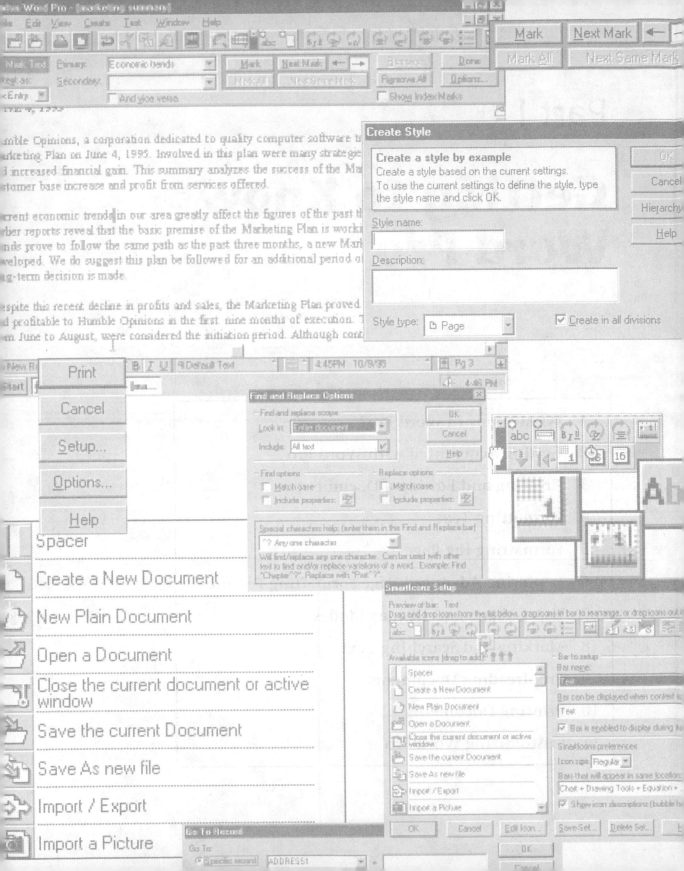

Lotus Word Pro - [marketing summary]

File   Edit   View   Create   Text   Window   Help

| Mark | Next Mark | ← |
| Mark All | Next Same Mark |

Mark Text   Primary: Economic trends   ▼ | Mark | Next Mark | ← → | Remove | Done
Text as: Secondary: ▼ | Remove | Next Same Mark | Remove All | Options...
<Entry ▼   □ And vice versa   □ Show Index Marks

June 4, 1995

Humble Opinions, a corporation dedicated to quality computer software tr
Marketing Plan on June 4, 1995. Involved in this plan were many strategie
and increased financial gain. This summary analyzes the success of the Ma
customer base increase and profit from services offered.

Recent economic trends in our area greatly affect the figures of the past th
Earlier reports reveal that the basic premise of the Marketing Plan is worki
trends prove to follow the same path as the past three months, a new Mark
developed. We do suggest this plan be followed for an additional period of
a long-term decision is made.

Despite this recent decline in profits and sales, the Marketing Plan proved
and profitable to Humble Opinions in the first nine months of execution. T
from June to August, were considered the initiation period. Although cont

Create Style

Create a style by example
Create a style based on the current settings.
To use the current settings to define the style, type
the style name and click OK.

Style name:

Description:

Style type: □ Page   ▼   ☑ Create in all divisions

OK
Cancel
Hierarchy
Help

New R...   Print   B   I   U   ¶ Default Text   4:45PM 10/8/95   Pg 3
Start   Cancel   hxx...   4:46 PM

Print
Cancel
Setup...
Options...
Help

Find and Replace Options

Find and replace scope
Look in: Entire Document   ▼
Include: All text   ▼

OK
Cancel
Help

Find options
□ Match case
□ Include properties

Replace options
□ Match case
□ Include properties

Special characters help: (enter them in the Find and Replace bar)
"? Any one character   ▼
Will find/replace any one character. Can be used with other
text to find and/or replace variations of a word. Example: Find
"Chapter"?", Replace with "Part"?".

Spacer

Create a New Document

New Plain Document

Open a Document

Close the current document or active window

Save the current Document

Save As new file

Import / Export

Import a Picture

Smarticons Setup

Preview of bar: Text
Drag and drop icons from the list below, drag icons in bar to rearrange, or drag icons out

Available icons (drag to add)
Spacer
Create a New Document
New Plain Document
Open a Document
Close the current document or active window
Save the current Document
Save As new file
Import / Export
Import a Picture

Bar to setup
Bar name:
Text

Bar can be displayed when context is
Text

☑ Bar is enabled to display during

Smarticons preferences
Icon size: Regular ▼

Bars that will appear in same location
Chart + Drawing Tools + Equation +

☑ Show icon descriptions (bubble h

OK   Cancel   Edit Icon...   Save Set...   Delete Set...

Go To Record

Go To:
● Specific record   ADDRESS1   ▼   =

OK
Cancel

What's New in Word Pro?

by Sue Plumley

Word Pro 96 for Windows 95 is the next version of Ami Pro 3.11, made for Windows 95. Lotus has changed the name, added hundreds of features, improved hundreds of features more, and created a fantastic new product from the old. Nevertheless, you will recognize many of Ami Pro's features and advantages in this new word processor.

You may wonder why it took so long for Lotus to develop and release Word Pro. After you become familiar with this version, you'll understand. Word Pro is based on a totally new programming code that makes it a powerful and effective word processor. This version's new functionality guarantees congruity, consistency, and ease of use.

The extra time Lotus spent developing Word Pro makes the program simpler to use, intuitive, and packed with time-saving features—Lotus boasts 1,500 new features. New development methods provide more integration within the program, so you can do anything anywhere—for example, you can easily switch between table, frame, and text formatting.

Word Pro is a purely object-oriented application, meaning easier editing and more flexibility within the program. Additionally, the new programming code contributes new editing and formatting features, improved proofreading, easier viewing of documents, and more efficient document revision. Other new features and enhancements include fewer menus, floating icons, parallel columns, and more.

In this chapter, you learn how to:

■ Understand object orientation and live action

■ Use InfoBoxes

■ View new formatting, proofreading, and viewing features

■ Understand new integration features

Understanding the New Structure

The foundation for many of the new features and enhancements to Word Pro lies in the way Word Pro was written. New programming codes enhance the core of the application. In addition to the core engine, supplementary codes are affixed in layers. These layers enable Word Pro to perform more tasks more efficiently.

This version's structure presents a new way of working without changing the graphical interface too much. Word Pro looks somewhat similar to Ami Pro 3 and behaves similarly in many cases; however, the more you use the program, the more you notice the improvements.

A major goal of Word Pro is to present a word processing program that enables both beginning and advanced users to complete their work quickly and easily, creating useful, professional-looking documents. Word Pro attains its goal of consistency and simplicity by presenting an object-oriented application that uses live action to perform tasks and carry out commands.

Understanding Object Orientation

▶ See "Changing Character Formatting," p. 79

Objects in Word Pro can consist of text, frames, tables, clip art, and graphs; and every object has properties. For example, *text properties* include the font or typeface, the size of the text, spacing, tabs, and so on. Due to certain additions to the program, manipulation and modification of objects and their properties are easier and faster than ever before.

One addition that makes assigning properties to objects easy is the InfoBox. An *InfoBox* (similar to a dialog box) presents all properties associated with the object, divided into different tabs, or folders, from which you can choose. Right-clicking an object displays a *quick menu* from which you can choose the properties or InfoBox. You can also access the InfoBox through the menu of the object you are modifying: text, frame, table, and so on. The Frame InfoBox, for example, contains tabs with properties related to the frame: size, lines, margins, and tabs. Figure 1.1 shows the Frame InfoBox.

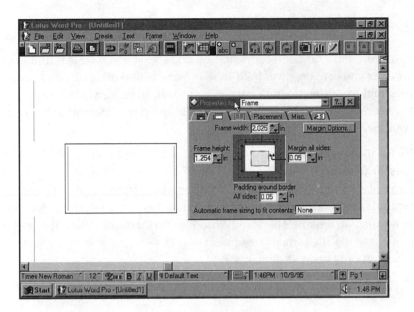

Fig. 1.1
Choose from
various tabs in the
Frame InfoBox to
assign properties
to the frame.

From the InfoBox, you choose the properties you want to apply to the object.
You can choose as few or as many properties as you want. When you're finished formatting an item, you can close the InfoBox or leave it open for future use.

▶ See "Formatting
Frames," p. 398

▶ See "Formatting
Tables," p. 338

Another major benefit of InfoBoxes is that when you open an InfoBox, you
can choose to view and modify text properties and then you can view and
modify frame or table properties, without closing the InfoBox and opening
another. You choose the element you want to modify, and the InfoBox displays the choices for that particular element.

Understanding Live Action

Word Pro's new WYSIWYG (what you see is what you get) augments object
orientation. The program is centered around objects (text objects, frames,
tables, and pictures), which means Word Pro is a more enhanced and efficient application than previous versions of Ami Pro. When you enter text,
for example, each character appears on-screen as you type it; no more waiting
for the cursor and the program to catch up to you as you type.

Similarly, the choices you make in the InfoBoxes immediately appear on-
screen—this feature is called live action. *Live action* means that when you
apply a font, resize a frame, or assign another property from an InfoBox, the
changes take place immediately. The InfoBox remains open but the object
in your document is modified. You can continue to make changes in the
InfoBox, viewing the changes on-screen, until you're happy with the results.

Doing Anything Anywhere

▶ See "Creating Styles," p. 254

With Word Pro's new object orientation and live action, you can find many shortcuts and conveniences built-in that make your work easier and faster. The structure of the program enables you to effortlessly switch between tasks, easily access InfoBoxes, manipulate objects, and create and assign styles that save time.

The InfoBoxes are an ingenious way of organizing and managing object properties. You can access and make use of any object's InfoBox at any time and in any place within the program. In addition to formatting objects, object manipulation is more flexible and functional than ever before, conforming to the *do anything anywhere* basis for Word Pro. Furthermore, Word Pro enables you to save specific formatting options—styles—for use within the same document or in other documents.

> **Note**
>
> You're probably used to paragraph styles that you can apply to the text in your document; paragraph styles give your document a consistent look and generally make your life easier. Word Pro now offers you the same type of styles for frames, tables, table cells, and even the page. Now your life is truly easier!

Accessing InfoBoxes

InfoBoxes present multiple tabs containing properties you can assign to specific objects. When applying properties to the text, for example, you may change the font, size, or color of the text in the InfoBox. As you work, you can choose to modify any of the properties in the InfoBox and view the changes on-screen as you make them.

> **Tip**
>
> To view an object's InfoBox, point to the object and click the right mouse button. From the quick menu, choose the Properties command.

When you're finished with the InfoBox, you can do one of two things: close the box or collapse the box. If you close the box, you can always display it again. Alternately, you can *collapse* the box—hide all the box except its title bar and tabs—and leave it on-screen for later use. Figure 1.2 shows a collapsed InfoBox. Close an InfoBox by clicking the Close button (x) in the title bar.

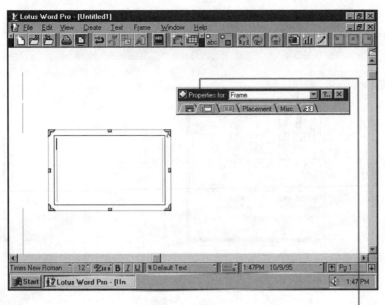

Fig. 1.2
Collapse an
InfoBox for quick
access later in the
work session.

Double-click here to expand or collapse the InfoBox

Nesting Objects

Because of Word Pro's object orientation, you find greater versatility in creating, formatting, editing, and manipulating objects in the program. Word Pro provides a unique feature called object nesting. *Nesting* objects means placing one object within another; for example, you can place a frame within a frame, and even place those frames within another frame, a table, or other object. In other words, you can nest any object in any other object anywhere in the document.

Figure 1.3 illustrates three nested objects: a graphics frame containing a drawing within a table within another frame.

▶ See "Filling a
Frame," p. 391

You may want to nest objects to create a special effect or to illustrate specific elements. You can control the properties of each object you use and therefore better control the look of your document by nesting objects.

Tip

When working with nested objects, you can access the InfoBox and quickly switch between the objects for easy formatting.

Fig. 1.3
Nesting objects gives you more control over the elements in your documents.

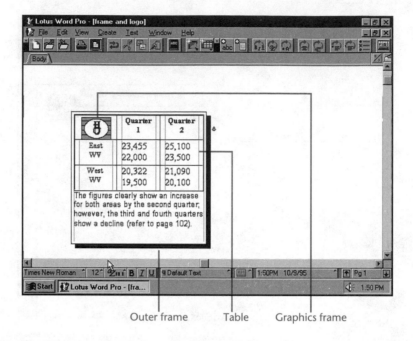

Outer frame   Table   Graphics frame

Using Frame and Text Styles

When formatting text and frames, you can spend a great deal of time creating just the right look for your document. You might apply text formatting such as font, text size, spacing, borders, and alignment to a heading, for example, only to repeat that formatting for every heading in your document.

▶ See "Formatting Frames," p. 398

The same is true for frame formatting. Suppose that you create a specific size frame, with margins, text wrap, shading, and borders for that frame. To create consistency in your document, you want to use that same style of frame elsewhere in the document.

Rather than create heading or frame styles over and over again in your document, you can assign a text or frame style to the formatted object and apply that style with the click of a mouse. In addition to saving time by creating and using styles, you can apply the styles anywhere in your document and at any time. Figure 1.4 illustrates a document with heading styles and frame styles applied.

Tip

Using similar text and frame styles in a document creates unity and consistency, thus making the text easier to read and the document more attractive.

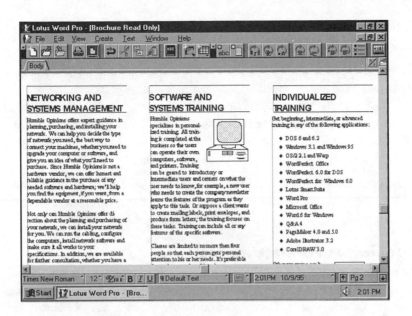

Fig. 1.4
Create a text or
frame style one
time and then
apply the style to
other text and
frames in your
document.

Troubleshooting

I've nested 14 objects and now my computer runs super slow.

The number of objects you can nest is limited by your computer's memory. Try
nesting fewer objects. You can also add RAM to your computer to better handle the
situation.

I changed the font in one of my styles and now all my styles are in that font.

In Word Pro, styles are hierarchical—based on other, similar styles. When you change
a property of one style, however, Word Pro displays a message box asking if you
want to change all styles or just the one. You must have chosen to change all styles.
Choose Edit, Undo and try again.

Viewing Added Features

Lotus revealed an amazing 1,500 new features added to Word Pro. Although
this chapter cannot cover all new features, most are covered somewhere in
this book. This section introduces you to a few of the most interesting new
features that you can use.

One of Word Pro's goals is to make document creation and formatting easier.
Although Word Pro is not strictly a desktop publishing program, many of its

enhancements point in that direction. Document formatting is one area in which Lotus has added new features that help accomplish this goal.

Another area of vast improvement is in proofreading documents. Added features make the jobs of spelling and grammar checking faster and more efficient. Along with proofreading documents, viewing documents has changed in Word Pro, enabling the user to arrange and look at various document types in multiple views. Document revision is a task that Word Pro addresses with more features that are useful and advantageous.

Long document management and organization has always been an arduous task in any word processing program. Word Pro has formulated a system for dealing with long documents more effectively and reasonably.

Looking at Formatting Features

In addition to InfoBoxes—which are a major improvement in formatting text, frames, and tables—Word Pro has included several new ideas to help you format documents. Two new features in particular are CycleKeys and the Format Checker.

CycleKeys

▶ See "Changing Paragraph Formatting," p. 88

CycleKeys are the function keys on your keyboard. In Word Pro, the function keys are assigned formatting commands, and each time you press a key, the selected text is formatted. Each time you press F6, for example, Word Pro cycles the alignment from left to centered to right and then to left again.

Other CycleKeys include F4 to change font size, F3 to cycle fonts, and F2 to cycle styles. Additionally, Word Pro provides cycle SmartIcons for users who prefer to use the mouse, such as the Indent, Numbering, Face, Attribute, Alignment, Bullet, Paragraph, and Point Size cycle SmartIcons.

Tip

Customize CycleKey commands by choosing File, User Setup, CycleKey Setup and selecting the formatting commands you want to assign to the function keys.

Format Checker

In addition to spelling and grammar checkers, Word Pro includes a Format Checker to help you maintain consistency and professionalism in your documents. The Format Checker scans your document to check for such items as inconsistent use of spaces, bulleted lists, acronyms, and so on. Figure 1.5 shows the Format Checker bar.

▶ See "Using the Format Checker," p. 192

Fig. 1.5
Let the Format Checker help you maintain consistency within your documents.

The Format Checker is especially useful when you import a document from another word processor and you want to check for changes that occurred during the conversion process.

The Format Checker bar appears below the SmartIcons when you choose Edit, Check Format. Format check highlights questionable areas of the document and displays the problem in the Format Check bar. You use the bar to correct or ignore the problem and to choose options for format checking.

Reviewing Proofreading Changes

Word Pro now uses a UI (user interface) or modeless bar to represent many features, including the spell checker, grammar checker, find and replace, table of contents, and index features. The bar remains on-screen while you work and can be activated when you need it. In fact, you can display several UI bars on-screen at the same time so you can alternately check the spelling and the grammar, for example.

The Check Spelling feature highlights all questionable words in the document (see fig. 1.6). You can quickly scan the words to see which are misspelled and which are correct names, technical terms, and so on. After you check the spelling in your document and skip questioned words, the spell checker remembers those words and does not highlight them again if you check the spelling in the same document during the same session.

▶ See "Using Spell Check," p. 172

Fig. 1.6

The Check Spelling feature highlights the questionable words so you can quickly recognize the ones that are misspelled.

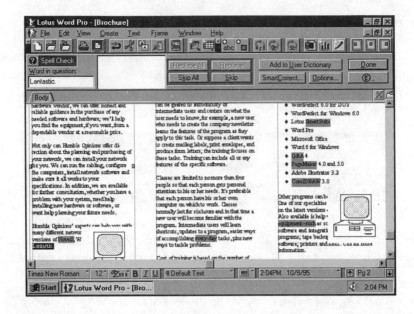

▶ See "Using Grammar Check," p. 185

> **Note**
>
> The Check Grammar feature works in a similar manner as the Check Spelling feature. It's on a UI bar and highlights all questionable grammar in the document.

SmartCorrect is a useful feature that automatically corrects typographical errors as you type. Word Pro lists some common errors, such as *teh* (the) and *thier* (their); however, the handy part of this feature is that you can add your own entries.

▶ See "Editing Text," p. 66

Not only can you add any typos you commonly make, you can add shortcuts that help speed up your work. Instead of typing Word Pro, for example, enter *wp* as the item to replace and *Word Pro* as the replacing item. You can also use shortcuts for personal names, cities, company names, and so on.

Working with Long Documents

▶ See "Using Master Documents," p. 318

Word Pro includes several features that can help you organize and manage long documents. Ami Pro 3 used Master Documents as a method of working with many smaller documents you wanted to combine into one large one, such as many chapters in a book or many sections to a report. Word Pro uses Master Documents, plus division tabs and the Page Gauge, to make long document management much easier.

Word Pro includes features that enable you to create *division tabs*, similar to worksheet tabs used in 1-2-3, in which you can store your document. You can name tabs, place any amount of text and objects in each tab, and even import and link data from other documents and programs to a division tab. Additionally, you can easily create, move, and delete division tabs, and you can collapse and expand division tabs for easier management.

▶ See "Creating and Using Divisions," p. 308

As a bonus, you can divide tabs into sections and then format each section differently. You can change the page orientation, SmartMaster (style sheet), styles, contents, and so on. You can also create tables of contents and indexes across sections and divisions.

Word Pro includes a special feature on the scroll bar for long documents. As you scroll, a small box called the Page Gauge tells you which page you are on. Now you can quickly and easily find the page you want without guessing where you are on the scroll bar.

Figure 1.7 illustrates a set of division tabs for a report and the Page Gauge in use.

Division tabs   Page Gauge

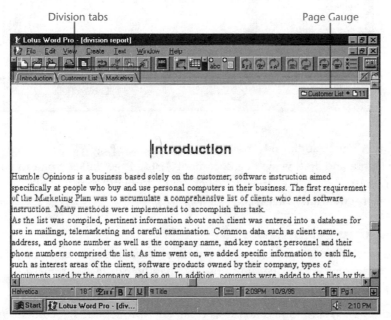

Fig. 1.7
Use division tabs to divide long documents for easier management and better organization.

Viewing Documents

In addition to the regular views and modes in Ami Pro 3, Word Pro has added special views to help you work on your documents. Naturally, you can view one page in various magnifications or you can easily split the screen to view two different areas of one document. Word Pro, however, has enhanced viewing far beyond these basic methods.

In Word Pro, you can view and sort pages using Page Sorter view (see fig. 1.8). In Page Sorter view, you can display any or all of the pages in your document, select and move any page, and otherwise organize your document by viewing all of it on-screen.

Fig. 1.8
Use Page Sorter view to organize your document pages and see any possible layout or design problems.

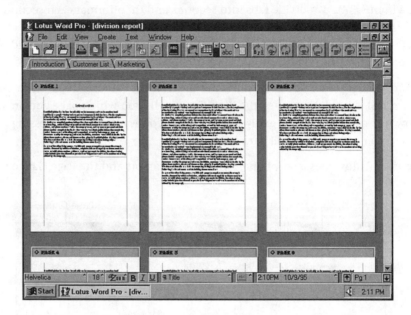

▶ See "Using Views," p. 143

Another handy addition is the PageWalker. Use the PageWalker to view both the layout and draft views of a document. Using PageWalker, you can edit text on one side of the screen while checking formatting on the other side. Figure 1.9 illustrates PageWalker view.

Revising Documents

▶ See "Making Document Revisions," p. 479

This version's document revision features are similar to those in version 3, but with some impressive additions. Two handy features—comment notes and team revisions—make editing a shared document easier.

Comment notes are commentaries you can add throughout a document. A marker in the text shows where the note is and the topic to which it refers. When you open the note, you can read it, add to it, respond to it, or delete it.

Comment notes are perfect for editors or proofreaders to question part of the text without changing the text. Figure 1.10 illustrates a comment.

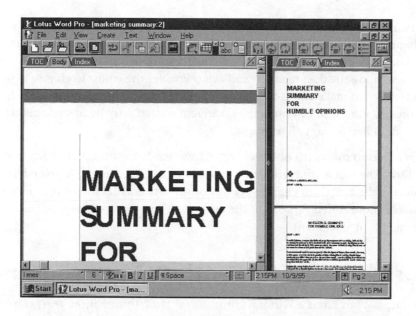

Fig. 1.9
The PageWalker enables you to examine two views of the document at the same time.

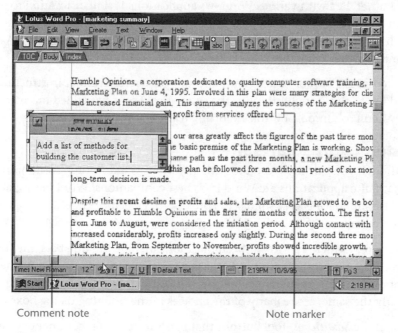

Comment note   Note marker

Fig. 1.10
Use a comment note to enter your thoughts or suggestions without actually changing the document.

In addition to the revision marking and review features of Ami Pro 3, Word Pro has added team revision features—called *TeamReview* and *TeamConsolidate*—to help with revisions made by more than one person.

▶ See "Consoli-
dating Edits,"
p. 502

The more revisions made to a document, the more difficult it is to review them. The team revision features enable one person to control document revisions. Suppose an editor sends a document to two people for review. Before sending the document, TeamReview enables the editor to choose which reviewer can make changes and how elaborate those changes can be. Additionally, the editor can mark the document so that only he or she can make the final decision on all revisions.

Each person makes his or her changes, then sends the document back to the editor. The editor compares and consolidates the documents. As the editor reviews the suggested changes, TeamConsolidate enables the editor to view two or more edited versions of the document and then save or reject changes made to the document.

Using Word Pro with Other Programs

Because Word Pro is a Windows program, sharing information, text, graphics, and other data with various Windows applications is similar to Ami Pro version 3. You can cut, copy, paste, link, and embed elements just as you can with other applications. However, a few enhancements exist for using Word Pro with other programs.

Word Pro is a part of Lotus SmartSuite and is therefore similar in structure and use to those applications in the suite. Also, Lotus has added more power to Word Pro's importing and exporting features.

Using Lotus SmartSuite

Although you can use Word Pro with any other Windows application, the SmartSuite applications are Word Pro's best companions. Word Pro's graphical user interface is very similar to Lotus 1-2-3, Freelance Graphics, Approach, and Organizer.

Common elements between the applications include the title bars, menus, scroll bars, and status bar—but Lotus takes the mutual items a step further. Not only are the menu names similar, but commands on each menu are nearly the same, as are many of the choices in the resulting dialog boxes.

Use of the *SmartIcons*, tool buttons that perform common commands, are nearly the same in the SmartSuite applications. Use of the ruler and status bar are similar as well. Customizing the programs, linking, importing, use of styles—all are the same, as are many other features and commands. Because the SmartSuite applications are similar, you not only can share data between the programs easily, but you can learn each of the applications faster through familiarity.

Increasing Your Importing and Exporting Power

Importing and exporting documents in Word Pro is more powerful and much easier than ever before. Word Pro provides a handy dialog box that enables you to quickly and effortlessly import or export a file. Additionally, you can choose to export or import ASCII characters as well as other file types, and you can choose to automatically check the format of an imported file and correct common conversion errors such as spaces in place of tabs.

▶ See "Importing and Exporting Text and Data Files," p. 513

Additionally, Word Pro makes it easy to import various files and documents into a Master Document for organization and management of your work. Suppose that you're writing a report and you want to use several charts and spreadsheets in the report. You can easily import those files to a Word Pro Master Document that also contains your text files and perhaps even some database files. You thereby create a document that contains all the files you need for easy referencing, printing, reviewing, and revising.

From Here...

Now that you're familiar with some of the new and improved features of this version, you're ready to further explore working with Word Pro. Refer to the following chapters:

- Chapter 2, "Getting Acquainted with Word Pro," presents an overview of the Word Pro screen and shows you how to use the mouse and keyboard, start and exit the program, and use the Help feature.

- Chapter 3, "Creating and Editing a Document," explains how to enter and select text, copy and move text, save a document, close and open documents, and begin a new document.

- Chapter 4, "Formatting Text," shows you how to apply character and paragraph formatting and how to apply paragraph styles.

Chapter 2

Getting Acquainted with Word Pro

by Elaine Marmel

Word Pro is one of the most powerful word processing software packages available for the Windows environment. Word Pro has all the basic features you expect from a word processing program, and it contains a wide variety of advanced features for more complicated operations.

> ### Tip
> Word Pro rewards you for the time you spend getting acquainted. The shortcuts are a great boon, but only if you know how to use them.

With Word Pro's numerous shortcuts, you can easily perform operations quickly and efficiently. The designers of Word Pro thoughtfully created simple efficiencies for users; for any operation you are likely to repeat often, Word Pro seems to offer a shortcut.

In this chapter, you learn how to:

- Review Word Pro features
- Start Word Pro and get around the application
- Understand the Word Pro screen
- Get help

An Overview of Word Pro Features

Word Pro is a word processing program that meets the needs of a variety of professionals in different industries. Word Pro can easily support basic word processing features such as enhancing text with underlined, boldface, or italic type; checking for spelling errors; and checking basic grammar. Word Pro also supports far more sophisticated features such as creating, editing, and publishing documents; automating work by using scripts and glossaries; building tables and outlines; and merging text with graphics.

If you're upgrading from an earlier version of Word Pro (which Lotus Corporation previously called Ami Pro), you can learn about the new features in Word Pro by choosing Help, For Upgraders. The Help menu is discussed later in this chapter; you can also go back to Chapter 1 for an overview of the new features.

The following list contains just a few of the features available in this version of Word Pro:

- Word Pro is a WYSIWYG (what you see is what you get) user interface, and also provides you with the capability of working in several different views of a document.

- You can get context-sensitive Help anywhere in the program. To get help at any time, press F1. You can also use a new Word Pro feature, Ask the Expert, that enables you to formulate questions in your own words; Word Pro then shows you the answers.

- You can format characters in different fonts and sizes and add emphasis by using underlined, boldface, or italic type. You can use Word Pro's Fast Format feature to quickly repeat text formatting with the mouse.

▶ See "Editing Text," p. 66

- You can move or copy text in Word Pro by dragging the text with the mouse.

> **Tip**
>
> If you want to see the function of a particular SmartIcon, just move the mouse pointer over the icon and a bubble appears with a brief description.

- With the SmartIcon bars, you can execute many Word Pro menu commands without opening a menu. The SmartIcon bars change to reflect the current location of the insertion point, making SmartIcons relevant to a particular task. For example, if you place the insertion point in the header area of a document, you see additional SmartIcons used to insert common header elements (such as page numbers or dates).

You can customize the SmartIcon palette so it provides the commands you use most often. You can create your own sets of SmartIcons to use under different editing conditions.

■ Word Pro enables you to define paragraph styles and apply them throughout a document. To easily set up a new style, Word Pro mimics settings you create.

■ The status bar provides status information and quick access to paragraph styles, page setup, font types, sizes, and colors, as well as text enhancements such as bold or underline.

■ Word Pro provides spell checking, a thesaurus, and a grammar checker. In addition, Word Pro includes a SmartCorrect feature that checks your typing as you go. You also now have the capability to check your document formatting for any inconsistencies.

■ Use any of the SmartMasters that Word Pro supplies or create your own SmartMasters to store text and formatting you use regularly, such as a layout for a monthly report. A SmartMaster preview feature enables you to view a SmartMaster before you attach it to a new document. Because many of the SmartMasters that Word Pro supplies are automated, Word Pro prompts you through actions such as creating a memo or a newsletter. See Chapters 12 and 13 to learn more about using SmartMasters.

■ Glossaries enable you to automate repetitive work.

■ You can easily print envelopes and labels.

■ Create tables of contents and indexes, and use the Master Document feature to print multiple documents and create one table of contents and index for multiple documents.

■ Use the team editing features of Word Pro—TeamConsolidate and TeamReview—to share documents and collaborate during document creation. Using these team editing features, Word Pro indicates edited passages, comments, and questions within the document. Word Pro identifies who made each comment and numbers the lines of a long document so reviewers can refer to the line numbers when commenting. To incorporate changes from many sources, use the TeamConsolidate feature to compare the files and combine the changes.

■ Create newspaper-style columns or use tables to create columnar text.

■ Add rows or columns anywhere in a table and change column sizes in a table by dragging. You can also use the drag-and-drop feature to move or copy columns and rows.

I

Getting to Know Word Pro

In the rest of this chapter, you become acquainted with some of these features while you learn your way around Word Pro—you'll find information about the rest of them throughout the rest of the book. This version of Word Pro has made the software a versatile document generator; with its capabilities, you can achieve professional—and useful—results.

Starting Word Pro

Word Pro must operate in the Windows environment. To start Word Pro, follow these steps:

1. Click the Start button.

2. Highlight Programs to see the list of available program folders. Usually, you find the Word Pro icon in the Lotus SmartSuite folder.

3. Highlight the folder containing Word Pro and click the Word Pro icon.

Windows starts Word Pro and the Welcome to Lotus Word Pro dialog box appears (see fig. 2.1). You see the Welcome to Lotus Word Pro dialog box every time you first start Word Pro.

Fig. 2.1
You are prompted to base the new document on a SmartMaster in the opening dialog box.

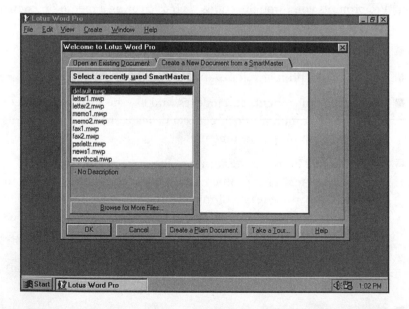

▶ See "Changing the User Setup," p. 212

Tip

The first time you start Word Pro, you'll see the Personal tab of the Word Pro Preferences dialog box, where you can enter personal information about your company.

If you choose DEFAULT.STY as the SmartMaster, the program creates a new document temporarily named [Untitled1], in which you can start typing.

▶ See "Under-standing SmartMasters," p. 241

> **Note**
>
> SmartMasters in Word Pro are the same as style sheets in Ami Pro 3. Many Smart-Masters are automated and walk you through processes before you see an opening screen.

You can open as many Word Pro documents at a time, each in its own window, as the memory on your computer permits. Word Pro titles the first document you open as [Untitled1], and numbers additional new documents sequentially: [Untitled2], [Untitled3], and so on. When you exit and restart Word Pro again, the program starts with [Untitled1].

Identifying Screen Parts

To work efficiently in any program, it's important to understand the screen. Figure 2.2 shows various parts of the Word Pro screen labeled to make the following pages easier to understand.

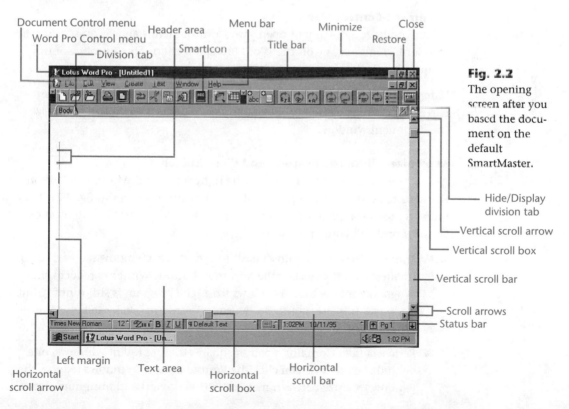

Fig. 2.2
The opening screen after you based the document on the default SmartMaster.

Title Bar

The title bar appears at the top of the screen and displays the name of the program and the name of the document in which you are working.

When you start Word Pro, the program window and [Untitled1] document window are *maximized*, which means that they fill all the available work space on-screen. Working in a maximized window is not essential but is usually easiest. You can change the size of either the document window or the Word Pro application window by using the Control menu or the Minimize or Maximize button, described a bit later.

Word Pro Control Menu

The Word Pro Control menu contains commands that enable you to change the size of the application window or exit the application. If you minimize the size of the Word Pro application window, you automatically minimize the size of the document in which you're working along with the application.

The Restore command performs the same function as the Restore button, which you'll learn about later in this chapter.

Document Control Menu

When you have a document open, two Control menus appear on-screen. The top Control menu controls the Word Pro application. The bottom Control menu controls the document.

Using the commands on the document Control menu, you can close the current document, switch to the next open document, and change the size of the document window.

Maximize, Minimize, Restore, and Close Buttons

Also at the top of the screen, but on the right side, are the Minimize button, the Restore or Maximize button, and the Close button (refer to fig. 2.2). These buttons provide a quick way to change the size of the Word Pro application window or the document window:

- *Minimize button.* Contains a dash to symbolize a window reduced to its smallest size. If you click the Minimize button, Windows reduces the program window to its Windows icon. The program is still running but no longer fills the screen. To return to Word Pro, click the Lotus Word Pro box on the taskbar.

- *Restore button.* Contains a pair of squares that represent windows, one behind the other. If you click the Restore button, Windows reduces the window to a size between maximum (full screen) and minimum (icon) size, and the Restore button changes to the Maximize button. When the window is reduced, you can resize the window to any desired size.

You might have noticed the Restore command on both the Program Control menu and the Document Control menu. The Restore command on these menus performs the same function as the Restore button performs.

■ *Maximize button.* Appears only if you previously chose the Restore button. This button contains a single square with a black top border that represents a window. If you click the Maximize button, Windows maximizes the window and the Maximize button changes to the Restore button.

▶ See "Closing and Opening Documents," p. 74

■ *Close button.* Contains an x. If you click the Close button, you start the process for closing Word Pro or the current document.

Menu Bar

The menu bar contains the names of the Word Pro menus; these menus contain Word Pro commands that are grouped by function. For example, the File menu contains commands that open, close, save, and print documents, and find information in document files. Word Pro executes some commands, such as the Save command, as soon as you choose that command. For other commands, the program requires additional information to execute the command. Choosing Word Pro menu commands and supplying additional information are discussed in detail later in this chapter. Table 2.1 shows a short description of each main menu option.

Table 2.1	Main Menu Options
Option	**Function**
File	Provides access to the disk, creates new or opens existing documents, closes documents, saves documents, interacts with other applications, and prints documents.
Edit	Provides options that enable you to manipulate or edit text and complete various document-checking tasks.
View	Changes the display of the page to draft, layout, page sorter, full page, special modes. Also adjusts your own view preferences.
Create	Provides commands to create special elements such as tables, frames, drawings, footnote/endnote, or even a comment note. From this menu, you can partition a document into divisions and sections.

(continues)

Table 2.1 Continued	
Option	**Function**
Text	Contains commands that manipulate the appearance of text. This menu is actually context-sensitive and may disappear, depending on what is selected on-screen. When the selection is a frame, this menu disappears—you'll see only the Frame menu. When the insertion point rests in text inside a frame, you see both the Text menu and the Frame menu.
Frame	Appears only when a frame is selected or the insertion point rests in a frame. This menu contains commands to modify frames that have been previously created.
Table	Appears only when a table is selected or the insertion point rests in a table. This menu contains commands to modify cell or table properties, change the size of rows/columns, as well as insert and delete rows/columns.
Window	Moves the insertion point between document windows and arranges or closes document windows.
Help	Accesses Word Pro Help, enables you to type a question in your own words by Asking the Expert, and provides a tour of Word Pro.

SmartIcon Bars

While it may look like one long SmartIcon bar, two default SmartIcon bars actually appear just below the menu bar when you start Word Pro. Each SmartIcon bar has a list box tab at the left edge of the bar (see fig. 2.3). If you click the list box tab, you see a menu pertaining to the SmartIcon bar. You can change the placement of a SmartIcon bar by dragging the area below the list box tab.

SmartIcons, which comprise the SmartIcon bars, provide shortcuts to Word Pro menu commands. By choosing a command from a SmartIcon bar, you execute menu commands without opening menus, and you save keystrokes. To execute the spell check command, for example, you choose the Edit, Check Spelling command, or you can click the SmartIcon that represents the Spell Checker (it has ABC on it). You can find more discussion of SmartIcons and their properties later in this chapter.

Tip

To hide the SmartIcons and provide a wider work area on-screen, choose View, Show/Hide, SmartIcons. To quickly toggle between hiding and showing the SmartIcons, press Ctrl+Q.

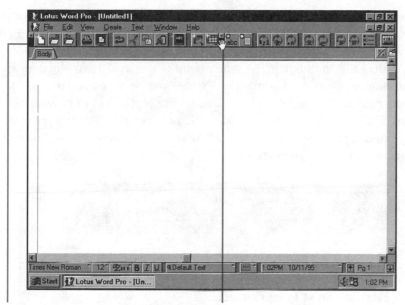

Fig. 2.3
The mouse pointer
changes to the
shape of a hand
when you high-
light the area you
use to move the
SmartIcon bar.

Drag here   Mouse pointer before dragging

Text Area

The text area, located below the SmartIcon bar, is where you type text and
insert tables and graphics. In Layout mode, the left and right margins are
visible—note the gray line representing the left margin (refer to fig. 2.2). At
the top of the screen, you see a break in the gray margin line. The area above
the break represents the header area of the document, and the area below
represents the main area where you type document text. Notice a similar area
for the footer when you scroll down to the bottom of the page.

The insertion point (a flashing vertical bar) appears in the upper left corner of
the text area. The insertion point indicates where text will appear when you
begin to type.

▶ See "Typing
Text," p. 58

Scroll Bars

The scroll bars are located at the bottom and the right side of the screen (refer
to fig. 2.2). You use the horizontal scroll bar to move the text on-screen from
side to side. You use the vertical scroll bar to move up and down in the document.

Often, an entire document does not fit on one screen. To scroll through the
document, use the mouse in conjunction with the vertical scroll bar. To
move one line at a time, click a scroll arrow once. To move in a particular
direction continuously, point to the scroll arrow and hold down the mouse

▶ See "Moving Around in a Document," p. 61

button. To move up or down one window at a time, click above or below the scroll box, respectively. To move to a particular place in a document, drag the scroll box to that location (for example, to move to the middle of the document, drag the scroll box to the center point of the scroll bar). A marker appears to give you an approximation of where you are when you release the mouse button (see fig. 2.4). When you click in the text area of your document, you move the insertion point to the new location. This last point is very important; until you click the mouse at the new location, the insertion point remains at the previous location.

Fig. 2.4
As you drag the scroll box, the location marker gives you an idea of where the insertion point will appear in the document.

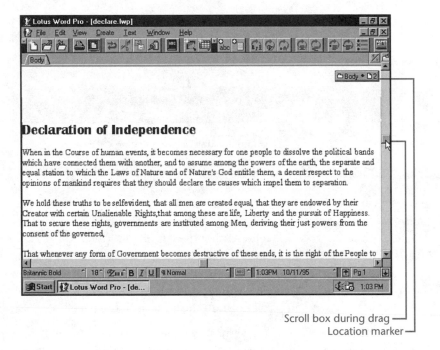

Scroll box during drag
Location marker

Status Bar

In Word Pro, the status bar is not a passive line on-screen that describes your document; it is an interactive tool you can use to implement commands (see fig. 2.5). The appearance of the status bar changes depending on the function you are using. The buttons provide information about the current document and shortcuts to execute commands. Click the buttons to make changes.

Table 2.2 summarizes the buttons on the status bar.

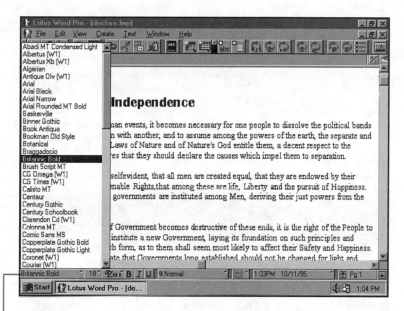

Fig. 2.5
In addition to providing information, use the status bar to format your document. From this figure, you can see that you can select a font using the Font list on the status bar.

Status bar

Table 2.2	Status Bar Buttons
Button	**Function**
Font	Displays the name of the current typeface at the insertion point. Click to choose from a list of available typefaces.
Point size	Indicates the point size at the insertion point. Click to choose from a list of available point sizes.
Font color	Selects the color of the font.
Bold	Adds boldface to text.
Italics	Adds italics to text.
Underline	Adds single underlining to text.
Style	Indicates the paragraph style for the current paragraph (such as Text). Click to choose from a list of available styles.
Statistics	Switches between various statistics available while working on a document (see fig. 2.6). For example, when you open this pop-up menu, you can determine if you are working in Insert mode or Typeover mode. You switched between these two modes using the Insert key on your keyboard. Insert mode inserts new text to the left of the insertion point. Typeover mode replaces old text with new text as you type, and pressing Enter doesn't move the insertion point to the next line.

(continues)

Table 2.2 Continued	
Button	**Function**
Page status	Displays the current page number. Click the button to display the Go To dialog box and specify the page to which you want to move.
Page arrows	Moves the insertion point up one page (click the up arrow) or down one page (click the down arrow). Click the button between the two arrows to display the Go To dialog box to move to a different page.

Fig. 2.6
Using the Statistics button, you can observe date/time or cursor position or display whether you are in Insert or Typeover mode.

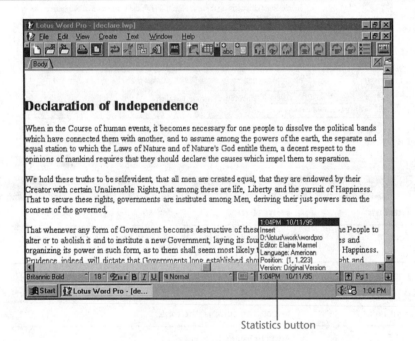

Statistics button

Recognizing Mouse Pointer Shapes

You can use the keyboard or the mouse for most Word Pro activities. Sometimes the keyboard method is faster because you can press a combination of keys more quickly than you can click a series of commands with the mouse. At other times, however, the mouse method is faster because you can move the mouse pointer across the screen more quickly than you can move the insertion point with a series of keystrokes. Most users become familiar with both methods of moving the insertion point and employ the fastest or most comfortable method in each situation.

The shape of the mouse pointer changes depending on the operation. When you type text, for example, the mouse pointer is an I-beam when it appears in the text area. The pointer becomes an arrow when you move outside the text area and when you point at something other than text—for example, a menu item. The mouse pointer also can take a number of other shapes.

Table 2.3 summarizes the mouse pointer shapes in Word Pro.

Table 2.3   Mouse Pointer Shapes

Name	Icon	Appears When
Pointer		The mouse pointer is pointing at a menu, a command, a scroll bar, a SmartIcon, a ruler, or the status bar.
I-beam		The mouse pointer is in the text area.
Hand		The mouse pointer is over selected text or a selected frame, or on the edge of an empty frame. You're about to move or copy the text, or move or select the frame.
Move Text Pointer		You are dragging text from one location to another. Place the vertical bar of the pointer where you want the text to appear.
Copy Text Pointer		You are copying text from one location to another. Place the vertical bar of the pointer where you want the copy of the text to appear.
Fast Format Pointer		You have extracted text attributes or paragraph styles and are applying them.
Frame Icon		You click the Add a Frame SmartIcon (or choose manual frame creation). You use this shape to create and position the frame.

Making Choices

When you're working in Word Pro, you choose SmartIcons, menu commands, and items from dialog boxes and InfoBoxes to perform specific functions. This section describes how to choose items and what to do if you change your mind.

Choosing Menu Commands

To choose a command from a menu, you may use the mouse, the keyboard, or one of the shortcut key combinations available for many of the commands.

To open a menu with the mouse, move the mouse pointer into the menu bar. Point to the name of the menu you want to open and click the left mouse button. Word Pro opens the menu and displays the commands. To choose a command from the menu, point to the name of the command you want and click the left mouse button.

If the command is followed by an arrow, Word Pro displays another menu with additional commands. If the command is followed by an ellipsis (...), Word Pro displays a dialog box or an InfoBox to request more information. Otherwise, Word Pro executes the command immediately. A *grayed* or *dimmed* command indicates that command is not available currently (see fig. 2.7).

Fig. 2.7
When the insertion point rests in a frame, the Insert Page Break command on the Text menu is grayed and not available.

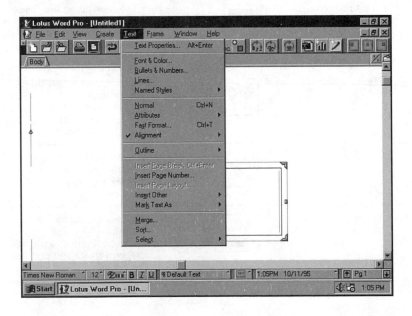

If you open a menu and then change your mind, you can close the menu by clicking the mouse anywhere in the text area, or you can open a different menu by clicking the name of that menu.

To open a menu and choose a command with the keyboard, press the Alt key and then press the underlined letter in the menu name you want to open. To open the Window menu, for example, press Alt+W.

Word Pro opens the menu and displays the commands of that menu. To choose a command from the menu, press the underlined letter in the command, or press the up- and down-arrow keys to highlight the command and then press Enter.

If you open a menu and then change your mind, you can do any of the following:

- Close the menu by pressing Esc two times.

- Open a different menu by pressing Esc one time and then pressing the underlined letter in another menu name.

- Open a different menu by pressing the arrow keys to highlight the menu name.

Word Pro also provides keyboard shortcuts for many commands; you may find the shortcuts easier than using the mouse. Table 2.4 summarizes the Word Pro keyboard shortcuts.

Table 2.4 Word Pro Keyboard Shortcuts	
Command	**Keyboard Combination**
Bold	Ctrl+B
Center-align	Ctrl+E
Copy	Ctrl+C or Ctrl+Insert
Cut	Ctrl+X or Shift+Delete
Delete the next word	Ctrl+Delete
Delete the preceding word	Ctrl+Backspace
Exchange the current paragraph with the preceding paragraph	Alt+up arrow

(continues)

Table 2.4   Continued

Command	Keyboard Combination
Exchange the current paragraph with the following paragraph	Alt+down arrow
Fast Format	Ctrl+T
Find and Replace	Ctrl+F
Go To dialog box	Ctrl+G
Insert a Glossary entry	Ctrl+K
Insert a page break	Ctrl+Enter
Italics	Ctrl+I
Justify	Ctrl+J
Left-align	Ctrl+L
Normal	Ctrl+N
Open	Ctrl+O
Paste	Ctrl+V or Shift+Insert
Print	Ctrl+P
Right-align	Ctrl+R
Save	Ctrl+S
Show/Hide SmartIcons	Ctrl+Q
Underline	Ctrl+U
Word underline	Ctrl+W

Choosing SmartIcons

With SmartIcons, you can execute many Word Pro menu commands without opening menus. You see two default SmartIcon bars on the opening screen of Word Pro. SmartIcon bars work a little differently—and a little smarter—in this version. The SmartIcons that appear on-screen are the SmartIcons you need, to do whatever you're trying to do at the moment. For example, if you insert a frame, you see that a few SmartIcons change at the right edge of the current set (see fig. 2.8). If you select the frame, the entire right SmartIcon bar changes (see fig. 2.9).

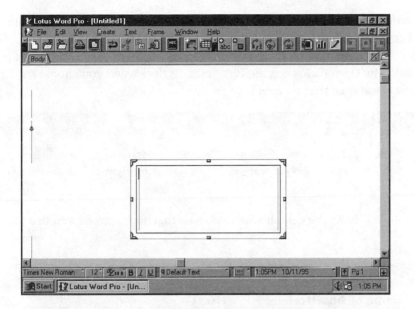

Fig. 2.8
If you insert a frame, new SmartIcons appear at the right.

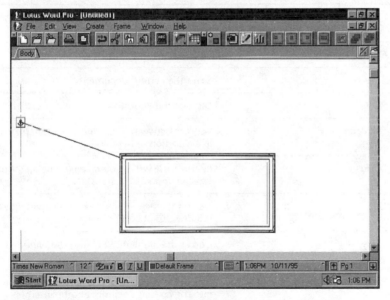

Fig. 2.9
The right set of SmartIcons changes entirely when you select a frame.

If you drag a SmartIcon bar, you can display SmartIcons on the left, right, top, or bottom of the screen, or you can leave the SmartIcons floating and move them around as you want.

▶ See "Customizing SmartIcons," p. 222

To use the SmartIcons, position the mouse pointer on the SmartIcon and click. Suppose that you want to open an existing document without opening the File menu. Position the mouse pointer over the File Open SmartIcon and click. The Open dialog box appears, just as it does when you choose the Open command from the File menu.

Tip

Remember, to learn the purpose of any SmartIcon, position the mouse pointer on the SmartIcon, and a bubble appears with a brief description of the SmartIcon's function.

Table 2.5 shows the default SmartIcon bars that appear when you first start Word Pro.

Table 2.5   Default SmartIcons

Name of SmartIcon	Effect
New	Displays the New dialog box so you can base a new document on a SmartMaster.
Open	Opens an existing document.
Save	Saves the current document.
Print	Displays the Print dialog box.
Full Page View	Toggles between displaying the entire page or just a portion of the page.
Undo	Reverses the last action taken (by default Word Pro can undo 100 actions).
Cut	Deletes the highlighted text and copies it to the Windows Clipboard.
Copy	Copies the highlighted text to the Windows Clipboard.
Paste	Inserts the contents of the Windows Clipboard into the current document at the insertion point.
Spell Check	Checks the spelling in the document.

Name of SmartIcon	Effect
Frame	Creates a frame on the current page in the position you specify.
Table	Creates a table at the insertion point.
Text InfoBox	Opens the Text Properties InfoBox so you can define multiple characteristics for text.
Page InfoBox	Opens the Page Layout Properties InfoBox so you can define multiple characteristics for the right or left pages or the entire document.
Attribute Cycle	Cycles through and applies various combinations of boldface, underlining, and italics.
Typeface Cycle	Cycles through and applies the available fonts in alphabetical order.
Point Size Cycle	Cycles through and applies available point sizes going larger with each cycle.
Alignment Cycle	Cycles through and applies left, center, right, or justified alignment.
Indent Cycle	Indents the current paragraph over to the next tab setting each time the SmartIcon is pressed.
Bullet Cycle	Cycles through and applies various bullet formats.
Numbering Cycle	Cycles through and applies the different numbering options.
Skip Bullet/Number	Enables you to skip using a bullet or number paragraph style for the next paragraph but keeps text aligned properly.

Using Shortcut Menus

Throughout Word Pro, you can find shortcut menus available to help you with particular tasks. If you select text or an object and then click the right mouse button, you see a shortcut menu relevant to that area or object. Figure 2.10 shows the shortcut menu for text, figure 2.11 shows the shortcut menu for a selected frame, and figure 2.12 shows the shortcut menu for a table. Each shortcut menu contains commands relevant to the selected object.

▶ See "Selecting Text," p. 63

▶ See "Creating Columns," p. 112

Fig. 2.10
When you click the right mouse button, this shortcut menu appears.

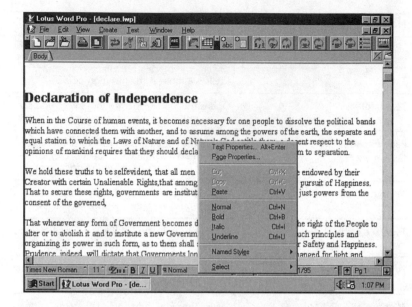

Fig. 2.11
When you select a frame and then click the right mouse button, you see this shortcut menu.

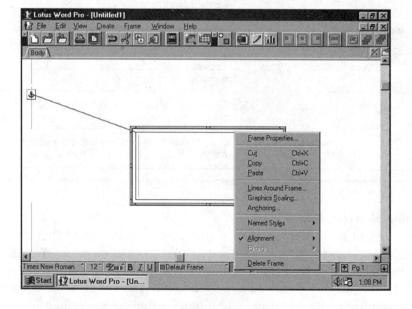

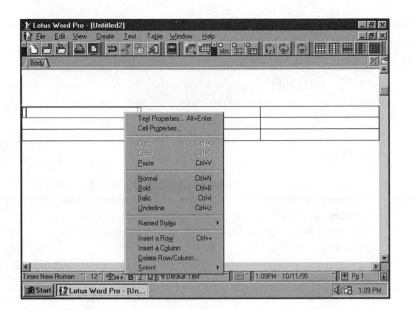

Fig. 2.12
Place the insertion point in a table and click the right mouse button to see this shortcut menu.

Using Dialog Boxes

Whenever you choose a menu command followed by an ellipsis (...), Word Pro displays a dialog box in which you supply additional information (see fig. 2.13).

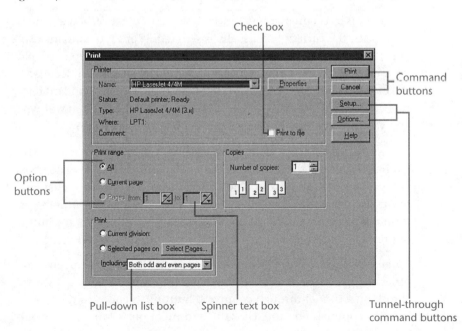

Fig. 2.13
The Print dialog box contains examples of the various elements you may need to use while working in a dialog box.

Like figure 2.13, each dialog box can contain any or all of the following types of elements:

■ A *list box* contains a list of options. Word Pro has two kinds of list boxes. The I̲ncluding list box is an example of a *pull-down* list box. Pull-down list boxes are closed when the dialog box first appears; to open one, click the down arrow at the right side of the box.

> **Note**
>
> Another type of list box doesn't appear in figure 2.13. This type of list box is open when the dialog box first appears. To choose an option from either type of list box, click the option. If the list box is not long enough to display all available options, hold down the down arrow to move beyond the options that appear in the box.

■ An *option button* is a small round button you use to choose one option from a group of related options, such as the Cu̲rrent Page button in the Print Range box. To choose an option button, click the button. A black dot appears in the currently selected option. In a group of option buttons, you can choose only one at a time. You cannot, for example, choose both Cu̲rrent Page and A̲ll Pages.

■ A *text box* is a rectangular box in which you enter text. When a dialog box opens, the current text usually is selected. Word Pro contains two kinds of text boxes. The Pages Fro̲m and T̲o boxes are examples of *spinner text boxes* in which you can use the arrows to increase or decrease the current selection. The C̲opies box is an example of a standard text box. In this type of text box, Word Pro may predict what you will type, and you can type new information to replace the prediction.

■ A *command button* is a rectangular button that performs an action. The OK button accepts the settings in the dialog box, closes the dialog box, and performs the command. The Cancel button cancels your changes to the settings in the dialog box and closes the dialog box without performing the command. To choose a command button, click the button, or press Tab until the button is highlighted and then press Enter.

■ A *tunnel-through command button* is a command button that opens another dialog box, such as the S̲etup and O̲ptions buttons. You'll see an ellipsis on a tunnel-through command button. To choose a tunnel-through command button, click the button, or press Tab until the button is highlighted and press Enter. You can also press and hold the Alt key and then press the underlined letter in the command button.

■ A *check box* is a square box you use to choose an option. You can choose more than one check box from a group of related options. A check mark appears in the check boxes of activated options. To choose a check box, click the check box, or press and hold the Alt key and then press the underlined letter in the option name. To deactivate the option and remove the check mark from the box, choose the check box again.

You also may notice a black, dotted box surrounding an option. This dotted line highlights the current pointer location.

To choose dialog box options using the mouse, click the button or box. To choose dialog box options using the keyboard, press and hold down the Alt key and press the underlined letter in the option name. To choose the OK button or the Cancel button using the keyboard, press the Tab key to high-light the button, and then press Enter.

Using InfoBoxes

InfoBoxes are new to this version of Word Pro; they simplify assigning prop-erties to objects. An *InfoBox* is similar to a dialog box, but it presents all the properties associated with one object in one box.

As you can see in figure 2.14, an InfoBox is divided into tabs from which you choose to change attributes of an object. The Text InfoBox, for example, contains tabs with properties related to text and paragraphs: fonts, align-ment, border lines, bullets/numbers, and so on. When applying properties to the text, for example, you can change the font, size, or color of the text at the same time using the InfoBox.

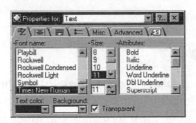

Fig. 2.14
Choose from various tabs in the Text InfoBox to assign various properties to text and paragraphs.

From the InfoBox, choose the tab containing the properties you want to ap-ply to the object. You can choose as few or as many properties as you want.

The choices you make in the InfoBoxes immediately appear on-screen. This *live action* feature means that changes take place immediately when you apply a font, resize a frame, or assign another property from an InfoBox. The Info-Box remains open but the object in your document is modified.

▶ See "Chang-ing Character Formatting," p. 79

> **Tip**
>
> To view an object's InfoBox, point the mouse at the object and click the right mouse button. From the quick menu that appears, choose the appropriate Properties command.

You can access an InfoBox through the menu of the object you select. You can read about opening InfoBoxes in various chapters throughout the book.

When you're finished with the InfoBox, you can do one of two things: close or collapse the box. If you close the box, you can always display it again.

Alternatively, you can *collapse* the box, which hides all the box except its title bar and tabs. To collapse an InfoBox, double-click its title bar. You may want to collapse an InfoBox so you can better see your work while you're making the changes. After you collapse an InfoBox, expand it again by double-clicking the title bar. Figure 2.15 shows a collapsed InfoBox.

Double-click here to expand the InfoBox

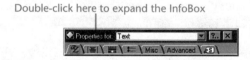

Fig. 2.15
You can collapse an InfoBox for quick access later in the work session.

> **Tip**
>
> You can move a collapsed or expanded InfoBox by dragging its title bar to a new location with the mouse.

Using Help

Using Word Pro Help, you can move through lists of topics to find information or search for information using keywords related to the information. Word Pro will demonstrate the information contained in a Help topic and show you a list of cross-references to which you can jump. If you need to, you can print a Help topic.

Word Pro's Help is context-sensitive. To get Help when a Word Pro dialog box or InfoBox appears, press F1 or click the Help button.

Using Ask the Expert

Ask the Expert is a new Help feature in Word Pro. Using this feature, you type questions in your own words. The Expert responds by supplying a Help window and a list of other possible topics that may answer your question.

To "Ask the Expert," choose <u>H</u>elp, Ask the E<u>x</u>pert. Your screen changes so you can ask a question. Type a question in your own words in the box provided (see fig. 2.16).

Type a question here →

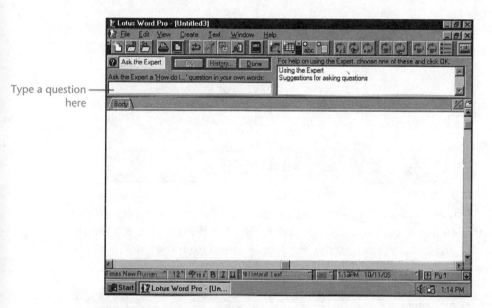

Fig. 2.16
Type a question using your own words and click OK.

The questions you ask should be task-oriented—that is, you should be able to start the question with "How do I...." Also, the question should cover only one subject. If you provide too much information in the question, the Expert may not answer your question directly. Instead, you may see a topic that covers a portion of your question and a series of related topics.

After you click OK, Word Pro evaluates your question; in most cases, Word Pro displays a Help topic and you see related topics listed in the Expert's list box. Double-click a related topic to see the Help window for that topic (see fig. 2.17).

Fig. 2.17
If you ask "How do I insert a bookmark?," Word Pro displays a Help window for that topic and gives you exact instructions.

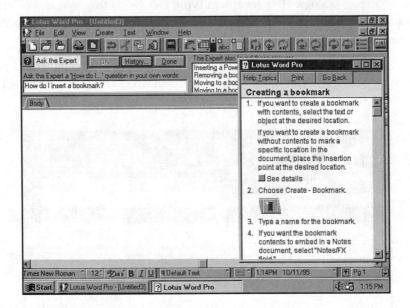

Suppose that you asked a question before (maybe two or three weeks ago) and you cannot remember the answer. You don't need to reenter the question; just click the History button and select your question from the list. Then click OK as before.

> **Tip**
>
> Leave the Expert open while you perform an unfamiliar task. That way, you can ask a question whenever you get stumped.

When you finish using the Expert, click the Done button to return the screen to its original appearance.

Viewing Help Topics

If you choose Help, Help Topics, you see the window in figure 2.18.

Fig. 2.18
Tht three tabs in
the window let
you approach
getting help in
three different
ways: using a table
of contents, using
an index, or typing
a keyword to
display topics by
subject.

When you click a book on the Contents tab, you see additional books. If you
continue clicking books, eventually you see topics, like those in figure 2.19.

When you display Help topics (see fig. 2.20), you may see a button at the
bottom of the topic indicating that related topics are available. If you need
more information on related topics, click the box.

Fig. 2.19
When you open
enough books, you
see topics, which
are represented by
pieces of paper
containing
question marks.

Fig. 2.20
When you click
See Related Topics,
Word Pro displays
a list of related
Help topics.

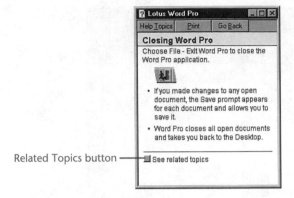

Related Topics button

Instead of using the Help window as you work with a command, you may want to use a printout of the Help information on that command. To print a Help topic, click the Print button at the top of the Help window (refer to fig. 2.20).

Note

When you print from Help, you cannot change the format; Word Pro always prints in a defined style to the printer you specify.

Exit from the Help window in any of the following four ways:

- Click the x in the upper left corner of the Help window.

- Click the Control menu icon in the upper left corner of the screen, and then choose the Close command.

- Double-click the Control menu icon.

- Press Alt+F4.

Searching for Topics

If you want, search Word Pro Help by using keywords. Click the Index tab of the Help Topics dialog box (see fig. 2.21).

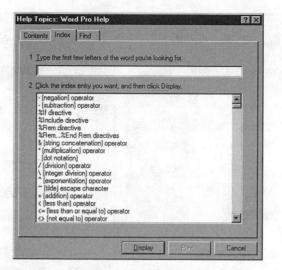

Fig. 2.21
When you choose the Index tab in the Word Pro Help Topics window, you can use a keyword to search for Help topics.

You either type the keyword you want Word Pro to find in the text box or choose a keyword from the list box. After you type or choose a keyword, click the Display button. Word displays the Help topic.

Using Context-Sensitive Help

Instead of moving through the Help index topic by topic, you can get Help when you're in any Word Pro dialog box. Press F1 or choose the Help button in the dialog box.

To demonstrate getting context-sensitive Help in a dialog box, the following steps use the Go To dialog box:

1. Choose Edit, Go To. The Go To dialog box appears (see fig. 2.22).

2. Press F1 or choose the Help command button. The Help topic appears for that specific dialog box. In figure 2.22, the Help topic appears to the right of the Go To dialog box.

Fig. 2.22
You can get help when you're in a dialog box by pressing F1 or by clicking the Help command button.

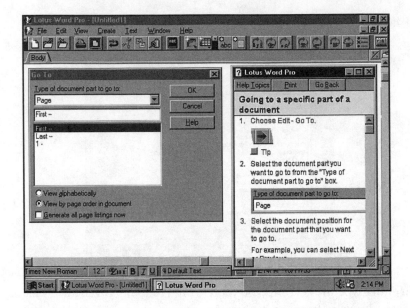

Exiting Word Pro

You can exit Word Pro using one of the following ways:

- Choose File, Exit Word Pro.

- Open the application Control menu and choose Close.

- Double-click the application Control menu icon.

- Press Alt+F4.

- Click the Close button (marked with an x) in the upper right corner of the Word Pro title bar.

Regardless of the method you use, if you have made changes to any open document, you see a message asking whether you want to save the document. Choose Yes, No, or Cancel.

From Here...

In this chapter, you learned the basics of starting Word Pro and understanding what you see when the opening screen appears. Now that you have learned how to use the mouse and the keyboard, dialog boxes and InfoBoxes, and of course, how to get help, you're ready to create a document.

To learn how to create, edit, and format a document, explore these chapters:

- Chapter 3, "Creating and Editing a Document," presents the basics of editing and typing in Word Pro—you learn how to open, close, and save documents as well.

- Chapter 4, "Formatting Text," shows you how to apply and modify character attributes such as fonts. You also learn how to format paragraphs and apply paragraph styles.

- Chapter 5, "Formatting the Page," continues with document formatting by explaining how to set margins, add headers and footers, and work in columns.

- Chapter 6, "Exploring Advanced Page Formatting Features," explores advanced page formatting techniques such as inserting page breaks and numbers, working with rulers, and using borders, lines, and shading in your document.

Chapter 3

Creating and Editing a Document

by Elaine Marmel

Now that you have explored the Word Pro screen and understand its components, you're ready to start using Word Pro. In this chapter, you learn how to create a new document, type text, and correct simple mistakes.

Basic editing techniques are an important part of using Word Pro on a day-to-day basis; this chapter covers some of these techniques, including how to move and copy text. In addition, you learn some time-saving techniques such as undoing and redoing actions and using Word Pro's new SmartCorrect feature.

In this chapter, you learn how to:

- Start a new document

- Move around in the document

- Select text

- Move, copy, and delete text

- Undo and redo actions

- Save a document

- Open a previously saved document

Placing Text in a Document

Typing text in a word processing program can be much faster and easier than writing on paper. Making revisions is quicker with word processing; if you change your mind about the structure of a sentence or the organization of a paragraph, you can insert words and sentences, delete phrases, move information from one location to another, and more.

Typing Text

◀ See "Recognizing Mouse Pointer Shapes," p. 36

The *insertion point* is the flashing vertical bar in the text area of the document. The insertion point marks the place where Word Pro inserts text into the document (see fig. 3.1). In a new document, the insertion point appears in the upper left corner of text area. As you type, text appears to the left of the insertion point, and the insertion point moves to the right. You can move the insertion point by using the keyboard or the mouse, but you cannot move the insertion point beyond the last character in the document.

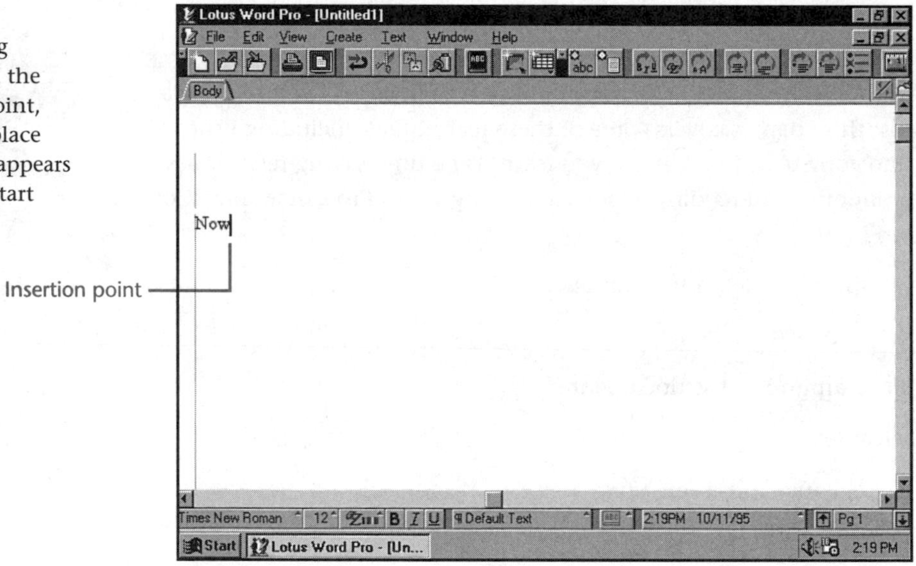

Fig. 3.1
The flashing vertical bar, the insertion point, marks the place where text appears when you start typing.

Insertion point

> **Note**
>
> Don't confuse the insertion point with the mouse pointer. The two are completely separate entities with no connection to each other besides the word *point* in their names. The insertion point marks the place where text appears when you type. The mouse pointer, on the other hand, marks the location of the mouse. The insertion point never changes shape—it always remains a vertical bar. The mouse pointer, however, does change shape. When the mouse pointer rests in the menu area, it looks like an arrow. When the mouse pointer rests over the text area, it looks like an I-beam. Also, you can have both an insertion point and a mouse pointer on-screen simultaneously—just move your mouse.

When you reach the end of a line while entering text in the document, the insertion point automatically moves to the next line. This action, known as *word wrap*, occurs because Word Pro calculates when you reach the right margin and "returns the carriage" for you.

▶ See "Changing Paragraph Formatting," p. 88

Sometimes, however, you may want to start a new line in a specific location—like when you want to start a new paragraph. When you press Enter, Word Pro single spaces the insertion point to the beginning of the next typing line. How does Word Pro know to single space? By default, Word Pro assigns spacing above and below the paragraph—and the default spacing is 0.

If you're like most typists, you make mistakes that you notice immediately and want to correct. You can use the Backspace key or the Delete key to remove one character at a time.

When you press Backspace, you delete the character immediately to the left of the insertion point. If you type the line shown in figure 3.2, for example, you can correct the mistake by pressing Backspace twice to remove the letters *t* and *y* (in that order). After you remove incorrect letters by pressing Backspace, you can type the correct letters immediately, without having to move the insertion point.

> **Tip**
>
> Ctrl+Backspace deletes from the insertion point left to the beginning of the word. Similarly, Ctrl+Delete deletes from the insertion point right to the end of the word, including the space after the word.

Fig. 3.2
Correct the typing mistake at the end of the sentence by pressing the Backspace key twice to delete the last two characters.

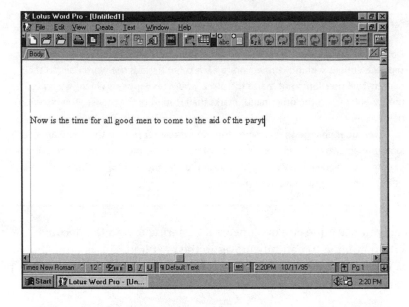

Backspace deletes the character to the left of the insertion point, and Delete removes the character immediately to the right of the insertion point. To use Delete to correct the typed line shown in figure 3.2, press the left-arrow key twice to position the insertion point between the *r* and the *y*, as shown in figure 3.3, and then press Delete twice to remove the letters *y* and *t* (in that order).

Fig. 3.3
In this example, reposition the insertion point before using the Delete key to remove the incorrect characters.

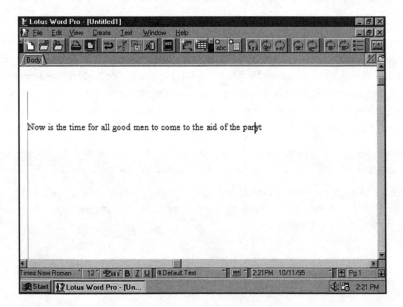

Moving Around in a Document

As you create longer documents, being able to move the insertion point around (*navigate*) the document efficiently becomes important. You can move the insertion point using the mouse or the keyboard.

To move the insertion point with the mouse, position the mouse pointer where you want the insertion point, and then click the left mouse button. As you position the mouse pointer in the text area, the mouse pointer changes shape to the I-beam pointer, which you learned about in Chapter 2, "Getting Acquainted with Word Pro." If you want to move the insertion point to a place in the document that doesn't appear in the window, you can display that part of the document by using the Page Up and Page Down buttons on the status bar or by using the vertical scroll bar. In Chapter 2, you learned how to use the mouse and the scroll box to help you position the insertion point.

◀ See "Identify-ing Screen Parts," p. 29

You can also use the arrows at the ends of the scroll bar (the *scroll arrows*) to move to a different area of the document. Follow these steps:

1. To scroll toward the beginning of the document, position the mouse pointer on the up arrow at the top of the vertical scroll bar. To scroll toward the end of the document, position the mouse pointer on the down arrow at the bottom of the vertical scroll bar.

2. Press and hold down the left mouse button. The text of the document scrolls toward the beginning or end of the document.

3. Release the mouse button when the text you want to view appears in the window.

4. Move the mouse pointer into the text area. The mouse pointer becomes an I-beam pointer.

5. Position the I-beam pointer where you want the insertion point, and then click the left mouse button.

> **Caution**
>
> Remember, the insertion point doesn't move until you click the new location. If you start typing before you click the new location, Word Pro inserts the text at the original insertion point location.

Moving the insertion point with the keyboard can be very efficient. To move the insertion point, you use the direction keys individually or in combination with the Ctrl key (see table 3.1).

Table 3.1 Keyboard Methods for Moving the Insertion Point	
Key or Key Combination	**Effect**
Left-arrow key	Moves the insertion point one character to the left
Right-arrow key	Moves the insertion point one character to the right
Up-arrow key	Moves the insertion point up one line
Down-arrow key	Moves the insertion point down one line
Ctrl+left-arrow key	Moves the insertion point one word to the left
Ctrl+right-arrow key	Moves the insertion point one word to the right
Home	Moves the insertion point to the beginning of the line
End	Moves the insertion point to the end of the line
Ctrl+up-arrow key	Moves the insertion point to the beginning of the paragraph
Ctrl+down-arrow key	Moves the insertion point to the end of the paragraph
Page Up	Moves the insertion point up one screen
Page Down	Moves the insertion point down one screen
Ctrl+Page Up	Moves the insertion point to the top of the preceding page
Ctrl+Page Down	Moves the insertion point to the top of the next page
Ctrl+Home	Moves the insertion point to the beginning of the document
Ctrl+End	Moves the insertion point to the end of the document
Ctrl+period	Moves the insertion point to the beginning of the next sentence
Ctrl+comma	Moves the insertion point to the beginning of the preceding sentence

You can use the Go To dialog box to go directly to a specific location in a document (see fig. 3.4). Open the Go To dialog box in any of these ways:

- Press Ctrl+G.

- Choose Edit, Go To.

- Click the page number button near the right end of the status bar.

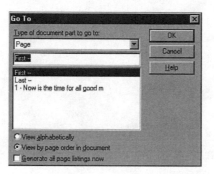

Fig. 3.4
In the Go To dialog box, specify the page to which you want to move the insertion point.

Using the Go To dialog box, you can reposition the insertion point by typing a page number or by choosing from the list box. After choosing a target location, click OK; the insertion point moves to that location. If you change your mind and don't want to move to another location, click Cancel.

Selecting Text

If you want to change text in some way, you must identify the text you want to change before you can change it. To identify the text you want to change, you *select* it by using the mouse or the keyboard.

Tip
When you need to delete more than a few characters at a time, you can select the text you want to delete and then press Enter, Backspace, or Delete.

Selecting with the Mouse

To select text with the mouse, position the mouse pointer (which changes shape to look like the I-beam mouse pointer) at the beginning of the text you want to select. Then drag the mouse (press and hold down the left mouse button while you move the mouse) until the text is highlighted (see fig. 3.5).

Fig. 3.5
The highlighted
text in this figure
is selected.

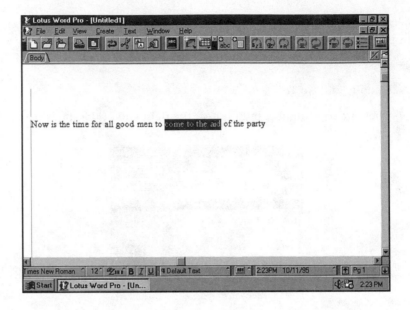

▶ See "Changing
Character
Formatting,"
p. 79

In table 3.2, you find some shortcut techniques you can use to select text with the mouse.

Table 3.2   Selection Methods Using the Mouse

Selection	Technique
One word	Place the mouse pointer on the word and double-click.
Multiple words	Position the mouse pointer on the first word, double-click, and, keeping the mouse button depressed, drag the mouse pointer across the other contiguous words.
One sentence	Place the mouse pointer in the sentence, press and hold down Ctrl, and click.
Multiple sentences	With the mouse pointer in the first sentence, press and hold down Ctrl, click, and drag the mouse pointer across the sentences you want to select.
One paragraph	Place the mouse pointer in the paragraph, press and hold down Ctrl, and double-click.
Multiple paragraphs	With the mouse pointer in the first paragraph, press and hold down Ctrl, double-click, and drag the mouse pointer across the paragraphs you want to select.

Tip

You can change the font, point size, color, or apply boldface, italics, or underlining to a single word without selecting the word. Simply place the insertion point anywhere in the word and complete the action.

Troubleshooting

I tried to select multiple words by double-clicking and then dragging. Instead, I seemed to move the first word I meant to select.

When you double-clicked, you released the mouse button after the second click and before dragging. Undo your mistake and then try again. This time, however, hold the mouse button down after the second click and then drag.

Selecting with the Keyboard

Table 3.1 (shown earlier in this chapter) provides information on moving the insertion point with the keyboard. To select text with the keyboard, add the Shift key to the key combination used to move the insertion point. Table 3.3 lists key combinations for selecting text.

Caution

If you touch any key on the keyboard except an arrow key, or if you press Enter while text is selected, Word Pro deletes the highlighted text. You can reverse an accidental deletion by using Word Pro's Undo feature, covered later in this chapter.

Table 3.3 Selection Methods Using the Keyboard

Key Combination	Effect
Shift+left-arrow key	Selects one character to the left
Shift+right-arrow key	Selects one character to the right
Shift+up-arrow key	Selects one line up
Shift+down-arrow key	Selects one line down

(continues)

Table 3.3 Continued	
Key Combination	**Effect**
Shift+Home	Selects from the insertion point to the beginning of the line
Shift+End	Selects from the insertion point to the end of the line
Shift+Ctrl+up-arrow key	Selects from the insertion point to the beginning of the paragraph
Shift+Ctrl+down-arrow key	Selects from the insertion point to the end of the paragraph
Shift+Page Up	Selects up one screen from the insertion point
Shift+Page Down	Selects down one screen from the insertion point
Shift+Ctrl+Page Up	Selects all text from the insertion point to the beginning of the preceding page
Shift+Ctrl+Page Down	Selects all text from the insertion point to the end of the current page
Shift+Ctrl+Home	Selects text from the insertion point to the beginning of the document
Shift+Ctrl+End	Selects text from the insertion point to the end of the document
Shift+Ctrl+period	Selects text from the insertion point to the end of the sentence
Shift+Ctrl+comma	Selects text from the insertion point to the beginning of the sentence

Editing Text

Editing text is what you do most in word processing, so you want to edit as efficiently as possible. This section explores several editing features:

- As you may expect, Word Pro enables you to move and copy text in several different ways—you choose the method that works best for your circumstances.

- Word Pro now enables you to undo more than just the last action you took. You also learn about the new Redo feature.

- Word Pro's SmartCorrect feature helps you catch typing mistakes as you type.

Moving Text

Moving text involves removing the text from its current location (*cutting*) and placing it in a new location (*pasting*). You can move text in three ways:

- Use the Cut and Paste commands.

- Click the Cut and Paste SmartIcons.

- Use the mouse to drag-and-drop the text.

In the first two methods, when you cut text from the document, Word Pro places the cut text on the Windows *Clipboard*. The Clipboard is a temporary holding area for the information you cut or copy. The text remains on the Clipboard until you exit Windows or place other text or graphics on the Clipboard. The Clipboard can hold only one entry at a time; each time you place information on the Clipboard, you replace any information previously stored there.

> **Tip**
>
> The Cut and Paste commands are available on the shortcut menu that appears when you press the right mouse button after selecting text.

To move text and place it on the Clipboard during the move operation, follow these steps:

1. Select the text you want to move.

2. Click the Cut SmartIcon, press Ctrl+X or choose Edit, Cut. Word Pro removes the text from the document and stores the text on the Clipboard.

3. Position the insertion point where you want the text to appear.

4. Click the Paste SmartIcon, press Ctrl+V or choose Edit, Paste. The text appears in the new location.

You can also use the mouse to move text by dragging the text. To drag the text to a new location, follow these steps:

1. Select the text you want to move.

2. Position the mouse pointer anywhere in the selected text; then click and hold down the left mouse button. The mouse pointer changes shape, showing an insertion point and a hand grabbing text.

3. Continue holding down the mouse button as you drag the mouse pointer to the new location where you want to insert text.

4. Release the mouse button. The text disappears from its original location and reappears in the new location.

Copying Text

Copying text involves making a duplicate of the text (*copying*) and placing the duplicate in a new location (*pasting*). The original text remains in its original location. As with moving text, you can copy text in three ways:

- Use the Copy and Paste commands.
- Click the Copy and Paste SmartIcons.
- Use the mouse to drag-and-drop the text.

Again, the first two methods use the Clipboard as a temporary storage area for the text you are copying. See the preceding section, "Moving Text," for information on the Clipboard.

> **Tip**
>
> The Copy and Paste commands are available on the shortcut menu that appears when you click the right mouse button after selecting text.

To copy text and place it on the Clipboard, follow these steps:

1. Select the text you want to copy.

2. Click the Copy SmartIcon, press Ctrl+C or choose Edit, Copy.

3. Position the insertion point where you want a duplicate of the text to appear. Click the left mouse button to move the insertion point from its previous location.

4. Click the Paste SmartIcon, press Ctrl+V or choose Edit, Paste. A duplicate of the text appears in the new location.

You can use the mouse to copy text by dragging the text. Follow these steps:

1. Select the text you want to copy.

2. Position the mouse pointer anywhere in the selected text, then press and hold down the Ctrl key and the left mouse button. As you begin to move the mouse pointer, the pointer changes shape. You see an insertion point and a hand containing a plus sign (+) dragging text.

3. Without releasing the mouse button, drag the mouse pointer to the new location for the text. Use the red insertion point portion of the mouse pointer shape to align the text.

4. Release the left mouse button. The text remains at its original location and a copy appears in the new location.

Undoing and Redoing Actions

Occasionally, you may need to undo actions and commands. Perhaps you deleted text unintentionally or made changes you don't want to keep. Use the Undo SmartIcon or the Undo command on the Edit menu to undo your last action.

Using Undo

In the Word Pro Preferences dialog box, you can specify how many prior actions you want to be able to undo. Word Pro enables you to undo virtually an unlimited number of actions, but usually, you don't need to undo too many. By default, you can undo up to 100 previous actions, which ought to be plenty.

▶ See "Setting General Preferences," p. 213

After you set up the number of actions you want to be able to undo, you can undo an action by clicking the Undo SmartIcon or by choosing Edit, Undo. With either method, no prompt appears; Word Pro immediately reverses the last action.

If the undo level is set above 1 in the Word Pro Preferences dialog box, and you use the Undo SmartIcon or the Edit, Undo command again, Word Pro undoes actions in reverse order. If you delete and then paste a word, for example, and click the Undo SmartIcon or choose Edit, Undo twice, Word Pro first undoes the paste operation and then restores the deleted word.

Undoing or Redoing a Specific Action

So, what if you undo an action and *then* change your mind—that is, you didn't mean to undo. Well, you could go through the original steps again—for example, you could retype text you deleted—or, you can *redo*. When you redo an action, you undo the effectiveness of an Undo command.

> **Note**
>
> In this version of Word Pro, the number of actions you can undo and redo is virtually unlimited. You set the number of actions you want Word Pro to remember in the Word Pro Preferences dialog box. While you can specify any number up to 32,000, each action you ask Word Pro to remember (to be able to undo or redo) costs a little in memory. And the more memory you allocate to undoing and redoing, the less memory you have available for other actions such as opening additional documents.

Say, for example, that you insert a frame and then delete it. You then decide you want the frame after all. Choose Edit, Undo/Redo Special. The Undo/Redo dialog box appears (see fig. 3.6).

Fig. 3.6
Use this dialog box to undo or redo an action.

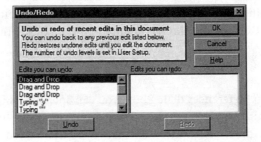

To undo an action, select the action from the list on the left and choose Undo. To redo an action, select the action from the list on the right and choose Redo. The theory here, of course, is that you must have undone something before you can redo it, so you may not see anything in the Redo list unless you undo something.

▶ See "Changing the User Setup," p. 212

> **Note**
>
> Notice, as you select an action and choose either the Undo or Redo button, that Word Pro performs the action immediately—without closing the dialog box. You see the action on-screen behind the dialog box. You may have heard the term *modeless;* the term refers to a dialog box that you don't need to close or click an Apply button to see changes. Because of this *live action* method of operating, you don't see a preview window inside a non-modal dialog box such as Undo/Redo.

Using SmartCorrect

SmartCorrect is the friend of the typist who makes habitual typing mistakes. Do you often type *the* as *teh*? How about *document* as *docuemtn*? Well, now you just teach Word Pro about your own favorite typos and let Word Pro fix them each time you type them. You don't take any action when you make a mistake—just keep typing.

To identify your favorite typos for Word Pro, follow these steps:

1. Choose <u>E</u>dit, S<u>m</u>artCorrect. The SmartCorrect dialog box appears (see fig. 3.7). Notice that *teh* already appears in the <u>S</u>martCorrect Entries list. If you click *teh* in the list, you see the replacement text Word Pro supplies when you accidentally type it.

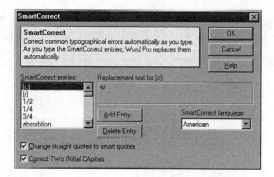

Fig. 3.7
Here you see the common typing mistakes Word Pro already knows how to handle.

2. Click <u>A</u>dd Entry. You see the Add SmartCorrect Entry dialog box shown in figure 3.8.

Fig. 3.8
In this dialog box, you teach Word Pro to correct your common typing mistakes.

3. In the <u>S</u>martCorrect Entry box, type the *incorrect* spelling of the word you want Word Pro to fix.

4. In the <u>R</u>eplacement Text box, type the entry as you want it to appear after Word Pro fixes it.

5. Choose OK. Word Pro redisplays the SmartCorrect dialog box.

6. Notice the two check boxes in the dialog box. The first box determines whether Word Pro uses straight quotes or smart quotes, which are curled. The second box tells Word Pro to use lowercase on the second of two consecutively typed capital letters. Check one or both boxes if you want.

7. To delete an entry in the list, highlight the entry and choose <u>D</u>elete Entry.

8. When you're finished, choose OK.

Caution

When you delete a SmartCorrect entry, Word Pro doesn't warn you or give you a chance to change your mind. And you cannot undo the action.

Troubleshooting

I accidentally deleted a SmartCorrect entry. How can I get it back?

You must recreate the entry using the <u>A</u>dd Entry button in the SmartCorrect dialog box.

Saving a Document

While you're working on a document, it's a good idea to save the document periodically. When you save a document, different actions can take place. Word Pro's behavior depends on whether you have saved the document previously or whether you are saving the document for the first time.

Naming a Document

 You save the active document by choosing a command from a menu or by using the Save SmartIcon. The <u>F</u>ile menu provides two commands for saving documents: <u>S</u>ave and Save <u>A</u>s. You generally use <u>S</u>ave if the document has already been saved on disk and you want to save the current version of the document with the same name. If you're saving a new document or saving a revised document under a new name, use Save <u>A</u>s.

Tip

If you choose the Save SmartIcon, Word Pro figures out for you whether to use the Save or the Save As command, based on whether the document has been previously saved.

To save a new document—one that you haven't yet saved—follow these steps:

1. Choose File, Save; or choose File, Save As; or click the Save SmartIcon. Word Pro displays the Save As dialog box (see fig. 3.9).

Fig. 3.9
In this dialog box, you describe your document so you can save your work and find the document the next time you need it.

2. In the File Name text box, type a name for the document. You don't need to supply an extension. For this example, type **SAMPLE** for the name of the document.

3. In the Description box, type a description of the document. This step is optional, but a description helps remind you what the file contains when you need to reopen the document.

4. Use the Save In list box to specify the drive and folder where Word Pro is to save the document.

5. Word Pro can convert documents to other file formats. Use the Save as Type list box to choose an alternate format.

6. Choose OK.

Saving Changes to an Existing Document

After you provide a name for a document, saving it becomes almost immediate. Choose File, Save or click the Save SmartIcon. Word Pro doesn't display any dialog boxes or ask any questions; instead, the mouse pointer changes to an hourglass shape while Word Pro saves the document.

Each time you make changes to a document, save the document to save those changes. When you save a document, Word Pro writes over the previous version of the document.

> **Tip**
>
> You can rename a document using the Save <u>A</u>s command. Simply follow the steps outlined in the previous section and supply a new name for the document. Word Pro leaves both files on your disk.

Opening and Closing Documents

Saving documents transfers changes from the document on-screen to disk, but saving doesn't clear your screen. Although you don't need to clear the screen, you may want to put a document away when you're done working with it. And after you close a document, you may need to open it again to make changes. Or you may want to start a new document. You may even want to leave one document open while you work in another document. In this section, you learn how to open a document you already saved, start a new document, and close a document.

Opening an Existing Document

You can open an existing document with a command from a menu or with a SmartIcon. To open an existing document, follow these steps:

1. Click the Open Existing File SmartIcon, or choose <u>F</u>ile, <u>O</u>pen. The Open dialog box appears (see fig. 3.10).

Fig. 3.10
Use this dialog box to reopen a document you have already created.

2. Use the Look <u>I</u>n list box to navigate to the drive and folder containing the file you want to open.

3. If the document is not a Word Pro document, open the Files of <u>T</u>ype list box and choose the file type.

4. Highlight the name of the document in the File <u>N</u>ame list box. If you typed a description when you created the document, it appears in the Description text box.

5. Choose OK to open the document.

Word Pro can remember the documents you open. In the Word Pro Preferences dialog box, you can instruct Word Pro to remember up to the last five documents you saved. Word Pro lists the documents at the bottom of the <u>F</u>ile menu (see fig. 3.11). You can open any of the documents by clicking the document or by typing the number that appears in front of the document name.

▶ See "Setting General Preferences," p. 213

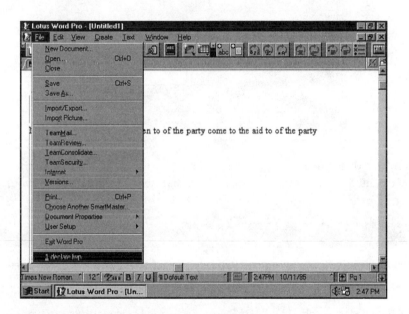

Fig. 3.11
Open a document by choosing it from the bottom of the File menu.

Note

You can open more than one document at a time. You are limited only by the amount of memory you have on your computer. Opening more than one document at a time enables you to cut or copy information from one document and then switch to another document to paste the information. To switch between documents, open the <u>W</u>indow menu. At the bottom of the menu, click the name of the document to which you want to switch.

Starting a New Document

When you first start Word Pro, you see the Welcome to Lotus Word Pro dialog box. You can use this dialog box to start a new document or open an existing document.

But suppose that you already started Word Pro and you need to start a new document. Click the Create New File SmartIcon or choose File, New. Word Pro displays the New dialog box (see fig. 3.12).

Fig. 3.12
The New dialog box closely resembles the dialog box you see when you start Word Pro.

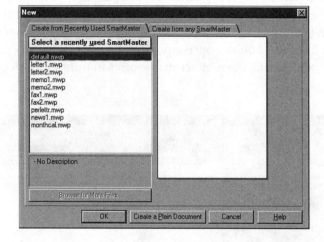

▶ See "Understanding SmartMasters," p. 241

From this dialog box, you can select a SmartMaster on which to base the document. SmartMasters contain settings that help Word Pro format your document.

> **Note**
>
> In Ami Pro (the previous version of Word Pro), SmartMasters were called style sheets.

The SmartMaster called DEFAULT provides some basic settings, such as a general-use typeface (the specific typeface and point size depend on your printer), and margins. If you choose this SmartMaster, Word Pro displays a blank document called [Untitled1], and you can begin typing text.

Closing Documents

Because you can open more than one document at a time, you may find that closing documents when you finish working with them is easier and less confusing.

To close a document, follow these steps:

1. Make the file you want to close the active document. If you need to switch documents, use the Window menu.

2. Choose File, Close. If you haven't named (saved) the document yet, Word Pro displays a message asking if you want to save the document. If the document has a name but you have changed the document since the last time you saved it, Word Pro displays a message asking if you want to save the changes.

3. Choose Yes, No, or Cancel.

   If you choose Yes, you save the document with the changes and close it. (If the document is new, Word Pro displays the Save As dialog box and prompts you for a name.)

   If you choose No, you close the document without saving the changes.

   If you choose Cancel, Word Pro closes the dialog box, but not the document.

After closing the document, Word Pro displays another open document; If no other documents are open, Word Pro displays the blank application screen.

If you exit Word Pro, you close the active document and all other open Word Pro documents. Again, Word Pro asks if you want to save changes you have made.

From Here...

You've learned the basics about creating and editing a document in this chapter. Consider exploring the following chapters:

- Chapter 4, "Formatting Text," shows you how to apply and modify character attributes such as fonts. You also learn how to format paragraphs and apply paragraph styles.

- Chapter 5, "Formatting the Page," continues with document formatting by explaining how to set margins, add headers and footers, and work in columns.

- Chapter 6, "Exploring Advanced Page Formatting Features," explores advanced page formatting techniques such as inserting page breaks and numbers, working with rulers, and using borders, lines, and shading in your document.

Chapter 4

Formatting Text

by Elaine Marmel

As you work in Word Pro, you may encounter times when you want to change the appearance of text in a document. You may want to enhance the appearance of a word, phrase, or paragraph, for example, by using underlining or boldface type.

Formatting is the process of specifying the appearance of text. Word Pro divides formatting into three categories: character formatting, paragraph formatting, and page formatting. Within each category, you can format text in different ways.

▶ See "Formatting the Page," p. 105

In this chapter, you learn how to:

- ■ Modify fonts
- ■ Apply character attributes
- ■ Align and indent text
- ■ Set line spacing

Changing Character Formatting

Characters are letters, numbers, and punctuation marks. When you format characters, you specify their appearance by changing the font, point size, or color of characters, or by applying attributes such as boldface or underlining.

You can apply character formatting before you type the characters, or you can type the characters and then apply the formatting. The following sections explain how you can use the keyboard, SmartIcons, or the Text InfoBox to change character formatting.

Word Pro has defined *CycleKeys* and *Cycle SmartIcons* that serve as shortcuts so you can see all the options available when changing character formatting. Each time you press a CycleKey or click a Cycle SmartIcon, you "cycle through" the options available for that key. Using these CycleKeys or Cycle SmartIcons, you can apply fonts, point sizes, and attributes (such as boldface or italics).

Modifying Fonts

Fonts are collections of typefaces that share a common style. Each font has a distinctive look. Two common fonts are Courier and Times New Roman. Most fonts are available in a range of sizes. You measure the size of a font in points (one point is equal to 1/72 inch); smaller point sizes produce smaller text.

▶ See "Using Type Sizes," p. 465

In Word Pro, you can use preset point sizes from 6 to 48 points. Or, if you are using a laser printer with adjustable or scalable fonts, you can specify the point size. To print documents, use the hardware fonts and point sizes available on your printer (these are fonts supplied with your printer or fonts you add to your printer using font cartridges). Or you can use software fonts (also called soft fonts) if your printer supports them.

▶ See "Changing Printing Options," p. 197

Word Pro doesn't control printing or your display; Windows controls both. Screen fonts, printer fonts, and the way they work in Windows are complex subjects. For more information, consult *Special Edition Using Windows 95* or *Using Windows 95* (published by Que Corporation) or the *Windows User's Guide*.

You can choose a font before you type the characters, or you can select existing characters and then change the font.

To change an existing font, follow these steps:

1. Select the text you want to modify.

> **Tip**
>
> To change the font of just one word, place the insertion point in that word instead of selecting each character of the word.

2. Click the Font list on the status bar and select a font (see fig. 4.1).

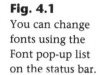

Tip

To cycle through available fonts, press F3 or repeatedly click the Face Cycle
SmartIcon.

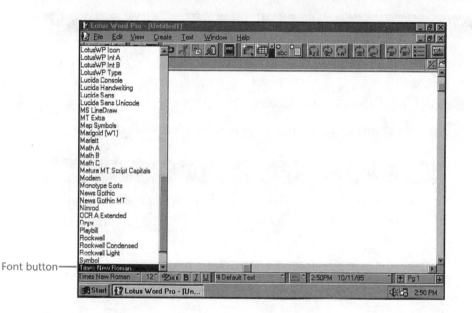

Font button

Fig. 4.1
You can change
fonts using the
Font pop-up list
on the status bar.

Alternatively, you may prefer to use the Text Properties InfoBox, particularly
if you want to change more than one characteristic of the selected text (see
fig. 4.2). Click the Text InfoBox SmartIcon or press the right mouse button
and choose Text Properties from the shortcut menu.

Font tab

Fig. 4.2
From the Font tab
of the Text
Properties InfoBox,
you can change
the font, point
size, color, and
attributes of the
selected text.

Adjusting Text Size

You can set the point size of the current font before you type, or you can select existing characters and then change the point size.

To change the point size of existing text, follow these steps:

> **Tip**
>
> To change the point size of a single word, place the insertion point in that word.

1. Select the text you want to modify.

2. Click the Point Size list on the status bar and select a size (see fig. 4.3).

> **Tip**
>
> To cycle through point sizes, press F4 or repeatedly click the Point Size Cycle SmartIcon.

Fig. 4.3
Using the Point Size pop-up list on the status bar, you can change the size of a font.

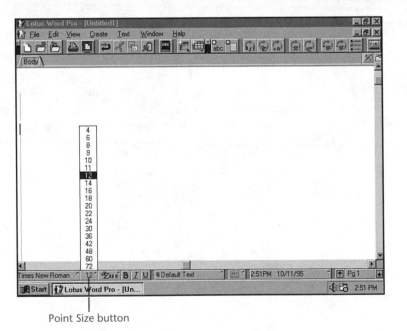

Point Size button

Alternatively, you may prefer to use the Text Properties InfoBox, particularly if you want to change more than one characteristic of the selected text (refer to fig. 4.2). Click the Text InfoBox SmartIcon or press the right mouse button and choose Text Properties from the shortcut menu.

Table 4.1 briefly describes the options available on the Font tab of the Text InfoBox.

Table 4.1 Font Options in the Text InfoBox

Option	Action
Font Name	Controls the typeface used for the text.
Size	Changes the point size for the typeface—the greater the point size, the larger the typeface.
Attributes	Controls the application of character attributes such as underlining or italics.
Text Color	Controls the color of the characters on color printers; on other printers, controls the shading of the characters.
Background	Controls the color behind characters on color printers; on other printers, controls the shading behind characters.
Transparent	Placing a check in this check box tells Word Pro to ignore any selection you made for the Background color.

Adjusting Text Attributes

Tip

To cycle through available attributes, press F5 or repeatedly click the Attribute Cycle SmartIcon.

You can use character attributes to enhance the appearance of text in many ways. Figure 4.4 shows the striking differences you can achieve by applying text attributes such as boldface, italics, and underline.

Fig. 4.4
Sample text after
applying various
character formats.

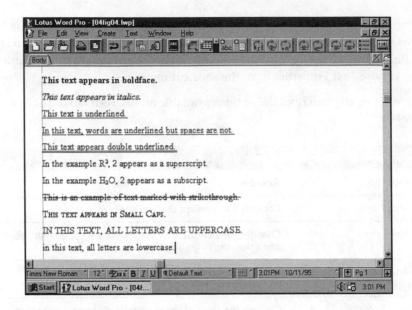

Table 4.2 lists the various character attributes that are available in this version
of Word Pro.

Table 4.2 Character Attributes	
Character Attribute	**Effect**
Bold	Characters appear in boldface type.
Italic	Characters appear in italic type.
Underline	Both words and spaces are underlined.
Word underline	Words are underlined, but spaces are not.
Double underline	Both words and spaces have a double underline.
Superscript	Characters are raised above the regular line of type and are in a smaller point size.
Subscript	Characters are lower than the regular line of type and are in a smaller point size.
Strikethrough	Characters appear with a straight line through them.
Small caps	Characters are all uppercase, but initial caps are in the assigned point size and the rest of the characters are in a slightly smaller point size.
Uppercase	Characters are all uppercase.

Character Attribute	Effect
Lowercase	Characters are all lowercase.
Hidden	Hidden text doesn't print.
Protected	Used along with document protection, text can be protected from changes.
Normal	Removes all character attributes and returns selected text to its original paragraph style settings.

▶ See "Formatting Text," p. 464

Getting to Know Word Pro

Tip

The Uppercase and Lowercase attributes can save you from retyping text that you want to change to the other case. For example, you may have an entire paragraph in lowercase that you want to change to uppercase. You can select the paragraph and then select the Uppercase attribute.

Note

You remove character attributes either by following the steps to apply the attribute or by pressing Ctrl+N to choose the Normal command from the Text menu.

You can choose a character attribute before you type the characters or you can type the characters and then choose an attribute. If you have already typed text, select the text to which you want to apply attributes. Then use one of the following methods:

- Repeatedly click the Attribute Cycle SmartIcon.

- Repeatedly press F5, the Attributes CycleKey.

- Choose Text, Attributes, and then choose Bold, Italic, or Underline.

Tip

Choosing Text, Attributes, Other also opens the Text Properties InfoBox.

- Click the Text InfoBox SmartIcon, or press the right mouse button and choose Text Properties from the shortcut menu to display the Text Properties InfoBox. Use the Font tab to apply one or more attributes.

■ Press any of the shortcut key combinations listed in table 4.3. Remember, you can apply an attribute before you type by pressing the shortcut key combination, typing, and then pressing the shortcut key combination again when you finish using the attribute. Alternatively, you can select typed text and then press the shortcut key combination for the character attribute you want to assign.

Table 4.3 Keyboard Shortcuts for Applying Character Attributes	
Attribute	**Shortcut**
Normal	Ctrl+N
Boldface	Ctrl+B
Italics	Ctrl+I
Underline	Ctrl+U
Word underline	Ctrl+W

Copying Character Formatting with Fast Format

Suppose that you italicized a few words in the first paragraph of the document and you decide to apply italics to the entire third paragraph. You can use the Fast Format command to copy the formatting of the italicized words in the first paragraph to the entire third paragraph. To use this feature, you must have a mouse.

To use the Fast Format feature, follow these steps:

1. Apply any kind of character formatting to text. You can apply the formatting using any of the methods mentioned previously in this chapter.

> **Tip**
>
> Make sure you drag to select. Placing the insertion point in a word to select just that word has a different effect when using Fast Format.

2. Select the text that contains the formatting you want to apply.

3. Choose Text, Fast Format, or press Ctrl+T. The mouse pointer becomes an I-beam with a paintbrush attached.

4. Use the mouse to select the text to which you want to apply the formatting. When you release the mouse button, Word Pro applies the formatting. Fast Format remains active, so you can continue selecting text and applying the formatting.

5. To turn off Fast Format, choose <u>T</u>ext, Fa<u>s</u>t Format again or press Ctrl+T again.

Note

If you use the <u>T</u>ext menu method to turn on Fast Formatting, note that a check mark appears to the left of the Fa<u>s</u>t Format command on the menu. Choosing the command again removes the check mark.

If you select a single word by placing the insertion point in that word, Word Pro doesn't automatically copy and apply formatting. Instead, you see the dialog box shown in figure 4.5. You learn more about paragraph styles in "Using Paragraph Styles" later in this chapter. Choosing the other option in this dialog box, The Look of the Text at the Insertion Point, has the same result as following the steps above, except that you don't need to highlight the selection containing the formatting before you turn on Fast Format. Word Pro assumes that the "selection" is the text at the insertion point, and applies the formatting of that text to whatever text you subsequently select.

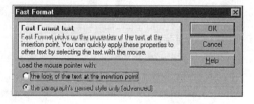

Fig. 4.5
From this dialog box, you can choose to copy character attributes or the paragraph style.

You can use Fast Format to apply any character formatting previously discussed in this chapter, including the fonts. Word Pro can copy more than one type of character formatting at a time, but the text you select to copy must contain all the formats. In figure 4.6, for example, the phrase `for all good men` appears in boldface type and the phrase `to come to the aid` appears in both underlined and boldface type.

Fig. 4.6
This sample text contains mixed attributes, including boldface and underlined boldface.

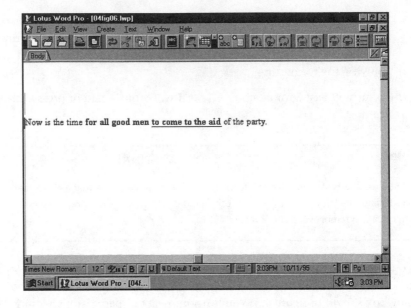

If you select both formatted phrases, turn on Fast Format, and then select the unformatted phrase Now is the time, Word Pro applies boldface and underlining to Now is the time. If you select only the phrase for all good men, turn on Fast Format, and then select the phrase Now is the time, Word Pro applies only boldface to Now is the time.

Changing Paragraph Formatting

The traditional definition of the term *paragraph* is "a series of related sentences." In Word Pro, the word *paragraph* has a special meaning: any amount of text or graphics followed by a paragraph mark (¶). See figure 4.7 for an example. If you have chosen to display paragraph marks, when you press Enter, Word Pro inserts a paragraph mark symbol into your document at the end of the paragraph.

To display paragraph marks, choose View, Set View Preferences. The View Preferences dialog box appears (see fig. 4.8).

Click the Show Marks list box. If no check mark appears next to Returns, click Returns. The list box remains open in case you want to mark or unmark other options. For example, you may also want to see Tabs. When you finish choosing items to display, click anywhere outside the list. Then choose OK to close the dialog box.

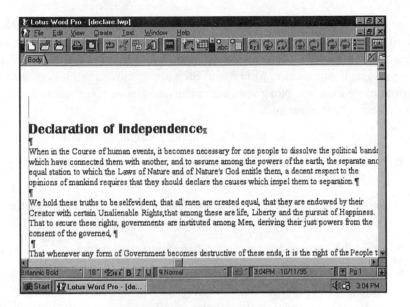

Fig. 4.7
Paragraph marks indicate the end of a paragraph.

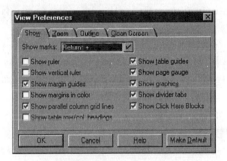

Fig. 4.8
From this dialog box, you can specify the information you want to see on-screen.

You can control the following attributes of paragraph formatting:

- Alignment
- Tab settings
- Indention
- Line spacing

You can also apply bullets or numbers to paragraphs. To enhance the appearance of a paragraph or to call attention to a paragraph, you may want to draw lines around it or apply a shadow border to it. These types of formatting are described later in this section.

Just as with character formatting, you can apply paragraph formatting before or after you type the text, but you may find it easiest to apply paragraph formatting after typing the paragraph. To do this, place the insertion point in the paragraph you want to format and then apply the format. If you want to format more than one paragraph, select the paragraphs you want to format and then apply the format.

Again, several methods are available to apply paragraph formatting:

- Repeatedly click either the Alignment Cycle SmartIcon or the Bullet Cycle SmartIcon.

- Repeatedly press the appropriate CycleKey: F6 for Alignment, F7 for Indention, F8 for Bullet List, or F9 for Number List.

- Open the Text menu and choose the appropriate command.

- Click the Text InfoBox SmartIcon or press the right mouse button and choose Text Properties from the shortcut menu to display the Text Properties InfoBox. Use the Alignment tab, the Lines and Shadows tab, the Bullets and Numbers tab, or the Misc tab to apply one or more attributes.

The Text Properties InfoBox provides the most complete way to format paragraphs; through this InfoBox you can access all the paragraph formatting options.

Adjusting Alignment

Alignment refers to the position of text within the margins of the page. In tables or frames, Word Pro measures alignment from the margins of the column, frame, or cell. In Word Pro, you can align text to the left or right margins, center the text, or justify the text.

As figure 4.9 shows, left alignment aligns text at the left margin and produces a ragged right margin.

When you use center alignment, the text is centered between the left and right margins, and both margins appear ragged (see fig. 4.10).

Figure 4.11 shows right alignment. Aligning text at the right margin produces a ragged left margin.

If you justify text, Word Pro aligns the text at both margins by expanding the spaces between words (see fig. 4.12).

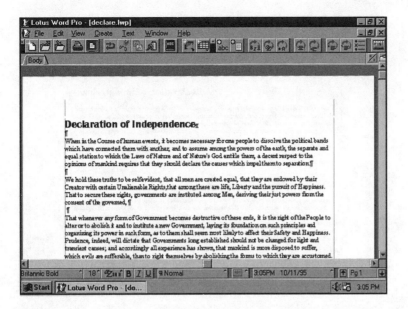

Fig. 4.9
This text is left-aligned.

Getting to Know Word Pro

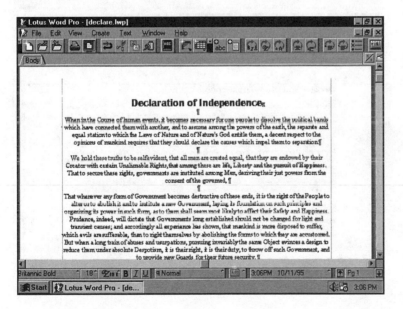

Fig. 4.10
This text is center-aligned.

Fig. 4.11

This text is right-aligned.

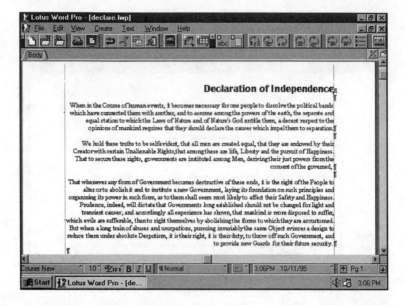

Fig. 4.12

This text is justified.

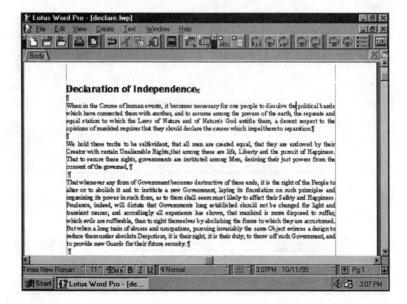

When you change the alignment, you don't need to select the entire paragraph. You can select any part of the paragraph, or just place the insertion point somewhere in the paragraph, because Word Pro aligns only entire paragraphs. To align text, follow these steps:

▶ See "Applying Text Alignment," p. 468

1. Place the insertion point anywhere in the paragraph you want to align, or select multiple paragraphs to align.

> **Tip**
>
> To cycle through the available alignment options, repeatedly click the Alignment Cycle SmartIcon or repeatedly press F6, the Alignment CycleKey.

2. Click the Text InfoBox SmartIcon, or press the right mouse button and choose Text Properties from the shortcut menu. When Word Pro displays the Text Properties InfoBox, click the Alignment tab (see fig. 4.13).

Alignment tab

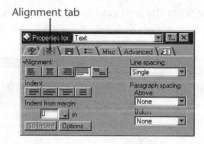

Fig. 4.13
Using this tab, you can set alignment for the selected paragraph.

3. Click one of the five Alignment options in the InfoBox.

If you prefer keyboard shortcuts, use those shown in table 4.4 to align paragraphs. To use a keyboard shortcut, place the insertion point in the paragraph you want to align and then press an alignment key combination.

Table 4.4   Alignment Keyboard Shortcuts

Alignment	Shortcut
Left	Ctrl+L
Center	Ctrl+E
Right	Ctrl+R
Justify	Ctrl+J

> **Note**
>
> To remove alignment, choose a different alignment or press Ctrl+N to choose Text, Normal and return the paragraph to the default left alignment.

Setting Tabs

By default, Word Pro places tabs every half inch in your document. You may want to change the tab settings. For example, if you have columns of numbers, dates, lists, and so on, you may want to set a tab for each item. You can change tab settings using the ruler or the Misc tab of the Text Properties InfoBox.

You can create left tabs, center tabs, right tabs, or decimal (numeric) tabs. You can add a *leader* to the tabs in your document. A leader is a series of characters that precedes the tab and its following text. For leader characters, you can use periods, dashes, or underlines. In a right tab, for example, you may want a series of periods (a *dot leader*). You use a dot leader when you want to lead the reader's eye from the text on the left to the text on the right. Examples of each type of tab are shown in figure 4.14.

Fig. 4.14
You can format
text using
different tab types.

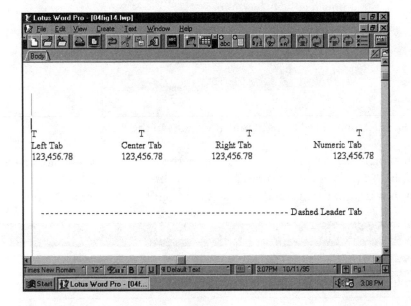

To set tabs *without* leaders, follow these steps:

1. Display the ruler by choosing View, Show/Hide, Ruler. The horizontal ruler appears at the top of the document (see fig. 4.15).

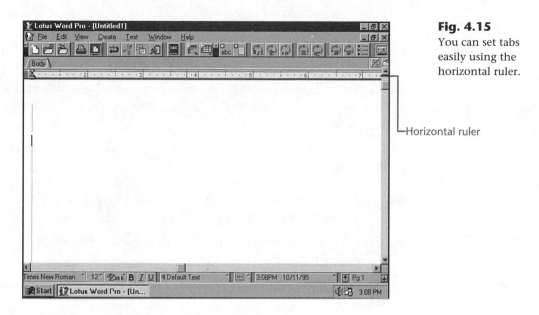

Fig. 4.15
You can set tabs
easily using the
horizontal ruler.

Horizontal ruler

2. Move the mouse pointer into the ruler.

3. (Optional) If you don't want to use the predefined tabs, click the right
   mouse button and choose Clear All Tabs from the shortcut menu (see
   fig. 4.16).

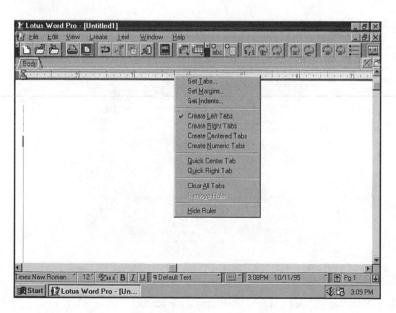

Fig. 4.16
From this shortcut
menu, you can
clear all tabs and
set tab alignment.

Getting to Know Word Pro

4. If you want to insert a left-aligned tab, move the mouse pointer to the location where you want to place the tab and click the left mouse button.

5. If you want to insert a right-aligned, centered, or numeric tab, click the right mouse button to open the shortcut menu. Choose the appropriate alignment from the menu.

6. Click the left mouse button on the ruler at the location where you want the tab to appear.

If you want to use a leader character or set tabs using exact measurements, you must use the Set Tabs on Ruler dialog box. Follow these steps:

1. Make sure the horizontal ruler appears. If it doesn't, choose View, Show/Hide, Ruler.

2. Move the mouse pointer into the ruler to the location where you want to place the tab.

> ### Tip
> You can open the Set Tabs on Ruler dialog box from the Text Properties InfoBox. Choose the Misc tab and then click Set Tabs.

3. Click the right mouse button to display the shortcut menu.

4. Choose Set Tabs. The Set Tabs on Ruler dialog box appears (see fig. 4.17).

Fig. 4.17
Use this dialog box to set a tab and define a leader character for it.

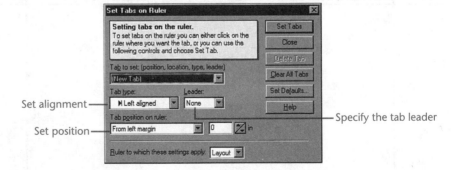

5. Click the Tab Type list box and select the type of tab.

6. Click the Leader list box and choose a leader character.

7. Use the Tab Position on Ruler list box and the number spinner box next to it to position the tab.

8. Click Set Tabs, then click Close.

To move an existing tab, click its marker and drag the marker with the mouse to its new location. To delete a single tab, drag it down off the ruler. To delete all tabs on the ruler, choose the Clear All Tabs button in the Set Tabs on Ruler dialog box.

Modifying Indentions

Using *indention*, you can indent one line or an entire paragraph of text from the margins. Creating special document effects is easy using a variety of indents available in Word Pro. You can create bibliographies, for example, using outdents (also known as hanging indents), which align the first line of the paragraph at the left margin and indent subsequent lines of the paragraph.

You can change indention using the Alignment tab of the Text Properties InfoBox, which contains Quick Indention buttons (see fig. 4.18).

Indent left margin ———

Indent first line   Outdent first line

Indent both left and right margins

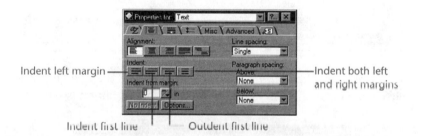

Fig. 4.18
Using the Quick Indention buttons, you can easily indent the selected paragraph.

Tip

Use F7, the Indention CycleKey, to cycle incrementally from the left margin through the indentions available in Word Pro. The Indention CycleKey does not cycle through right indents or outdents.

Figure 4.19 shows examples of paragraphs indented using each of the Quick Indention buttons:

■ The first paragraph is indented one-half inch from the left margin.

■ In the second paragraph, the first line is indented one-half inch from the left margin.

■ The third paragraph uses a hanging indent, where the first line is not indented and all the other lines in the paragraph are indented one-half inch from the left margin.

■ The last paragraph is indented one-half inch from both margins.

Fig. 4.19
You can indent
text in four
different ways.

Left margin ─────

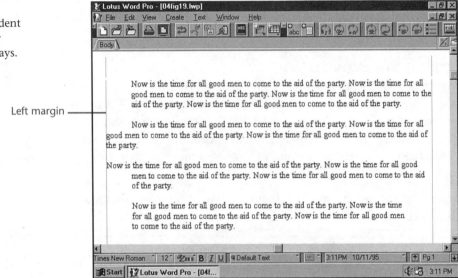

To set indents, click the Text InfoBox SmartIcon to open the Text Properties InfoBox. Click the Alignment tab then click the Options button (see fig. 4.20).

Fig. 4.20
You can control the
amount Word Pro
indents text from
the Indent Options
dialog box.

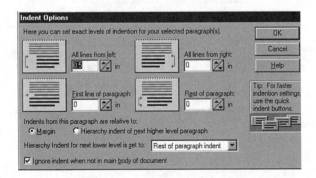

Type the exact amount in the spinner text box following the indention style you have chosen, or click the up- and down-arrow buttons located at the ends of the text box. Each time you click the arrow button, you increase or decrease the amount by .05 inch.

Setting Line Spacing

Line spacing refers to the amount of space between lines in a document. For text in the *single-space* format, no blank line appears between lines of text. In the *double-space* format, a blank line (the height of one line of text) appears between lines of text. Word Pro offers half, single, double, and 1 1/2-line spacing, and also enables you to specify multiple, leading, and custom spacing formats.

You set line spacing from the Alignment tab of the Text Properties InfoBox. Word Pro directly changes the spacing when you click most options in the list box, but you see dialog boxes if you choose Multiple (see fig. 4.21), Leading (see fig. 4.22), or Custom (see fig. 4.23).

Fig. 4.21
Use this dialog box to specify a number of lines between text.

Fig. 4.22
Use this dialog box to vary spacing as it relates to font size.

Fig. 4.23
Here you can control spacing when printing to preprinted forms.

With the Multiple option, you specify a multiple number of lines between text. For example, you can create triple spacing by specifying 3.

The Leading option helps you vary spacing as it relates to font size. For example, if your text is 11 points and you specify the leading option at 13 points, Word Pro sets line spacing by adding two points to the line height of your text.

Using the Custom option, you set a fixed distance, in inches, centimeters, picas, or points, between lines of text. For example, if you specify one-half inch, each base line is one-half inch from the next line. Custom spacing is useful if you need to fit text into a preprinted form.

Using Bullets and Numbers

Bullets are often used to set off a list of items in a document. Typically, a character appears before each item in a bulleted list; the first line of the text is indented from the bullet and subsequent lines are aligned with the first line of the text, not with the bullet.

Using the Bullet Cycle SmartIcon or F8, the Bullet CycleKey, you see the series of characters you can use to create a bulleted list and their varying alignments.

You can also apply a bullet to a paragraph using the Bullet tab of the Text Properties InfoBox (see fig. 4.24). From this tab, you can control the amount of space Word Pro leaves between the margin and the bullet and between the bullet and the text.

If you need to create a two-paragraph bullet, where the bullet appears before the first of the two paragraphs, and the second paragraph is aligned with the text of the first (bulleted) paragraph, place a check in the Skip Bullet/Number check box.

You can control the font and character Word Pro uses for bullets. Click the Font button to change to a different font. Click the arrow next to the Other list box to select a character you want Word Pro to use for the bullet.

Bullet tab

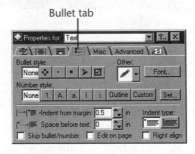

Fig. 4.24
Using this tab of the Text Properties InfoBox, you can control the appearance of bullets and numbers.

Occasionally, you may need to list information in your document, and the order of the information is important. You can easily create a numbered list in Word Pro.

Tip

Press F9 or click the Numbering Cycle SmartIcon repeatedly to cycle through the available numbering options for a paragraph.

Use the Bullet tab of the Text Properties InfoBox to add a number to a paragraph (refer to fig. 4.24). With the insertion point in the paragraph you want to number, click a number style. Word Pro places that number style in front of the paragraph, aligning the number on the left margin. By default, the first line of text is indented and the rest of the lines in that paragraph are aligned with the first line of text. Use the Indent Type buttons to change the alignment of the text in the paragraph in relation to the number. You can also use the indent text spinner boxes to control the amount of space Word Pro leaves between the margin and the number, and the amount of space between the number and the text.

When you press Enter to start a new paragraph, Word Pro assigns the next sequential number, based on the style you chose, to the new paragraph. If you need to create a two-paragraph numbered item (where the second paragraph is a continuation of the first paragraph and doesn't get a number of its own), place the insertion point in the paragraph that should not be numbered and select the Skip Bullet/Number check box. Word Pro does not number the current paragraph, but when you press Enter, Word Pro assigns the next sequential number to the new paragraph.

If you place a check in the Edit On Page check box, Word Pro lets you edit the paragraph number and change it to anything you want.

Outline and custom numbering are also available. When you click either the Custom button or the Set button, the Numbered List Options dialog box appears (see fig. 4.25).

▶ See "Using Out-
line Numbering,"
p. 281

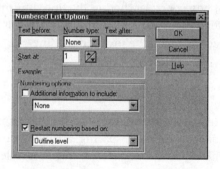

Fig. 4.25
In this dialog box,
you can define a
custom numbering
scheme.

Customize your numbering scheme by adding text before numbers or including section names as part of the number. For example, to include a section name as part of a number, place a check in the Additional Information to Include check box, then open the list box and choose Section.

Adding Lines and Borders

Lines and borders are two other devices often used to set off paragraphs. Using the Lines and Borders tab of the Text Properties InfoBox, you can define the way you highlight these paragraphs (see fig. 4.26).

Lines and Borders tab

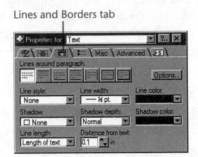

Fig. 4.26
Add lines or shadow borders to paragraphs from this tab of the Text Properties InfoBox.

Use the buttons on this tab to specify how you want the lines to appear around the paragraph containing the insertion point. The last button places a shadow box around the paragraph.

The Line Style and Line Width boxes control the appearance and thickness of the line you draw; use the Line Color list box to change the color of the line. The Shadow list box determines where the shadow appears—for example, you can draw a single line around a paragraph and add a shadow to it. The Shadow Depth list box controls the size of the shadow, and, of course, the Shadow Color list box controls the color of the shadow.

The Line Length list box controls whether the line runs from margin to margin or extends the length of the text it surrounds. The Distance from Text box controls the space between the text and the line.

Using Paragraph Styles

A *paragraph style* consists of all elements discussed earlier in this chapter—font, alignment, indenting method, spacing, attributes, and special effects such as bullets, numbers, lines, or borders. Paragraph styles can also include hyphenation. Creating, using, and—when necessary—modifying paragraph styles ensures uniformity in a document.

▶ See "Modifying SmartMasters," p. 247

Word Pro stores paragraph styles in SmartMasters. A *SmartMaster* is a collection of paragraph styles and page layouts well-suited for a certain type of work. Word Pro comes with many SmartMasters containing different collections of paragraph styles and page layout information.

When you open a new document, you generally work with the default SmartMaster. The default SmartMaster contains margin and tab defaults and a number of paragraph styles, including Default Text. The Default Text style, used for the majority of the text in most documents, contains information about the default font, point size, and text alignment.

You can change the Default Text style and the default SmartMaster if they don't meet your everyday work needs.

▶ See "Creating Styles," p. 254

▶ See "Managing Styles," p. 257

From Here...

In this chapter, you learned about the ways you can format characters and paragraphs in Word Pro. Now you're ready to explore page formatting. See the following chapters:

■ Chapter 5, "Formatting the Page," continues with document formatting by explaining how to set margins, add headers and footers, and work in columns.

■ Chapter 6, "Exploring Advanced Page Formatting Features," explores advanced page formatting techniques such as inserting page breaks and numbers, working with rulers, and using borders, lines, and shading in your document.

Getting to Know Word Pro

Chapter 5

Formatting the Page

by Elaine Marmel

In Chapter 4, "Formatting Text," you learned some different ways to change the style of a document: by modifying fonts and character attributes and by applying paragraph formatting.

◄ See "Changing Character For-matting," p. 79

Style also occurs within the larger context of *page formatting*. Page formatting features include changing margins, columns, page orientation, paper size, borders, lines, shading, and more. This book divides the coverage of page formatting, often called page layout formatting, into three chapters.

◄ See "Changing Paragraph Formatting," p. 88

In this chapter, you learn how to:

- Change the size and orientation of a page
- Change the page margins
- Create and work in columns
- Add headers and footers to your page

In subsequent chapters, you explore the use of page lines, shading, boxes, automatic page numbering, using page layout styles, and displaying your document in different views in Word Pro.

► See "Exploring Advanced Page Formatting Features," p. 125

Understanding the Default Page Layout

As you learned in earlier chapters, when you open a document in Word Pro, you associate a SmartMaster with the document. The SmartMaster contains instructions to Word Pro regarding page formatting and specialized para-graph styles. Not only does Word Pro provide you with a general-use default

▶ See "Using
Word Pro's
SmartMasters,"
p. 242

SmartMaster, it also provides over 50 specialized SmartMasters for memos, envelopes, letters, invoices, and other documents. You can also create your own SmartMasters. Although the SmartMaster is the source of the default values for page layout parameters such as margin size, number of columns, tabs, and so on, the page formatting in the SmartMaster may not meet all your needs for your document. The changes you make to the page formatting apply only to the current document. The SmartMaster you used to open the document remains intact even if you change the page formatting for that particular document.

▶ See "Creating
a New
SmartMaster,"
p. 261

◀ See "Using
Paragraph
Styles," p. 102

You learned earlier in this book that you can create paragraph styles that contain formatting characteristics you want to apply to a particular paragraph. In the same way, you can save the page formatting settings you establish so you can use them in other documents or other sections of the same document. You store page formatting characteristics in a *page style*.

You use the Page Properties InfoBox to change most page layout settings. Like the Text Properties InfoBox, the Page Properties InfoBox has several different tabs, each controlling one aspect of page settings. In figure 5.1, you see the first tab of the Page Properties InfoBox.

▶ See "Saving
Page Format-
ting Settings,"
p. 134

When you change page formatting options, you affect the entire document. If you want to change the page settings for just a portion of a document, you must divide the document into sections and then change the page layout for a particular section.

Fig. 5.1
The first tab of the Page Properties InfoBox enables you to control page size, orientation, and margins.

Page Settings tab

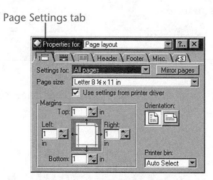

Setting Page Size and Orientation

Page size refers to the physical size of the paper on which you want to produce your document. *Orientation* refers to the direction in which you want text to print on that paper. Orientations are named *portrait* and *landscape* based on the way artists position their canvases when they paint pictures of people or the countryside.

▶ See "Under-standing Divisions and Sections," p. 306

Changing the Page Size

To change the size of your page, you use the first tab of the Page Properties InfoBox, which is the Page Settings tab (refer to fig. 5.1).

To display the Page Properties InfoBox, click the Page InfoBox SmartIcon or click the right mouse button to open a shortcut menu, and then choose Page Properties.

For standard page sizes, you can choose Letter (8 1/2 by 11 inches) or Legal (8 1/2 by 14 inches), or you can choose from several envelope sizes. Word Pro also offers European paper size setting A4, which is 8.27 inches long and 11.69 inches wide, which actually is 210×297 mm. If the paper is a custom size, choose Custom and specify the dimensions of the paper in the Custom Page Size dialog box (see fig. 5.2).

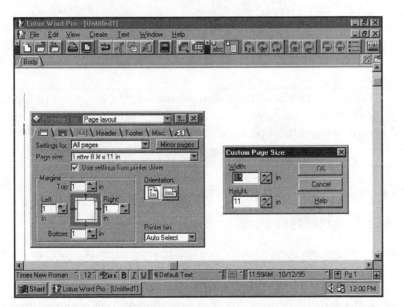

Fig. 5.2
Using the Custom Page Size dialog box, you can define specific page size measurements.

Note

Not all printers support all sizes of paper, and some may require manual feed of custom sizes. Check your printer manual to determine your printer's capabilities.

Setting Page Orientation

Page orientation refers to the direction of the longest measurement of the page. The orientation you choose usually depends on the kind of document you are creating. For letters, reports, and most business documents that emphasize text rather than tables or graphics, portrait orientation (upright, with the short side of the paper at the top) is preferable. If you are printing trifold brochures, some forms, flyers, books, or charts with multiple columns, you may want to print in landscape orientation (sideways, with the long side of the paper at the top).

As you can see from figure 5.3, you click an orientation button to select the orientation you want.

Fig. 5.3
Click one of these two buttons to set page orientation.

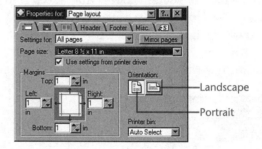

▶ See "Printing
Documents,"
p. 203

▶ See "Types of
Documents,"
p. 450

In most cases, to print landscape, your printer must be able to print in landscape orientation. If you try to print in landscape orientation with a printer that doesn't support this option, Word Pro displays a warning message; you must reconfigure the printer or change printers before continuing.

Setting Margins, Page Tabs, and Columns

▶ See "Under-
standing Divi-
sions and
Sections,"
p. 306

From the Page Properties InfoBox, you can change tabs, columns, and margins for the entire document at one time. Regardless of where the insertion point is in the document, the changes you make will change the default settings for the entire document. You can use different page layout settings for parts of your document by inserting a section, which is described in Chapter 16, "Managing Long Documents."

At first glance, Word Pro's variety of settings and options may appear overwhelming. Remember, however, as you use each option, the change appears immediately in the document, making the whole process fast and simple.

Setting Page Margins

Margins are the white space between the text and the edges of the page. The page has margins along the top, bottom, left, and right sides. Default margins are set by the SmartMaster you use when you open the document. You can change these margins whenever you choose.

The changes you make to margin settings affect the appearance and amount of text you can fit on a page. The larger the margins, the less space for text remains. You may want to increase the left margin to allow room for notes or binding, or you may want to decrease all margins to fit more text on a page.

To change margins, follow these steps:

1. Open the Page Properties InfoBox by clicking the Page InfoBox SmartIcon or by clicking the right mouse button and choosing Page Properties from the shortcut menu (see fig. 5.4).

2. Position the insertion point in the Left text box and type the size of the margin (in inches) for the left margin. You can also use the arrow buttons next to the spinner text box to select the number.

3. To change the right, top, and bottom margins, repeat step 2 for each spinner text box.

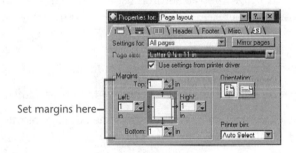

Set margins here—

Fig. 5.4
The options for setting margins appear on the Page Settings tab of the Page Properties InfoBox.

Setting Page Tabs

As you know, each Word Pro SmartMaster establishes a set of default tab settings for each document you base on that SmartMaster. Earlier in this book, you learned to change tabs for the paragraph containing the insertion point. But what if you want to change the tabs for the entire document? Do you need to change the tabs paragraph by paragraph? Or select the whole document and change the tabs? Nope. Use the Page Properties InfoBox to change the page tabs.

◄ See "Setting Tabs," p. 94

Just as you can create different kinds of tabs for a particular paragraph, you can create page tabs that include evenly spaced tabs, left tabs, and right tabs. The page tabs affect the entire document, not just the paragraph containing the insertion point.

To create page tabs, follow these steps:

1. Open the Page Properties InfoBox by clicking the Page InfoBox SmartIcon or by clicking the right mouse button and choosing Page Properties from the shortcut menu.

2. Click the Misc tab of the Page Properties InfoBox (see fig. 5.5).

Fig. 5.5
Use the Misc tab of the Page Properties InfoBox to set tabs that affect your entire document.

Set tab measurement for entire document

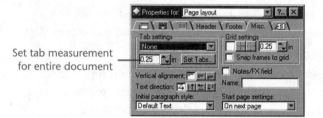

3. Open the Tab Settings list box and choose the tab type you want. Then use the spinner box below the Tab Settings list box to change the default distance you want between tabs. You can choose from these tab types:

- None, which uses default tabs set every 1/4 inch.

- Evenly Spaced, which creates tabs every 1/4 inch by default.

- From the Left Edge, which sets one tab at the left edge of the document, 1/4 inch from the left margin by default.

- From the Right Edge, which sets one tab at the right edge of the document, 1/4 inch from the right margin by default.

- Custom, which enables you to set tabs at varying locations.

If you want custom tabs or you want to use a leader character, click the Set Tabs button to display the Set Tabs on Ruler dialog box shown in figure 5.6.

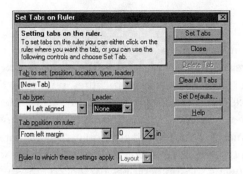

Fig. 5.6
Use the Set Tabs
on Ruler dialog box
to specify options
for custom tabs
or to set leader
characters.

To set a page tab with a leader, follow these steps:

> **Tip**
>
> Because you cannot insert a new tab where a tab already exists, remove unwanted
> tabs first. To remove a tab, click the Tab to Set list box, select the tab, and click
> Delete Tab.

1. Click the Leader list box and choose a leader character.

2. Use the Tab Position on Ruler list box and the number spinner box next
   to it to position the tab.

3. Click Set Tabs.

> **Tip**
>
> To delete all tabs on the ruler, move the mouse pointer into the ruler, click the
> right mouse button, and choose Clear All Tabs from the shortcut menu.

To move an existing tab, you can just drag the tab marker on the ruler, the
same way you move a paragraph tab. If you don't see the ruler on-screen,
choose View, Show/Hide, Ruler. You must also be in Layout mode to see the
ruler.

Creating Columns

▶ See "Desktop
Publishing
with Word
Pro," p. 441

Columns have many uses in word processing. Text in two or three columns is often easier to read and more pleasing to the eye than text that spans the entire width of the page. Newsletters, brochures, price lists, flyers, forms, and even books can use multiple-column formats. Word Pro offers newspaper-style columns; the text flows from the bottom of column one to the top of column two automatically. Alternatively, you can create parallel columns, where an entry in the first column corresponds to an entry in the second column. (The following section describes parallel columns.)

Working with multiple columns of text is very difficult if you try to use tabs to create parallel columns, and impossible if you want to create newspaper columns. Use tabs to set up columns of numbers or lists; use Word Pro's column feature for newspaper columns or parallel columns. As you type, Word Pro enters the text into formatted columns. As with the other page layouts, the default number of columns is determined by the SmartMaster you use when you open the document. If you use the default SmartMaster, your document formats into one column by default.

Creating Newspaper Columns

Suppose that you want to place columns in a sample document, such as the document shown in figure 5.7.

Fig. 5.7
The sample text appears in one column.

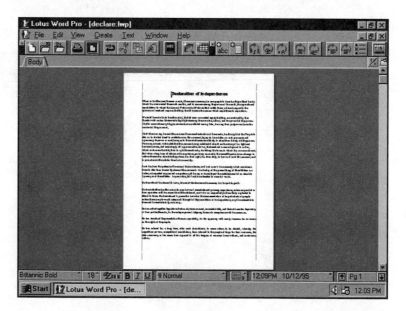

To create newspaper columns, follow these steps:

1. Click the Page InfoBox SmartIcon, or click the right mouse button and choose P̲age Properties from the shortcut menu.

2. Click the Columns tab of the Page Properties InfoBox (see fig. 5.8).

I

Getting to Know Word Pro

Fig. 5.8
Use the Columns tab of the Page Properties InfoBox to create newspaper columns in your document.

> **Tip**
>
> Remember, too many columns on a page make reading difficult.

3. Use the Number of Newspaper Columns spinner box to specify how many columns you want to create.

> **Tip**
>
> In most documents the default gutter width of .17 makes the text too close for comfortable reading. To ensure that your columnar text is easy to read, make the gutter at least .25 inches, and even more if possible (up to .5 inches).

4. Use the Space Between Columns spinner box to change the distance between columns. The space between columns is known as the *gutter*.

5. Use the options in the Vertical Line Between Columns area to describe any lines you want Word Pro to place between each column. Open the Line Style list box and choose a line style (see fig. 5.9).

6. Set the thickness of the line using the Line Width list box.

> **Tip**
>
> Remember, line colors will appear on printed copies only if your printer supports color printing.

Fig. 5.9
Word Pro offers a
wide variety of
line styles you can
use when placing
lines between
newspaper
columns.

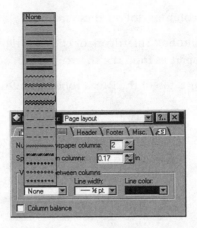

7. Set the color of the line using the Line Color list box.

> **Tip**
>
> Wait until you have completely entered your text before you turn on Column Balance. Otherwise, the columns balance as you type, making text jump in unexpected ways between the columns.

8. Click the Column Balance check box to evenly fill columns when text does not fill the entire page (see figs. 5.10 and 5.11).

> **Note**
>
> Word Pro automatically balances columns on all but the last page without using the Column Balance option.

In figure 5.7, you saw sample text in one column. In figure 5.11, you saw a two-column layout. Figure 5.12 shows the same text in three columns.

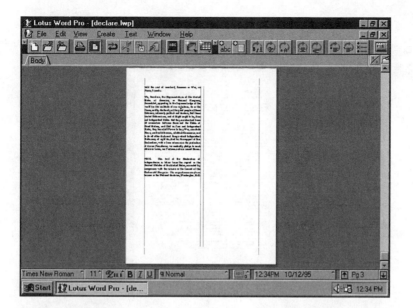

Fig. 5.10
This figure shows columnar text without balanced columns. Unbalanced columnar text completes one column before flowing to another.

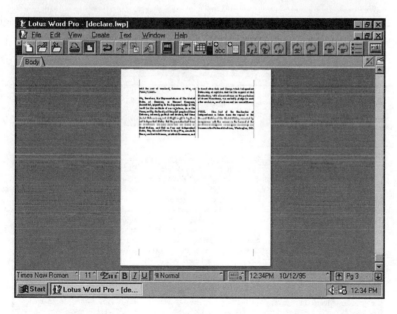

Fig. 5.11
This figure shows columnar text with balanced columns.

▶ See "Formatting Frames," p. 398

▶ See "Balancing Design Elements," p. 455

▶ See "Producing Newsletters," p. 452

Fig. 5.12
This figure shows the sample text in three columns.

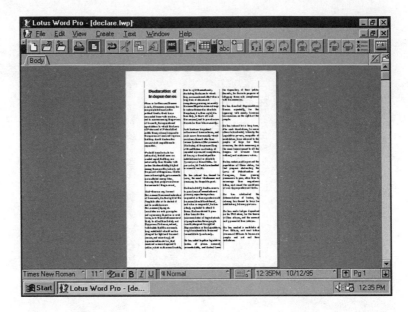

You can modify columns using the ruler. Place the mouse pointer in the gray area on the ruler between margins. The pointer changes shape (see fig. 5.13).

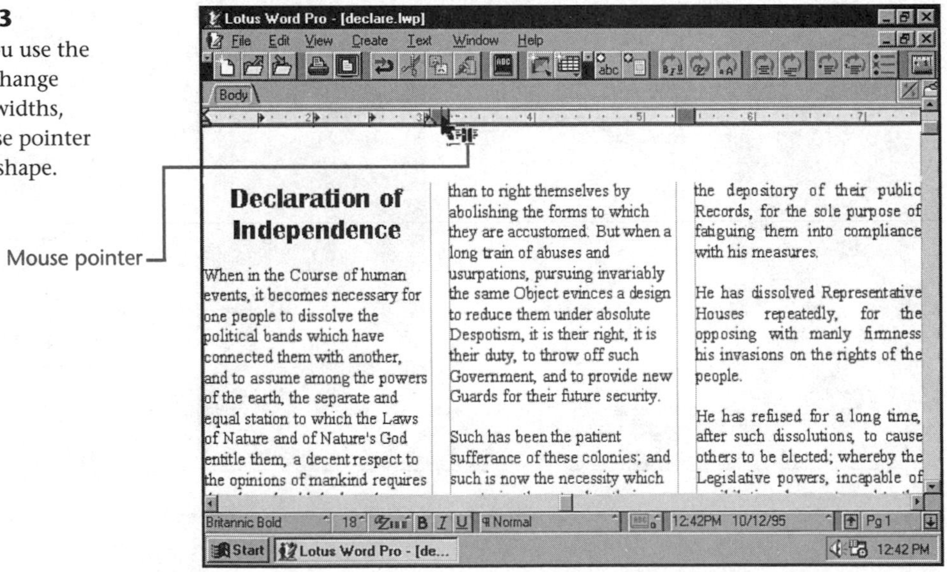

Fig. 5.13
When you use the ruler to change column widths, the mouse pointer changes shape.

Mouse pointer

Drag the column boundary. Dragging to the left makes the column to the left smaller. Dragging to the right makes the column to the right smaller.

Creating Parallel Columns

You can create *parallel columns* to enter text where the information in one column relates directly to the information in the next column. Glossary entries provide a good example—the entry in the first column (the word being defined) corresponds to the entry in the second column (the definition).

Suppose that you want to create columnar text like the sample in figure 5.14.

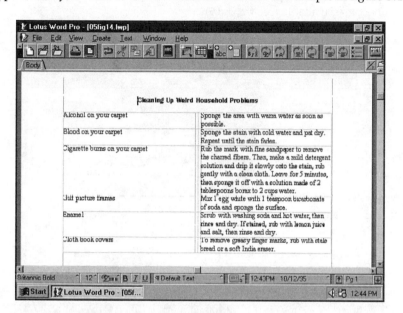

Fig. 5.14
Parallel columns enable you to type one entry in the first column and a related entry in the second column.

To create parallel columns like the ones shown in figure 5.14, follow these steps:

1. Place the insertion point where you want parallel columns to begin.

2. Choose the Create, Parallel Columns command. The Create Parallel Columns dialog box appears (see fig. 5.15).

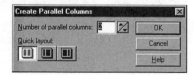

Fig. 5.15
Use this dialog box to create parallel columns in your document.

3. Use the Number of Parallel Columns spinner box to specify how many columns you want to create.

4. Click one of the Quick Layout buttons to create evenly sized parallel columns or columns where either the left or right column is smaller than the other columns.

5. Click OK.

When you click OK, columns appear in your document and the Columns menu becomes available (see fig. 5.16).

Fig. 5.16
After you create parallel columns, you can adjust and format them using the commands on the Columns menu.

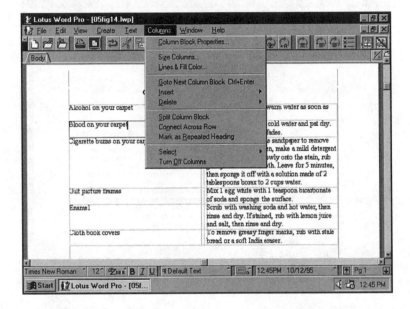

The first three commands on the menu all open the Column Properties InfoBox, which, like other InfoBoxes, contains multiple tabs. Each of the following figures shows a different tab of the Column Properties InfoBox (see figs. 5.17, 5.18, 5.19, and 5.20).

> **Tip**
>
> You'll find more information on the settings you see on each tab of the Column Properties InfoBox earlier in this chapter and in other chapters of this book.

First tab

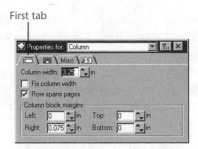

Fig. 5.17
From the first tab
of the Column
Properties InfoBox,
change column
size and format
settings.

Second tab

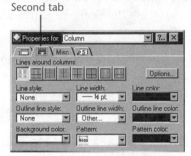

Fig. 5.18
From the second
tab of the Column
Properties InfoBox,
add lines and
colors to parallel
columns.

Misc tab

Fig. 5.19
From the Misc tab
of the Column
Properties InfoBox,
change tab settings
and vertical
alignment within
a column.

Style tab

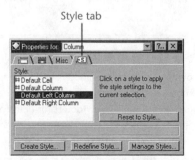

Fig. 5.20
From the Style tab
of the Column
Properties InfoBox,
assign a column
style.

To type in parallel columns, place the insertion point in the first column and type as usual. Word wrap still operates within the column, so you don't need to press Enter when you reach a column's right boundary. When you finish typing in one cell (Word Pro calls each box in the table a *cell*) and want to move to the next, press Ctrl+Enter. The insertion point jumps to the next cell. When you reach the end of a row, pressing Ctrl+Enter inserts a new row in the parallel columns.

Use the Insert and Delete commands on the Columns menu to add or remove rows or columns. Use the Split Column Block command to divide one cell into multiple cells. Similarly, use the Connect Across Row command to connect all cells in a particular row.

When you don't want to type in parallel columns any longer, place the insertion point at the location where you no longer want a column format and choose the Columns, Turn Off Columns command.

Adding Headers and Footers

You can use headers or footers to convey information about the document or your company. A *header* is information (text or a picture) that appears in the top margin of a document page. For example, a header may contain the date and recipient in a letter; or it can contain the date, volume number, and issue number of a newsletter. A *footer* is information that appears in the bottom margin of a document page, such as a chapter name or a page number.

A sample header may look like this:

```
07-15-95   The ABC Company Page 1
```

▶ See "Under-
standing Divi-
sions and
Sections,"
p. 306

Typically, a header or footer displays the same information on each page where it appears. You have some flexibility in using headers and footers; the header or footer can appear on all pages or it can begin on any page you specify.

> **Note**
>
> You may want to use different headers and footers in different parts of your document. When writing a book, you may want to enter chapter names in the header for each chapter. To create different headers or footers for different parts of your document, you insert section breaks to divide your document. Then you can create different header and footer information in each section.

When you create a header or footer, Word Pro uses the Header and Footer settings specified in the current SmartMaster for your document. (If you have changed the SmartMaster, the most recent settings apply.) The SmartMaster settings for your main document text, therefore, also apply to your headers and footers.

You can use all of Word Pro's text formatting and editing features on headers and footers (paragraph styles, indenting, spell checking, text enhancements, and so forth). You can also set special margins and tabs for headers and footers by using the Header tab of the Page Properties InfoBox.

▶ See "Designing the Page in Layout Mode," p. 140

To create a header or footer, display the document in Layout mode so you can see the header or footer area (see fig. 5.21). (If the footer area is not visible, scroll the page down until it is.) Then, place the insertion point in the header or footer area. You can type the header or footer first, and then format it; or you can format the header or footer, then type it into your document.

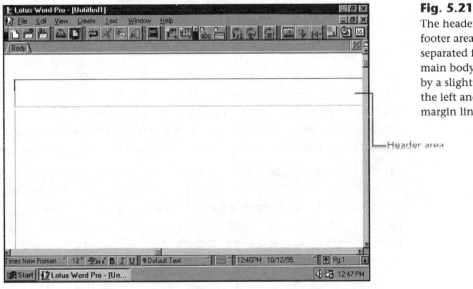

Fig. 5.21
The header and footer areas are separated from the main body of text by a slight break in the left and right margin lines.

Header area

The formats for headers and footers operate independently of the format for the body of the document. You can set some formats from the Page Properties InfoBox, but you have access to more formats using either the Header Properties InfoBox (see fig. 5.22) or the Footer Properties InfoBox (see fig. 5.23). To open either of these InfoBoxes, place the insertion point in the appropriate area (header or footer) of the document and then click the right mouse button. Depending on the location of the insertion point, you'll see either the Header Properties command or the Footer Properties command.

Fig. 5.22
The Header
Properties InfoBox
has four tabs of
related options.

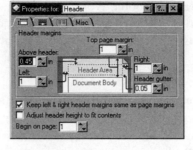

Fig. 5.23
The Footer
Properties InfoBox
strongly resembles
the Header
Properties InfoBox,
but the options
apply to footers.

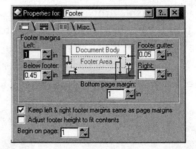

In general, the settings you change while creating headers or footers do not affect the main text. Note, however, that the Top Page Margin and the Bottom Page Margin settings take into account the settings for the whole page. Word Pro remembers the size of the page when you choose a top or bottom margin and prevents you from setting a margin that cannot fit on the page.

For headers, the top page margin measures the distance from the top edge of the page to the beginning of text and includes header text. The distance above the header measures the distance from the top edge of the paper to the beginning of header text. The header gutter margin measures the distance between the header text and the document text. The margins work similarly (but in reverse order) for footers.

Note

Laser printers do not print within one-half inch of the edge of the page. Therefore, the distance between a header or footer and the edge of the page must be at least one-half inch.

Troubleshooting

My header doesn't print. What's wrong?

If header or footer text doesn't print, it is probably in the nonprint zone, or you haven't provided a large enough area to accommodate the font and paragraph spacing.

The first page of a document often shows the company logo, letterhead, or newsletter nameplate at the top of the page. Headers containing information to identify subsequent pages (such as the name of the person receiving the letter) usually begin on the second page, to avoid printing over the logo or letterhead. If you want the header (or footer) to begin on the second page, type **2** in the Begin on Page spinner box.

Note

The header or footer area disappears from page 1 when the header or footer begins on a page other than 1. To include fixed header or footer information on page 1, return to the Page Properties InfoBox and reset the Begin on Page spinner box to 1.

The other tabs of the Header or Footer Properties InfoBox provide additional formatting options, such as drawing lines around and applying colors to your headers and footers, creating columns, and setting tabs, vertical alignment, and paragraph styles in your headers and footers.

You type the text for the header or footer the same way you type any other text. Place the insertion point in the header or footer area and type the header or footer text. The insertion point doesn't need to be on the first page of the document to create a header or footer. You can create headers and footers while working on any page in a section.

You can then format the text by applying text attributes. Note that additional SmartIcons appear when you place the insertion point in the header or footer area to make it easy for you to insert a page number, date, or both the date and time.

Note

You can create alternating headers or footers by placing the header or footer text in a frame. Then, use the Frame Properties InfoBox to set the Frame placement to Pages Left/Right. This principle works within sections as well, so you can create alternating headers that vary within a document.

▶ See "Creating a Frame," p. 385
You can delete a header or footer at any time by simply cutting the text from the header or footer area.

Tip

To remove headers or footers with lines around them, delete the text, reopen the Header or Footer Properties InfoBox, and remove special formatting that you applied.

From Here...

In this chapter, you explored some of the opportunities of working with page layout. You now know how to set up margins, page tabs, columns, page size, orientation, and headers and footers. Go on to look into these related topics:

- Chapter 6, "Exploring Advanced Page Formatting Features," explores advanced page formatting techniques such as inserting page breaks and numbers, as well as using borders, lines, and shading in your document.

- Chapter 7, "Using Views and Display Modes," teaches you about Word Pro display modes and the purpose of using each view.

Chapter 6

Exploring Advanced Page Formatting Features

by Elaine Marmel

You've already learned about modifying fonts and character attributes and applying paragraph formatting as ways to change the style of a document. You've also learned about such page formatting features as changing margins, columns, page orientation, and paper size.

Now let's explore some of the more advanced page formatting functions Word Pro has to offer.

In this chapter, you learn how to:

- Specify page breaks and column breaks
- Use automatic page numbering
- Use page lines and borders
- Apply shading
- Apply page layout styles

◀ See "Changing Character Formatting," p. 79

◀ See "Changing Paragraph Formatting," p. 88

◀ See "Setting Page Size and Orientation," p. 106

◀ See "Setting Margins, Page Tabs, and Columns," p. 108

◀ See "Adding Headers and Footers," p. 120

Using Page and Column Breaks

Word Pro automatically places page breaks according to the directions you specify for the page formatting. For example:

- Based on the margins you set, Word Pro fills up a page and then inserts a page break.

- On the Options tab of the Document Properties dialog box, you can deselect widow/orphan control, which prevents single lines of a paragraph at the top or bottom of a page.

- You can anchor a frame to certain text so that the text and frame stay on the same page.

- You choose line spacing for the document.

In addition to all the page breaks Word Pro inserts automatically based on the directions you specify, you also can place a manual page break or column break wherever you need it in the text.

To insert a manual page break, place the insertion point where you want to begin the new page or column and press Ctrl+Enter. Word Pro inserts a page break in your document (see fig. 6.1).

Fig. 6.1

When you insert a page break, Word Pro shifts to the next page. You see a page break marker on the previous page.

Page break marker —

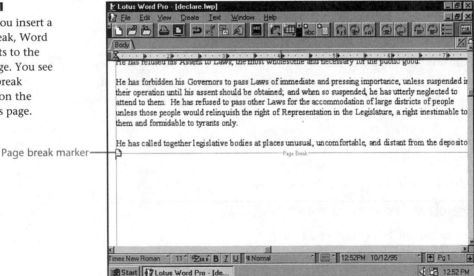

A column break is useful if you want to place certain text in particular columns. If you use a manual column break, you can control the division of text in columns. Follow these steps to insert a column break:

1. Place the insertion point at the location where you want the current column to end.

2. Choose Text, Insert Other, Insert Column Break.

Word Pro inserts a column break (see fig. 6.2).

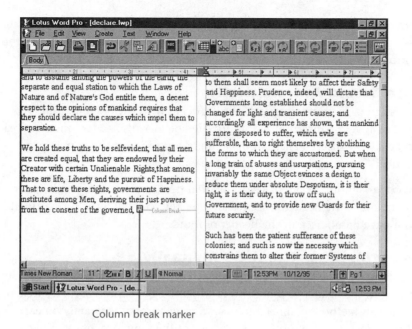

Column break marker

Fig. 6.2
When you insert a column break, Word Pro moves the insertion point to the top of the next column.

Getting to Know Word Pro

If you insert a column break when your document contains only one column, Word Pro automatically moves to the top of the next page (as if you inserted a page break).

> **Tip**
>
> To quickly move the insertion point to a page break or column break marker, choose Edit, Go To. In the Go To dialog box, click the Type of Document Part to Go To list box and choose Page Break or Column Break. Then choose OK or press Enter.

To remove page and column breaks, place the insertion point immediately before the break and then press the Delete key.

◀ See "Changing Character Formatting," p. 79

In addition to changing the appearance of the printed page, you can change how the document appears on-screen as you work, as explained later in this chapter.

Numbering Pages

Word Pro offers several ways to handle page numbering. You can assign page numbers for your entire document, or you can start page numbering on any specified page. You can specify the starting page number (for example, 2 or 3

◀ See "Adding Headers and Footers," p. 120

rather than 1). You also can use leading text (such as *Page* 1) with page numbers. By using headers and footers, you can locate page numbers in the top or bottom margin, at the left, right, or in the center of the margin.

Numbering Automatically

To assign page numbers automatically, begin with the document in layout mode. Move the insertion point into the document's header or footer area and click the Insert a Page Number SmartIcon to insert the correct page number.

▶ See "Designing the Page in Layout Mode," p. 140

Word Pro automatically places sequential numbers on each page of your document in the header or footer. If you need to modify the formatting for your page numbers, edit the header or footer.

Inserting Page Numbers Manually

If you prefer to control the location of page numbers and don't want them to appear in the header or footer, you can place a page number on a single page. Using this method, you need to place a page number separately on each page of your document. Word Pro keeps track of the sequence, but you need to insert the numbers manually. Follow these steps:

> **Tip**
>
> If you place the insertion point in the header or footer area, the resulting page number appears on each page where the header or footer appears.

1. Place the insertion point where you want the first page number to appear in the document.

2. Choose the Text, Insert Page Number command. The Insert Page Number dialog box appears (see fig. 6.3).

Fig. 6.3
In the Insert Page Number dialog box, describe the way you want page numbers to appear.

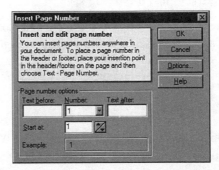

3. In the Text <u>B</u>efore box, type any text you want to appear before the page number. For example, type **Page**.

> **Note**
>
> If you type leading text that includes a following space, as *Page* in the example *Page 1*, you must type the space, too.

4. In the <u>N</u>umber list box, specify the numbering style you want to use for the page numbers. To see a list of available styles, click the down-arrow button.

5. In the Text <u>A</u>fter box, type any text you want to appear after the page number.

6. If you want to start numbering with a number other than 1, click the <u>S</u>tart At spinner box and specify the starting page number.

7. Choose the <u>O</u>ptions button. Word Pro displays the Page Number Options dialog box (see fig. 6.4).

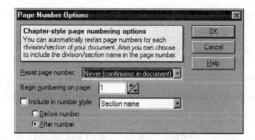

Fig. 6.4
Use the Page Number Options dialog box to set numbering options for sections and divisions, and to start numbering pages after page 1.

8. If your document is divided into sections or divisions, you can reset the page number so it starts over for each new section or division. Use the <u>R</u>eset Page Number list box.

9. If you want to start numbering pages after page 1, use the Begin <u>N</u>umbering on Page spinner box to specify the page on which you want numbering to begin.

10. Using the Include in Number <u>S</u>tyle list box, you can include the section name or the division name either before or after the page number.

11. After you finish specifying numbering features, choose OK to redisplay the Insert Page Number dialog box.

12. Choose OK. Word Pro places a page number in the document at the location of the insertion point.

Remember, these steps insert a page number for only one page. You must repeat the steps for each page of your document on which you want page numbers to appear. If you insert additional page numbers onto subsequent pages, Word Pro places sequential page numbers in your document according to your page numbering specifications.

◀ See "Changing Character Formatting," p. 79

If you want, you can enhance the page numbers and accompanying text with italics, boldface, and other character formatting. Simply select the page number and format it.

Adding Lines, Borders, and Shading

Just as you were able to add borders, lines, and shading to paragraphs, you also can add these elements to pages. These elements may be particularly effective if you're creating a cover page for a report.

Adding Lines

With the Page Properties InfoBox, you can draw lines around an entire page. A box around the page, or lines bordering the top and bottom margins of a page, make your document more attractive and noticeable.

You can specify whether you want lines on all sides or only certain sides of the page. You can also indicate the line position and choose the width of the lines.

To place lines on a page, position the insertion point on that page. Then choose the Page InfoBox SmartIcon, or click the right mouse button and choose Page Properties from the shortcut menu. From the Page Properties InfoBox, click the Page Lines and Colors tab (see fig. 6.5).

Fig. 6.5
From the Page Lines and Colors tab of the Page Properties Info-Box, you can add lines to a page.

Tip

You may see the results of your actions better if you click the Full Page View SmartIcon.

If you want lines to appear all the way around the page, choose one of the Lines Around Page buttons. Using these buttons, you can add simple lines to your page or create a shadow-box effect. In either case, the corners can be squared or rounded.

If you don't want lines all the way around your page, use the Show Lines list box (at the bottom of the dialog box) to select the sides on which you want lines to appear. You can choose more than one item from this list box, and you click anywhere outside the list to close it.

Note

Use caution when choosing Page Edge from the Line Placement list box. If you use a laser printer, these lines won't print; in addition, you may find them difficult to see on-screen. Click the Line Placement list box and choose another option, such as On Margin, to both see and print the lines. If you choose Other, you can specify the distance from the edge of the page. Remember to specify at least one-half inch if you use a laser printer.

From the Line Style list box, choose a line style (see fig. 6.6).

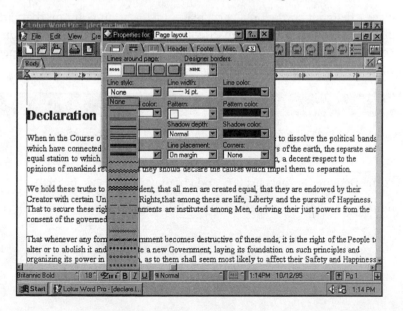

Fig. 6.6
You can insert one of 19 styles of lines.

Use the Line Color box to specify the color for the lines. From the palette that appears when you open the box, click the color you want to use for the line.

Using Designer Borders

As you just learned, you can draw lines around an entire page. Word Pro also lets you draw custom borders around the page that are particularly effective for title pages (see fig. 6.7).

Fig. 6.7
Spruce up a report's title page with a designer border.

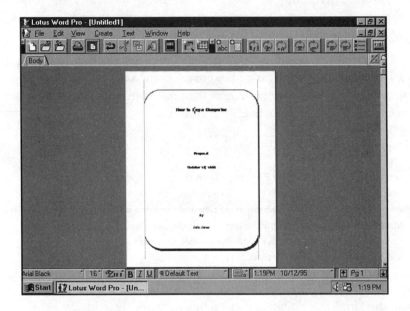

 To place a designer border on a page, place the insertion point on that page. Then choose the Page InfoBox SmartIcon, or click the right mouse button and choose Page Properties from the shortcut menu. From the Page Properties InfoBox, click the Page Lines and Colors tab (refer to fig. 6.5).

Tip

 Click the Full Page View SmartIcon to better see the results of your actions.

Click the Designer Borders list box and choose a border (see fig. 6.8).

To remove a designer border, reopen the list box and choose None.

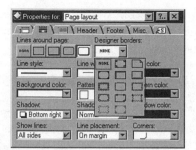

Fig. 6.8
Choose any of
these designer
borders.

Adding Shading to a Page

Page shading is another effective publishing tool you can use to draw attention and create an impact on the reader (see fig. 6.9).

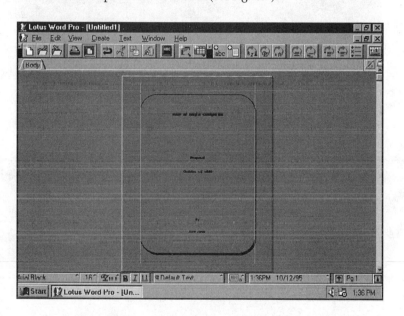

Fig. 6.9
Page shading adds
impact to a page.

To shade a page, place the insertion point on that page. Then choose the Page InfoBox SmartIcon, or click the right mouse button and choose Page Properties from the shortcut menu. From the Page Properties InfoBox, click the Page Lines and Colors tab (refer to fig. 6.5).

> **Tip**
>
> You may see the results of your actions better if you click the Full Page View SmartIcon.

The Background Color list box controls the color of the page; you can use this option to provide shading. Or you can set a pattern to appear in the background of your page (see fig. 6.10).

Fig. 6.10
Background patterns create interest, but be careful—they can also make reading difficult.

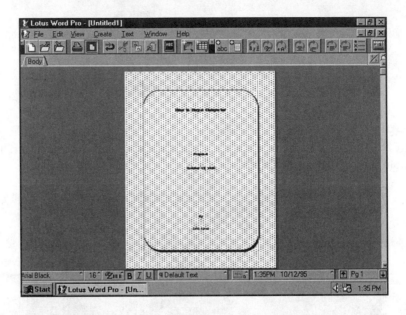

> **Tip**
>
> Remember, colors appear on printouts only if your printer supports color. You can use patterns without setting any colors; just choose a light enough pattern so you can still read the text on the page.

Use the Pattern Color list box to choose a color for the patterned area of the page.

To remove shading, reset the Background Color, the Pattern, and the Pattern Color list boxes back to white.

▶ See "Formatting the Section," p. 317

▶ See "Copying Styles to Other SmartMasters," p. 260

Saving Page Formatting Settings

Sometimes you spend a great deal of time setting up page formatting, and you know you will want to use these same settings again. You can save page formatting settings as a *page style*, which enables you to use these settings in another section of the same document or in a different document.

Creating a page style isn't difficult. Follow these steps:

1. Set up the page to include all the formatting you want—margins, headers and footers, columns, page tabs, borders, lines, shading, and so on.

2. Then choose the Page InfoBox SmartIcon, or click the right mouse button and choose P**a**ge Properties from the shortcut menu. From the Page Properties InfoBox, click the Style tab (see fig. 6.11).

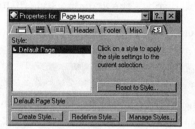

Fig. 6.11
Using the Style tab, you can create, redefine, or manage page styles.

3. Click the Create Style button. Word Pro displays the Create Style dialog box shown in figure 6.12.

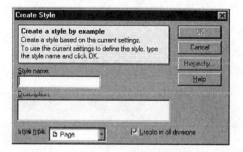

Fig. 6.12
Using the Create Style dialog box, you create a page style by example.

4. In the **S**tyle Name text box, type the name you want to give this page style. In the **D**escription box, you may want to include some information that describes the page formatting settings this style includes.

5. Choose OK to save the page style.

6. To apply a page style, simply highlight it in the Style tab of the Page Properties InfoBox.

You can change the settings of a page style you've already created by following these steps:

1. Apply the style and make the changes you want. For example, change the margins.

2. Redisplay the Style tab of the Page Properties InfoBox.

3. Making sure the correct style is highlighted, click the Redefine Style button. Word Pro displays the Redefine Style dialog box (see fig. 6.13).

4. Change the description of the page style and choose OK.

> **Tip**
>
> If you don't like the changes you made to a page style, click the Reset to Style button on the Style tab of the Page Properties InfoBox to return the style to its original settings.

Fig. 6.13
When you redefine a page style, you get the opportunity to change its description, noting the new settings contained in the style.

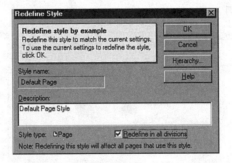

▶ See "Managing Styles," p. 257

You can manage page styles the same way you manage paragraph styles.

From Here...

In this chapter, you learned about additional page layout features you can use to customize your documents—features such as page numbering, borders and lines, and shading. Take a look at these chapters:

■ Chapter 7, "Using Views and Display Modes," describes how to change the display of text on-screen and the uses of the draft, layout, and outline modes.

■ Chapter 8, "Marking and Searching Text," and Chapter 9, "Proofreading Documents," help you master the editing process.

■ Chapter 13, "Using Advanced SmartMasters," helps you understand styles and teaches you how to manage them.

■ Chapter 16, "Managing Long Documents," teaches you how to divide your document into manageable parts.

■ Chapter 22, "Desktop Publishing with Word Pro," shows you how to spruce up your documents.

I

Getting to Know Word Pro

Chapter 7

Using Views and Display Modes

by Elaine Marmel

Word Pro provides several different ways you can look at your document on-screen. Some of these ways are called *views*, and the others are called *display modes*. In general, display modes present your document in one window, while views present your document in two or more windows, each serving a different purpose.

In this chapter, you learn how to:

- Design in Layout mode
- Edit in Draft mode
- Use Page Sorter mode to help you organize your document
- Zoom in and out to see your document from varying perspectives
- Use Word Pro's special views—Page Sorter, Panorama, DocSkimmer, and Zoomer

Using Display Modes

Display modes affect how the document appears on-screen; they also provide you with different options for working with the document.

Word Pro provides three display modes for presenting documents on-screen. In *Layout mode*, you see the document as it will look when you print it. In *Draft mode*, you do not see exactly how the document appears on the page; instead, you see a less formatted, working version of the document. In *Page Sorter mode*, you see full pages of the document that you cannot read, but they help you see the overall visual effects on a given page.

Modes help you work in the same document in different ways; you can move from one display mode to another at any time while working with a document. Choose the mode you want from the View menu.

Designing the Page in Layout Mode

To see a WYSIWYG (what you see is what you get) view of a document, choose View, Layout. Word Pro presents the document as it will appear when you print it (see fig. 7.1). Notice that you see the columns in Layout mode.

Fig. 7.1
In Layout mode, your document appears on-screen the same way it will appear when you print it.

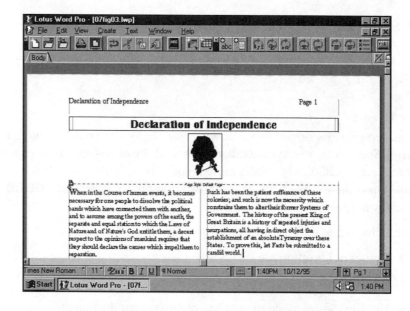

The text is displayed with specified attributes, alignment, indentation, columns, and spacing. Tables, pictures, headers, footers, and footnotes also appear.

Although this view provides you with complete information about the appearance of your document, you may find it somewhat slower to work in than Draft mode. In Layout mode, screen redrawing takes longer because of the number of objects that Word Pro displays on-screen.

Editing in Draft Mode

For quick maneuvering and editing within a document, choose View, Draft. You see a less formatted view of the document, as shown in figure 7.2. The program displays text enhancements and attributes, but no page breaks, columns, headers, footers, footnotes, unanchored frames, drawings, or charts.

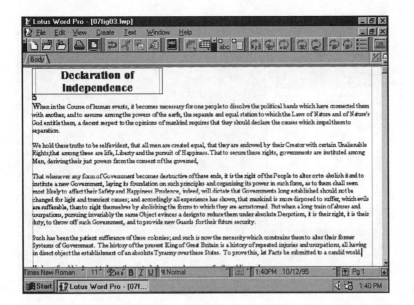

Fig. 7.2
Contrast this document in Draft mode with figure 7.1, which shows the same document in Layout mode.

> **Tip**
>
> With the Clean Screen options, you can show or hide parts of the Word Pro screen such as the menu bar and the SmartIcons.

▶ See "Setting View Preferences," p. 230

Text and pictures in anchored frames appear in the correct locations, but other kinds of frames don't appear at all. You can edit the contents of a frame in Draft mode, but you cannot create, cut, copy, or move a frame.

Organizing in Page Sorter Mode

To switch to Page Sorter mode, choose <u>V</u>iew, <u>P</u>age Sorter. When you first display a multipage document in Page Sorter mode, you see only the first page. At the top of the page, you see a gray bar containing a plus sign and the number of pages in your document. You can use this plus sign to expand the view (see fig 7.3).

Page Sorter mode shows how text and graphics look on the page; this mode is most useful for reorganizing the pages of a document.

When you click the plus sign, Word Pro shows you up to three rows, each containing up to three pages of your document (see fig. 7.4).

Fig. 7.3
When you initially display a document in Page Sorter mode, you see only the first page in a reduced size.

Click this symbol to expand your document

Fig. 7.4
After you expand a document, Word Pro changes the plus sign to a minus sign so you can reduce the view again.

The plus sign changes to a minus sign so you can reduce the view again

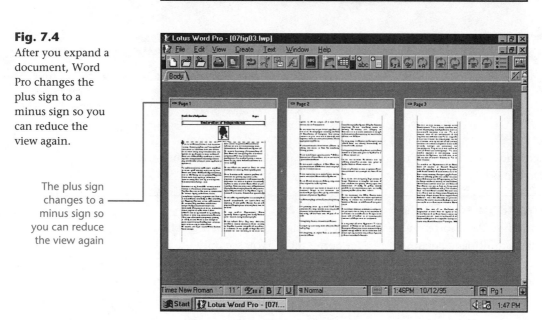

To move a page in Page Sorter mode, use the gray area that appears at the top of the page. Drag by clicking in the gray area of the page you want to move to the new location. As you begin to drag, the mouse pointer shape changes and you see a red vertical line to the left of the page you're moving. This line represents the current location of the page and always appears to the left of the current location (see fig. 7.5). As you drag to move a page, release the mouse button when the red vertical line appears to the left of the location where you want the page.

> **Note**
>
> Although the text is tiny, you can edit in Page Sorter mode—notice the tiny insertion point. However, because the text is so small, it's easy to make a mistake.

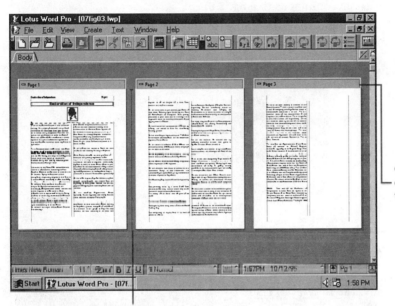

Fig. 7.5
Drag a page to reorder your document.

Click here and drag to move the page

Line indicates where page 3 will appear after releasing the mouse button

Using Views

Typically, you work in Draft or Layout mode in Word Pro—the document appears on-screen in a certain fashion, with your favorite options available. Sometimes, however, you may need to enlarge the view. Or, alternatively, you may want to work in different modes simultaneously, which you now can do in Word Pro.

Using Zoom

With the Zoom view in Word Pro, you can change the size of the text as it appears on-screen. Zoom works in either Layout or Draft mode.

> **Note**
>
> You cannot zoom in Page Sorter mode, but you can access the Zoom feature while in Page Sorter mode. If you choose a Zoom option, Word Pro automatically switches to the last mode you were using before you switched to Page Sorter mode.

Using the Zoom options available, you can zoom in or out to see your document in just about any size you want. Open the View menu and choose one of the Zoom commands (see fig. 7.6).

Fig. 7.6
From the View menu, you can zoom out to see a full page, zoom to see your document at 100% of its size, or zoom to one of several custom sizes.

For the purpose of this discussion, we will work in and talk about Layout mode. As you can see from figure 7.6, the Zoom To submenu contains the Margin Width and Page Width commands. If you zoom to Margin Width, you will see the margin lines but you will no longer see the margins of your document (see fig. 7.7).

If you zoom to Page Width, Word Pro displays the text so you can see all of each line on the page (see fig. 7.8).

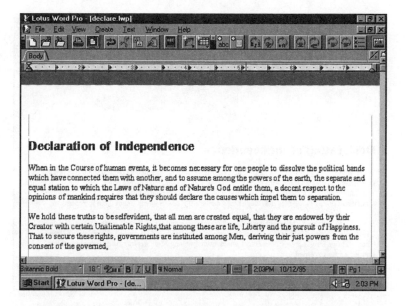

Fig. 7.7
This document was zoomed to Margin Width.

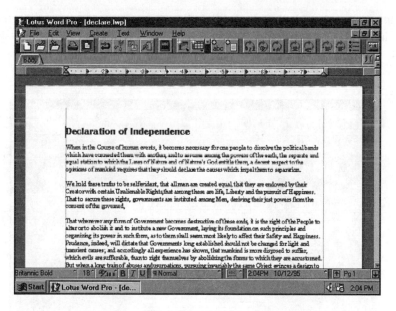

Fig. 7.8
This document was zoomed to Page Width.

When you zoom to 100%, you see your document at 100% magnification (see fig. 7.9).

Fig. 7.9
This document
was zoomed to
100%.

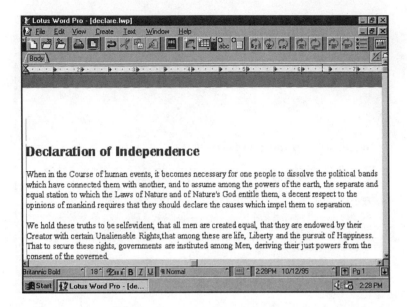

Fig. 7.9
This document
was zoomed to
100%.

When you zoom to Full Page, the document appears similar to Page Sorter
mode. If you compare figure 7.10 to figure 7.3, notice that you don't see a
plus or minus sign on figure 7.10 and you cannot move pages around in Full
Page view.

Fig. 7.10
This document
was zoomed to
Full Page view.

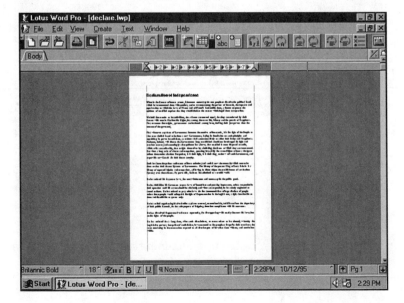

You'll find many choices available on the Zoom To submenu. Some of the larger views can be particularly helpful for positioning frames precisely on a page, for viewing text set in a small typeface, for creating equations, or for making fine edits in a drawing.

▶ See "Setting View Preferences," p. 230

By choosing Zoom To, Other, you can set the zoom percentage you want to use as a default (see fig. 7.11).

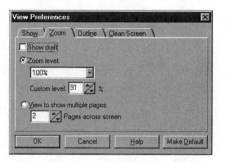

Fig. 7.11
From the Zoom tab of the View Preferences dialog box, you can select a custom zoom setting.

Notice also in figure 7.11 that you can show more than one page on-screen simultaneously by selecting the View to Show Multiple Pages option button. In figure 7.12, you see two pages on-screen as a result of setting the Pages Across Screen spinner box to 2.

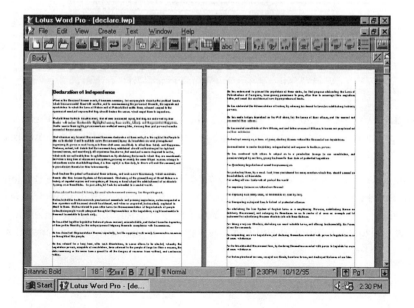

Fig. 7.12
From the Zoom tab of the View Preferences dialog box you can control the number of pages you view on-screen.

Using Special Views

You can work in more than one of the display modes or views simultaneously using Word Pro's special views. These special views present a single document in more than one window—each window presents the document differently. Word Pro provides four special views:

- Page Walker displays the document in two columns: one in Layout mode and one in Full Page view.

- Panorama displays the document in two rows: one in Layout mode and one in Full Page view.

- DocSkimmer displays the document in Draft mode, with outline tools, and Full Page view.

- Zoomer displays the document in Draft mode, Layout mode, and Full Page view.

To switch to any of these special views, choose View, Special Views to open the Special Views dialog box (see fig. 7.13).

Fig. 7.13
Using the Special Views dialog box, you can display your document in a combination of display modes.

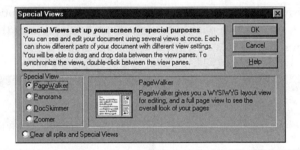

To clear any view you select from this dialog box, you can choose View, Clear All Splits or reopen this dialog box and choose the Clear All Splits and Special Views option button.

In Page Walker view shown in figure 7.14, you see Layout mode on the left and Full Page view on the right—the same view you see when you choose the View, Zoom to Full Page command. You can edit your document in either view, although editing in Full Page view may be quite difficult because the text is so tiny.

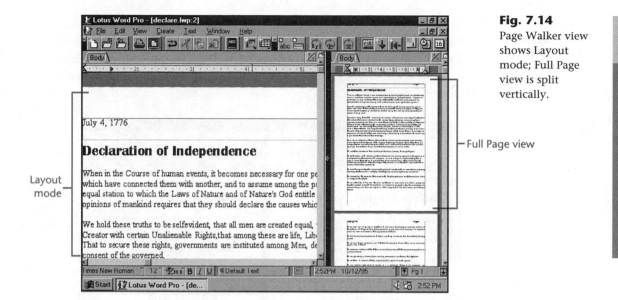

Fig. 7.14
Page Walker view
shows Layout
mode; Full Page
view is split
vertically.

Full Page view

Layout mode

Panorama view is similar to Page Walker view, but the view in Layout mode
runs horizontally across the screen rather than vertically down the left side
(see fig. 7.15).

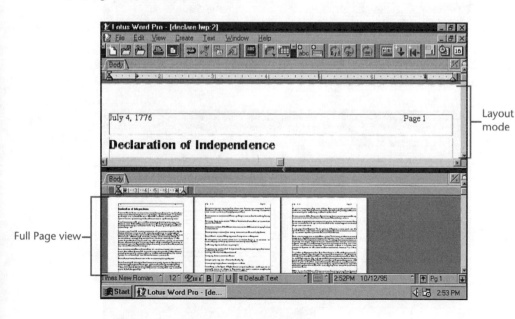

Fig. 7.15
Panorama view
shows Layout mode
and Full Page view
split horizontally.

Layout mode

Full Page view

▶ See "Under-
standing Out-
line Mode,"
p. 268

DocSkimmer view shows a view of Draft mode on the left side of the screen, outline tools in the upper right portion of the screen, and a Full Page view in the lower right portion of the screen (see fig. 7.16). You can edit in the Draft mode view, organize your document with outline tools, and see the layout of the document with Full Page view.

Fig. 7.16
DocSkimmer view
combines Draft
mode, outline
tools, and Full
Page view.

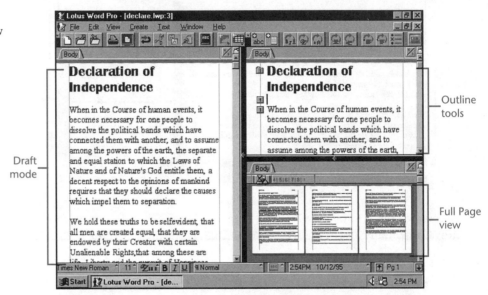

The Zoomer view gives you a view in Draft mode, a view in Layout mode, and a Full Page view (see fig. 7.17).

Fig. 7.17
The same
document in
Zoomer view.

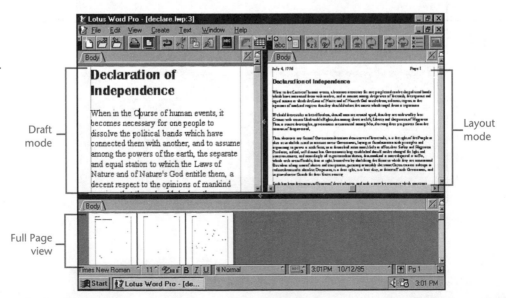

From Here...

In this chapter, you learned how to change the display of text on-screen using the various modes and views available in Word Pro. From here, you may want to explore the following:

- Chapter 11, "Customizing Word Pro," teaches you how to set up various defaults such as your viewing preferences.

- Chapter 14, "Outlining a Document," explains how to use Word Pro to organize a document.

- Chapter 22, "Desktop Publishing with Word Pro," shows you how to spruce up your documents.

I

Getting to Know Word Pro

Chapter 8

Marking and Searching Text

by Lisa Bucki

Word Pro has long provided numerous tools to make it easier to revise and edit documents you're creating—even long documents or ones that need to go through numerous revision cycles. The latest version of Word Pro makes a good thing even better, offering several new features for moving through text and replacing text.

In this chapter, you learn how to search through documents using methods that include bookmarks, the Find and Replace feature, and the Edit, Go To command. With these techniques, you can edit your documents swiftly and efficiently.

In this chapter, you learn how to:

- Create bookmarks so you can easily go to a specific point in a document
- Use Word Pro's Go To feature to move to a particular page, document object (like a footnote), bookmark, and more
- Find and replace text and formatting attributes

Using Bookmarks

Just as you insert a piece of paper between the pages of a book so you can find your place again, you can use *bookmarks* in Word Pro documents. With a document bookmark, you can jump quickly to the bookmark location to insert text, make revisions, and so on.

▶ See "Showing and Hiding Screen Elements," p. 231

▶ See "Creating Divisions," p. 309

You can add a bookmark anywhere in a document by positioning the insertion point where you want the bookmark to appear and then inserting and naming the bookmark. Even though the bookmark appears on-screen, it does not print, so you don't have to worry about hiding the bookmarks before printing. However, you can turn off the display of bookmarks if you prefer a cleaner screen appearance.

> **Tip**
>
> Bookmarks located in other divisions are listed with first the division name and then the bookmark name.

Note that you don't need to create a bookmark when the information you want to jump to starts on a new page, is in a footnote, or is in a frame. You can use the Go To command, described later in this chapter, to jump to those kinds of elements in a document. However, if you do want to mark and name a *particular* page or element, create a bookmark for it.

Adding and Removing a Bookmark

To add a bookmark, you begin by positioning the insertion point at the document location where you want to place the bookmark. For example, if you are creating a draft for an annual report, you can create a bookmark for each section right beside the title or subheading for the section. After positioning the insertion point, use the following steps:

> **Tip**
>
> If your iconbar doesn't include the Bookmarks SmartIcon, you can add it. See Chapter 11, "Customizing Word Pro," for details on customizing iconbars.

1. Choose Create, Bookmark, or click the Bookmarks SmartIcon. The Bookmarks dialog box appears (see fig. 8.1).

2. Type a name for the bookmark in the Bookmark Name text box. (A bookmark name may be up to 36 characters long and may include any combination of letters, numbers, and spaces.) For example, you may type **1995 in Review** for the name.

3. After you type the bookmark name, choose Mark. Word Pro creates a bookmark at the insertion point and assigns the specified name to the bookmark. The Bookmarks dialog box closes, and Word Pro returns to

the document, displaying the new bookmark (see fig. 8.2). Although the mark may cover a letter or two, the text remains intact, and the bookmark does not print.

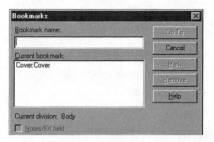

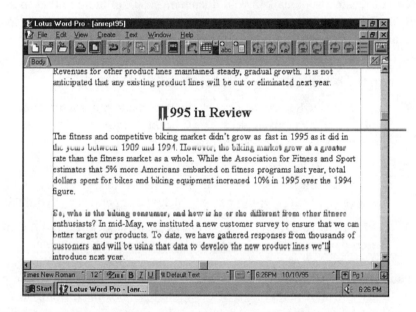

Fig. 8.1
The Bookmarks dialog box enables you to create and move to bookmarks in the current document, including all divisions.

Fig. 8.2
A mark appears to show where you inserted a new bookmark.

Bookmark appears in file but doesn't print

Tip

You can use the same bookmark name more than once in a document by assigning the same name to bookmarks in different divisions of a document. So if you have a document with two chapters and each chapter is in a separate division, you can create a bookmark called Chart 1, for example, in each chapter.

If a bookmark is no longer useful, you can remove it from your document. You don't need to move to or select a bookmark in any way before you delete it. You can handle the entire operation from the Bookmarks dialog box.

To remove a bookmark, follow these steps:

1. Choose Create, Bookmark, or click the Bookmarks SmartIcon. The Bookmarks dialog box appears, as shown earlier in figure 8.1.

2. In the Current Bookmark list box, click the name of the bookmark you want to remove.

3. Click Remove. The Bookmarks dialog box closes. Word Pro removes the specified bookmark and returns to the document. The bookmark no longer appears in the document.

Finding a Bookmark

After you create a bookmark in your document, you can jump to that spot quickly. For example, suppose that you're still working on your annual report text and you have some new facts to add to the 1995 in Review section, which you've marked with a bookmark.

To return to a bookmark in your document, follow these steps:

1. Choose Create, Bookmark, or click the Bookmarks SmartIcon. The Bookmarks dialog box appears. The Current Bookmark list box lists all the bookmarks in your document.

2. In the Current Bookmark list box, click the name of the bookmark where you want to jump. For example, you can click Body:1995 in Review. Body: is the division name, which was appended by Word Pro.

3. Click the Go To button. The Bookmarks dialog box closes, and the insertion point moves to the specified bookmark.

◀ See "Using Special Views," p. 148

◀ See "Organizing in Page Sorter Mode," p. 141

If you're working with a special view such as PageWalker or DocSkimmer, you can still use the Bookmarks dialog box to jump to a bookmark. Doing so automatically scrolls the display and moves the insertion point in the currently selected window of the special view. The display for other view windows doesn't scroll until you click the part of the display where you want to go. If you find a bookmark while you're working in Page Sorter mode, you need to expand the display so the page containing the found bookmark is displayed (you can see the insertion point blinking on the found bookmark). Otherwise, you cannot see the found bookmark, even though the insertion point moved to it.

You also can use Edit, Go To to find bookmarks, footnotes, page breaks, notes, and so on as explained in the next section.

Using Go To

Word Pro's Go To feature enables you to move around quickly in your document—to a bookmark, a particular page, a specific item (header, footer, frame), and so on. Go To automatically moves the insertion point to the location you select—whether it's 1 or 20 pages away.

You can use Go To in any Display mode or any of the special views. You may find working in special views a bit difficult, as described in the previous section.

When you need to go to a particular area of a document, follow these steps:

1. Choose <u>E</u>dit, <u>G</u>o To. Alternatively, you can click the page number on the status bar or click the Go To SmartIcon. The Go To dialog box appears (see fig. 8.3).

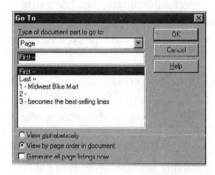

Fig. 8.3
Using the Go To dialog box, you can move the insertion point to various parts of your document.

2. Click the down arrow beside the <u>T</u>ype of Document Part To Go To drop-down list to display its choices (see fig. 8.4). Scroll through the list and click the name of the kind of document part you want to go to. For example, you can choose Page Break.

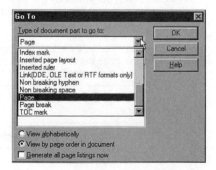

Fig. 8.4
From the drop-down list entitled Type of Document Part To Go To, you can specify a document area to go to.

3. From the list box below Type of Document Part To Go To, select one of the options. For example, if you chose Page Break in step 2, you can choose either Next or Previous for this step. If you want to view the options in this list alphabetically rather than by the order they appear in the document, click the View Alphabetically option button (the default is View by Page Order in Document).

4. Click OK. The Go To dialog box closes and Word Pro moves the insertion point to the specified location or item. In some cases, the insertion point is positioned on or near the document part you choose to go to. In other cases, such as for non-breaking spaces, Word Pro selects the document part.

In the Go To dialog box, the drop-down list box entitled Type of Document Part To Go To enables you to specify whether to move to a page, bookmark, or element. After you select a document part from this list, options for that document part appear in another list box. These options vary depending on the document element you select from the Type of Document Part To Go To drop-down list.

For example, as in figure 8.4, if you choose to go to a Page, Go To lists First--, Last--, and each page in the document (identified by the page number and the first line of text in the page). Selecting one of these options from the list and clicking OK takes you to the top of the selected page. Table 8.1 lists the choices in the Type of Document Part To Go To drop-down list and explains the options available for each choice.

Table 8.1 Types of Document Parts You Can Go To	
Document Part	**Options and Description**
Bookmark	Enables you to go to any bookmark in the document; identifies each bookmark by the page number the bookmark is on, its division name, and the bookmark name.
Click Here	Enables you to go to a Click Here block; identifies each block by the page number the block is on, its block number, and its prompt text.
Column Break	Goes to the Next or Previous column break in the document.
Comment Note	Goes to the Next or Previous comment-note mark.

Document Part	Options and Description
Doc Info Field	Selects the Next or Previous document info field inserted in the document.
Footer	Goes to the Next or Previous footer.
Footnote Mark	Goes to the Next or Previous footnote mark in the text of the document.
Footnote Text	Goes to the text of the Next or Previous footnote.
Frame	Goes to the Next or Previous frame in the document.
Header	Goes to the Next or Previous header.
Index Mark	Selects the Next or Previous index mark inserted in the document.
Inserted Page Layout	Goes to the Next or Previous page layout mark inserted in the document.
Inserted Ruler	Goes to the Next or Previous ruler mark inserted in the document.
Link (DDE, OLE)	Goes to the Next or Previous linked or embedded object in the document.
Non-Breaking Hyphen	Selects the Next or Previous non-breaking hyphen inserted in the document.
Non-Breaking Space	Selects the Next or Previous non-breaking space inserted in the document.
Page	Goes to the top of the first or last page or any other page in the document (identified by the page number and the first line of text in the page).
Page Break	Goes to the Next or Previous page break in the document.
TOC Mark	Selects the Next or Previous TOC mark inserted in the document.

As you have seen, Word Pro's Go To feature enables you to move the insertion point to specific locations in the document. The next section describes another valuable Word Pro feature, Find and Replace, which enables you to find a specific section of text and replace it with different text.

Troubleshooting

When I use Go To, nothing happens or I get a message that Word Pro can't do what I'm asking. What happened?

If Word Pro cannot find the specified item in your document, you generally see an error message. The message indicates that the item doesn't exist or that you directed the Go To process in the wrong direction (for example, search for the Next page break when the document has no more page breaks). To clear the message, click OK or press Enter. Word Pro returns to the document so you can restart the Go To operation.

Using the Find and Replace Bar

▶ See "Customizing Smart-Icons," p. 222

Word Pro's Find and Replace feature can find a particular word, symbol, or text attribute in your document and replace the found item with something different. You can find and replace words (replace *alive* with *lively*), symbols (replace *$* with *%*), or attributes (find text formatted with the Arial font and change it to Times New Roman).

When you choose Edit, Find & Replace or click the Find and Replace SmartIcon, Word Pro displays a modeless Find and Replace bar at the top of the document window. This bar offers more convenience than the old Find and Replace dialog box because the bar stays on-screen as you work, enabling you to perform multiple searches or find repeated occurrences of the text you're looking for. The term *modeless bar* means you can still edit your document when the bar is on-screen, something you cannot do with dialog boxes. Figure 8.5 shows the Find and Replace bar.

The text you specify in the Find or Replace With text boxes can be a few letters, a word, a phrase, or a short sentence containing no more than 40 letters, characters, spaces, and wild-card characters (see the section later in this chapter called "Finding and Replacing with Wild Cards and Special Characters").

Tip

To remove the Find and Replace bar from your screen, click the Done button or press Alt+D.

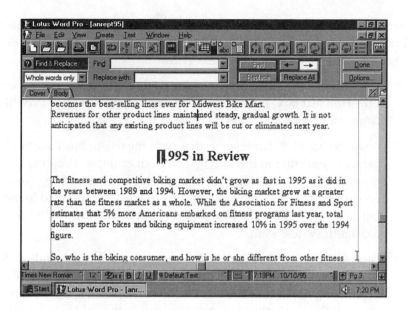

Fig. 8.5
The Find and Replace bar stays open at the top of the document until you're completely finished with it.

For information regarding using Find and Replace with text attributes, see the later section of this chapter, "Finding and Replacing Attributes."

After you perform your first Find and Replace operation, a Search Finished dialog box appears informing you about the number of Words found and Words replaced. This dialog box gives you the option of closing Find and Replace. Clicking Yes removes the modeless bar from the screen. Clicking No simply closes the dialog box; on the Find and Replace bar, the Find button turns into the Continue Find and Replace button. Change the entries as needed in the Find and Replace With text boxes, then click the Continue Find and Replace button to search for and replace the new entries you specified.

Find and Replace is smarter in this version of Word Pro than in previous versions. While the Find and Replace bar is on-screen, it stores your various entries in the Find and Replace With text boxes. Then for subsequent Find or Replace operations, you can click a down arrow to display the Find or Replace With drop-down lists and choose one of your previous entries.

Searching for Text

Most of the time, you'll probably use Find and Replace to locate an entire, exact word or phrase. By default, Word Pro searches the text of the current document for the word or text you specify, starting from the location of the insertion point and moving to the end of the document. However, you can search for parts of words and change the direction of the search. Specifically, Word Pro enables you to use the drop-down list in the lower left corner of the Find and Replace bar to search for these items:

- *Whole Words Only*. Finds exact matches of the word or phrase you enter in the Fin<u>d</u> text box. For example, you can search for single words like *Midwest* or phrases like *Midwest Bike Mart*.

- *Words Starting With*. Finds words that have the one or more starting characters you enter in the Fin<u>d</u> text box. For example, choosing this option and entering **sail** in the Fin<u>d</u> text box finds *sail, sailing, sailor,* and *sailboat*. This option replaces only the characters specified in the Fin<u>d</u> text box with the characters specified in the Replace <u>W</u>ith text box, not the whole word.

- *Words Ending With*. Finds words that have the one or more ending characters you enter in the Fin<u>d</u> text box. For example, choosing this option and entering **ike** in the Fin<u>d</u> text box finds *bike, mike,* and *like*. This option replaces only the characters specified in the Find text box with the characters specified in the Replace <u>W</u>ith text box, not the whole word.

- *Words Containing*. Finds words containing a group of one or more characters you enter in the Fin<u>d</u> text box. For example, choosing this option and entering **id** in the Fin<u>d</u> text box finds *Midwest, identification,* and *bid*. This option replaces only the characters specified in the Fin<u>d</u> text box with the characters specified in the Replace <u>W</u>ith text box, not the whole word.

Note

To search a specific area of the document, select the text before clicking the <u>F</u>ind or <u>R</u>eplace buttons in the Find and Replace bar. Word Pro searches the selected text only. If you do not preselect text and begin a Find and Replace operation, Word Pro searches from the location of the insertion point to the end or beginning of the document, depending on the direction you specify.

Note

You cannot search for text in Comment Notes or drawings.

Each time Word Pro finds text that matches the text you specified, it highlights the matching text. To perform a typical search through the entire document, follow these steps:

1. Click to position the insertion point in the document at the location where you want to begin a Find operation.

2. If the Find and Replace bar isn't on-screen, click the Find and Replace SmartIcon or choose Edit Find and Replace Text. The Find and Replace bar appears (refer to fig. 8.5).

3. If you don't want to use the default Whole Words Only option from the drop-down list in the lower left corner of the Find and Replace bar, select another option.

4. Type the word, phrase, or partial word you want to find in the Find text box (see fig. 8.6).

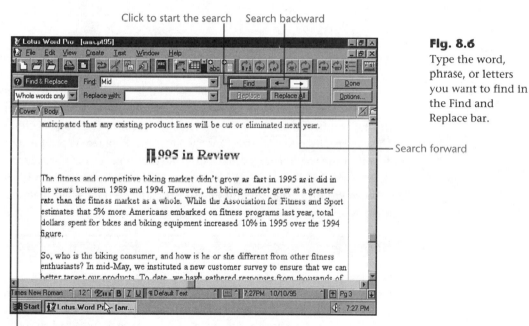

Click to start the search   Search backward

Fig. 8.6
Type the word, phrase, or letters you want to find in the Find and Replace bar.

Search forward

Select whether to search for a whole word or partial word

5. Click an arrow to determine whether to search forward or backward through the document. The left-pointing arrow searches from the insertion point backward to the beginning of the document. The right-pointing arrow searches from the insertion point forward to the end of the document.

6. Click Find. Word Pro moves to the first occurrence of the word, phrase, or partial word you specified and highlights it. To end the search operation, click Done, and skip the following steps.

7. To find the next occurrence of the matching text, click Find again. Continue clicking Find to find as many occurrences of the matching text as you need to review.

8. If you click Find and the document has no more matching instances of the text you're finding, Word Pro displays a dialog box telling you how many instances of matching text were found and asking whether you want to close Find and Replace. Click Yes to do so or No to perform additional Find and Replace operations.

9. If you want, enter new text to find, then click the Continue Find and Replace button to rerun the search, or enter new text to find and then click Find.

Replacing Text

When you make an entry in the Replace With text box of the Find and Replace bar, then click Find, you can indicate whether you want Word Pro to replace the occurrences of matching text one at a time or all occurrences of the specified text at one time. You can replace any word, phrase, or partial word that you find with the up to more than 40 characters you specify. Note that if you specify part of a word for the Find and Replace, Word Pro replaces only part of the word. For example, suppose that you select Words Starting With and type **Mid** in the Find text box and **North** in the Replace With text box. Word Pro finds *Midwest* and replaces the *Mid* characters with *North*, yielding *Northwest*.

> **Note**
>
> In addition to using SmartCorrect (see Chapter 3, "Creating and Editing a Document," for more on this feature), you can use Find and Replace to ease the burden of typing long, unique words or words you often misspell. Simply type an abbreviation for a difficult word or phrase and then replace it. For example, use *qp* when you type your document, and then find *qp* and replace it with *quantum physics*.

Follow these steps to replace matching text Word Pro finds:

1. Position the insertion point in the document at the location where you want to begin a replace operation.

2. If the Find and Replace bar doesn't appear on-screen, click the Find and Replace SmartIcon or choose <u>E</u>dit, <u>F</u>ind and Replace Text. The Find and Replace bar appears.

3. If you don't want to use the default Whole Words Only option from the drop-down list in the lower left corner of the Find and Replace bar, select another option.

4. Type the word, phrase, or partial word you want to find in the Fin<u>d</u> text box.

5. Type the word or phrase that you want to insert as the replacement for each occurrence of found text in the Replace <u>W</u>ith text box.

6. Click an arrow to determine whether to search forward or backward through the document. The left-pointing arrow searches from the insertion point backward to the beginning of the document. The right-pointing arrow searches from the insertion point forward to the end of the document.

7. Click <u>F</u>ind. Word Pro moves to the first occurrence of the word, phrase, or partial word you specified and highlights it.

8. Click the <u>R</u>eplace button to replace the found text with the text you specified and then continue with the rest of the steps for this procedure. You can also click Replace <u>A</u>ll to have Word Pro replace all matches with the replacement text you specified.

9. To find the next occurrence of the matching text, click <u>F</u>ind again, and then click <u>R</u>eplace to change the found text. To find the next occurrence of matching text without replacing, simply click <u>F</u>ind without clicking <u>R</u>eplace. Continue clicking <u>F</u>ind and <u>R</u>eplace to find as many occurrences of the matching text as you need to review.

10. If you click <u>F</u>ind and the document has no more matching instances of the text you're finding, or if you chose Replace <u>A</u>ll in step 8, Word Pro displays a dialog box telling you how many instances of matching text it found and asking whether you want to close Find and Replace. Click <u>Y</u>es to do so or <u>N</u>o to perform additional Find and Replace operations.

11. If needed, type new text to find and replace, then click the <u>C</u>ontinue Find and Replace button.

Getting to Know Word Pro

Finding and Replacing with Wild Cards and Special Characters

You use *wild cards* and *special characters* to search for and replace different words that share similar characteristics. When you're performing a Find or Replace operation in Word Pro, you can enter the wild-card characters in both the Fin̲d and Replace W̲ith text boxes of the Find and Replace bar. To enter a wild-card character, you precede it with the caret (^) symbol. After the caret, you enter the wild card or special character you want to find or replace. Table 8.2 lists the wild cards and special characters you can use. You can find more information about these characters by clicking the O̲ptions button in the Find and Replace bar and then using the S̲pecial Characters Help drop-down list in the Find and Replace Options dialog box.

Table 8.2 Wild Cards and Special Characters for Finding and Replacing	
Type This...	**To Find or Replace...**
^?	A single character in a word
^*	A group of any characters in a word
^+	Phrases matching the word(s) preceding ^+ through the word(s) in the phrase you enter after ^+, including any intervening characters; for example, if you enter *1995* ^+ *Review* in the Fin̲d text box, Word Pro finds phrases like *1995 in Review* and *1995 Annual Review*, and replaces the entire found phrase with the Replace W̲ith text.
^p	Phrases matching the word(s) preceding ^p through the end of the paragraph, including any intervening characters
^t	Tabs
^r	Hard returns
^^	The caret (^) character

The question mark wild-card character replaces a single character in the word, and the asterisk wild-card character replaces any number of characters.

To search for words beginning with *part* (such as *particle* and *participate*), for example, you type **part^***. To search for words with one letter between the letters *c* and *t*, you type **c^?t**. To search for words with two letters between the letters *n* and *t*, you type **n^?^?t**. To search for words with one letter between *th* and *n* and any number of letters following (such as *thinning* or *thence*), you type **th^?n^***.

To search for tabs, enter **^t** in the Find text box. To search for hard returns, which create paragraphs, enter **^r** in the Find text box.

To find or replace an entire paragraph starting with the phrase *Midwest Bike Mart*, enter **Midwest Bike Mart^p**.

Setting Find and Replace Options

Word Pro enables you to search different parts of a document or match the case of the word you enter in the Find or Replace With text boxes of the Find and Replace bar. You also can find and replace text with particular formatting attributes; this feature enables you to replace text formatting quickly and easily. To perform all these special Find and Replace functions, you use the Find and Replace Options dialog box (see fig. 8.7), displayed by clicking the Options button in the Find and Replace bar.

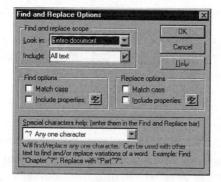

Fig. 8.7
You can specify several different options for a Find and Replace operation.

The top area of the dialog box enables you to specify the Find and Replace Scope. By default, Find and Replace Scope is set for Entire Document and All Text. If you want to search and replace only in the division or the section that currently contains the insertion point, choose Current Division or Current Section's Text from the Look In drop-down list.

If you want to search only certain elements in the document rather than all parts of the text (specified by All Text), use the Include drop-down list. Word Pro treats the different parts of a document separately. The main document text is considered one text stream, text in frames is another text stream, and so on. When you perform a Find and Replace operation in Word Pro, you can search these different document parts:

■ All Text

■ Main Document Text

- Headers & Footers
- Tables
- Frames
- Footnotes

If you choose All Text in the Include drop-down list, Word Pro searches all the document parts. If you prefer not to search the entire document, you can specify that Word Pro search one or more of the other kinds of document parts. To do so, click the check mark beside the Include drop-down list. When the drop-down list appears, click each of the document parts you want to search. When a document part is selected in the list, a check mark appears to the left of it. For example, you can click the Tables and Footnotes options to select them. After you have selected each of the document parts to search, click the check mark for the drop-down list again to close it.

If you want to Find and Replace for text of a certain case, you can use the Match Case check boxes in either the Find Options or Replace Options areas of the Find and Replace Options dialog box. If you click the Match Case check box in the Find Options area, Word Pro finds text matching the case of the text you entered in the Find text box of the Find and Replace bar. So Word Pro finds *Mom* if you search for it, but not *mom*. If you mark the Match Case check box in the Replace Options area, Word Pro finds matching text and assigns case according to the capitalization of the matching text found. For example, if you told Word Pro to find *Mom* and replace it with *Dad* and you mark the Match Case check box in the Replace Options area, Word Pro replaces *Mom* with *Dad*, *MOM* with *DAD*, and *mom* with *dad*.

When you're finished choosing the options you want in the Find and Replace Options dialog box, click the OK button. You return to the Find and Replace bar so you can click the Find button or Continue Find and Replace button to proceed with the search through your document. The Find and Replace Options dialog box also enables you to find text with particular attributes and replace those attributes. This capability is described next.

Finding and Replacing Attributes

Word Pro's Find and Replace Options dialog box enables you to find enhanced text (boldface, italics, underline) or to enhance replacement text. You display the Find and Replace Options dialog box by clicking Options in the Find and Replace bar (refer to fig. 8.7).

Word Pro offers an Include Properties check box and button in both the Find Options and Replace Options areas of the Find and Replace Options dialog box. You can use the Include Properties check boxes in a couple of ways:

■ Using the Find & Replace Text Properties dialog box (see fig. 8.8) you can choose to find and replace several properties at one time—including the Font Name, Size, Attributes, Text Color, and so on—applied to the text entered in the Find text box.

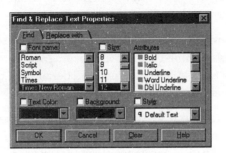

Fig. 8.8
The Find & Replace Text Properties dialog box enables you to specify several font properties at one time.

■ If you don't enter any text to find or replace, you can still click one or both of the Include Properties check boxes in the Find and Replace Options dialog box and replace properties within the entire text instead of specific text.

You can limit the search to enhanced text by indicating the enhancements you want Word Pro to find (Font Name, Size, Bold, Italic, Underline, Word Underline, Double Underline, Text Color, Background, Style, or Small Caps) on the Find tab of the Find & Replace Text Properties dialog box. You can choose combinations of attributes to search for. For example, you can search for both boldface and underline. If you select the Style check box and a paragraph style name in the Find & Replace Text Properties dialog box, Word Pro finds or replaces the selected paragraph style.

To enhance the replacement text (for example, if you want the replacement text to be in italics), you indicate the enhancements you want on the Replace With tab of the Find & Replace Text Properties dialog box.

After you have finished selecting attributes, choose OK to close the Find & Replace Text Properties dialog box. Word Pro returns to the Find and Replace Options dialog box. Choose OK again to return to the Find and Replace bar. Then you can click Find or Continue Find and Replace to proceed with the search.

From Here...

This chapter covered a lot of ground, but you should find it was worth the trip. In this chapter, you learned how to use bookmarks to find locations or items in your document, use the Go To function to locate certain parts of the document, and use the Find and Replace function to find and replace text and formatting.

For other topics that can make you more effective in managing and refining your documents, review these chapters:

- Chapter 9, "Proofreading Documents," provides you with information about the tools for fine-tuning your document contents. The chapter explains how to use Spell Checker, the Thesaurus, Grammar Checker, and the Format Checker.

- Chapter 11, "Customizing Word Pro," explains how to set some of the preferences that this chapter briefly touched on. The chapter explains how to control which document elements appear on-screen, how to change your personal user info such as your user name and initials, how to set up the SmartFill feature, and more.

- Chapter 16, "Managing Long Documents," introduces you to several tools for better organizing information in your documents. There, you learn how to create divisions and sections in a document, as well as how to control formatting within a section, set up a table of contents and index, and insert data from other applications.

Chapter 9

Proofreading Documents

by Lisa Bucki

Before you print a document, you need to check it for errors. This action saves you time (from reprinting the document) and embarrassment (from releasing a document that contains errors). One of the most important proofreading tools in word processing is a spelling checker that rapidly finds and highlights possible misspellings in a document.

In addition to Spell Check, Word Pro offers several other proofreading tools to help ensure and even improve the quality of your text. The Thesaurus enables you to search for the perfect word to convey your meaning. Grammar Check double-checks your sentence structure and style, and the new Format Checker feature helps you achieve formatting consistency with options such as the number of space characters you insert between sentences.

Lotus has taken great pains in developing Word Pro features to help you create documents that not only look great but also have polished and professional language. Use the tools described in this chapter to improve on your already brilliant work and cut down on the length of time you spend editing documents.

In this chapter, you learn how to:

- Use Spell Check to proof a document for spelling errors and repeated words

- Create and edit your own user dictionaries

- Select the perfect word with the Thesaurus

- Use the Grammar Check to search your documents for grammar errors by choosing grammar and writing style options

■ Clean up your document's appearance, especially elements such as extra spacing after sentences and bullet list formatting, with the new Format Checker feature

Using Spell Check

The Spell Check feature, like other Word Pro tools, is powerful and flexible. Word Pro checks the spelling of each word in a document against a dictionary with more than 100,000 words that comes with the program. This dictionary includes legal, business, finance, and insurance terms. Spell Check can find misspelled words, suggest correctly spelled replacements, and find words that appear twice, such as *the the*.

You can check a single word or an entire document, including all divisions and sections. Unless you specify otherwise, the program checks the spelling in the main body of the document and in frames, headers and footers, and other special locations. Spell Check compares words in the selection or document against the entries in the main dictionary. If the document contains words not included in Word Pro's default main dictionary, you can add those words to a *user dictionary*, which Word Pro uses in addition to the main dictionary for future spell check operations. Although you cannot edit Spell Check's main dictionary, you can create and customize one or more user dictionaries, adding new words as needed. Employing a user dictionary along with the main dictionary can cut down on Spell Check time by avoiding frequent stops at custom words, like *AT&T*.

◀ See "Using SmartCorrect," p. 70

Spell Check even enables you to update Word Pro's SmartCorrect feature (as mentioned in the next section), which corrects words automatically as you type them.

Running a Spell Check

When you start Spell Check, Word Pro enters spell check mode and displays a Spell Check bar at the top of the screen. If you select part of a document, Word Pro checks only your selection; otherwise, it checks the whole document. Spell Check finds all unrecognized words—words that don't appear in the main dictionary or in any user dictionary. Word Pro highlights the questionable words and enables you to review them one by one. After Spell Check finishes, the insertion point returns to the location where you started Spell Check.

Unlike the spell checkers in other word processing programs, Word Pro's Spell Check feature doesn't close automatically when you perform a spell check. The Spell Check bar stays on-screen until you click the Done button. As long as the Spell Check bar appears on-screen, you can continue to edit your document; as you do so, Spell Check automatically compares the words you add or change in the document to the dictionary, highlighting any misspellings as you make them.

Spell Check remembers all your directives during a spell check session. For example, if you tell Spell Check to skip a particular word like *RockMaster*, it skips that word every time you check the document until you remove the Spell Check bar from the screen. (However, you need to tell Spell Check to skip the word again if you close and then redisplay the Spell Check bar.)

To display the Spell Check bar, follow these steps:

1. Make the document you want to check the active document by selecting the document name from the Window menu.

   (Optional) To check only part of the document, highlight the part of the document to check.

2. Choose Edit, Check Spelling or click the Spell Check SmartIcon. The Spell Check bar appears, as shown in figure 9.1. Spell Check highlights any word not found in the main dictionary or in any user dictionaries you have included in the spell check. The highlighted word appears in the Word in Question text box. Spell Check lists possible correct spellings for the word in the box just to the right of this text box.

   If Spell Check doesn't find any words it suspects are misspelled, a message is displayed. In this case, go to step 7 of this procedure.

Tip

You can click in the document and edit the highlighted word rather than using the Spell Check bar.

Suggested replacements

Fig. 9.1
Use the Spell
Check bar to
review and correct
misspelled words
in a document.

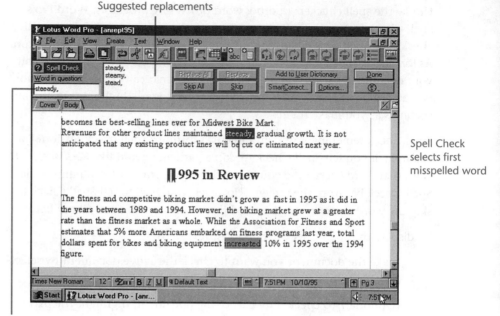

Spell Check
selects first
misspelled word

Word not found
in dictionary

3. To replace or skip the word that appears in the <u>W</u>ord in Question text
   box, choose from the following:

   ■ To replace only the current instance of the word, either edit the
     word in the <u>W</u>ord in Question text box or select one of Spell
     Check's replacement suggestions, then click the <u>R</u>eplace button.

   ■ To replace all instances of the word, either edit the word in the
     <u>W</u>ord in Question text box or click one of Spell Check's replace-
     ment suggestions. Then click the Replace <u>A</u>ll button.

   ■ To bypass the current instance of the word, click the <u>S</u>kip button.

   ■ To bypass all instances of the word, click the S<u>k</u>ip All button.

Caution

This version of Word Pro doesn't enable you to undo Replace <u>A</u>ll operations, so
be sure to double-check the replacement you're choosing.

---

4. To add the highlighted word to any user dictionary, click the Add to <u>U</u>ser Dictionary button (see "Working with User Dictionaries" later in this chapter.) For example, if you use an unusual word (such as *whizbang*) in the document and Spell Check finds it, you can add this word to the user dictionary. If you want, you can edit the word in the <u>W</u>ord in Question text box before clicking the Add to <u>U</u>ser Dictionary button.

5. If you want to add the word and its correction to SmartCorrect so that Word Pro will be able to make that correction automatically as you're creating other documents, click the Smart<u>C</u>orrect button. The Add SmartCorrect Entry dialog box appears, as shown in figure 9.2.

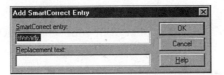

Fig. 9.2
Use Spell Check to add an entry to SmartCorrect so Word Pro will automatically correct words you frequently misspell.

The misspelled word appears in the <u>S</u>martCorrect Entry text box. Type the correction in the <u>R</u>eplacement Text text box, then click OK.

6. Word Pro selects the next misspelled word, which appears in the <u>W</u>ord in Question text box. Choose the necessary option as described in step 3 to replace or skip the word. Repeat this process for all the highlighted words that Spell Check questions.

7. After you review all the misspelled words, Word Pro displays the dialog box shown in figure 9.3, asking whether you want to close Spell Check. Click <u>Y</u>es to close Spell Check, or click <u>N</u>o and follow the rest of these steps to leave the Spell Check bar on-screen. With Spell Check on, Word Pro highlights any mistakes you make as you continue editing your document.

Note

If you selected only a section of text before starting Spell Check, and it finds no misspelled words, Spell Check displays a dialog box asking whether you want to finish checking the entire document. Click <u>Y</u>es to do so or <u>N</u>o to exit Spell Check and remove the bar from the screen. If you continue and when you finish checking the remaining document, you see the dialog box shown in figure 9.3, asking whether you want to close Spell Check. Click <u>Y</u>es to remove the Spell Check bar from the screen or <u>N</u>o to keep the Spell Check bar open.

Fig. 9.3
After you replace or skip all the words in your document, this dialog box asks whether you want to close Spell Check.

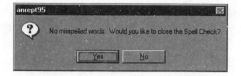

8. Edit your document as needed. If you type a word that doesn't appear in the main dictionary or any user dictionary, Spell Check highlights the word and displays it in the Word in Question text box. Use the options in step 3 to handle the questioned word, then continue working.

9. To rerun the Spell Check on the whole document or a selection, click the Continue Spell Check button.

10. To remove the Spell Check bar from your screen, click the Done button.

Setting Options

You can specify several options to customize the way you want Spell Check to check the current document. Click the Options button on the Spell Check bar to display the Spell Check Options dialog box, as shown in figure 9.4.

Fig. 9.4
You can set up Spell Check to control how it checks your document.

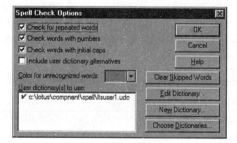

In addition to using this dialog box to set various options, you can use it to choose and edit user dictionaries for a spell check. This topic is described in the next section, "Working with User Dictionaries."

The following options in the Spell Check Options dialog box enable you to control Spell Check features other than the user dictionaries:

■ *Check for Repeated Words.* Select this option to tell Spell Check to look for duplicate words, such as *and and*. Selected by default.

■ *Check Words with Numbers.* Select this option to ensure that Spell Check reviews words that contain numbers, such as *beta12*. If you don't select this option, Spell Check skips these types of words. Selected by default.

■ *Check Words with Initial Caps.* Select this option to check words that begin with a capital letter. If you use titles and subtitles, for example, and you want Spell Check to check those words, you must select this option. Otherwise, Spell Check skips text that begins with a capital letter. Selected by default.

■ *Color for Unrecognized Words.* Click the down arrow to the right of the color box for this choice to display a palette of colors. Then click a color on the palette to have Spell Check use that color to highlight unrecognized words in a document. The default color is turquoise, but you may prefer a brighter color to make the misspellings easier to view.

■ *Clear Skipped Words.* Click this button to tell Spell Check to clear all words skipped in the current document (and therefore be found the next time you spell check the document).

To close the Spell Check Options dialog box, click OK.

Note

Remember that if you open the Spell Check bar for another document, you must reset the Spell Check options as needed for the document.

Working with User Dictionaries

As you learned earlier in this chapter, you can add words to a separate user dictionary already created in Word Pro as you perform a spell check, making those words available for future spell checks. By default, Word Pro has a user dictionary set up for you called LTSUSER1.UDC. In addition to that default user dictionary, you can create and edit more user dictionaries, and you can specify one or more user dictionaries for Spell Check to use with a particular document. You can also edit the user dictionary, adding new words or deleting unwanted words as necessary, and even specifying a language or replacement text for a particular word.

Choosing User Dictionaries for a Spell Check

You work with user dictionaries via the Spell Check Options dialog box. You can choose to use additional dictionaries you've created (as explained in the next section), dictionaries you've purchased, or dictionaries from other applications. To specify one or more user dictionaries to use when spell checking a document, follow these steps:

1. Display the Spell Check Options dialog box by clicking the Options button on the Spell Check bar (refer to fig. 9.4).

2. Select the Include User Dictionary Alternatives check box.

3. In the User Dictionary(s) to Use box, select each user dictionary you want to use. You can use more than one dictionary at a time. A check mark appears beside each selected dictionary, as shown in figure 9.5.

Fig. 9.5
You can specify user dictionaries to use during a Spell Check of the current document.

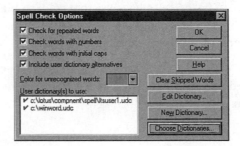

4. Click OK to close the Spell Check Options dialog box.

5. Click the Continue Spell Check button on the Spell Check bar to restart the spell check operation. When a word appears in the Word in Question text box, the user dictionary words may be listed as suggested replacements along with words from the main dictionary.

6. You can either edit the highlighted word in the text box or select a replacement for it in the list of suggestions.

   If you want, click the Add to User Dictionary button to add the misspelled word (so Spell Check recognizes it as a misspelling) and its replacement to all user dictionaries in use for the current spell check.

7. Choose to skip or replace the word in question.

8. After you review and replace or skip all the misspelled words, Word Pro displays a dialog box asking whether you want to close Spell Check. Click Yes to do so. Or click No and follow the rest of these steps to leave the Spell Check bar on-screen. With Spell Check on, Word Pro highlights any mistakes you make as you continue editing your document.

9. Edit your document as needed. If you type a word that doesn't appear in the main dictionary or any user dictionary, Spell Check highlights the word and enters it in the Word in Question text box. Use the options in the Spell Check bar to handle the questioned word, then continue working.

10. If you want to rerun the Spell Check on the whole document or a selection, click the Continue Spell Check button.

11. When you're finished using the Spell Check bar, click the Done button to remove it from your screen.

Troubleshooting

My user dictionary doesn't appear in the Under Dictionary(s) to Use box. How can I find it?

If you display the Spell Check Options dialog box and the user dictionary you want (and created previously) isn't available, click the Choose Dictionaries button. The Word Pro Preferences dialog box appears with the Default files tab selected. Click in the Default User Dictionary(s) text box, then use the right arrow key to move to the right of the last entry in the text box. Click the Browse button and choose the user dictionary (UDC) file you want to use. Click Open, then click OK to close the Word Pro Preferences dialog box. Your user dictionary will appear among the choices.

Creating a User Dictionary

Adding a new user dictionary to Spell Check is fairly painless. To add a dictionary, click the New Dictionary button in the Spell Check Options dialog box. The New User Dictionary dialog box appears (see fig. 9.6). Enter a name for the new user dictionary file in the New File Name text box. When you create a new dictionary, Word Pro saves it in the default dictionary directory that's currently in use (more on this in a moment). If you want, you can specify a full path to tell Word Pro the disk and directory in which to store a user dictionary. Click OK to close this dialog box. Word Pro automatically adds the UDC file name extension to the dictionary file.

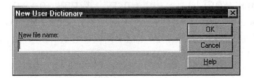

Fig. 9.6
This dialog box enables you to create a new user dictionary.

The User Dictionary(s) to Use list now includes the new user dictionary. You can edit the new user dictionary as described in the next section, or you can simply click it in the User Dictionary(s) to Use box.

Editing a User Dictionary

Most of the time, you add words to the selected user dictionary(s) by clicking the Add to User Dictionary button during a spell check. The Spell Check Options dialog box also enables you to add words by editing any user dictionary. With this dialog box, you can add and remove words, set a language, and set options for each word such as replacement text or special hyphenation. To edit a user dictionary, follow these steps:

1. Display the Spell Check bar.

2. Click the Options button to display the Spell Check Options dialog box.

3. Click the Edit Dictionary button to display the Edit User Dictionary dialog box (see fig. 9.7).

Fig. 9.7
Use this dialog box to change the contents of the selected user dictionary.

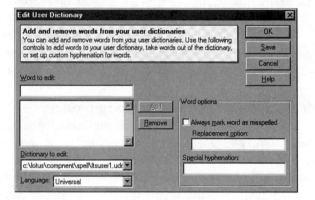

4. Click the Dictionary to Edit list box and select the dictionary you want to edit.

5. To add a new word to the dictionary list, type the word in the Word to Edit text box. If you want, set the following options for the new dictionary word, then click Add to add the word to the dictionary:

   ■ Click the Language list box to select a language (more on this later in the chapter) for the new dictionary word.

   ■ In the Word Options box, select the Always Mark Word as Misspelled option to have Spell Check recognize the word only when it has the capitalization you specified or to always question a particular word; for example, you might use this option for abbreviations.

- In the Replacement Option text box, you can enter a replacement that Spell Check can use for the word you're adding. For example, you can enter *type* to have Spell Check always use it as the replacement for *teyp*.

- In the Special Hyphenation text box, you can specify the exact hyphenation for the word added to the dictionary, so Spell Check recognizes that hyphenation and questions anything different.

6. To delete an unwanted word from the user dictionary, select the word in the list box below the Word to Edit text box. Click the Remove button.

7. To change the options specified for a user dictionary word, select the word in the list box, and then select the options you want for the word.

8. Repeat steps 5, 6, and 7 to add, remove, and alter additional words in the user dictionary.

9. Save the updated user dictionary by clicking the Save button.

10. Click the OK button to close the Edit User Dictionary dialog box, and click OK again to close the Spell Check Options dialog box.

Choosing Default User Dictionaries

The Spell Check Options dialog box includes a Choose Dictionaries button (refer to fig. 9.5). Clicking this button displays the Word Pro Preferences dialog box. In the Default Files tab, the Default User Dictionary(s) text box enables you to specify which user dictionaries appear by default in the Spell Check Options dialog box. On the Locations tab, enter a new directory in the User Dictionaries text box where Word Pro can automatically access the new user dictionaries you create.

▶ See "Setting Locations," p. 217

▶ See "Setting Default Files," p. 219

Chapter 11, "Customizing Word Pro," provides more detail on using this dialog box.

Changing Languages

By default, Word Pro spell checks your documents using the language that is currently in use with Windows 95 on your system. Word Pro comes with dictionaries in many different languages and even provides dictionaries with medical terms.

If you chose another language for the document when you set the document's properties, you should choose that same language when you perform a spell check so that Spell Check doesn't stop for every foreign term in the document. (Spell Check could get particularly tedious if your document is written completely in a foreign language!)

To change the language for a spell check, click the globe button on the Spell Check bar. The Current Language for Spelling list box appears (see fig. 9.8).

Fig. 9.8
Spell Checker provides for 23 languages, plus several variations of American and British; only American and British IZE are installed with Word Pro.

Scroll through the list of choices, then click the language to use. The list box closes so you can proceed with the spell check. If you add words to a user dictionary with the foreign language dictionary in use, Spell Check uses that language for the added word in the user dictionary. To return to the original language dictionary (usually the System choice), click the globe button again and select that language.

Using the Thesaurus

You may be accustomed to using a printed thesaurus to help you find synonyms for words as you compose documents. A thesaurus helps you find more descriptive or lively words to help you improve your writing and make your documents more interesting. For example, you may want to refer to a thesaurus to replace a somewhat mundane word like *good* with something jazzier like *exceptional* or *valuable*.

> **Tip**
>
> Brainstorm with Word Pro's Thesaurus. Suppose that you're looking for names for a new road racing bike. Find synonyms for *fast* (like *fleet*, *rapid,* and *swift*). You might then settle on a name like *RapidTransit* or *StreetFleet.*

The electronic thesaurus provided with Word Pro enables you to find the perfect word choice, but it's much faster than browsing through a printed thesaurus. Besides providing synonyms, the Word Pro Thesaurus provides definitions and enables you to place a selected synonym directly into a document. The Word Pro Thesaurus contains more than a million definitions, variations, and synonyms for thousands of root words.

To look up a word in Word Pro's Thesaurus, follow these steps:

1. In the document, select the word you want to find a synonym for by double-clicking it or placing the insertion point in it. For example, select a common word like *led.*

   > **Note**
   >
   > Be sure to select only one word. If you select more than one, the Thesaurus looks up only the first word.

2. Choose Edit, Check Thesaurus, or click the Thesaurus SmartIcon. The Thesaurus dialog box appears, as shown in figure 9.9.

Open the list to see other words you've looked up

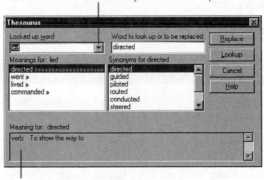

Definition for selected meaning

Fig. 9.9
The Thesaurus dialog box shows synonyms, in this case for the word "led."

3. The Meanings For box displays words with the same or similar meaning as the word *led*. A >> symbol to the right of the word indicates that the Thesaurus does have synonyms for the word. A series of >> symbols after the word indicates that the synonyms for the word appear in the Synonyms for Directed list box. You can take several different actions to find the right word for your document:

   ■ Select a word in the Meanings For box. The word's synonyms appear in the Synonyms for Directed list box. You can browse this list to find the word to insert in your document.

   ■ Select a word in the Meanings For box or Synonyms for Directed list box, then click <u>L</u>ookup. The word you clicked appears in the Looked Up <u>W</u>ord list box, and meanings and synonyms appear for it in the Meanings For box and Synonyms for Directed list box.

   ■ If you want to return to a word displayed earlier in the Looked Up <u>W</u>ord list box, click the down arrow beside that list to display its choices, then click the word to display its meanings and synonyms.

4. When you find the word you want to use, click it in either the Meanings For box or Synonyms for Directed list box. A faint, dotted selection outline appears around the word in addition to the highlight.

5. Click the <u>R</u>eplace button. The Thesaurus replaces the original word with the new word.

6. If you change your mind, you can choose a different word. Repeat steps 3 through 5 to do so.

7. Click Cancel to return to your document.

Troubleshooting

When I try to use the Thesaurus to find a word, I get a dialog box telling me the Thesaurus doesn't have that word. What am I doing wrong?

You may have one of three problems. First, you may have made a typing error in the word you selected. If so, scroll through the Replace With list box in the Can't Find Word in Thesaurus dialog box (see fig. 9.10), click the correct spelling, and click OK. If you haven't mistyped, make sure you selected a word (not a space) and only a single word (not a phrase), then rerun the Thesaurus check. Finally, the word may really not exist in the Thesaurus. Try entering an alternate word in your document and looking up that word in the Thesaurus instead.

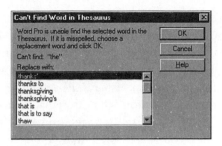

Fig. 9.10
The Thesaurus tells
you if it cannot
find a word you
want to look up.

Using Grammar Check

To communicate effectively, you need to tailor your writing for the audience
and situation. Word Pro's Grammar Check proofreading tool enables you to
check a document for correct grammar and use of language. You can specify
grammar rule and writing style options to customize Grammar Check to meet
your needs for a particular document and a particular audience. For example,
you need a much more formal style of writing for a business report or letter
to a potential client than you do for a letter to an acquaintance.

When you perform a grammar check, Word Pro displays a Grammar Check
bar that includes options for replacing or skipping any grammar errors (see
fig. 9.11).

Brief explanation of error

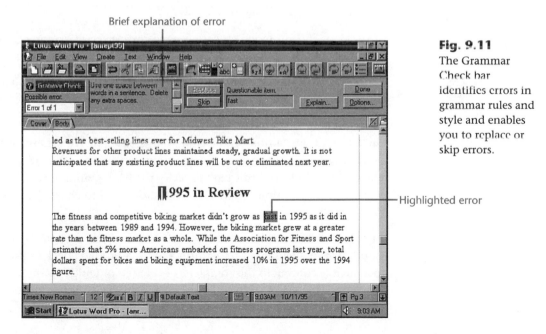

Fig. 9.11
The Grammar
Check bar
identifies errors in
grammar rules and
style and enables
you to replace or
skip errors.

Highlighted error

In Word Pro, you can proofread a document for correct grammar and use of language. Grammar Check examines each sentence in the document and determines whether the text conforms to various grammar, style, usage, and punctuation rules. If a sentence or word appears to break one or more of these rules, the Grammar Check bar displays the sentence or word that contains the error and suggests a revision. You can replace the error with Grammar Check's suggestion, you can edit the suggestion, or skip the error. In this way, you respond to the errors one by one. After you have responded to all the errors found, Grammar Check displays the readability statistics for your document, valuable information you can use to fine-tune your writing.

However, before you get to that point, you need to make some decisions about your audience and the writing style you want. To control how the Grammar Check operates, you need to select grammar rules and styles as described in the next section.

Selecting Grammar Rules and Styles

You can customize Grammar Check by specifying grammar rule and style options to meet your specific needs. For example, you can disable rules that don't apply to the writing style you want to use in a particular document, or you can specify options for finding errors you frequently make, such as split infinitives.

To set grammar options, follow these steps:

1. Open the document in which you want to perform the Grammar Check or make it the active document.

2. Choose <u>E</u>dit, Check Gramm<u>a</u>r, or click the Grammar Check SmartIcon. The Grammar Check bar appears on-screen and highlights the first error in the document (refer to fig. 9.11).

3. Click the <u>O</u>ptions button on the Grammar Check bar. The Grammar Options dialog box appears as shown in figure 9.12, with the <u>R</u>ules tab selected by default. Use this tab to specify the basic grammar rules, usage, and punctuation Grammar Check should use to check the grammar in the document.

4. If needed, click the down arrow to display the Grammar Check <u>L</u>evel list box. Choose Full Proof to perform a more thorough check of the document according to the complete 44-rule set, or Quick Proof to perform a faster check of the 28 most essential rules and style issues.

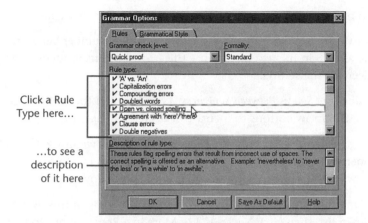

Click a Rule
Type here...

...to see a
description
of it here

Fig. 9.12
The Rules tab in
the Grammar
Options dialog box
enables you to
choose rules for
Grammar Check.

5. Click the down arrow in the Formality list box. You can choose from
the following styles: Standard (normal business language), Formal (for
extremely formal documents like business proposals or academic articles), or Informal (for more casual correspondence with acquaintances
like customer newsletters).

6. In the Rule Type list box, click to select and deselect rules as needed. A
check mark appears beside selected rules that Grammar Check will use.
By default, all the rules are selected, so you need to deselect the rules
you don't want to use. You can have one rule selected, none selected, or
any number in between. Table 9.1 lists the rules you can select.

7. Click the Grammatical Style tab to display its options (see fig. 9.13).
These options help Grammar Check determine how simple or complex
the language in the document should be.

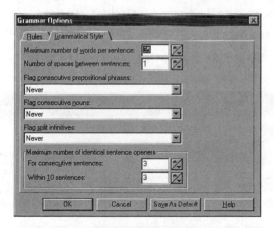

Fig. 9.13
You can choose
the Style options
for your grammar
check.

You can make the following choices in the <u>G</u>rammatical Style tab:

- *Maximum Number of <u>W</u>ords Per Sentence.* Type a number between 25 and 75 in the text box, or use the arrow buttons to increase or decrease the setting.

- *Number of Spaces <u>B</u>etween Sentences.* Type **1** or **2** in the text box or use the arrow buttons to increase or decrease the setting.

- *Flag <u>C</u>onsecutive Prepositional Phrases.* Click the down arrow to open this drop-down list, then choose Never, If 3 or More in a Row, If 4 or More in a Row, or If 5 or More in a Row.

- *Flag Consecutive <u>N</u>ouns.* Click the down arrow to open this drop-down list, then click Never, If 3 or More in a Row, If 4 or More in a Row, or If 5 or More in a Row.

- *Flag <u>S</u>plit Infinitives.* Click the down arrow to open this drop-down list, then click Never, Always, If 2 or More Intervening Words in a Row, If 3 or More Intervening Words in a Row, or If 4 or More Intervening Words in a Row.

- *For Consec<u>u</u>tive Sentences.* This setting controls the Maximum Number of Identical Sentence Openers using the same words or phrases. Type a value between 0 and 9 in the text box or use the arrow buttons to increase or decrease the setting.

- *Within <u>1</u>0 Sentences.* This setting controls the Maximum Number of Identical Sentence Openers within each group of 10 sentences. Type a value between 0 and 9 in the text box or use the arrow buttons to increase or decrease the settings.

8. If you want to use the Grammar Options you have specified for all Grammar Checks going forward, click the Sa<u>v</u>e As Default button.

9. Click OK to close the Grammar Options dialog box.

Table 9.1 Rules for Controlling a Grammar Check	
Rule	**Description**
"A" vs. "An"	Finds incorrect choices for a/an articles preceding nouns.
Capitalization errors	Identifies the common capitalization errors, including sentences that don't begin with a capital letter.

Rule	Description
Compounding errors	Lets you know if you've incorrectly hyphenated a word.
Doubled words	Finds repeated words or situations where you've mistakenly repeated two words of the same type, like *for about*.
Open vs. closed spelling	Finds spelling errors where you've unnecessarily inserted spaces in a phrase such as *a lot* rather than *alot*.
Spelling errors	Performs a spell check, comparing words with the main dictionary.
Agreement with "here"/"there"	Ensures that a predicate noun agrees with the subject of a sentence when that subject is *here* or *there*.
Clause errors	Alerts you to sentence structure problems, such as when you've joined too many clauses together.
Double negatives	Finds instances when you've used two negatives to indicate a positive, which can potentially confuse readers.
Formatting errors	Checks number, date, address, time, and currency formatting.
Inappropriate prepositions	Finds prepositions used incorrectly.
Mass vs. count errors	Makes sure you use singular adjectives with singular nouns and plural adjectives with plural nouns.
Misspelled expressions	Finds phrases that are misspelled in the context of the surrounding text.
Misspelled foreign expressions	Identifies foreign expressions you may have misspelled.
Misused words	Finds words that are easy to use incorrectly, such as *hopefully*.
Nonstandard modifiers	Ensures that you use adverbs to modify verbs, adjectives to modify nouns, and so on.
Nonstandard terms	Finds terms that aren't part of standard English usage.
Noun phrase consistency errors	Makes sure you use singular modifiers with singular nouns and plural modifiers with plural nouns.
Pronoun errors	Checks your usage of pronouns.

(continues)

Table 9.1 Continued	
Rule	**Description**
Punctuation errors	Finds incorrect or duplicated punctuation.
Spacing errors	Identifies errors in spacing between words.
Subject-verb agreement errors	Ensures that verbs agree with subjects, as in *I go* rather than *I goes.*
Ungrammatical expressions	Identifies phrases that aren't accepted in standard English.
Verb group consistency errors	Lets you know if your verb forms don't agree in a sentence.
Word order errors	Tells you if you've mistakenly misordered multiple noun modifiers.
Commonly confused words	Finds words that sound similar but are distinctly different, such as *casual* and *causal.*
Homonyms	Identifies when you've mixed up words that sound very much alike, like *ensure* and *insure.*
Possible word confusion	Identifies words that may be confused because they're similar in meaning.

After making your choices in the Grammar Options dialog box, you are ready to make corrections to the errors in grammar or style in your document.

Running a Grammar Check

You can use the Grammar Check to review the grammar, usage, style, and punctuation of sentences in your document. You can check the whole document or any part of a document.

To check grammar in a document, follow these steps:

1. Make the document you want to check the active document. Position the insertion point at the point in the document where you want to start checking grammar. If you want to check the grammar in only part of the document, highlight just that part of the document.

2. Choose <u>E</u>dit, Check Gramma<u>r</u>, or click the Grammar Check icon. The Grammar Check bar appears on-screen (refer to fig. 9.11) and highlights the first sentence or error in the document.

3. If you need to, set the Grammar Options as described in the preceding section.

4. When Grammar Check locates a grammar or style error in a sentence or word, the program highlights the sentence in the document and displays a description of the error in the text box beside the Possible Error list box. To learn more about the possible error, click the Explain button. The Rule Explanation dialog box appears to provide more detail about the correction Grammar Check thinks the sentence or word needs (see fig. 9.14). Click OK to close the Rule Explanation dialog box.

Fig. 9.14
Learn more about a suggested correction in the Rule Explanation dialog box.

5. Correct the sentence or ignore it using one of these steps:

- If the sentence is incorrect, first make any changes you want in the Replace With text box. Then click the Replace button to replace the incorrect sentence with the suggested sentence.

- To ignore Grammar Check's suggestion, click the Skip button.

6. When you are finished checking your document, click the Done button. The Readability Statistics dialog box appears and displays the number of words, sentences, paragraphs, and syllables in the text, as well as several standard measurements of the document's readability (see fig. 9.15).

Note

Included in the Readability Statistics are scores that identify the grade level of the writing, based on the average number of letters per word and per sentence, number of sentences per 100 words, and number of syllables per word.

Fig. 9.15
Grammar Check provides you with statistics about your document, including comparisons between it and certain standard readability tests.

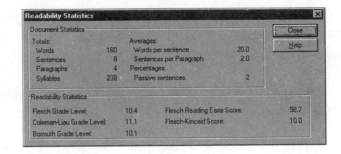

7. Click Close to close the Readability Statistics dialog box and return to the document.

The grammar check is complete. Word Pro returns to the text of the document, leaving the insertion point at the last sentence checked.

> **Tip**
>
> Many readability statistics are tied to the number of words per sentence and sentences per paragraph. To keep your writing easy to understand, use Grammar Check to help you keep your sentences and paragraphs short.

If the Grammar Check feature finds inappropriate word usage, you may need to substitute synonyms that improve the readability of the text. In these situations, consider using Word Pro's handy Thesaurus, described earlier in the chapter.

Using the Format Checker

Even though word processing programs make creating documents quick and convenient, many users may not be typing and formatting experts. In addition, typing conventions tend to vary between typewriters and word processors. Breaking old typing habits is often hard. For example, the conventional typewriter standard was to insert two spaces after every sentence. With a word processor, you need to insert just one space after each sentence because most fonts in word processors are proportional, allowing smaller spacing sizes for letters but larger spaces for words. Then your eye can more easily distinguish each word or sentence.

▶ See "Using Word Pro's SmartMasters," p. 242

The Format Checker looks at the formatting details in your document. (Use Word Pro's SmartMasters to quickly control the formatting of your document.)

When you perform a Format Checker, you can specify a Quick Check, which checks only basic typing issues, or you can specify the formatting options you choose. The following sections describe both these approaches.

Running a Format Check

As with the Spell Check and Grammar Check bars, Word Pro displays a Format Checker bar at the top of the screen to enable you to replace or skip text for which Format Checker suggests changes. To perform a Quick Check on the format of your document, use the following steps:

1. Make the document you want to check the active document. Position the insertion point at the beginning of the document or highlight part of the text to use Format Checker only on that selection.

2. Choose <u>E</u>dit, Check Fo<u>r</u>mat or click the Format Check SmartIcon. The Format Checker bar appears (see fig. 9.16).

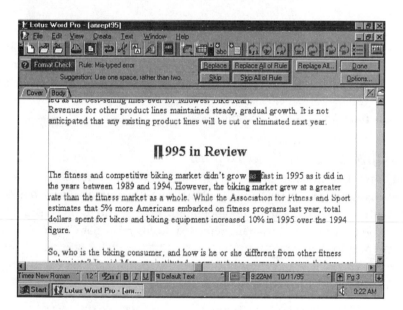

Fig. 9.16
You can perform a Quick Check of the basic formatting for your document.

3. The Format Checker selects the first text for which it finds a suggested change. It identifies the rule it uses to suggest the change and the suggested formatting change.

4. Choose a button to deal with the suggestion. The following options are available on the Format Checker bar:

- *Replace.* Replaces the highlighted text with the text that appears in the Suggestion box.

- *Replace All of Rule.* Replaces all text occurrences similar to the highlighted text with the text in the Suggestion box.

- *Skip.* Skips the highlighted text without making the suggested change.

- *Skip All of Rule.* Skips all text occurrences similar to the highlighted text without replacing the text with the suggested change.

- *Replace All.* Replaces all formatting that doesn't match the rules with suggested formatting, and displays a message dialog box to confirm your choice.

5. When the Format Checker has finished checking your document, a message box appears telling you the Format Check has finished. Choose OK to return to the document. The Format Checker bar changes to display the Continue Format Check button. You can click this button to resume format checking, or click the Done button to remove the Format Checker bar from the screen.

Setting Options

You don't need to settle for the default Format Checker options, such as checking spacing between sentences, improving the format of bulleted lists, replacing quote marks with true typographic quotes, and so on. Word Pro gives you control over the parameters used during a Format Check. You make the changes to these options in the Format Checker dialog box, which you access by choosing the Options button on the Format Checker bar (see fig. 9.17). You can set the following options:

- *Check Spacing between Sentences.* Click this check box, then select either the 1 Space or 2 Spaces option. This selection tells Format Checker to find sentences with too many or too few spaces after them and then correct the spacing by adding or deleting spaces as needed.

- *Improve Format of Bulleted Lists.* When this option is clicked, Format Checker finds lists you have created and changes dashes and asterisks, which you used to identify each list entry, into typographical bullets. Format Checker also sets up consistent indentations for the list items.

- *Improve the Appearance of Acronyms.* When clicked, this option lets Format Checker suggest font and punctuation improvements for acronyms like AM and PM.

- *Replace with Proper Character.* To select an option in this list box, click the option so a check mark appears to the left of it. You can select as many or as few list options as you want. Format Checker suggests typographical replacements for all the selected (checked) items. For example, Format Checker typesets items like fractions, quotes, and register marks when these items are selected in the list.

- *Mis-Typed Correction Options.* In this box, you can select punctuation typing errors you want Format Checker to find and remove. You can select one, two, or all of these options for correction: Trailing Space Underline, Double Spaces, Double Commas.

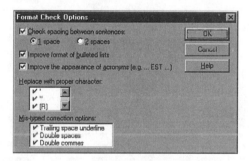

Fig. 9.17
The Format Check Options dialog box enables you to set the options Format Checker uses.

From Here...

In this chapter, you learned how to use Spell Check, the Thesaurus, Grammar Check, and Format Checker to proofread and improve the writing and word choice in your documents. Later chapters explain how to create output and fine-tune the appearance of your document. If you need to learn more about such topics now, review these chapters:

- Chapter 10, "Printing Documents," explains how to output your professional documents on paper. This chapter covers issues such as choosing and setting up a printer to use with Windows and performing the actual print operation.

- Chapter 11, "Customizing Word Pro," gives you details on setting up Word Pro to better suit your needs. For example, this chapter teaches you how to set default locations for files such as your user dictionary files.

■ Chapter 12, "Working with SmartMasters," introduces you to using Word Pro's SmartMasters to enhance the appearance of your expertly written and proofread text with a minimum of fuss.

Chapter 10

Printing Documents

by Lisa Bucki

After you develop and proofread a document, you are ready to print it. Although more cases may exist today where you can share documents electronically—via e-mail or on a network, for example—you still may have instances where your work on a document is not complete until you print it.

Windows 95 helps applications handle printing more effectively; however, you're likely to encounter numerous printing issues. You may use different printers; you may print documents created by other users on other systems; or you may print on a printer that offers multiple options. This chapter helps you manage the key issues of printing your documents in Word Pro.

In this chapter, you learn how to:

- Choose and set up a printer in Windows 95 to use with Word Pro
- Specify the options you want to use for printing the document
- Print a document and any notes it contains
- Print envelopes

Changing the Printing Options

Like other Windows programs, Word Pro uses the printer installed to work with Windows and uses the current setup for that printer. If you don't change the printer, and you are satisfied with the results you get when you print, you can simply print a document without worrying about the setup.

Often, though, you may need to change printers or change requirements for the current printer. Perhaps you want to print at a lower resolution. Or you want to change the default page setup to landscape orientation (sideways, with long edges at top and bottom) rather than the usual portrait orientation (upright, with short edges at top and bottom). The following two sections explain how to choose and set up the printer, and how to set print options in Word Pro.

Modifying the Printer Setup

You may have access to more than one printer with your computer. For example, you may have a local printer in your office and have access to a network printer. Or perhaps you create a file on a computer with one kind of printer attached, then need to print that document from a computer with a different kind of printer. In either of these cases or others, you need to choose a new printer before printing your Word Pro document. Microsoft Windows controls the printer; you specify how you want Windows to handle the necessary setup options (such as paper size, printer cartridges, and optional soft fonts).

To select and set up the printer you want to use, follow these steps:

1. Choose File, Print. Or press Ctrl+P or click the Print SmartIcon. The Print dialog box appears (see fig. 10.1). The top of the dialog box tells you which printer is the currently selected printer.

Fig. 10.1
The Print dialog box is the starting point for selecting a new printer and setting it up so you can print from Word Pro.

Current printer

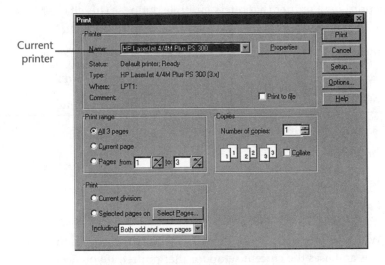

2. Click Setup to begin the setup process and display the Print Setup dialog box (see fig. 10.2).

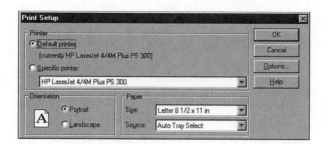

Getting to Know Word Pro

Fig. 10.2
The Print Setup
dialog box enables
you to choose
another printer
that was previously
installed to work
with Windows on
your computer.

3. To begin selecting another printer, choose the Specific Printer option
    button and then click the down-arrow to see the list choices.

4. Select a printer in the list.

5. In the Orientation area, select Portrait or Landscape to set the default
    paper configuration for the selected printer.

6. To change the options in the Paper area, click the Size down arrow and
    choose a new paper size. If the selected printer has more than one paper
    tray (such as a specialized envelope tray in addition to the regular paper
    tray), click the Source down arrow and choose a new tray.

7. To specify the setup options for the selected printer, click the Options
    button to open the specific printer's Setup dialog box (see fig. 10.3).

    Use the Help button in this dialog box and your printer's manual for
    more information on setting up your particular printer. The Help dialog
    box provides help for every selection in the specific printer's Setup dia-
    log box. Click OK to close this dialog box. If the specific printer's Setup
    dialog box offers other command buttons, such as the About and Fea-
    tures buttons shown in figure 10.3, you can use them to display other
    dialog boxes to further fine-tune your printer setup.

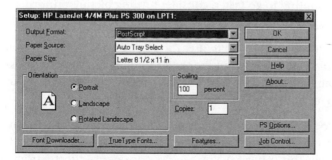

Fig. 10.3
The Properties
dialog box enables
you to set the
options for your
printer. The
available choices
depend on the
printer you select.

8. Click OK to close the specific printer's Setup dialog box.

9. Click OK again to close the Print Setup dialog box.

Keep in mind the following issues when you specify the printer setup:

■ When you change printer setup options, you affect the current document and all documents subsequently printed on that printer. You also affect other Windows programs using that printer.

◄ See "Adjusting Text Attributes," p. 83

◄ See "Adding Lines and Borders," p. 102

■ You may need to change some formatting options in your documents depending on the printer you select. For example, if you have a document with many colors applied to text and other elements but your printer doesn't handle color very well or washes out lighter colors so they're unreadable, consider changing some of the colored elements to black so they will print in the most readable and attractive fashion.

■ To use landscape orientation, you need to change both the Windows printer setup and the page layout for the document in Word Pro (to landscape orientation). If a document uses both portrait and landscape orientation, you must create a new division or section and change the orientation to accommodate landscape or portrait orientation. See Chapter 16, "Managing Long Documents," for instructions on working with sections and divisions, and see Chapter 5, "Formatting the Page," to learn how to change the page orientation.

■ If you change the graphics resolution setting, remember that the more dots per inch (dpi) you choose, the better the printout but the slower your printing. A greater dpi setting makes the printout look more realistic and less grainy; the printer uses more dots to create the image and places those dots closer together for a smoother image appearance.

■ If your document has many pictures inserted in frames and you want the printing to go faster, consider turning picture printing off. The next section describes this printing option and others.

■ To ensure that Word Pro uses the settings you choose for your printer, display the Page Layout Properties InfoBox and select the Use Settings From Printer Driver check box. Otherwise, settings you make in Word Pro may override the changes you specify for your printer.

■ If you have a fax modem installed in your computer and have installed software for sending and receiving faxes in Windows (most fax modems include this software), you can fax documents directly from Word Pro. Use the Print Setup dialog box to select the fax modem printer driver from the Specific Printer drop-down list (for example, QuickLink II Fax on FAX/MODEM). Specify all other print options and print the document. Your fax modem software's send component loads and prepares the document for faxing, including a cover page if you specify. All you need to do is enter the fax phone number.

Troubleshooting

I need to print to a specific printer, but it doesn't appear in the Specific Printer drop-down list of the Print Setup dialog box. Where is the printer I need?

The Specific Printer drop-down list displays the different types of printers available. If the printer you need doesn't appear on the list, you may not have the correct printer installed, or the correct printer driver may not be available. For information on installing printer drivers, consult your Windows 95 documentation.

Choosing Printing Options

After you specify your printer setup, you can choose Word Pro printing options for the current document and print the document. To start this process, display the Print dialog box by choosing File, Print. Or press Ctrl+P or choose the Print SmartIcon. The Print dialog box appears (refer to fig. 10.1).

Choose the Options button. Word Pro displays the Print Options dialog box, shown in figure 10.4. Click each option you want to select; table 10.1 describes the print options. Remember, the options you set don't affect any other documents. Then click OK to close the dialog box and return to the Print dialog box.

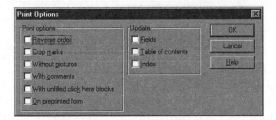

Fig. 10.4
The Print Options dialog box enables you to specify options for the current print job in Word Pro.

Tip

The Reverse Order choice in the Print Options dialog box is helpful if you need to photocopy the document, and your photocopier reverses the order of the original it's copying.

Table 10.1 Choices in the Print Options Dialog Box	
Option	**Description**
<u>R</u>everse Order	Prints pages in reverse order, starting with the last page of the last division and moving toward the first page.
Crop <u>M</u>arks	Adds printer crop marks, which are used for trimming the page to the document when it prints. For example, if you're creating a document that's 5.5"×8.5" in size but you can print only on 8.5"×11" paper, turn on this option so Word Pro prints crop marks to help you precisely trim away the excess paper to reach the 5.5"×8.5" finished size.
Without <u>P</u>ictures	Prints the document using picture placeholders rather than the actual images. This option provides quicker printing so you can produce drafts of your document or use a slower printer or printer with less memory.
With <u>C</u>omments	Prints the contents of Comment Notes inserted in your document as well as the document text. See the section "Printing Comment Notes" later in this chapter for more information.
With Unfilled Clic<u>k</u> Here Blocks	Prints the entire document but does not print your entries in any Click Here blocks. This method enables you to create blank preprinted forms.
<u>O</u>n Preprinted Form	Provides the reverse effect of the preceding option. When you select this option, Word Pro prints only the contents of Click Here blocks, so you can fill in your preprinted form.
<u>F</u>ields	Ensures that Word Pro updates the contents of all fields before printing.
<u>T</u>able of Contents	Tells Word Pro to check for TOC entry changes and update the TOC if necessary before printing.
<u>I</u>ndex	Tells Word Pro to check for Index entry changes and update the Index if necessary before printing.

If you don't enable the <u>F</u>ields, <u>T</u>able of Contents, and <u>I</u>ndex options, Word Pro prints the document as it currently appears on-screen, whether you've saved the document to update the elements or not.

Troubleshooting

In the Print Options dialog box, I selected the Crop <u>M</u>arks check box, but they didn't print. What could be wrong?

You can print crop marks only if the size of your paper exceeds the page layout size you set for the document by a comfortable margin (most printers require one-quarter inch to one-half inch all around). Otherwise, Word Pro has no space to print the marks. Try reducing the size of the printed image by using the Scaling option (if it's in the Options dialog box for your printer). Or, if you need an original that's 100% size, print to a larger paper size if you can. Otherwise, you may need to take a disk copy of your document to a local print shop and have them print it on the correct paper size for you.

I'm trying to print to a preprinted form, but it doesn't line up. Any suggestions?

Unless you're sure your form setup is perfect, it's a good idea to print the fill-in contents on a blank piece of paper first. Then place the page with the printed fill-in contents on top of the form and hold the two up to the light. See whether the fill-in contents line up with the form. On the fill-in contents page, mark any adjustments you need and measure them. Then go back to your document and make the changes. When your fill-in contents page lines up perfectly with the form page, you are ready to print to the form page.

Printing Documents

Now you have selected and set up the printer, but you're not finished yet. You can specify additional print choices in the Print dialog box before printing. These choices include the number of copies to print, page range to print, and more. After you specify the choices in this dialog box, you can finally print the document. Some Print dialog box choices are described in more detail later in this section.

> **Note**
>
> If you're using a laser printer to print to letterhead paper or preprinted forms, make sure you insert the letterhead paper or blank forms correctly in the paper tray. Some printers require that you insert the paper face up, and some require that you insert it face down.

To use the Print dialog box to finally (whew!) print a document, follow these steps:

1. If the Print dialog box isn't open, choose File, Print. Or press Ctrl+P or click the Print SmartIcon. The Print dialog box appears (refer to fig. 10.1). Select and set up a printer and specify print options as described in the previous sections, if needed.

> **Tip**
>
> If you choose to print the Current Division, you can use the Select Pages option to print only selected pages in that division or the entire division.

2. Specify the page(s) to print in the Print Range area of the dialog box:

   ■ To print the entire document, choose All Pages.

   ■ To print noncontiguous pages, choose Selected Pages Only, then click the Select Pages button. The Select Pages dialog box appears (see fig. 10.5). You can Select Pages to Print By in one of two ways. You can click the List of Pages button and then enter the pages to print in the List the Pages text box (separating each page or range with a comma and using hyphens to specify ranges, such as 2-4). Or you can click the Whole Divisions button and then choose the name of the division to print in the Divisions to Print list. Click OK to return to the Print dialog box.

   ■ To print only a range of pages (for example, pages 1 to 3 or 5 to 8), select the Pages option. Then use the From text box or spinner arrows to specify the beginning page number, and the To text box or spinner arrows to specify the ending page number.

   ■ Choose Current Division to print only the division containing the insertion point.

   ■ Choose Current Page to print only the page containing the insertion point.

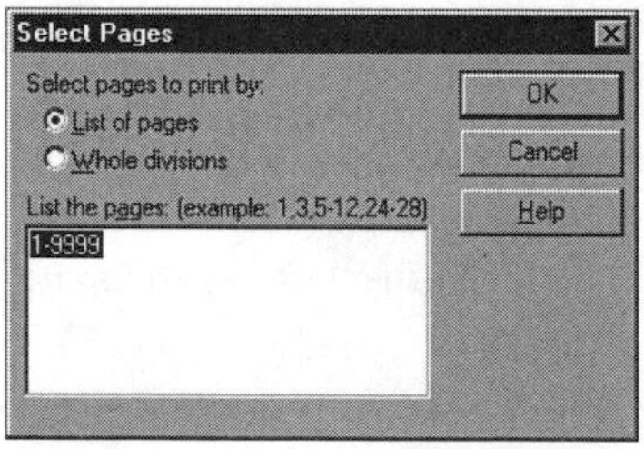

Fig. 10.5

The Select Pages dialog box enables you to print by entering lists of noncontiguous pages or by selecting divisions.

3. Still in the Print dialog box, click the down arrow beside the Including drop-down list and specify the type of pages (Odd, Even, or Both Odd and Even Pages) you want to print.

4. Specify Print Quality using that drop-down list. The available choices depend on the selected printer.

5. Select the Print to File check box if you want to print the document to a disk file rather than to the selected printer.

6. Specify the number of copies to print by clicking the Copies text box and typing the number of copies you want.

7. Select the Collate Copies check box to print the entire document before printing another copy. If you request more than one copy in the Copies text box and don't choose this option, Word Pro prints the requested number of copies for page 1, for page 2, and so on. Note that printing collated is slower than printing uncollated.

8. If you want to make the print job a low-priority activity for your computer so you can continue working at top speed in your document, make sure that the Print This Document in Background check box is selected.

9. To print the document, click Print.

Word Pro displays a message that indicates the document is printing. This message remains on-screen until the entire document is sent to the printer. The screen disappears and you can continue your work.

> **Note**
>
> You can use a laser printer to apply color foil to part of a document. Simply lay the foil over the part of the already-printed document that you want to decorate, insert the page in the paper tray, print a blank page, and peel off the excess foil. One source for this foil is Paper Direct, 1-800-A-PAPERS.

Printing Duplex Pages

In the preceding section, you learned that the Print dialog box offers many choices for printing specific pages of a document. These options may come in particularly handy for one special printing situation—when you need to print original two-sided, or *duplex*, documents instead of using a photocopier to create two-sided copies.

You can accomplish two-sided printing even if you don't have a printer capable of printing on both sides. The process involves using the Including drop-down list in the Print dialog box and making two printing passes for the document. To print two-sided pages for your document, follow these steps:

1. Choose File, Print. Or press Ctrl+P or click the Print SmartIcon. The Print dialog box appears (refer to fig. 10.1).

2. Click the down arrow beside the Including drop-down list and choose Odd, which prints only odd-numbered pages (right-hand pages if you're planning to bind the duplexed pages in a report). You want to choose Odd first, of course, because page 1 is an odd page.

3. Set any other printing options you want, then click Print to send the document to the printer.

4. Take the printed pages, flip them over, and insert them again into the paper tray for your printer. It may take some practice to learn the correct way to insert the paper in the paper tray, and you may need to change the order of the pages. The objective here is to insert the paper so Word Pro prints on the blank side of the paper in the direction you want.

5. Choose File, Print. Or press Ctrl+P or click the Print SmartIcon. The Print dialog box appears (refer to fig. 10.1).

6. Click the down arrow of the Including drop-down list and choose Even, which prints only even-numbered pages (left-hand pages if you're planning to bind the duplexed pages in a report).

7. Set any other printing options you choose, then click Print to send the document to the printer.

After the second printing pass, you should have clean, original, two-sided pages that you can bind as a report.

Printing Envelopes

You can easily print envelopes in Word Pro, which automates the process of creating an envelope with the correct dimensions, if your printer has these capabilities.

To start the process, make sure the tray containing envelopes is inserted in your printer. Choose Create, Envelope. Word Pro displays a special Envelope bar at the top of the screen and inserts a new division in the document for the envelope (see fig. 10.6).

If your document is a letter that includes a name and address block, Word Pro automatically inserts that name and address in the addressee frame. Word Pro also automatically inserts a frame for your return address.

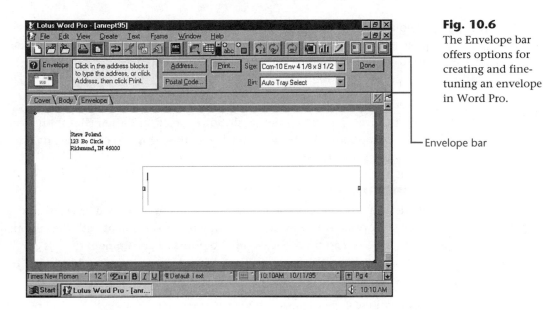

Fig. 10.6
The Envelope bar offers options for creating and fine-tuning an envelope in Word Pro.

Envelope bar

To change either address, click its frame and edit the frame text. Or you can click the frame and then choose the Address button on the Envelope bar. The Address dialog box appears (see fig. 10.7). To insert a previously saved name and address in the frame you selected, click the Address Names drop-down list, select the name you want, then click OK. Word Pro closes the dialog box and inserts the correct name and address.

To create a new address in the Address dialog box, type the new name in the Address Names text box. Then type the new name and address in the Address text box and click the Add Address button. Click OK to insert the new address in the frame you selected before displaying the Address dialog box.

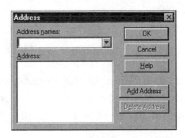

Fig. 10.7
The Address dialog box enables you to select an address you saved previously, or to enter and save a new address to use when creating envelopes later.

Use the Size list to change the size of the envelope layout if needed. To change the positioning of the addressee or return address frame, drag the frame to a new position just as you do any other frame.

If you want to add printed postal bar codes to the bottom of the envelope to help your postal office sort the mail more efficiently, click the Postal Code button on the Envelope bar. In the Bar Codes dialog box that appears, select a Bar Codes type from that drop-down list, then click OK.

To print your envelope, choose the Print button. In the Print dialog box, select Current Division if it isn't already selected, and then click Print to print the envelope only. In the Envelope bar, choose Done to close the Envelope bar when you're finished.

Printing Comment Notes

By default, Word Pro doesn't print the comment notes you insert in a document. However, if you want a hard copy of the document with the comments included, you can print one. Word Pro prints each comment note as a frame in the document; the frame overlays other document text and includes the author's user name and the note's creation date and time.

Follow these steps to print comment notes:

1. Choose File, Print. Or press Ctrl+P or click the Print SmartIcon. The Print dialog box appears (refer to fig. 10.1).

2. Choose the Options button. The Print Options dialog box opens (refer to fig. 10.4).

3. Select the With Comments check box.

4. Click OK to close the Print Options dialog box and return to the Print dialog box.

5. Click Print again to print your document with the comment notes.

Printing an Outline

▶ See "Outlining a Document," p. 267

When you outline your document in Word Pro and work with the various outline levels, Word Pro prints only the levels currently on-screen. To print an outline for your document, choose Text, Outline, and use the options on the submenu that appears to collapse the document text and heading levels you don't want to include in your document. Then choose File, Print. Specify any printing options you want, then click Print to print the outline.

From Here...

You've learned the ins and outs of printing all or part of a Word Pro document. You learned how to choose a Windows printer, set it up, specify printing options, and print. You also learned to print duplex (two-sided) pages, envelopes, and notes.

You may be interested in moving beyond printing to publishing—creating cohesive documents that have visual impact and allow you to communicate effectively. Part III, "Producing Professional Output with Word Pro," contains chapters that enable you to explore document publishing. Consider these chapters for starters:

- Chapter 19, "Using Frames," explains how to use frames to arrange text and graphics in a document to better organize and call attention to information.

- Chapter 21, "Using Draw," gives you an introduction to Word Pro's tools for creating your own drawings of logos, scenes, and more.

- Chapter 22, "Desktop Publishing with Word Pro," defines desktop publishing and how to use tools in Word Pro to create professional-quality flyers, brochures, newsletters, and more.

Chapter 11

Customizing Word Pro

by Lisa Bucki

Everyone has preferences. Some people like a spartan, modern decor while others prefer a living and working space overflowing with knick-knacks. Some people like vanilla ice cream and others prefer chocolate. Some people run alone to exercise, while others play basketball or indulge in another team sport.

Your preferences apply when you work with software, as well. Word Pro offers a myriad of settings you can customize to adjust Word Pro's appearance and performance to suit your choices and needs. When working with a new software program, you may be tempted to get started quickly and not spend much time setting up. Developing a sense of what you need before you spend much time on setup is probably a good idea, but setting up the software in such a way that it perfectly suits your purposes can save time. Adding a particular SmartIcon to the icon bar, for example, may not sound like a time-saver, but this small change can be important if you repeat a command 50, 100, or 500 times daily.

Word Pro makes customizing easy; nowhere is the software's versatility more apparent than in the number of options Word Pro enables you to preset. This enables you to create a working environment offering precisely the features you want.

In this chapter, you learn about Word Pro's many default settings. The chapter explains how to set general preferences and specific preferences for paths and views, how to work with and customize SmartIcons, and how to change settings for CycleKeys and SmartFill.

In this chapter, you learn how to:

- Set general preferences to control things like how often Word Pro performs autotimed saves of your files

- Control the default paths where certain files are stored and default files for features such as user dictionaries

- Edit your user information, including items such as your company name and fax number

- Modify SmartIcon bars and SmartIcons and create custom SmartIcons

- Customize CycleKeys for quick formatting

- Set view preferences to control such features as whether rulers or graphics appear on-screen, control Zoom and Outline views, and set Clean Screen options such as whether you see title bars and other program features

- Create custom SmartFill entries so that you can automatically enter series of data in consecutive table cells

Changing the User Setup

You can customize the way Word Pro works by setting the many defaults the program offers. You can indicate whether you want automatic backups, set the number of actions Word Pro can undo, change the markup options for document revisions, disable some features and warning messages, specify default paths (locations) and files, or enter and update personal information about yourself that Word Pro stores to track file information or to use in documents like fax cover sheets.

As you use the program and establish a special style of working, you can set up Word Pro to suit that style. If you prefer not to use SmartCorrect so that you can work more quickly, for example, you can turn SmartCorrect off by default when you start up Word Pro.

To set defaults, you use the Word Pro Preferences dialog box (see fig. 11.1). To display the Word Pro Preferences dialog box, choose File, User Setup. Click Word Pro Preferences in the User Setup submenu that appears.

The Word Pro Preferences dialog box offers four tabs, which contain a specific set of options you can adjust. By default, the General tab is selected when the Word Pro Preferences dialog box opens.

The next few sections describe the options available on each of the tabs in the Word Pro Preferences dialog box, starting with the General tab. After you finish setting defaults in the various tabs of the Word Pro Preferences dialog box, click OK or press Enter to close the dialog box. Word Pro then implements the choices you made in this dialog box each time you start Word Pro.

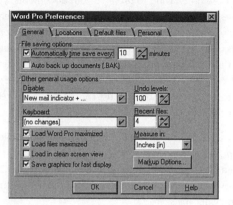

Fig. 11.1
The four tabs in the Word Pro Preferences dialog box enable you to set various program defaults.

Setting General Preferences

The General tab in the Word Pro Preferences dialog box (refer to fig. 11.1) enables you to control numerous automated and general features within Word Pro. For example, you can control whether Word Pro performs automatically timed saves of your document to preserve your work between full save operations; timed saves are not full saves but just keystroke recording. You can also control how many of the files that you've recently worked with appear at the bottom of the File menu.

After you choose the options you want in this tab, you can continue working in the Word Pro Preferences dialog box by clicking another tab to set its options, or you can click OK to close the Word Pro Preferences dialog box. Following are descriptions of all the options available in the General tab and how to set them:

■ *Automatically Time Save Every.* When this option is selected, Word Pro saves your document at designated intervals. After you turn on this option, specify how often you want the program to save the document (in minutes, using values of 1 or more) by typing a value in the text box beside the option or using the spinner arrows. When you are using a document and Word Pro is saving automatically, the message Time Saving document(s) appears in the status bar to indicate that your file is being saved. Word Pro assigns the .~ts file name extension to the timed save file and saves it in the directory specified in the Backups entry of the Locations tab (described in the next section).

> **Note**
>
> If you don't use time saving to preserve your documents, you could lose any work you've done since your last File, Save operation if there's a computer error or power loss to your system. It's a good idea to automatically time save documents every five to ten minutes. But be aware that automatically time saving isn't active when you work with the drawing, charting, or equations features of Word Pro. Timed saves only occur when you're working with the word processing features, so you must choose File, Save frequently if you're drawing or creating equations.
>
> If there is a situation where your computer does crash while you're working on a document, restart your system and start Word Pro. It displays a message telling you a timed save version of your document exists. Click Yes to open the timed saved document to reclaim all your work between the last timed save and your previous full save.

- *Auto Back Up Documents (.BAK).* Select this option so that each time you save the current document, Word Pro creates a duplicate copy of that document with the .BAK file name extension and saves it on disk. By default, Word Pro saves the backup file in the directory specified in the Backups entry of the Locations tab (described in the next section). For information on naming your backup directory, see the next section, "Setting Locations."

- *Disable.* By clicking the check mark to display this list box, you can choose several features and warnings to disable in the list. Choosing an option in the list box places a check mark beside it to indicate that the option is disabled. Select all the options you want to disable; then click the list box check mark to close the list. You can disable these features and warnings:

> **Caution**
>
> Only experienced users should disable version warning messages; these messages can help prevent irreversible mistakes that result in data loss.

◀ See "Using SmartCorrect," p. 70

Choose *SmartCorrect* to stop automatic spelling corrections as you type documents.

Choose *Drag & Drop* to disable drag and drop document editing with the mouse.

Choose *Version Warning Messages* to turn off messages that appear as you're creating and editing multiple versions of a file.

▶ See "Using Versions," p. 508

Choose *Application Startup Scripts* to disable any scripts (macros) you've specified to run when you start Word Pro.

Choose *Document Open Scripts* to disable any scripts (macros) you've specified to run when you open a document created with a particular SmartMaster.

Choose *Small File Format* to prevent automatic compression of files.

Choose *Multiple Cell Paste* to prevent simultaneously pasting information into multiple cells in a table.

Choose *Welcome Dialog* to prevent an opening welcome screen from displaying when you start Word Pro, so that the program loads more quickly.

Choose *SmartSelect* to turn off Word Pro's quick text selection features.

Choose *New Mail Indicator* to turn off the automatic indicator that lets you know when a message is waiting for you.

Choose *Envelope Return Address* to hide the default return address.

Choose *Background Spell Check* to force Word Pro to check the spelling in the foreground.

■ *Load Word Pro Maximized.* When this option is selected, the Word Pro application window appears maximized (full-screen size) when you start the program. Otherwise, the Word Pro window opens to the size it was when you last exited the program, either in a smaller window or minimized to an icon.

■ *Load Files Maximized.* Select this option to tell Word Pro to open all files at full window size.

■ *Load in Clean Screen View.* By default this option is not selected. When you turn it on, Word Pro loads using the Clean Screen options you've specified in the <u>C</u>lean Screen tab of the View Preferences dialog box (see "Setting Clean Screen Options" later in this chapter).

■ *Save Graphics for Fast Display.* If you select this option, Word Pro creates screen snapshot files, stores them as temporary files on the hard disk as you work, and includes them in the document when you save it. This

Getting to Know Word Pro

option increases the speed at which pictures can be displayed, but also increases the size of the document. Select this option if you have plenty of disk space and value the increased speed as you work. Snapshot files can be quite large, so monitor your free disk space often.

> **Tip**
>
> Although you can set dozens of undo levels, you probably should specify a smaller number between 2 and 5. For each additional undo level, Word Pro stores deleted or changed material. Storing this material takes time and disk space, and managing the undo levels takes system memory (RAM).

- *Undo Levels.* Use this option to specify how many successive actions you can undo with the Undo command. Then, each successive time you use Undo, Word Pro returns to the preceding action, up to the number you specify with the Undo Levels option. To change this setting, type a value other than 0 in the Undo Levels text box or use the spinner arrows. The default is 100.

> **Tip**
>
> The list of recent files really saves time in searching for files. If you use many documents during a given time period, choose 5 for the Recent Files option.

- *Recent Files.* At the bottom of the File menu, Word Pro lists the files you've most recently worked with and saved. (You can open one of the files by clicking its name in the list.) To control the number of files listed, enter a value (from 0 to 5) in the Recent Files text box, or use the spinner arrows to change the value. The default is 4.

- *Measure In.* Use this drop-down list to specify whether Word Pro uses Inches (in), Centimeters (cm), Picas (pi), or Points (pts) for rulers, indents, and other measures in documents. Each pica equals 1/6-inch, and each point equals 1/12-inch. The default is inches.

▶ See "Changing Revision Options," p. 489

- *Markup Options.* Select this option to display a dialog box to set default color and formatting for revisions you make when you're using Revision mode in Word Pro. Chapter 24 explains how to use revision marking, and the section in Chapter 24 called "Changing Revision Options" explains how to change the Markup Options after clicking this button.

Setting Locations

When you select the Locations tab in the Word Pro Preferences dialog box (see fig. 11.2), it offers other default settings that apply to paths. Word Pro uses default paths as you work—paths for the document, for example, and for SmartIcons. You can save time by setting defaults that correspond with the paths you use most.

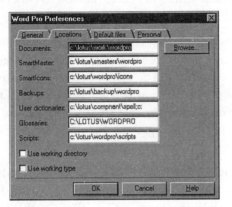

Fig. 11.2
Use this tab in the Word Pro Preferences dialog box to set the default locations where Word Pro stores and looks for certain kinds of files.

A *path* is like an address for a file; it consists of the letter to identify a disk (such as C) and a directory or directories (such as \LOTUS\SMASTERS\ WORDPRO). You can specify the default paths for documents, SmartMasters, backup files, scripts (macros), and more. Word Pro uses these paths to find and store files.

To change a default path, you need to change the entry for it in the appropriate text box in the Locations tab of the Word Pro Preferences dialog box. Use one of two methods to change a path entry:

- Click in the text box for a path and edit the entry (backspacing over and retyping characters as needed).

- Click in the text box for a path; then click the Browse button to display the Browse dialog box. Use the Look In lists to set a new path; then click OK to return to the Locations tab.

After you choose the options you want in this tab, you can continue working in the Word Pro Preferences dialog box by clicking another tab to set its options; or you can click OK to close the Word Pro Preferences dialog box. To set up default paths, change the path listed in each of the following text boxes:

■ *Documents.* Indicates where Word Pro automatically stores and looks for documents. You may want to change the default directory occasionally so that the default document directory reflects the projects you're working with most. For example, if you're performing a lot of work for a client and have a directory on disk for files created for that client, you may want to make the client directory your default Documents directory. The default setting here is C:\LOTUS\WORK\WORDPRO.

▶ See "Creating New Styles," p. 254

▶ See "Saving a New SmartMaster," p. 262

■ *SmartMaster.* Tells you where Word Pro automatically stores and looks for SmartMasters and styles. Unless you work with many SmartMasters and styles other than those that come with the program, you probably don't need to change the default. If you create custom SmartMasters, you may want to keep them separate from the ones that come with Word Pro. You can keep your custom style sheets in a different directory and set up a default path to that directory. The original entry in this text box is C:\LOTUS\SMASTERS\WORDPRO.

■ *SmartIcons.* Specifies where Word Pro stores and finds custom SmartIcon bars and SmartIcons. Word Pro stores the predefined bars and icons that come with the program in C:\LOTUS\WORDPRO\ICONS.

■ *Backups.* Indicates the path you want Word Pro to use for documents it saves with the automatic timed save and auto backup features (described earlier in this chapter). This directory is C:\LOTUS\BACKUP\WORDPRO.

■ *User Dictionaries.* Sets the directory where Word Pro stores new user dictionaries you create. (By default, Word Pro puts these files in C:\LOTUS\COMPNENT\SPELL.)

■ *Glossaries.* Tells Word Pro where to store glossaries you create. Word Pro uses the C:\LOTUS\WORDPRO directory for this purpose.

■ *Scripts.* Tells Word Pro where to store and look for scripts (macros) you create to automate various operations in Word Pro. To use a directory other than C:\LOTUS\WORDPRO\SCRIPTS, you must create it yourself before specifying it here.

■ *Use Working Directory.* The Locations tab also enables you to specify whether to use the working directory. Normally, when you choose File, Save or File, Open, Word Pro displays a list of Word Pro files located in the defined Documents directory. If you choose the Use Working Directory check box, each time you open or save a file, Word Pro looks at the current (working) directory of the last file opened rather than the Documents directory. For example, suppose that the Documents directory is C:\LOTUS\WORK\WORDPRO and you create a new document called API.LWP. Instead of saving the new document in C:\LOTUS\WORK\ WORDPRO, you use File, Save As to save it in the C:\API\DOCS directory. The next time you open a file during the current working session, Word Pro automatically displays the documents in C:\API\DOCS instead of C:\LOTUS\WORK\WORDPRO.

■ *Use Working Type.* When selected, this option uses only Word Pro files as the default file type in the Save As and Open dialog boxes. Deselected, Word Pro uses the first file type you choose when opening or saving a document until you choose another file type.

Troubleshooting

Word Pro lets me specify a directory in a particular Locations text box, but then I can't open the files from it. What's wrong?

The directory you specified may not exist. You need to actually create a directory before you can tell Word Pro to save files to it.

Setting Default Files

Click the Default Files tab in the Word Pro Preferences dialog box to display the options shown in figure 11.3. The files you specify here become the default files Word Pro uses or suggests for particular operations.

To change a default file, you need to change the entry for it in the appropriate text box in the Default Files tab of the Word Pro Preferences dialog box. If you need to change the default, you must include the entire path along with the name of the file to use. Use one of two methods to change a default file entry:

Fig. 11.3
Choosing the default SmartMaster, user dictionary, and glossary files.

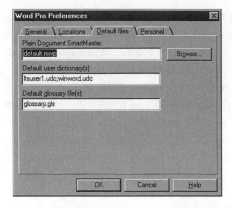

■ Click in the text box for a file and edit the entry (backspacing over and retyping characters as needed).

■ Click in the text box for a path; then click the Browse button to display the Browse dialog box. Use the Look In and File Name lists to choose a new file; then click OK to return to the Default Files tab.

After you choose the options you want in this tab, you can continue working in the Word Pro Preferences dialog box by clicking another tab to set its options, or you can click OK to close the Word Pro Preferences dialog box. To set up Default files, change the path and file listed in each of the following text boxes:

■ *Plain Document SmartMaster.* Enter the path and name of the file that you want to use as the default SmartMaster for normal (basic) documents.

◄ See "Choosing User Dictionaries for a Spell Check," p. 177

■ *Default User Dictionary(s).* Enter the path and name of a user dictionary file you want Word Pro to make available for use during a spell check.

► See "Using a Glossary," p. 292

■ *Default Glossary File(s).* Enter the name of the file holding glossary entries you've created so that Word Pro enables you to find and use those entries later.

> **Note**
>
> You can specify more than one file in the Default User Dictionary(s) and Default Glossary File(s) text boxes. To do so, click at the end of the entry(s) in this text box. Then, either type a semicolon and then the path and name of another file, or use the Browse button to append another file name to the text box entry.

Setting Personal Information

When you perform certain operations in Word Pro, the program requires information about you. For example, when you save a document, Word Pro remembers your user name along with the date and time you saved the document. Similarly, when you make document revisions or use TeamReview, TeamConsolidate, or other versions, Word Pro tracks the changes you make as opposed to changes made by another user. For these and other purposes, it's important to give Word Pro accurate personal information about yourself.

To do so, click the Personal tab in the Word Pro Preferences dialog box to display the options shown in figure 11.4. Word Pro uses the information you supply here for tracking files and other operations.

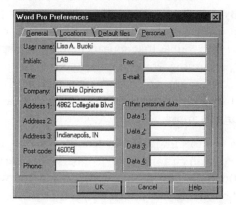

Fig. 11.4
Giving information about yourself as a user to Word Pro.

After you choose the options you want in this tab, you can continue working in the Word Pro Preferences dialog box by clicking another tab to set its options, or you can click OK to close the Word Pro Preferences dialog box. To set up Personal information, click in any of the following text boxes (most of which are self-explanatory) and edit the entry:

- *User Name*: Your name

- *Initials*: Initials to use to identify your notes and revisions

- *Title*: Your job title

- *Company*: Your company name

- *Address 1*: The first line of your address

- *Address 2*: The second line of your address

- *Address 3*: Your city and state

- *Post Code*: Your zip code

- *Phone, Fax*: Your phone and fax numbers, including area code (these are separated with different text boxes in the tab)

- *E-mail*: Your e-mail address

- *Data 1, Data 2, Data 3, and Data 4*: Any other data you want to store about yourself

Customizing SmartIcons

The latest version of Word Pro offers several sets of SmartIcons, in SmartIcon bars or *iconbars*. By default, the Universal iconbar appears just under the title bar and to the left on-screen. A *context iconbar* appears to the right of the Universal iconbar; the iconbar that appears here varies depending on the operation you're performing. For example, if you're creating a drawing, the Drawing Actions iconbar appears; if you're editing text, the Text iconbar appears. The next section, "Modifying SmartIcons," explains how to control when context iconbars appear.

Word Pro enables you to show and hide iconbars as you prefer and position them on-screen. You can customize the iconbars or create your own iconbars so that the SmartIcons you use most often appear as you work. You can even create your own SmartIcons and attach scripts (macros) to them.

Word Pro gives you a choice of whether to display iconbars. (However, because the major advantage of SmartIcons is that they let you execute commands with a single mouse click, hiding the SmartIcons defeats that benefit.) By default, you can use a pop-up menu to control whether iconbars appear at all or to control the display of a few of the default iconbars. To display this pop-up menu, point to the down-arrow button at the left end of either the Universal or current context iconbar. The pop-up menu shown in figure 11.5 appears.

In this pop-up menu, click Hide This Bar of SmartIcons to specify whether to hide the SmartIcon bar you displayed the pop-up menu for, or click Hide All SmartIcons to hide all iconbars from view. Click one of the other three iconbars listed at the bottom of the menu to control whether each of them appears. A check mark beside an iconbar name indicates that you've selected it to appear. After you click a choice in this pop-up menu, it closes automatically.

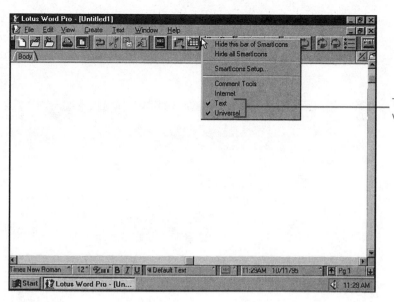

Fig. 11.5
Controlling the
display of the
iconbars.

The checked iconbars
will appear

You can also show or hide all SmartIcons by choosing <u>V</u>iew, Show/<u>H</u>ide. In
the submenu that appears, click SmartIcons.

Tip

The main reason to hide the SmartIcons is to create more room on-screen as you
work. You can press Ctrl+Q to quickly toggle between showing and hiding the
SmartIcons.

Most of the time when you are working on text, you probably want Word Pro
to display SmartIcons at the top of the screen. They're placed there for convenience because most users are accustomed to moving the mouse to the top of
the screen. However, if you are working with graphics, equations, or in one
part of the screen, you may prefer to set up the SmartIcons near the area
where you are working. In such a case, you can drag the iconbar away from
the top of the screen to position it in a *floating palette* anywhere else on-
screen. This palette behaves like any other window. You can drag it around or
resize it by dragging the palette border.

To specify the position of the SmartIcons, point to the square area beside the
down-arrow button at the left edge of the palette. The mouse pointer turns
into an open hand. Press and hold down the left mouse button so that the
pointer turns into a closed hand, then drag the palette to another position.

A dotted outline indicates the palette position, as shown in figure 11.6. When the palette reaches the position you want, release the mouse button. You can drag the palette back to its original position at any time. It will easily "snap" back in place when you do so.

Fig. 11.6
Dragging an iconbar to a new position on-screen.

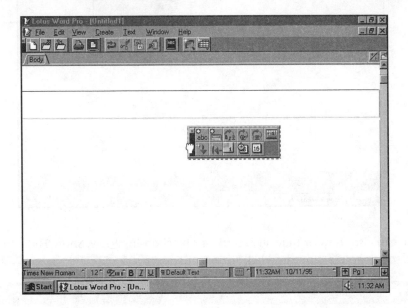

Beyond controlling iconbar display and changing an iconbar's location on-screen, you can customize iconbars by adding and deleting icons, specifying what context causes an iconbar to appear on-screen, or creating brand-new iconbars and icons. The next two sections describe making these kinds of changes.

Modifying SmartIcons

In addition to deciding when and where to display SmartIcon bars, you can specify the size of the SmartIcons, which SmartIcons you want to see on a particular iconbar, and the order in which you want to display them. You control all these options in the SmartIcons Setup dialog box.

You may prefer to create iconbars that are task- or document-oriented. Word Pro provides several preconfigured iconbars for you to use. You can edit any of these, or you can make changes to one of them and save those changes under a new name to create a new iconbar.

The SmartIcons Setup dialog box has a list containing SmartIcons and their descriptions. The list contains all available SmartIcons—those currently in use and any stored as .BMP files in the \LOTUS\WORDPRO\ICONS directory. You can add any of these icons to any iconbar.

When you begin using Word Pro, you may not be certain which SmartIcons you need most. You may want to tinker with an iconbar until it meets your needs. Perhaps you use the thesaurus often and want to use the SmartIcon that checks the thesaurus, or perhaps you want SmartIcons for Find and Replace operations, changing text to superscript, or toggling between Outline and Layout modes. There are more than 225 SmartIcons that you can choose from to add to any iconbar.

To modify an iconbar, use the following steps:

1. Choose File, User Setup. Click SmartIcons Setup in the submenu that appears. The SmartIcons Setup dialog box appears, as shown in figure 11.7.

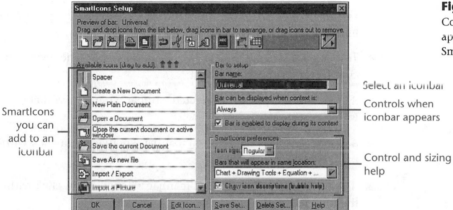

Fig. 11.7
Controlling the appearance of a SmartIcon set.

SmartIcons you can add to an iconbar

Select an iconbar

Controls when iconbar appears

Control and sizing help

2. In the Bar to Setup area of the dialog box, click the down arrow to display the Bar Name drop-down list; then click the name of the iconbar to which you want to make changes.

> **Tip**
>
> When you select an iconbar from the Bar Name drop-down list, its icons appear in the preview area at the top of the SmartIcons Setup dialog box. This enables you to see exactly which icons appear in a predefined iconbar.

Getting to Know Word Pro

3. Click the down arrow to display the Bar Can Be Displayed When Context Is drop-down list. Your choice from this list controls the context when an iconbar will automatically appear on-screen (unless you've hidden all iconbars). For example, if you choose Text in a Frame, the iconbar you selected in step 2 automatically appears on-screen every time you click to position the insertion point in text within a frame. Here are the available choices:

- *Always.* Displays the selected iconbar at all times unless you've hidden the iconbar display. (This is the default for the Universal iconbar.)

- *Text.* Displays the selected iconbar whenever you click in regular document text. (This is the default for the Text iconbar.)

- *A Frame.* Displays the selected iconbar whenever you select a frame. (This is the default for the Frame iconbar.)

- *Text in a Frame.* Displays the selected iconbar whenever you click in text within a frame.

- *Text in a Table Cell.* Displays the selected iconbar whenever you click in text within a table cell.

- *A Table Cell.* Displays the selected iconbar whenever you click within a table cell.

- *A Header.* Displays the selected iconbar whenever you click within the header area of a page.

- *A Footer.* Displays the selected iconbar whenever you click within the footer area of a page.

- *Text in Columns.* Displays the selected iconbar whenever you click within column text.

- *A Drawing.* Displays the selected iconbar whenever you're working within a drawing frame.

- *A Chart.* Displays the selected iconbar whenever you're working in a chart.

- *An Equation.* Displays the selected iconbar whenever you're working within a frame that contains an equation.

4. Make sure that the Bar is Enabled to Display During its Context check box is selected so that the iconbar you're working with isn't hidden.

5. You can change the order of the SmartIcons without changing which ones appear. In the SmartIcon bar preview area at the top of the SmartIcons Setup dialog box, point to the SmartIcon whose position you want to change. Drag the SmartIcon (see fig. 11.8) so that it covers the icon that will appear to the right of it in the selected iconbar. Release the mouse button. The other SmartIcons adjust to make room for the repositioned SmartIcon.

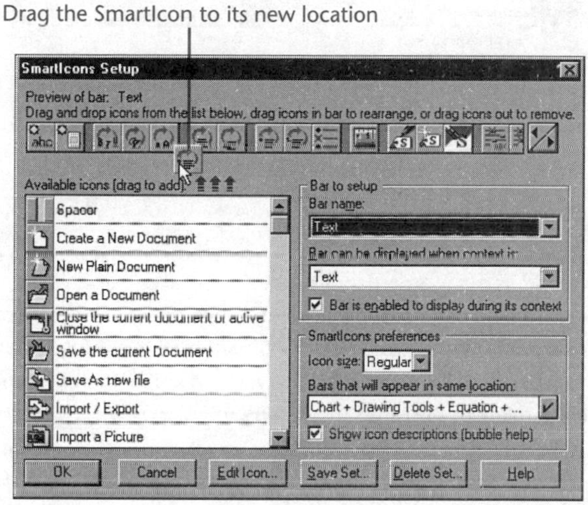

Drag the SmartIcon to its new location

Fig. 11.8
Dragging a SmartIcon to change its position on the iconbar.

6. To remove a SmartIcon or spacer from the current iconbar, point to it in the preview area at the top of the SmartIcons Setup dialog box. Press and hold down the left mouse button and drag the icon off the iconbar in the preview area. Release the mouse button. *Spacers* are gray vertical bars you can use to group icons for a more visually appealing and useful iconbar.

7. To add SmartIcons to the selected iconbar, point to the SmartIcon you want in the Available Icons list in the SmartIcons Setup dialog box. Because the list contains more than 225 icons, you may need to scroll down the list to find the one you want to add. Drag the SmartIcon (see fig. 11.9) to the desired position in the selected iconbar in the preview area at the top of the dialog box. The other SmartIcons in the previewed iconbar move to make room for the new SmartIcon.

Fig. 11.9
Selecting an icon
to add to the
selected iconbar.

...to the iconbar preview

Drag the icon
you want...

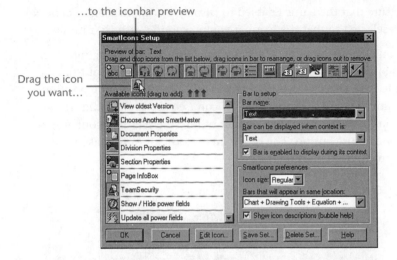

> **Note**
>
> You can add as many SmartIcons to the current iconbar as will fit, even using
> all the available SmartIcons, if you want. When you add a SmartIcon to the
> selected iconbar, Word Pro copies the SmartIcon from the Available Icons list.
> The Available Icons list never changes; you can create multiple SmartIcon bars
> containing many of the same SmartIcons.

8. Save your changes to the iconbar by clicking the Save Set button. The
   Save As SmartIcons File dialog box appears (see fig. 11.10).

Fig. 11.10
You can type a
new name in the
SmartIcon Bar
Name text box to
save your changes
as a new iconbar.

9. If you want to save your changes to a brand-new iconbar, edit the entry
   in the SmartIcons Bar Name text box; then click OK. Or, to simply save
   your changes to the iconbar you selected in step 2, click OK; then click
   Yes when Word Pro asks if you want to write over the existing iconbar.

10. Repeat steps 2 through 9 to make changes to other iconbars.

11. In the SmartIcons Preferences area of the dialog box, make sure that the
    Show Icon Descriptions (Bubble Help) option is selected (checked) to
    display that help when you point to an icon on any iconbar.

12. To change the size of the SmartIcons displayed in all iconbars, click the down arrow to display the Icon Size drop-down list. Word Pro sets the initial icon size based on your monitor type, but you aren't restricted to small if you have an EGA monitor or to large if you have a Super VGA monitor. Specify the size you want to use:

 Regular

 Large

> **Tip**
>
> If you're using the Large SmartIcon size, you should consider only displaying one iconbar at a time.

13. Click OK to close the SmartIcons Setup dialog box and resume your work in Word Pro.

To delete an iconbar, first display the SmartIcons Setup dialog box by choosing File, User Setup, and then choosing SmartIcons Setup. Click the Delete Set button. The Delete Set dialog box appears (see fig. 11.11). Click an iconbar in the Bars of SmartIcons To list; then click OK. When Word Pro asks you to confirm the deletion, click Yes.

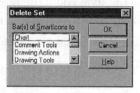

Fig. 11.11
Click an iconbar to delete in the list; then click OK to permanently remove it.

Customizing CycleKeys

CycleKeys enable you to progress through a variety of formatting choices. When you press the function key (F? key) Word Pro is using as a CycleKey to cycle to the next choice, Word Pro applies it to the selected text in your document. Chapter 4 explains how to use the various CycleKeys and CycleKey SmartIcons.

◀ See "Formatting Text," p. 79

You can control which styles Word Pro cycles through when you use a particular CycleKey. You do so in the CycleKey Setup dialog box. To display this dialog box, choose File, User Setup. In the submenu that appears, click the CycleKey Setup option. Word Pro displays the CycleKey Setup dialog box (see fig. 11.12).

Fig. 11.12
You can assign various functions for a particular CycleKey.

Select a CycleKey

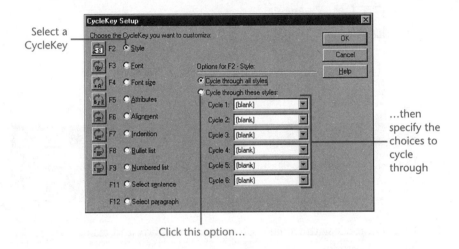

...then specify the choices to cycle through

Click this option...

Under Choose the CycleKey You Want to Customize, click a CycleKey's option button, such as Style, Font, or Font Size. Then click to select the Cycle Through These Styles option button (the name of the option button changes depending on the use of the CycleKey you select). Use the drop-down lists under that option to select the choices to cycle through, such as different style, fonts, or font sizes. Be sure you specify the correct order of priority. For example, you should choose the style you'll use most frequently for Cycle 1, the style you're next most likely to use for Cycle 2, and so on.

Repeat this process to customize additional CycleKeys as needed; then click OK to close the CycleKey Setup dialog box.

Setting View Preferences

The options in the View Preferences dialog box (see fig. 11.13) determine how the Word Pro screen appears. Word Pro sets initial defaults, but you can set your own view preferences and change them as necessary. To display the View Preferences dialog box, choose View, Set View Preferences. The View Preferences dialog box opens.

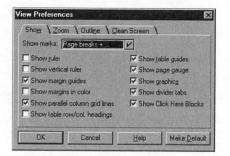

Fig. 11.13
The four tabs in the View Preferences dialog box enable you to determine how Word Pro appears on-screen.

In the View Preferences dialog box, you'll find four tabs containing related sets of view options. The following sections describe the contents of each tab. To select a tab to view it and set the options it contains, click the tab. The options you set in the View Preferences dialog box apply only to the current document unless you make them your default settings.

After you finish selecting the options on any tab, you can click another tab. When you've set the options you want for all tabs, click the Make Default button so that Word Pro will use your settings every time you start it—that is, until you change the View Preferences again. Then click OK to close the View Preferences dialog box and return to the document.

Showing and Hiding Screen Elements

The first tab in the View Preferences dialog box, Show, is selected when you first display the dialog box. The options on this tab represent various items; you can pick and choose which items you want to display in Word Pro. After you select the options you want in this tab, move on to another tab or click OK to close the View Preferences dialog box and implement your view choices. You can set the following options on this tab:

- *Show Marks.* Click the check mark for this option to display its drop-down list. The list displays all the kinds of marks you can display for non-printing elements in a document, such as section breaks, book-marks, and comment-note marks. To display marks of a particular type, click the mark type in the list so that a check mark appears beside it. Check all the mark types you want to display; then click the list check mark to close the list.

- *Show Ruler.* Check this option to show the ruler for formatting along the top of the screen when Word Pro's in Page Layout view.

- *Show Vertical Ruler.* Check this option to show another formatting ruler down the left edge of the screen when Word Pro's in Page Layout view.

- *Show Margin Guides.* Check this option to display non-printing margin guides for text.

- *Show Margins in Color.* Check this option to color margins in a dark shade so that you'll be able to see the working area of the document.

- *Show Parallel Column Grid Lines.* Check this option to display non-printing guidelines between parallel columns.

▶ See "Working with Tables and Charts," p. 325

- *Show Table Row/Col. Headings.* Check this option to have Word Pro display row (added numeric labels at the left side of the table) and column (added alphabetic labels along the top of the table) headings when you click in a table.

- *Show Table Guides.* Check this option to tell Word Pro to display non-printing grid lines to divide table cells.

- *Show Page Gauge.* Check this option to tell Word Pro to add a page gauge at the top of the vertical scroll bar.

- *Show Graphics.* Check this option to display graphics in frames. If this option is deselected, Word Pro displays a checkmark in any graphic frames you create; you lose the advantage of seeing the pictures in the frames, but Word Pro can run and work much more quickly because the pictures aren't taking up memory.

> **Tip**
>
> After you insert and view the graphics in a document, turn off the Show Graphics option to improve the speed at which Word Pro runs.

- *Show Divider Tabs.* Check this option to display tabs near the top of the screen for identifying and selecting divisions.

- *Show Click Here Blocks.* Check this option to display the placeholders for fill-in Click Here blocks.

Setting Zoom Options

Clicking the Zoom tab in the View Preferences dialog box displays the options shown in figure 11.14. After you select the options you want in this tab, move on to another tab or click OK to close the View Preferences dialog box and implement your view choices.

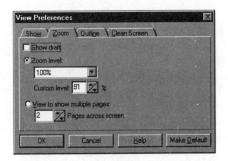

Fig. 11.14
Controlling the
view zoom of
documents you
open.

Here are the available options and how to set them:

■ *Show Draft.* Turn on this check box to always show the document(s) in Draft mode by default when you open it.

■ *Zoom Level.* Use this drop-down list to choose a zoom percentage for the document(s) when you open it. The options in this drop-down list are identical to the options on the View, Zoom To submenu.

■ *Custom Level.* Enter a zoom percentage in this text box or use the spinner arrows to change it. Changing this option sets the custom zoom percentage Word Pro applies when you choose View, Zoom To, Zoom To Custom Level or when you choose Custom from the Zoom Level drop-down list just described.

■ *View to Show Multiple Pages.* Click this option so that you can see more than one page of the document(s) by default on-screen when you open it. Use this choice in concert with the next option.

■ *Pages Across Screen.* If you selected the preceding option, type a value in this text box or use the spinner arrows to specify how many pages to display on-screen.

Setting Outline Options
The Outline tab in the View Preferences dialog box offers numerous options that enable you to control the Outline Mode view of your document. Figure 11.15 shows the Outline tab options. After you select the options you want in this tab, move on to another tab or click OK to close the View Preferences dialog box and implement your view choices. Here are the options that enable you to view an outline of your document:

▶ See "Outlining a Document," p. 267

Fig. 11.15
Controlling the
view zoom of
documents you
open.

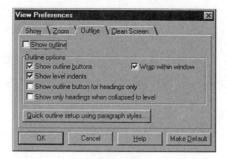

■ *Show Outline*. Check this option to show the document(s) in Outline mode.

■ *Show Outline Buttons*. Displays outline buttons to the left of each paragraph in the document when in Outline mode.

■ *Show Level Indents*. Applies indentation to the various outline levels in the document during Outline mode.

■ *Show Outline Button for Headings Only*. Select this option to hide outline buttons for body text in Outline mode.

■ *Show Only Headings When Collapsed to Level*. Displays only headings when the outline is collapsed to the highest level.

■ *Wrap Within Window*. Check this option to wrap the text for all outline levels to fit within the current document window.

▶ See "Setting
Outline Style
Sequences,"
p. 273

■ *Quick Outline Setup Using Paragraph Styles*. Click this button to display the Set Outline Style Sequences dialog box. This dialog box enables you to use the styles in a document SmartMaster to establish the various levels in your outline. Chapter 14, "Outlining a Document," explains how to work with this dialog box, outline buttons, and more.

Setting Clean Screen Options

The Clean Screen feature of Word Pro enables you to use more of the screen when displaying a document. To accomplish this, it takes a two-step process. First, you use the Clean Screen tab of the View Preferences dialog box (see fig. 11.16) to specify whether to display various parts of the Word Pro application window (as opposed to the window within Word Pro that holds your document) while in Clean Screen view. Then, you choose the Clean Screen view by choosing View, Show/Hide, and clicking Clean Screen in the submenu that appears.

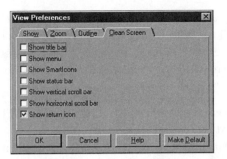

Fig. 11.16
Use the check boxes here to hide parts of the Word Pro program window in Clean Screen view.

In the <u>C</u>lean Screen tab, select whether to display the title bar, menu bar, SmartIcons, SmartStatus status bar, vertical scroll bar, horizontal scroll bar, and return icon (an icon you can click to return the document to its default view) by checking the corresponding check boxes; removing the check mark from a check box hides that element from screen display.

After you select the options you want in this tab, move on to another tab or click OK to close the View Preferences dialog box and implement your view choices.

> ### Troubleshooting
>
> *I turned on Clean Screen view, but I don't know how to return to regular viewing.*
>
> If you choose not to display the return icon in Clean Screen view, press Alt+V to display the <u>V</u>iew menu, and then choose Show/<u>H</u>ide, <u>C</u>lean Screen in that order. Display the View Preferences dialog box and click the <u>C</u>lean Screen tab. Click to put a check beside the Show <u>R</u>eturn Icon check box; then click OK. The next time you use Clean Screen view, the return icon appears at the lower left corner of the Word Pro screen. Click it to return to regular view.

Setting Up SmartFill

As you learn in Chapter 17, "Working with Tables and Charts," Word Pro's new SmartFill feature provides a quick and easy way to enter a series of data in consecutive table cells. For example, let's say that you want to enter the months of the year in the table. You could enter the month *January* in the first cell and have SmartFill enter the rest of the months of the year in subsequent cells. When it does so, SmartFill uses the formatting you applied to *January* to the rest of the entries it creates.

SmartFill works by using lists of table entries called *SmartFill lists*. When you select the table cell containing an entry in one of the SmartFill lists, SmartFill can complete the series of entries. However, if the word or number you enter doesn't exist in a SmartFill list, SmartFill won't know how to complete the series.

To solve this problem, you can create a custom SmartFill list so that Word Pro recognizes new text and knows how to complete the series. In fact, SmartFill enables you to create and store up to 100 custom SmartFill lists. For example, you could create custom SmartFill lists to enter categories in a budget, a list of clients, a list of products, and more.

Use these steps to create a custom SmartFill list:

1. Choose File, User Setup. In the submenu that appears, click SmartFill Setup. The SmartFill Setup dialog box appears (see fig. 11.17).

Fig. 11.17
This dialog box enables you to create custom SmartFill lists and make changes to existing lists.

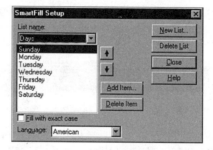

2. Click the New List button. The New SmartFill List dialog box appears.

3. In the New List Name text box, type a name for the custom SmartFill list you're creating. Make sure that the name adequately describes the contents of the list. For example, if you're creating a list of department numbers, name the list something like *Departments*. Click OK to continue.

4. When you add list items, you can add them in upper- and lowercase letters. If you want Word Pro to match your capitalization exactly when it enters the list items in a table, click to turn on the Fill With Exact Case check box. If you don't choose this option, SmartFill uses the capitalization in your first table cell entry to determine how to capitalize the list items it enters.

5. Click the <u>A</u>dd Item button to add your first item to the list. The New
   SmartFill Item dialog box appears (see fig. 11.18). Type the entry you
   want in the <u>N</u>ew SmartFill Item text box. Click OK to add the new item
   to the SmartFill list.

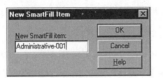

Fig. 11.18
Making a new
entry for SmartFill.

6. Repeat step 5 to add other list items.

7. When you've added all the entries you need, click the Close button.

You can use the SmartFill Setup dialog box to make changes to SmartFill lists,
as well. You can change the order of the entries in the SmartFill list, add and
delete list items, and delete whole lists. Choose <u>F</u>ile, <u>U</u>ser Setup. In the
submenu that appears, click SmartF<u>i</u>ll Setup. The SmartFill Setup dialog box
appears. Open the List Na<u>m</u>e drop-down list and click the name of the
SmartFill list to edit (see fig. 11.19).

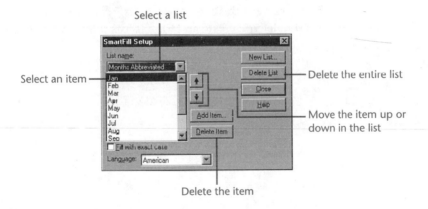

Fig. 11.19
Customizing a
SmartFill list.

Below the List Na<u>m</u>e list, click a list item to change. Use the arrow buttons to
move the item up or down in the list or the <u>D</u>elete Item button to remove it
from the list. Use the <u>A</u>dd Item button as you did when creating the list to
add more items to the list. Or, click the Delete <u>L</u>ist button to remove the
selected list from SmartFill. When you're finished making changes, click the
<u>C</u>lose button to return to your document.

From Here...

In this chapter, you learned how to set up your user preferences, SmartIcons, and display preferences. In addition, you learned how to customize the new CycleKey and SmartFill features so that they can help you work more effectively in Word Pro. You should now be able to set up Word Pro so that it perfectly complements your working style.

This chapter also mentioned several Word Pro features that you may want to learn more about. These features also help you work more quickly, enabling you to fine-tune the formatting for your document with a minimum of hassle. If you're ready to look at other automation features in Word Pro, check out these chapters:

- Chapter 12, "Working with SmartMasters," explains how to choose and use SmartMasters to apply predefined formatting to your documents, saving you the trouble of formatting your text paragraph by paragraph.

- Chapter 14, "Outlining a Document," teaches you how to use the Outline view and outlining tools to view and print an outline of your document so that you can examine and change the document's overall structure.

- Chapter 17, "Working with Tables and Charts," examines Word Pro's table features that let you create and format lists of data without worrying about setting tabs and the like.

Part II

Accelerating Your Word Processing

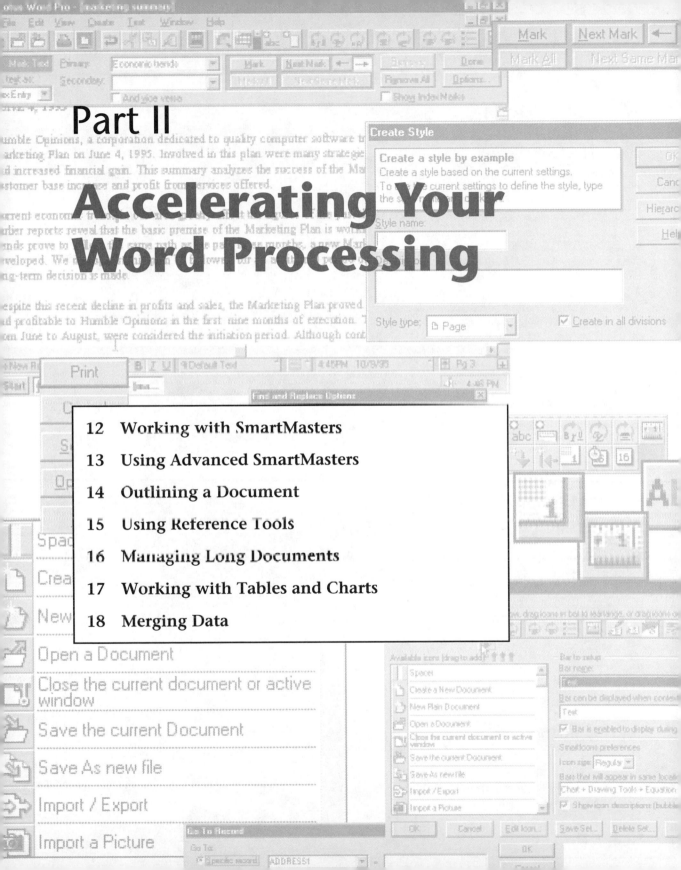

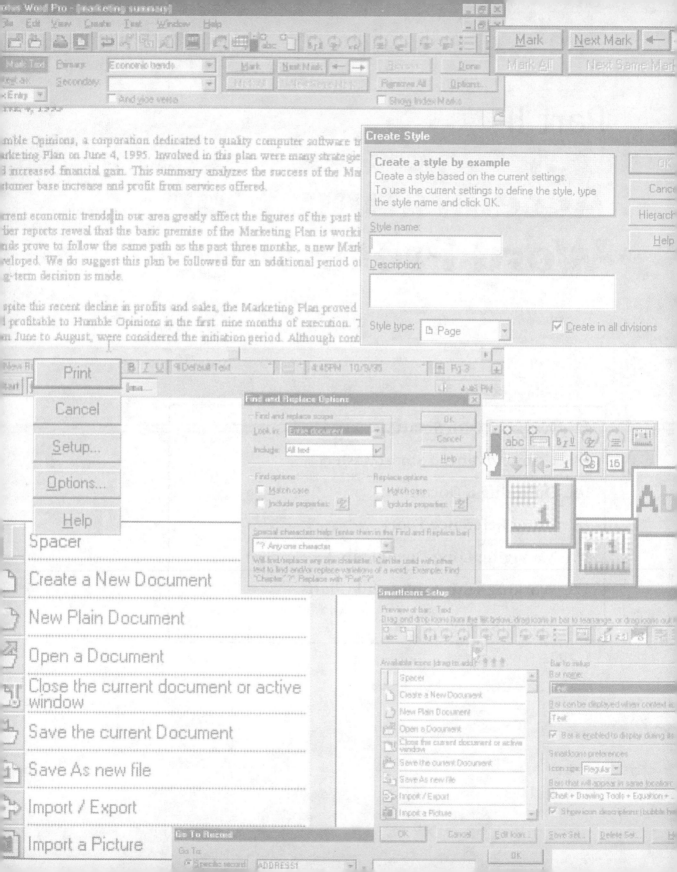

Lotus Word Pro - [marketing summary]

File Edit View Create Text Window Help

Mark | Next Mark | ←
Mark All | Next Same Mark

Mark Text
Primary: Economic trends
Secondary:
And vice versa

Mark | Next Mark | ← | →
Remove All | Options...
Show Index Marks

June 4, 1995

...mble Opinions, a corporation dedicated to quality computer software ti
...arketing Plan on June 4, 1995. Involved in this plan were many strategie
...d increased financial gain. This summary analyzes the success of the Ma
...stomer base increase and profit from services offered.

...rrent economic trends in our area greatly affect the figures of the past th
...ber reports reveal that the basic premise of the Marketing Plan is worki
...nds prove to follow the same path as the past three months, a new Mark
...veloped. We do suggest this plan be followed for an additional period of
...g-term decision is made.

...spite this recent decline in profits and sales, the Marketing Plan proved
...l profitable to Humble Opinions in the first nine months of execution. T
...n June to August, were considered the initiation period. Although cont

Create Style

Create a style by example
Create a style based on the current settings.
To use the current settings to define the style, type
the style name and click OK.

Style name:

Description:

Style type: [Page]

☑ Create in all divisions

OK
Cancel
Hierarch
Help

B / U 4 Default Text | 4:45 PM 10/9/95 | Pg 3

Print
Cancel
Setup...
Options...
Help

Spacer

Create a New Document

New Plain Document

Open a Document

Close the current document or active window

Save the current Document

Save As new file

Import / Export

Import a Picture

Find and Replace Options

Find and replace scope
Look in: Entire document
Include: All text

OK
Cancel
Help

Find options
☐ Match case
☐ Include properties

Replace options
☐ Match case
☐ Include properties

Special characters help (enter them in the Find and Replace bar)
*? Any one character
Will find/replace any one character. Can be used with other
text to find and/or replace variations of a word. Example: Find
"Chapter"?". Replace with "Part"?"

SmartIcons Setup

Preview of bar: Text
Drag and drop icons from the list below, drag icons in bar to rearrange, or drag icons out

Available icons (drag to add)
Spacer
Create a New Document
New Plain Document
Open a Document
Close the current document or active window
Save the current Document
Save As new file
Import / Export
Import a Picture

Bar to setup
Bar name:
Text
Bar can be displayed when context is
Text
☑ Bar is enabled to display during la
SmartIcons preferences
Icon size: Regular
Bars that will appear in same location:
Chart + Drawing Tools + Equation +
☑ Show icon descriptions (bubble he

OK | Cancel | Edit Icon... | Save Set... | Delete Set...

Go To Record
Go To
Specific record ADDRESS1
OK

Chapter 12

Working with SmartMasters

by Sue Plumley

SmartMasters are templates, or style sheets, containing preformatted styles that can help you create a document that looks attractive and professional. *Styles* are preformatted options applied to Word Pro features: text, characters, paragraphs, pages, frames, tables, and table cells. All features have a default style. You can use Word Pro's styles as they are, or you can modify them. Additionally, you can create your own styles to use with any of Word Pro's features.

You can choose any of Word Pro's SmartMasters to help you create a document such as a letter, memo, or brochure. Word Pro makes it easy for you to view various SmartMasters and choose the one that you want to use. Additionally, you can modify the styles to better suit your documents.

In this chapter, you learn how to:

- ■ View SmartMaster descriptions
- ■ Use SmartMaster styles
- ■ Use Click Here blocks
- ■ Modify SmartMasters
- ■ Change styles in a SmartMaster

Understanding SmartMasters

Every Word Pro document that you create starts with a SmartMaster, and each SmartMaster produces a different kind of document: memos, letters, newsletters, and so on. The SmartMaster that you've probably been using the most in Word Pro is the Default SmartMaster.

◀ See "Using Paragraph Styles," p. 102

Each SmartMaster has specific formatting and design that you can use as is or you can change to suit your purposes. All SmartMasters contain styles; you can choose to add Contents and Scripts. Contents consist of tables, Click Here blocks (preformatted placeholders that guide you to creating a document), frames, and so on. Scripts are automated tasks stored in a SmartMaster document that help you create the document.

> **Note**
>
> The Default SmartMaster consists of 12-point, Times New Roman as the default size and font, the most common styles used (Body Single, Bullet, Footer, Title, and so on), and an 8 1/2 by 11-inch page with 1-inch margins on all sides.

The biggest advantage to using a SmartMaster is consistency within a document and between similar documents. Suppose that you produce your company's newsletter each month. If you use a SmartMaster to help you create the document, the newsletter not only will be consistent each month but will be easier to produce than formatting the document from scratch each month.

The styles that you use for titles, subheads, body text, and so on are stored in a SmartMaster. Each time you create a headline in the newsletter, for example, you apply the Title style. All headlines look alike, and formatting is quick and easy—just select the text and apply the style. In addition, the page size and layout (columns, tabs, and so on) remain the same from month to month, and your newsletter looks more attractive because of it.

Using Word Pro's SmartMasters

You can create a new document and base it on any of Word Pro's SmartMaster style sheets. After opening a document based on a SmartMaster, you can apply Word Pro's styles, thus, quickly and easily creating a document. The Click Here blocks contained in many SmartMasters also help you enter text and/or graphics to make the document more attractive and effective.

Viewing SmartMasters

When you first open Word Pro, the Welcome to Lotus Word Pro dialog box appears (see fig. 12.1). Using this dialog box, you can choose any SmartMaster that you want to use as a foundation for a new document.

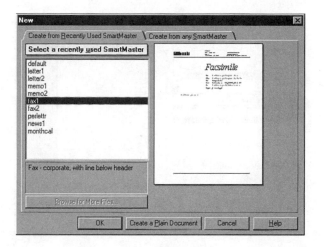

Fig. 12.1
Choose to create a
new document
from a specific
SmartMaster.

Notice that the Default style sheet, or SmartMaster, is the default choice. If
you want to choose another SmartMaster, you can select it from the list. The
list contains the ten most recently used SmartMasters only. To view other
SmartMaster choices, click the More SmartMasters button. The New dialog
box appears, as shown in figure 12.2.

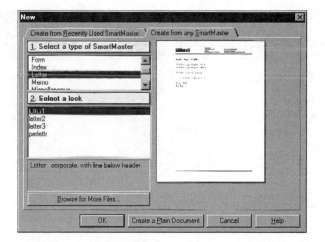

Fig. 12.2
The New dialog
box displays
various Smart-
Masters that you
can use to create
your document.

In the Create from any SmartMaster tab of the New dialog box, you first
choose a type of SmartMaster, such as a letter, memo, newsletter, and so on.

Next, you choose a specific look for the SmartMaster. When you select a specific SmartMaster from the second list, an example appears in the dialog box
so that you can see the page layout of the SmartMaster (see fig. 12.3).

Fig. 12.3
Select a type of
SmartMaster and
then choose a
particular look for
the document.

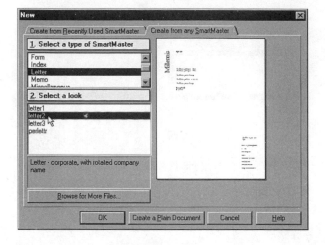

When you've selected the SmartMaster that you want to use, choose OK to
close the dialog box and reveal the SmartMaster. Figure 12.4 shows the Letter
SmartMaster. The Click Here blocks, displayed as gray type, do not print. Any
text or object (such as the date and the frame) that prints appears in black.
Click Here blocks only display in Layout mode.

Fig. 12.4
Use the letter
SmartMaster to
quickly enter your
company name,
address, text, and
more.

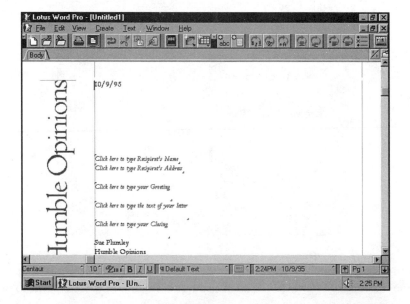

Tip

In addition to the dialog box that appears when you first start Word Pro, you can also
access the New dialog box by selecting File, New.

Using Click Here Blocks

Some SmartMasters, such as the Default SmartMaster, appear with no contents or scripts. All you do is enter your text and graphics. Other Smart-Masters, such as the Letter SmartMaster, contain Click Here blocks that help you enter text and graphics and complete the document more quickly.

To use a Click Here block, you simply click the mouse in the area and enter the text or picture called for. Figure 12.5 illustrates the Letter SmartMaster with the first Click Here block. Notice that Word Pro inserts user information, such as your name, your company's name, the date, and so on.

> **Tip**
>
> You can press Enter in a Click Here block and continue typing if your text takes up more than the allotted space.

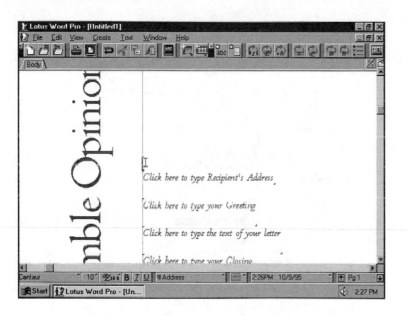

Fig. 12.5
Click a Click Here block to enter the text for that part of the document.

Click Here blocks work the same for pictures, tables, and other graphics as they do for text. Click in any Click Here block to add the object you want to insert.

If you change your mind about entering text or graphics in a Click Here block, just click anywhere else on the page to cancel. The gray text reappears but doesn't print.

Even if there is no Click Here block, by clicking the mouse and creating an insertion point (as you normally would), text can be added anywhere in the document. You can also add other frames, tables, and graphics.

Using SmartMaster Styles

Each SmartMaster comes with styles already formatted to help you complete your document. The SmartMaster styles include paragraph or text styles, frame styles, table styles (if applicable), and so on.

Most SmartMasters contain some basic paragraph styles, such as Default Text, Body Single, Bullet, Title, and so on, in addition to styles specific to the type of document that you're creating. You use SmartMaster styles as you would any style in Word Pro.

To apply a paragraph style to text in a SmartMaster, select the text and then click the Styles button on the status bar (see fig. 12.6).

Fig. 12.6

Apply Smart-Master styles by selecting the text and choosing the style from the Styles button on the status bar.

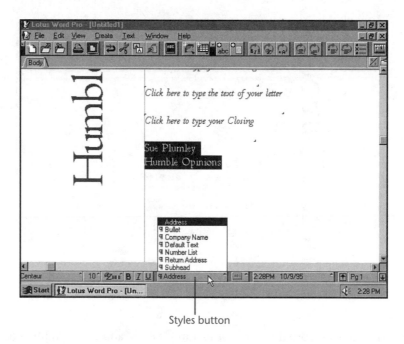

Styles button

▶ See "Formatting Tables,"
p. 338

▶ See "Formatting Frames,"
p. 398

A frame or table is created with the style elements—such as borders, margins, text wrap, and so on—that are embedded in the SmartMaster you use for the document. To view frame or table formatting, right-click the object and choose Properties from the quick menu. Use the Properties InfoBox to view any formatting options. You also can modify any of the table or frame formatting by using the Properties InfoBox.

Modifying SmartMasters

Word Pro makes it easy for you to create and format a document using a SmartMaster. You can use the SmartMaster's styles and page layouts and never need to change a thing. On the other hand, Word Pro also makes it easy for you to change formatting if you want to.

You can choose to change the page size or margins of a SmartMaster; you also can modify styles by changing fonts, sizes, alignments, and so on. Word Pro doesn't limit your creativity by making you adhere to a set of styles that may not suit your design.

Modifying Styles

You modify both text and object (frame, table, and so on) styles using the Properties InfoBox. You can change any of the formatting for text—such as font, alignment, spacing, and so on—and you can change formatting for frames and tables.

To change formatting for text, frames, or tables, right-click the element to be changed. From the quick menu, select the Properties command to display the Properties InfoBox (see fig. 12.7).

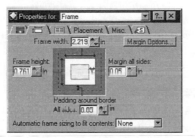

Fig. 12.7
To change frame styles, first display the Properties InfoBox, then change the formatting that you want to modify. Modifying table styles is similar.

In the Properties InfoBox, select the tab representing the attribute or format that you want to change. Change any of the formatting for text, frames, or tables, as you normally would.

When you're finished formatting, select the Style tab in the Properties InfoBox (see fig. 12.8).

If it's not already selected, select the style that you're modifying in the Style list. Choose the Redefine Style command button.

The Redefine Style dialog box appears as shown in figure 12.9. You can add a Description if you want, or you can simply choose OK to redefine the style.

◀ See "Using Paragraph Styles," p. 102

▶ See "Using Frame Styles," p. 416

▶ See "Formatting Tables," p. 338

II

Accelerating Your WP

Fig. 12.8
Modify the styles any way that you want, and then choose the Style tab of the Properties InfoBox.

Fig. 12.9
Redefine the modified style to match the current settings.

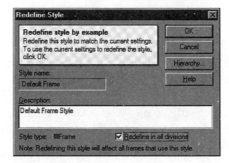

Tip

When you redefine a style, all paragraphs that use that style also are modified. You can quickly and easily change all frames, text, or tables in your document.

Modifying Page Layout

Modifying a SmartMaster's page layout is easy using the Properties InfoBox. You can change the size, orientation, margins, columns, headers, borders, and more.

◀ See "Setting Page Size and Orientation," p. 106

To access the Properties InfoBox, right-click the page to display the quick menu. Choose Page Properties; the Properties for Page Layout InfoBox appears (see fig. 12.10).

Using the Properties for Page Layout InfoBox, modify any of the settings that you want as you normally would.

◀ See "Changing Margins, Page Tabs and Columns," p. 108

◀ See "Adding Lines, Borders, and Shading," p. 130

When you're finished modifying the page, choose the Style tab of the Properties InfoBox. In the Style tab, choose Redefine Style. The Redefine Style dialog box appears (refer to fig. 12.9).

Choose OK in the Redefine Style dialog box to modify the page layout.

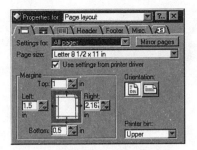

Fig. 12.10
Modify the page
layout for any
SmartMaster using
the Properties for
Page Layout
InfoBox.

Caution

Redefining the page layout style of a SmartMaster affects all pages that use that style.

Troubleshooting

*I redefined one of the styles in my SmartMaster, but now I realize that I should have
created a new style instead. Is there anything I can do?*

Yes. First, in the Properties InfoBox, choose the Style tab. Select the style in the Styles
list, and then click the Reset to Style command button. In the Reset to Style dialog
box, choose OK to remove all overrides that you made to the paragraph settings.

To create the new style, select the modified element and, in the Style tab, choose
Create Style. In the Create Style dialog box, name the new style and choose OK.

*I don't want the frames that are included with the SmartMaster I selected. Can I get rid of
them?*

Yes. Select the frame and press the Delete key.

▶ See "Creating
Styles," p. 254

▶ See "Editing a
Frame," p. 387

Changing SmartMasters

You may find that, after choosing a SmartMaster, you would prefer to use a
different look to the document. You can change SmartMasters at any time
without starting a new document. Additionally, you can choose to change
SmartMasters in the middle of a document containing divisions or sections.

▶ See "Using
Divisions,"
p. 306

To change a SmartMaster, follow these steps:

1. Choose File, Choose Another SmartMaster. The Choose Another
   SmartMaster dialog box appears (see fig. 12.11).

Fig. 12.11
Change Smart-
Masters in the
middle of creating
a document, if you
need to.

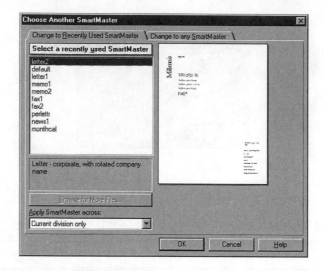

2. Choose one of the following tabs:

   Change To Recently Used SmartMaster to choose from a short list of recently used SmartMasters.

   Change To Any SmartMaster to choose from the complete list of SmartMasters.

3. Select the SmartMaster that you want to change to.

4. In the Apply SmartMaster Across list box, choose from the following options the location in the document at which you want to change the SmartMaster:

   Current division only. Changes the SmartMaster for the division in which the insertion point appears.

   All divisions at same level & below. Changes the SmartMaster for all divisions at the same level and below of the current division.

   Entire document. Changes the SmartMaster for the entire document.

5. Choose OK. The SmartMaster is applied to the document.

Viewing SmartMasters

Word Pro includes many SmartMasters that you can use in your daily work. Each SmartMaster comes with preformatted text blocks in which you can enter your own text. Additionally, some SmartMasters include column divisions, tabs, fields (such as insert date), and frames for tables, pictures, and other graphics.

Following are descriptions of a few of Word Pro's SmartMasters that you may want to use.

The Memo SmartMaster, shown in figure 12.12, provides a design you can use for your company memos. Enter your company's name, address, and other information in the Click Here blocks to quickly create the memo. Then enter the specific data in the from, to, and subject areas of the memo.

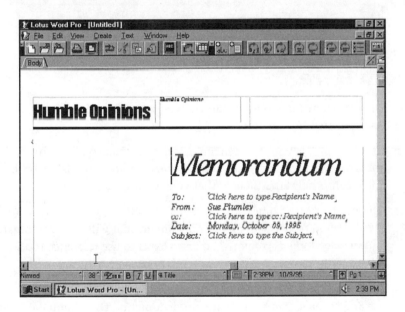

Fig. 12.12
In a hurry? Use Word Pro's Memo SmartMaster to quickly create your memo.

Notice the Fax SmartMaster, shown in figure 12.13, uses the same design as the Memo SmartMaster. You can easily create all of your company documents using Word Pro's SmartMasters so they'll have a consistent, professional look to them.

Fig. 12.13

Word Pro's Fax SmartMaster uses the same design as the Memo SmartMaster.

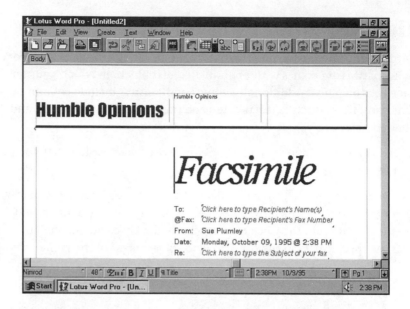

From Here...

Now that you know how to use SmartMasters, you can read the following chapters for related information:

- Chapter 13, "Using Advanced SmartMasters," tells you how to create and save new styles for your SmartMasters, rename and delete styles, and create a new SmartMaster that you can use repeatedly.

- Chapter 16, "Managing Long Documents," shows you how to create divisions and sections in a master document that will help you organize and manage long documents. You also learn to use reference tools across divisions.

- Chapter 20, "Using Advanced Frame Techniques," shows you how to use and manage frame styles in your documents. This chapter also tells you how to format frames and work with multiple frames.

Chapter 13

Using Advanced SmartMasters

by Sue Plumley

You use SmartMasters to help you create documents in Word Pro. Smart-Masters contain styles to apply to text, frames, and tables so that your document looks consistent and professional. You can modify a SmartMaster to suit your document design or contents by modifying styles and page layout.

Additionally, you can create new styles and save them to use repeatedly. The styles that you create also can be used in other SmartMasters in Word Pro. You can even create and save your own custom SmartMasters to use in your documents.

In this chapter, you learn how to:

- Create new styles
- Rename and delete styles
- Copy styles to other SmartMasters
- Create new SmartMasters
- Save and edit your SmartMasters

Creating Styles

◀ See "Using Paragraph Styles," p. 102

◀ See "Modifying SmartMasters," p. 247

SmartMasters contain styles that make formatting a document quick and easy. A SmartMaster includes text and paragraph styles, and may contain frame and table styles as well. You assign these styles to format the document and to create a consistent look to the pages of the document. You can also modify SmartMaster styles by changing fonts, lines, spacing, and so on.

Creating New Styles

After you work with SmartMasters and styles, you may find that you need to create your own styles to make your document more unique. You can create paragraph styles, frame styles, and table styles.

To create a new style, select the text, frame, or table that you want to change. Right-click the mouse to display the quick menu and choose the Properties command: Text Properties, Frame Properties, or Cell Properties. Alternatively, click the Redefine Style SmartIcon. The Properties InfoBox appears.

Note

Before creating a new style, apply an existing style to the text or other element that closely resembles the style you're about to create. For example, apply the Title style to text that you want to remain 18-point, bold, and centered; then, all you have to do is change the font from Helvetica to Bookman, for example, and save it as a new style.

Use the various tabs in the InfoBox to assign formatting to the text or element. When you're finished, choose the Style tab, as shown in figure 13.1.

Fig. 13.1
Use the Properties InfoBox to create a style.

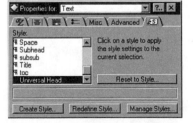

▶ See "Formatting Tables," p. 338

▶ See "Using Frame Styles," p. 416

In the Style tab of the Properties InfoBox, choose the Create Style button. The Create Style dialog box appears (see fig. 13.2). In the Style Name text box, enter the new name for the style. In Description, enter a description of the style, if you want.

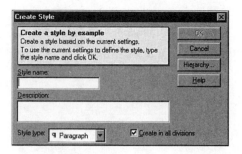

Fig. 13.2

To create a style, enter a new style name in the Create Style dialog box.

If the style displayed in the Style Type list box isn't the correct style type, choose the appropriate style and click OK. Word Pro adds the style to the Style list in the Style tab, and to the Style button on the status bar if the style is a paragraph style. You can now use the style in the current document by assigning it as you would any other style.

Using Style Hierarchy

When you create styles in Word Pro, you can link style properties—such as typeface, size, alignment, and so on—to the original style. If you link the properties, then your new style will change if and when you change the original style.

If, for example, you base a new style called Shelley Head on the Title style, and later you change the Title style, the Shelley Head style also changes. You might want to do this to maintain consistency across styles; for example, headings and subheadings. If you change the font of a subheading, for instance, you'll want the headings font to change as well so that the styles remain compatible.

Naturally, you can select the specific properties that you want to link and leave other properties alone. To use style hierarchy, follow these steps:

1. In the Create Style dialog box, click the Hierarchy button. The Style Hierarchy Definition dialog box appears (see fig. 13.3).

2. In the Choose the Properties You Want to Include as Part of the Definition of This Style list box, choose from the following options:

    ■ *All Properties.* All properties for the new style come from the new style's definition; no properties remain from the original style.

    ■ *All Local Settings of Current Selection.* Only the local settings come from the new style; all other properties come from the original style.

    ■ *Specific Properties.* Only specific properties come from the new style; all other properties come from the original style.

II

Accelerating Your WP

Fig. 13.3
Use the Style
Hierarchy
Definition dialog
box to choose the
properties that
you want to
include.

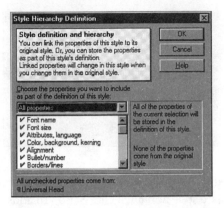

3. In the list box, click any property to select or deselect it. A property with a check mark in front of it is selected and defined as coming from the new style; an unchecked property comes from the original style.

4. Choose OK to close the Style Hierarchy Definition dialog box and return to the Create Style dialog box.

> **Tip**
>
> Style hierarchy is available and works the same in both the Create Style and the Redefine Style dialog boxes.

Redefining Styles

You can redefine any style that you've created or any style in an Word Pro SmartMaster. To redefine a style, select the text or other element and display the Properties InfoBox. Use the tabs to reformat the selected element, and then choose the Style tab in the InfoBox. Alternatively, you can click the Redefine Style SmartIcon.

Choose the Redefine Style command button; the Redefine Style dialog box appears (see fig. 13.4). Choose Hierarchy to display the Style Hierarchy Definition dialog box, if you want to change the style's hierarchy. Choose OK to close that dialog box. Choose OK in the Redefine Style dialog box to redefine the selected style.

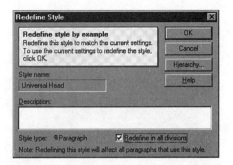

Fig. 13.4
Use the Redefine Style dialog box to apply a change to a new or original style in a Smart-Master.

> **Caution**
>
> When you redefine a style, it affects all paragraphs that use that style, depending on the selections in the Style Hierarchy Definition dialog box.

Managing Styles

Word Pro enables you to manage the styles that you create and the styles in any SmartMaster. You can rename or delete any style, but, more importantly, you can copy styles to other SmartMasters.

After you spend the time and effort to create new styles, you'll want to use them in other SmartMasters and other documents. Suppose that you create logo text or a special frame for your company's name. You'll want to use that text or frame in other documents as well. Do this by using Word Pro's style management feature.

> **Tip**
>
> You can't redefine the Default style properties.

Renaming Styles

You can change the name of a style in any Word Pro SmartMaster. If you rename a style, all attributes and formatting remain the same as they were before you changed the name.

To rename a style, follow these steps:

1. Open the Properties InfoBox and choose the Style tab.

2. Choose Manage Styles. The Manage Styles dialog box appears (see fig. 13.5).

Fig. 13.5
Choose Manage
Styles to enable
you to rename or
delete a style.

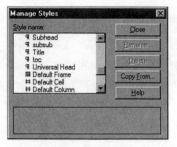

3. In the Manage Styles dialog box, choose the style that you want to rename in the Style Name list. A check mark appears beside the style.

4. Click the Rename button to display the Rename Style dialog box, as shown in figure 13.6.

Fig. 13.6
Select the style to
be renamed, and
then open the
Rename Style
dialog box.

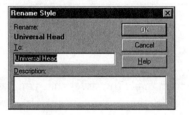

5. In the To text box, enter the new name for the style. You can enter a new name or in the Description text box, you can change the description, if you want.

6. Choose OK to close the Rename Style dialog box. The new name appears in the Style Name list box in the Manage Styles dialog box.

7. Choose Close to return to the Properties InfoBox.

The new style name appears in the style list and is available for use in the SmartMaster.

Deleting a Style

If you delete a style, it no longer appears in the style list; however, any text or frames assigned with the style remain formatted with the style's attributes. Additionally, the deleted style name appears in the Style list (in red type) whenever you select a paragraph or element formatted in that style.

To delete a style, follow these steps:

1. In the Style tab of the Properties InfoBox, choose the Manage Styles command button.

2. In the Manage Styles dialog box, select the style that you want to delete in the <u>S</u>tyle Name list box. A check mark appears beside the style name. You can select more than one style to delete by clicking each style.

> **Tip**
>
> If you accidentally select a style in the <u>S</u>tyle Name list, click it a second time to remove the check mark and deselect it.

3. Click the <u>D</u>elete button.

4. A message box appears asking you to confirm the deletion; choose <u>Y</u>es to delete or <u>N</u>o to cancel.

5. Choose <u>C</u>lose to close the Manage Styles dialog box and return to the Properties InfoBox.

Troubleshooting

I changed attributes of a style that came with the SmartMaster. I want to change it back to its original attributes, but I can't remember everything I changed. What can I do?

Open the Properties InfoBox and click the Style tab. In the Style list, select the style you changed and then click the Reset to Style button. The Reset to Style dialog box appears. Select the appropriate option in the Settings to Remove area and choose OK to reset the style. This sets the selected text back to its normal style formatting.

I accidentally deleted a style and now I want it back. Do I have to create the style all over again?

If you assigned the style anywhere in your document before deleting it, you can select the element and then choose Create Style in the Style tab of the Properties InfoBox. The assigned style in the document remains formatted with the deleted style's attributes until you reassign it a new style.

Copying Styles to Other SmartMasters

After creating styles to use in your document, you can copy those styles to other documents in Word Pro. Suppose that you created paragraph and table styles for a business report you produced in Word Pro. Now you need to create a second business report and you want to use those same styles. You can copy those styles using the Manage Styles dialog box.

To copy styles, follow these steps:

1. Choose the Style tab in the Properties InfoBox.

2. Choose the Manage Styles command button.

3. In the Manage Styles dialog box, choose Copy From. The Copy Styles From dialog box appears (see fig. 13.7).

Fig. 13.7
Copy styles from one document or SmartMaster to another using the Copy Styles From dialog box.

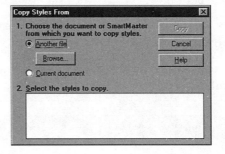

4. In number 1, Choose the Document or SmartMaster from Which You Want to Copy Styles, choose from one of the following options:

   ■ *Another File.* Click the Browse button to display the Browse dialog box. Select the drive, directory, and file name of the SmartMaster that you want to use to copy styles from.

   ■ *Current Document.* Choose to copy styles from the current document.

5. The styles from the selected file appear in number 2, the Select the Styles to Copy list box (see fig. 13.8).

6. To select a style, click it. A check mark appears beside the file. You can select as many styles to copy that you want.

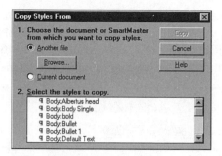

Fig. 13.8
The styles contained in the selected file appear in the Styles to Copy list.

> **Tip**
>
> Text styles are listed first in the Styles to Copy list, then the frame styles, cell styles, table styles, and page styles.

---

7. Choose Copy. Word Pro copies the styles and adds them to the style list.

Creating a New SmartMaster

You can create a SmartMaster from any document in Word Pro. You might want to use a SmartMaster to help you create your company's newsletter, for example. Then, after creating your own styles and customizing the newsletter, you can save it as a SmartMaster that you can use month after month. By creating the SmartMaster, you save the design of the newsletter so that each month's issue will be consistent and contain the elements that remain the same. Thus, you save time and produce a professional document.

Producing a SmartMaster

You can create a SmartMaster from any Word Pro document. Customize the SmartMaster by modifying styles, contents, and scripts, and then save the SmartMaster for future use.

◀ See "Modifying SmartMasters," p. 247

When creating a new SmartMaster, you can start with the default style or choose to create a plain document as a base (in the New dialog box). Alternatively, you can begin your new SmartMaster with any of Word Pro's preformatted SmartMasters as a foundation. If, for example, you plan to create a letter SmartMaster, you can use Word Pro's letter SmartMaster as a base and then add or delete the things you need to customize the style sheet.

◀ See "Setting
Page Size and
Orientation,"
p. 106

▶ See "Format-
ting Tables,"
p. 338

▶ See "Format-
ting Frames,"
p. 398

After choosing a SmartMaster to act as the groundwork for your new SmartMaster, modify the page properties, (if necessary) using the Page Properties InfoBox. Next, add some text, frames, tables, and other elements that you'll need in the SmartMaster. Modify them to appear the way you want.

> **Note**
>
> Perhaps the easiest way to create the SmartMaster is by making a whole new document. If you're working on a newsletter SmartMaster, for example, create the first issue of the newsletter with text, nameplate, frames, and all. When you're finished, you can save the newsletter document and then remove the text associated with this issue and save the newsletter SmartMaster.

As you create the SmartMaster, make sure to add any contents that you want to appear in the SmartMaster. Contents can include the company's name and address, a newsletter nameplate and logo, borders, and screened frames for announcements.

Saving a New SmartMaster

When you have created the SmartMaster and styles that you want for the new SmartMaster, you must save the style sheet so that you can use it later. To save a new SmartMaster, follow these steps:

1. Choose File, Save As. The Save As dialog box appears.

2. In Save as Type, choose Lotus Word Pro SmartMaster (see fig. 13.9).

Fig. 13.9
Choose to save
the formatted file
as a Lotus Word
Pro SmartMaster.

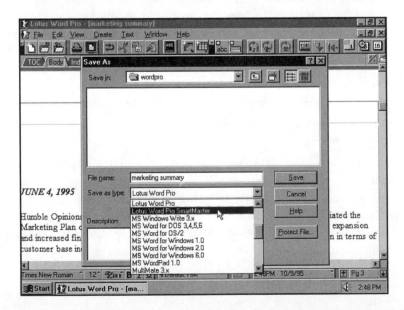

3. In File <u>N</u>ame, enter the name for the new SmartMaster. Don't enter an extension other than MWP, or the SmartMaster won't appear in the New dialog box.

4. In Save <u>I</u>n, choose LOTUS\SMASTERS\WORDPRO and then choose OK. Word Pro creates the new SmartMaster.

To use the new SmartMaster, choose <u>F</u>ile, <u>N</u>ew. The New dialog box appears with the new SmartMaster listed in the list box (see fig. 13.10). Select your SmartMaster and choose OK.

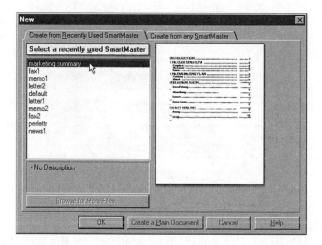

Fig. 13.10
You can select your own customized SmartMasters from the list in the New dialog box.

To edit a SmartMaster, start a new document based on the SmartMaster. Edit the styles or other elements any way that you want, and then save the Smart Master as described in steps 1 through 4.

Troubleshooting

I selected some styles to copy but got a warning about overwriting styles. What do I do?

The Overwrite Style message box appears if the style that you selected to copy already exists in the current document. You can choose to <u>O</u>verwrite the existing style, <u>R</u>ename the copied style, or Cancel the process. If you're unsure about overwriting a style, it's always best to rename the copied style.

Creating Click Here Blocks

You may want to create Click Here blocks in the SmartMasters you create so that others can easily use your SmartMaster as foundations. Suppose that you're creating a newsletter SmartMaster for your assistant to use each month. You can add Click Here blocks that will help your assistant in his or her work.

To create a Click Here block, follow these steps:

1. Choose the Create menu and the Click Here Block command. The Create Click Here Block dialog box appears (see fig. 13.11).

Fig. 13.11

Create your own Click Here blocks for use with your SmartMasters.

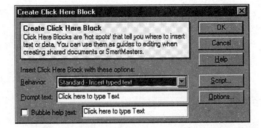

2. In Behavior, choose the appropriate option. You can choose to insert text, table, frame, OLE object, or other item from the list.

3. In Prompt Text, either accept the suggested text or enter your own text to accompany the behavior.

4. Choose whether to include Bubble Help Text and, if you want, edit the text to appear in the bubble.

5. Choose OK to accept the Click Here block.

Note

If you want, you can modify any of the behaviors using the Script button and the script language.

From Here...

Now that you can create and modify SmartMasters, you can use your knowledge by applying SmartMasters to your Word Pro documents. The following chapters give you more information about using SmartMasters in Word Pro.

- Chapter 16, "Managing Long Documents," shows you how to create divisions and sections to help organize long documents. Additionally, this chapter shows you how to use SmartMaster in formatting sections.

- Chapter 17, "Working with Tables and Charts," shows you how to create and edit tables. Additionally, this chapter shows you how to format table styles and save them to a document. You also learn to create a chart in Word Pro.

- Chapter 20, "Using Advanced Frame Techniques," shows you how to format frames and then save and use frame styles.

II

Accelerating Your WP

Chapter 14

Outlining a Document

by Sue Plumley

II

Accelerating Your WP

Writing an outline can be tedious and time consuming, but outlining is the best way to organize any writing project. An outline displays a document in an easy-to-read and quick-to-analyze layout. Word Pro's outlining features are powerful and make creating an outline a simple task.

Outlining in Word Pro is a matter of setting levels in the text, such as level one for the most important heading, level two for the second most important, and so on. Word Pro provides outlining tools, or buttons, for you to use in assigning outline levels to your text. When you assign a level, Word Pro identifies the level with a number and indents each level to set it apart from the others.

Additionally, you can assign levels using paragraph styles. When you assign a Title style, for example, Word Pro gives that style level one priority. You can change the levels of formatted text and use a combination of methods to assign levels.

◀ See "Using Paragraph Styles," p. 102

In this chapter, you learn how to:

- Create an outline by assigning levels
- Create an outline by assigning styles
- Promote and demote headings
- Collapse and expand an outline
- Print an outline
- Use outline numbering

Understanding Outline Mode

Outline mode is a powerful utility for managing and organizing a document. When you use Outline mode, you work with a multilevel structure; each level has a heading and contains subordinate headings and paragraphs of text. In Word Pro, you can create up to ten levels within the outline and each level can contain paragraph text as well as additional stepped levels.

You can choose to view only the main headings of the document (the first level); the first and second level headings; the first, second, and third level headings; and so on. You can change the level of a section, a heading, or a paragraph of body text any time (a heading and its subordinate headings and body text are known as a *section*). You can change a third-level section, for example, to a first-level section.

◀ See "Using Paragraph Styles," p. 102

Besides the outline structure, the *outline style* is an important facet of working in Outline mode. The outline style refers to the typeface, point size, and attribute for each level as well as the paragraph formatting, such as indents and line spacing. Each level is assigned a different outline style.

◀ See "Using Display Modes," p. 139

When you display outline tools, you're in Outline mode. There are no specific menu or icon bars that go with Outline mode, but there are outline buttons you can use to manipulate text. In addition, Outline mode has a few restrictions. Word Pro cannot display the outline tools in Layout mode; so when you choose to display the outline tools, Word Pro changes you to Draft mode. When you are not in Layout mode, you cannot view frames, pictures, tables, and so on when working with the outline tools. Additionally, you cannot switch to Layout mode until you hide the outline tools.

To display Outline mode, choose View, Show/Hide, Outline Tools. A check mark appears beside the Outline Tools command, and it remains active until you choose the command again.

Figure 14.1 shows a document in Outline mode. The paragraphs have been selected and assigned paragraph styles that are, in turn, assigned a level in the outline; for example, the Title style is level number one, Subhead is level two, and so on. The small gray buttons to the left of each paragraph show that paragraph's level.

Note

If the outline buttons don't appear after choosing Show/Hide Outline Tools, choose View, Set View Preferences to access the View Preferences dialog box. In the Outline tab, choose the Show Outline Buttons option; choose OK to exit the dialog box.

Level 1 outline buttons

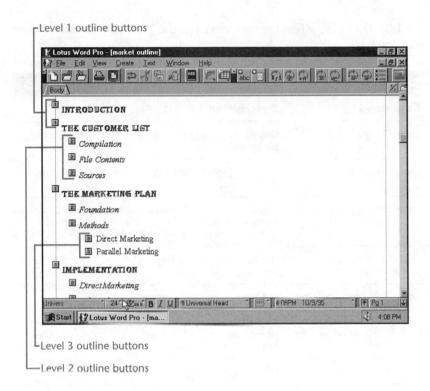

Fig. 14.1
Select and format
different outline
levels to help
organize the
document.

Level 3 outline buttons

Level 2 outline buttons

Changing the View Preferences

The View Preferences dialog box enables you to choose what you want to see on-screen when viewing Outline mode. You can choose to view all outline buttons or just the heading buttons. You also can choose to view the level indents.

To access the View Preferences dialog box, choose View, Set View Preferences. In the View Preferences dialog box, choose the Outline tab (see fig. 14.2).

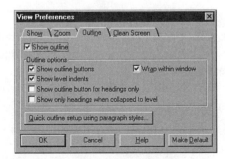

Fig. 14.2
Use the Outline
tab to choose
which outline
buttons you want
to view in Outline
mode.

II

Accelerating Your WP

Table 14.1 describes each of the commands in the View Preferences Outline Tab dialog box.

Table 14.1 View Preferences Outline Tab	
Command	**Description**
Show Outline	Displays Outline mode with level buttons beside each paragraph.
Show Outline Buttons	Shows or hides outline buttons; the default is to show the buttons.
Show Level Indents	Indents text for each level of the outline; level 2, for example, is indented 1/2 inch, level 3 is indented 1 inch, and so on. The default is to show indents.
Show Outline Button for Headings Only	Displays only the heading buttons, not the body text buttons.
Show Only Headings When Collapsed to Level	Hides text when levels are collapsed.
Wrap Within Window	Wraps headings and text within the window so you can view all.
Quick Outline Setup	Displays the Outline style.
Using Paragraph Styles	Sequences dialog box in which you can set style levels for the outline.

Tip

Choose the Make Default button in the View Preferences dialog box so you only have to set your preferences once.

Using the Outline Buttons

◀ See "Using Paragraph Styles," p. 102

The outline buttons that appear to the left of each paragraph indicate the level of the text. Level 1 is the highest level and level 9 is the lowest level. Generally, level 1 text is titles, level 2 consists of major headings, level 3 might be subheads, level 4 bulleted lists, and so on (although you can set up the outline however you want).

The outline buttons not only indicate the outline level of the text, they enable you to manipulate the text by moving it, changing the level, and so on, as described throughout this chapter.

To use an outline button, point the mouse at the button and right-click. A *quick menu*—a menu containing common commands related to outlining—appears beside the mouse that enables you to perform certain procedures, such as promoting and demoting outline levels. Additionally, take note of the keyboard shortcuts listed beside each command on the quick menu and use that shortcut instead of the menu the next time you need a command.

Creating an Outline

Outline mode has ten different outline levels: one to nine, and none; none usually represents body text. All Default text begins at level one; you assign the levels to the text. Level 1 is highest in the hierarchy, then level 2, and so on.

If you used styles in your document, such as Title, Subhead, and so on, Word Pro automatically assigns outline levels to the styles. Title, for example, is level one, Subhead is level two, and so on. Word Pro does enable you to change any level in the document. You also can create your own paragraph styles and assign levels to them.

> **Tip**
>
> If you want, you can modify the styles to your own preferences with or without changing the outline level assignment.

To assign outline levels in Word Pro, you can use the Text Properties InfoBox. Before beginning, make sure you choose <u>V</u>iew, Show/<u>H</u>ide, <u>O</u>utline Tools to display Outline mode.

◄ See "Modifying Styles," p. 247

Open the Text Properties InfoBox and then choose the Misc tab. Position the insertion point in the text or select the text to be assigned a level. In Outline Settings, enter a number in Document Level or use the arrows to enter the number. Figure 14.3 illustrates the Misc tab of the Text Properties InfoBox and the outline assigned with document levels.

When you're outlining a document, use the Smart Level and Heading Paragraph options to make outlining more efficient. Smart Level means that Word Pro "watches" your outline levels and keeps them consistent throughout; for example, if you accidentally assign level one to body text, Word Pro senses it's wrong and changes the level for you.

Fig. 14.3
When setting
outline levels,
select Use Smart
Level to help
keep the levels
consistent through
the outline
sequence.

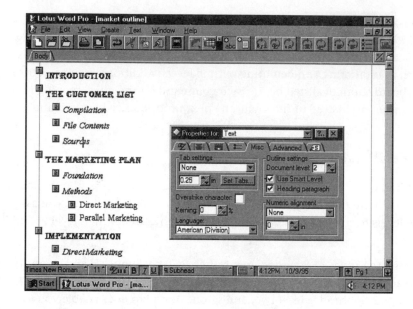

Additionally, the Heading Paragraph option promotes the selected text over
its body text. If you have a level 3 heading with level 3 text below it, for example, click the heading and choose Heading Paragraph in the Misc tab to
promote the heading to level 2.

> **Tip**
>
> To assign level none to any text, type **0** in the Document Level text box.

You can assign all outline levels using the Outline Settings area of the Misc
tab. If you have already assigned styles, such as Title, Subhead, and so on,
you can still use the Outline settings to assign different levels than the ones
Word Pro assigned with the styles. Figure 14.4 illustrates the same outline
using the Title style for level one.

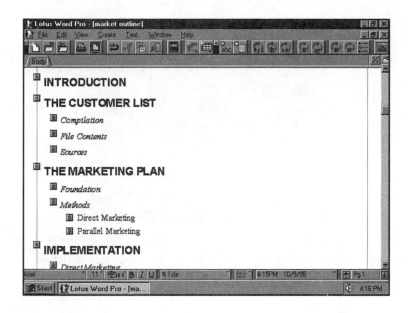

Fig. 14.4
Assign styles to any of the headings and reformat the styles, if you want.

Setting Outline Style Sequences

When you assign outline levels to a document, you're creating an outline sequence—level 1 is followed by level 2, and so on. When you use outline style sequences, you simply assign levels to the styles used to format the text—Title(level 1) is followed by Subhead (level 1), and so on.

When working with styles, you can change the level in the outline without changing the formatting of the paragraph styles. The reason you might want to change a style's level, or *sequence*—where that style falls into the outline's hierarchy—is to rearrange an outline without rewriting and reassigning style levels. Suppose, for example, you want to change the level 2 headings to level 3. Instead of reassigning all Subhead (level 2) paragraph styles to Outline3 (level 3) paragraph styles and then reassigning all level 3, 4, 5, and so on, you can simply rearrange the paragraph style's sequence within the outline.

To set the outline style sequences, follow these steps:

1. Point to any outline button and right-click the mouse. The Outline quick menu appears.

2. Choose Outline Styles and the Set Outline Style Sequences dialog box appears (see fig. 14.5).

Fig. 14.5

Use the Set Outline Style Sequences dialog box to rearrange your outline styles.

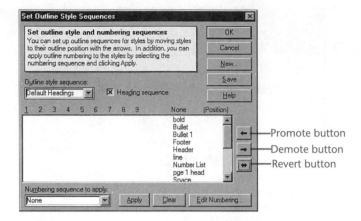

Promote button
Demote button
Revert button

3. To promote any paragraph style's level, select the style in the list box and click the Promote button. Each time you click the Promote button, the selected style moves to the left one level.

   To demote a level, select the paragraph style and click the Demote button; with each click of the button, the style moves one level to the right.

   To move a paragraph style all the way to the right quickly, click the Revert button. Figure 14.6 illustrates one way of arranging the styles in the Set Outline Style Sequences dialog box.

Fig. 14.6

Arrange the styles by level to make organizing your outline easier; use your own created paragraph styles as well as Word Pro's paragraph styles.

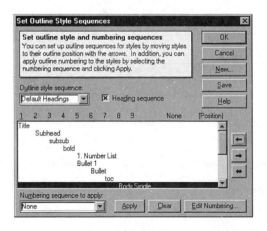

4. When you're finished arranging the levels, choose Save and then click OK to close the dialog box and apply the changes.

To assign a paragraph style to the outline, select the text and click the Style list on the status bar. Select the appropriate paragraph style.

To change any paragraph style's sequence in the outline, open the Set Outline Style Sequences dialog box and promote or demote the paragraph style in the level box. All assigned paragraph styles in your outline change levels accordingly.

Troubleshooting

I can't change to outline mode; the buttons won't show up.

You might be in Layout mode instead of Draft mode; choose View, Draft mode. If you still cannot see the outline buttons, choose View, Set View Preferences. Choose the Outline tab and choose Show Outline. Choose OK to close the dialog box.

I want to change outline style sequences but I also want to keep my original style sequences. Can I do that?

Yes, in the Set Outline Style Sequences dialog box, select the New button and name the new sequence. Now you can set the sequence without changing the original one. To select which sequence you want to use in the document, choose the named sequence from the Outline Style Sequence list box in the Set Outline Style Sequences dialog box. Default Headings is the original.

Editing in Outline Mode

You can easily edit an outline in Word Pro's Outline mode using the outline buttons and the Outline quick menu. When editing an outline, you might want to change the outline levels, move text, or view specific levels of the text. You can change outline levels by promoting or demoting the text. After you promote and demote text, you can show or hide specific levels of the outline and then perform such tasks as moving or deleting the text.

Promoting and Demoting Text

When you promote or demote text, you change the level of the text. Each level has a different indentation. For example, if you promote a heading from level 3 to level 2, the indentation of the level changes to the level 2 indentation. Also, if each level is assigned a different style, when you promote or demote a heading, you change the style of the text.

You can use the Promote in Outline Level and Demote in Outline Level SmartIcons to change levels. Alternatively, you can follow these steps:

1. Right-click the outline button to the left of the text you want to promote. The Outline quick menu appears (see fig. 14.7).

2. Choose Promote.

Fig. 14.7
Promote text to a higher level using the quick menu; you can also use the Alt+Left arrow keyboard shortcut.

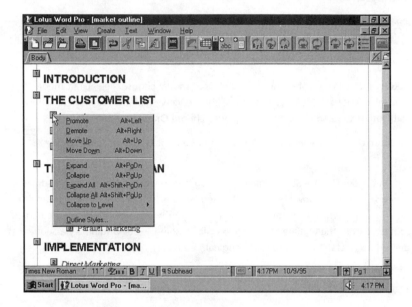

Tip

You can, alternately, choose Text, Outline, Promote to promote the selected text.

To demote text, follow these steps:

1. Right-click the outline button to the left of the text you want to demote to display the Outline quick menu.

2. Choose Demote; alternately, press Alt+Right arrow.

Repeat these operations as many times as needed to move the text to the desired level.

Note

To promote or demote a section of text (a heading and its subheadings and body text), select all of the headings and text, then click Promote or Demote.

Collapsing and Expanding the Outline

When you collapse an outline, you choose an outline level to appear, and all subordinate levels are hidden. When you expand an outline, the hidden levels reappear.

Caution

If you delete a heading while the outline is collapsed, any subordinate headings and paragraphs also are deleted. If you reposition a heading while the outline is collapsed, any subordinate headings and paragraphs are simultaneously repositioned.

You can choose to expand or collapse the entire outline, a section, or just a heading. To expand and collapse the outline, follow these steps:

1. Right-click an outline button to display the Outline quick menu.

Tip

Double-click the outline button to collapse the level and all levels below it; double-click the button again to expand the level.

---

2. Choose the Expand or Collapse command that suits your purpose, as described in table 14.2.

Table 14.2   Expanding and Collapsing an Outline

Command	Keyboard Shortcut	Action
Expand	Alt+PgDn	Expands selected level only.
Collapse	Alt+PgUp	Collapses selected level only.
Expand All	Alt+Shift+PgDn	Expands all levels under the selected level.
Collapse All	Alt+Shift+PgUp	Collapses all levels under selected level.
Collapse to Level	Alt+(level number)	Reveals a secondary menu from which you choose level **1** through **9** or None. The level you select is the level displayed; for example, choose level 3, and levels 1, 2, and 3 display.

You can also use the Expand and Collapse SmartIcons.

  You can also use the Expand All and Collapse All SmartIcons.

Figure 14.8 illustrates the secondary Collapse to Level menu.

Fig. 14.8
Choose a specific level to collapse the outline to; if you choose None then all levels are expanded.

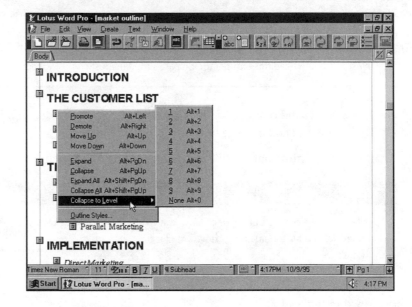

 You can use the Collapse to Level 1 SmartIcon to collapse an outline to the first level.

Figure 14.9 shows the sample outline collapsed to level 1.

Troubleshooting

◀ See "Using the Spell Check," p. 172

◀ See "Using the Find and Replace Bar," p. 160

I collapsed the outline and then spell checked the document; later, I found misspelled words in the text.

The spell checker checks only displayed text in an outline. To check the entire document, you must first expand all headings and text and then start the spell checker.

I was searching for specific text using the Find command and Word Pro could not locate the text; what happened to my text?

The Find and Replace features search only display text; collapsed text is ignored. Expand the entire outline and try again.

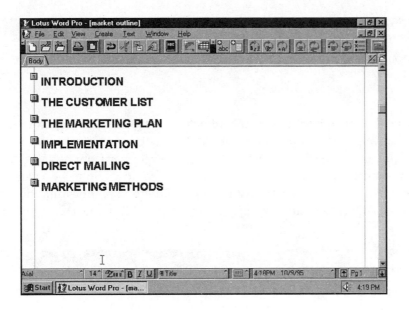

Fig. 14.9
When you collapse an outline, you can easily organize and manage the headings.

Moving Text

In Outline mode, you can move a heading, section, paragraph, or any combination of text up or down in the outline. You can choose to move a section or a heading and its paragraph together, or you can move only the heading or only the paragraph within the outline.

> **Tip**
>
> Always save your document before moving or deleting text; if you make a major mistake, you can close the document without saving it and then open the previously saved version.

To move a section up or down the outline, select the appropriate outline button to move one paragraph or select the text to move more than one paragraph. Right-click to display the Outline quick menu. Choose Move Up or Move Down. You can also use the keyboard shortcuts: Alt+Up arrow to move the text up or Alt+Down arrow to move the text down. The text moves one paragraph at a time; to move it above or below another paragraph, choose the Move command from the quick menu again.

II

Accelerating Your WP

Tip

You can also move text by selecting it and using the drag-and-drop method of editing.

 To move a heading without its subordinate headings and paragraphs, expand the heading. Place the insertion point in the heading you want to move and click the Move Up or Move Down in Outline Level SmartIcons or select the Move command from the Outline quick menu. You can also move a paragraph without its heading by first placing the insertion point within the paragraph, and then selecting the appropriate command from the Outline quick menu.

Troubleshooting

I moved some text but I messed up everything; what can I do?

Press Ctrl+Z or choose Edit, Undo. If you saved before altering the outline, you can close the file without saving it and open the previously saved version. Then try again.

Printing an Outline

You can print a document while in outline mode so you can better manage and organize your outline. When you print from Outline mode, Word Pro prints only the displayed text; therefore, you print only level 1 heads or only levels 1, 2, and 3 heads, for example. Printing your outline by levels can give you a better idea of how it's organized and what you need to do to edit the document.

◀ See "Printing Documents," p. 203
To print a document from Outline mode, follow these steps:

1. Expand or contract the document so that the text you want to print is displayed and the text you don't want to print is hidden.

2. Choose File, Print. The Print dialog box appears. Choose printer settings as necessary.

3. Choose OK or press Enter.

Using Outline Numbering

You can create a numbering scheme quickly and easily in Outline mode. A numbering scheme makes breaking down the document into its individual sections easier.

After you have the outline structured, follow these steps:

1. Position the insertion point in the paragraph where you want the numbering to begin.

2. Open the Text Properties InfoBox and choose the Bullet tab (see fig. 14.10).

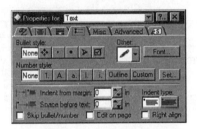

Fig. 14.10
Choose the numbering style and then set the numbers for the outline levels.

3. In Number style, choose Outline; the Set Outline Numbering Sequence dialog box appears (see fig. 14.11).

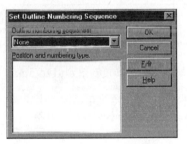

Fig. 14.11
You can choose to use the default outline sequence or create your own.

4. To choose the default outline sequence, select it in the Outline Numbering Sequence drop-down list.

5. The sample outline numbering sequence displays in the Position and numbering type box.

6. Choose the Edit button to display the Edit Numbering Sequence dialog box if you want to create a new numbering sequence.

Make choices according to the options listed in table 14.3.

Table 14.3 Numbering Options	
Option	**Description**
Sequence Position	Identifies the starting number's position and style, such as I, A, 1., and so on.
Text Before/Text After	Enters text you want to appear before or after the number.
Number Type	Chooses the numbering type.
Clear	Clears the Text Before and Text After text boxes.
Additional Information to Include	Chooses whether to include division or section name or number, for example.
Restart Numbering Based On	Chooses to restart numbers according to the outline or division.
Start At	Identifies the starting number.
Save	Saves to the outline sequence.
Save As	Saves to a new sequence you name.
Delete	Displays a list of outline sequences; select a sequence and choose Delete to erase that sequence.

▶ See "Creating Divisions," p. 309

7. Choose Save to close the dialog box and to apply the numbers.

8. In the Set Outline Numbering Sequences dialog box, choose OK to apply the numbering sequence (see fig. 14.12).

9. Close the Text Properties InfoBox to return to your document.

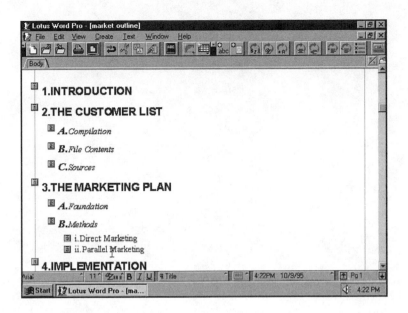

From Here...

Now that you understand the outlining features of Word Pro, you can explore other features and techniques to help you manage and organize your documents. Refer to the following chapters:

■ Chapter 12, "Working with SmartMasters," introduces you to understanding Word Pro SmartMasters and to using Word Pro's styles in your document.

■ Chapter 15, "Using Reference Tools," describes how to organize your documents by creating footnotes, a glossary, a table of contents, and an index.

■ Chapter 16, "Managing Long Documents," shows you how to divide your document into workable sections that you can individually format but collectively organize with a table of contents and index.

Using Reference Tools

by Sue Plumley

If you work with large documents in which you must create indexes, tables of contents, or footnotes, you'll love Word Pro's reference tools. Word Pro's reference tools let you track elements in your documents, designate sources, and otherwise accelerate your work automatically and easily. Using Word Pro's reference tools—such as glossaries, footnotes, indexes, and tables of contents—means more efficient and accurate work.

> **Note**
>
> Word Pro enables you to compile an index and table of contents over several files gathered together in a master document, as described in Chapter 16, "Managing Long Documents."

In many word processing programs, creating an *accurate* table of contents or index—in which all entries match in wording, capitalization, spacing, and spelling— can be surprisingly time-consuming and challenging. Word Pro automates the tasks of creating these reference tools and others so that your work is precise and easy to complete.

Footnotes and glossaries are excellent tools you can create, find, and edit in Word Pro. A *glossary* is a document in which you store frequently used text. Using a glossary in different documents saves time and energy. Use footnotes to help organize your document and refer readers to your sources.

In this chapter, you learn how to:

- Insert and edit footnotes
- Create and modify a glossary
- Create and modify a table of contents

- Mark and modify an index

- Generate an index and table of contents

Using Footnotes

Creating *footnotes* (notes at the bottom of the page) without using a word processing program, such as Word Pro, can be a headache. Fitting the footnotes onto the page can be tricky, and maintaining a consistent appearance for the footnotes from page to page can be difficult. If you have a line between the bottom of the text and footnotes, for example, you must be certain that the line is identical on each page. Similarly, the font, type size, numbering, and so on must be the same to create a professional-looking document. Finally, if you eliminate one footnote, you must renumber all other footnotes correctly. Word Pro makes creating, placing, and editing footnotes a breeze.

As an alternative to footnotes, you can choose to use *endnotes* with your document. Endnotes are placed at the end of the document (an approach often used in books) rather than at the bottom of each page, like footnotes.

Word Pro automates the process of creating footnotes and endnotes and builds in much of the consistency that is so difficult to maintain manually.

Inserting Footnotes

If you're writing footnotes as you write the text, you might not know how much space you need for them. It is difficult to plan for footnotes, and even harder to split them over additional pages as necessary. Word Pro takes care of all such problems for you. All you have to do is indicate in the text where the footnote number should appear and type the footnote's text.

Although typing a footnote can be a simple matter, you also have other choices to make. You must decide whether to use footnotes or endnotes. You also must choose the starting number and specify the length of the line on which the note appears.

When inserting a footnote, Word Pro inserts the reference number for the footnote in two places: at the location of the insertion point in the document and at the bottom of the page or table (the area that the program creates for the footnote text). The footnote can be any length and can have multiple paragraphs; Word Pro adjusts the text on the page to fit the footnote. After you have a footnote in place, you can use additional Word Pro features to go to the footnote, edit it, or remove it.

> **Tip**
>
> You can select the footnote text and format it to any size or font; alternately, format a footnote style for more consistency.

◀ See "Changing Character Formatting," p. 79

Follow these steps to create a footnote:

1. Place the insertion point where you want the reference number for the footnote. Change to Layout mode if you are in Draft mode.

◀ See "Paragraph Styles," p. 102

2. Choose Create, Footnote/Endnote. The Footnotes dialog box appears (see fig. 15.1).

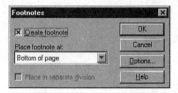

Fig. 15.1
Choose to insert a footnote or to specify options.

3. If you want to specify footnote options, choose the Options button. The Footnote and Endnote Options dialog box appears (see fig. 15.2).

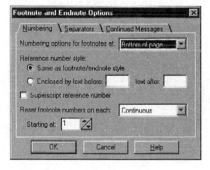

Fig. 15.2
You can change any numbering options in the Footnote and Endnote Options dialog box.

4. In the Numbering tab, choose any options (see table 15.1 for a description of all options in the Footnote and Endnote Options dialog box).

5. In the Separators tab, choose the options you want, such as the line length or space above and below the footnote (see fig. 15.3).

6. In the Continued Messages tab, choose options such as text alignment and repeated reference numbering (see fig. 15.4).

II

Accelerating Your WP

Fig. 15.3
Choose to place
a separator line
between the
document text
and the footnote.

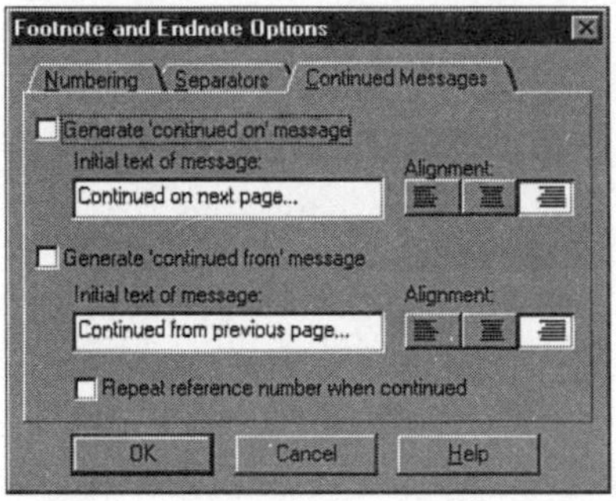

Fig. 15.4
Add "Continued
on" or "Contin-
ued from" to a
footnote carried
over to the next
page.

7. Choose OK to return to the Footnotes dialog box.

8. Choose where to place the footnote from the Place Footnote At drop-
down list: at the bottom of page, end of division, end of division group,
or end of document. Choose OK to close the dialog box. Word Pro inserts the reference number in your text and moves the insertion point
to the location where the footnote will be placed.

> **Note**
>
> If you choose to place the footnote at the end of the division, group, or docu-
> ment, you are choosing to create an endnote. Make sure all of your notes are
> placed in the same area within the document for consistency.

9. Enter the text for the footnote (see fig. 15.5). Click anywhere in the
document text to move out of the footnote area.

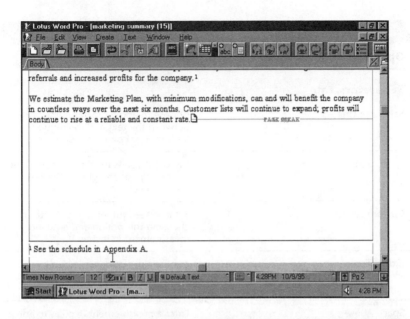

Fig. 15.5
Enter the footnote
text and then
select it; format the
text by changing
font, size, attri-
butes, and so on.

Table 15.1   Footnote and Endnote Options

Option	Action
Numbering Tab	
Numbering Options For Footnotes At	Choose which footnote to number: the one at the bottom of the page, end of the division, end of a division group, or end of the document
Reference Number Style	Choose to use the footnote/endnote style or to enter text that precedes or follows the footnote number
Superscript Reference Number	Select this option if you want the reference number to appear as superscript in the text and in the note
Reset Footnote Numbers On Each	Choose to run numbers continuously or reset at new division, division group, or new page
Starting At	Enter the number you want to start the reset numbers

(continues)

Table 15.1 Continued	
Option	**Action**
Separators Tab	
Separator Line For	Choose to add a separator line between the text and the regular footnotes or continued footnotes
Span to Margin	Choose if you want the footnote to use the same page margins as the text in the document
Custom Length	Set a line length for the footnotes by choosing this option and entering a measurement in inches
Indent From Left	Choose this option and enter a measurement in inches to indent the footnote from the left margin
Space Above	Enter a measurement in picas to add a space above each note
Space Below	Enter a measurement in picas to add a space below each note
Continued Messages Tab	
Generate "Continued On" Message	Choose to create a message telling the reader the note is continued on the next page
Alignment	Select an alignment for the text
Generate "Continued From" Message	Choose to create a message telling the reader the note is continued from the previous page
Alignment	Select an alignment for the text
Repeat Reference Number When Continued	Choose to add the reference number to continued text

▶ See "Creating and Using Divisions," p. 308

If you insert multiple footnotes, Word Pro fits them on the bottom of the page. Footnotes fill up from the bottom margin of the page as you create them. Sufficient space must be available for the note below the lowest frame on the page. If insufficient space is available below the lowest frame, Word Pro splits the footnote over additional pages.

Going to a Footnote

As you create a document, you can enter footnotes as you go along. Later, as you prepare the final version of the document, you can proof the footnotes by moving to each one in succession.

You can move easily from one footnote mark in the text to the next, and from footnote text to footnote text. Follow these steps to move from mark to mark:

◀ See "Using Go To," p. 157

1. Place the insertion point anywhere in the main document.

2. Choose Edit, Go To or press Ctrl+G. You can also click the Go To SmartIcon. The Go To dialog box appears (see fig. 15.6).

3. In the Type of Document Part to Go To list box, choose Footnote Mark.

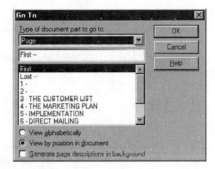

Fig. 15.6
Use the Go To dialog box to move from footnote to footnote.

4. Choose Next (or Previous) and click OK. The insertion point moves to the next (or previous) footnote reference number in the document. You can also choose to View Alphabetically or View by Position in Document.

Editing Footnotes

You can edit the footnote text just as you can edit main text. The trick is to get the insertion point where you want it before you begin editing. Follow these steps:

1. In Layout mode, choose Edit, Go To, Footnote Text.

2. Edit the footnote text as you would edit any other text.

3. After you finish editing, press the Esc key or click anywhere in the main text.

◀ See "Editing Text," p. 66

In Layout mode, you can move from footnote text to footnote text by pressing the down-arrow key. You can select text, however, only in a single footnote.

Note

You can change a footnote to an endnote by selecting the footnote reference number and choosing Create, Footnote/Endnote. Choose where to place the note and click OK. Word Pro displays the Move Notes dialog box; choose Move This Note. If you want to move all footnotes to the end, choose Move All Notes.

Removing Footnotes

You can easily remove a footnote by deleting the reference number. Word Pro deletes the footnote number, text, and then renumbers all other footnotes accordingly. To remove a footnote, follow these steps:

1. Move the insertion point to the reference number of the footnote you want to delete.

2. Select the reference number.

3. Press the Delete key. Word Pro deletes the footnote mark and its corresponding text.

Troubleshooting

When I chose the footnote mark in the Go To dialog box, Word Pro responded with `Go To could not find a match for that item.`

No footnote numbers exist after the location of the insertion point; move to the beginning of the document and try Go To again.

I accidentally removed a footnote reference number and the footnote text was erased as well.

When you remove the reference number, you remove the footnote. Choose Edit, Undo to cancel the last action.

Using a Glossary

A *glossary* is text you use over and over in various documents. A glossary might be a company name and address, a list of names, or a paragraph or two of boilerplate text. A glossary can consist of standard language for legal documents, a heading you use at the top of a document, or any text you use repeatedly. Instead of typing the text each time you need it, you can insert the text from the glossary.

> **Tip**
>
> Format your company's name and address and add a logo, for example, in a glossary so you can use it for letterheads, invoices, reports, and so on.

Entering Glossary Text

Word Pro has included an automated glossary assistant that helps you quickly and easily create glossaries for your documents. The first step to creating a glossary is to enter the text into a plain document. You can save the document and use it to enter several glossaries. Figure 15.7 illustrates a saved glossary document that contains several glossary entries. The glossary document makes it easy to edit the glossaries in the future.

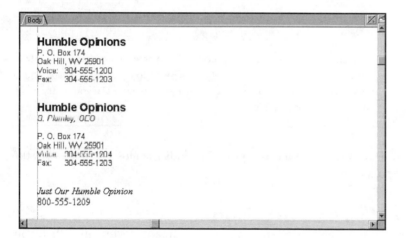

Fig. 15.7
Save similar glossaries in the same document so they'll be easy to find when you're ready to edit them.

> **Note**
>
> You can format the glossary text in large, boldface fonts; you can use bullets, different type sizes, alignments, and so on.

◀ See "Changing Character Formatting," p. 79

◀ See "Changing Paragraph Formatting," p. 88

After you set up and save the glossary document, you are ready to save the glossaries.

To save a glossary, follow these steps:

1. Select all of the text you want to include in one glossary.

2. Choose Edit, Glossary. The Glossary dialog box appears (see fig. 15.8).

Fig. 15.8
Create a new
glossary simply by
giving it a name.

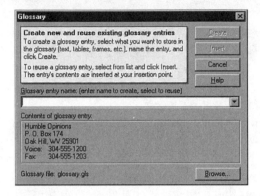

3. In Glossary Entry Name, enter a name for the new glossary.

> **Note**
>
> The glossary entry name can be up to 63 characters long. Since you only need to choose the name from a list when you want to insert the glossary, you do not have to worry about keeping the name short; so make your entry names as descriptive as possible.

4. Click the Create button. Word Pro adds the glossary and closes the dialog box.

Inserting a Glossary Entry

You can insert a glossary entry at any time in any document. When you choose to insert a glossary, the formatted glossary text is added to the document. To insert a glossary entry, follow these steps:

1. Open the document into which you want to insert the glossary entry and position the insertion point.

2. Choose Edit, Glossary. You can also click the Insert a Glossary Record SmartIcon. The Glossary dialog box appears.

3. Display the Glossary Entry Names by clicking the down arrow beside the text box (see fig. 15.9).

4. Choose the desired glossary name.

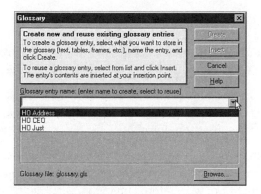

Fig. 15.9
All saved glossary
entries appear in
the Glossary Entry
Name list; choose
the one you want
to insert.

5. Choose <u>I</u>nsert. Word Pro closes the dialog box and inserts the glossary
   into your document (see fig. 15.10).

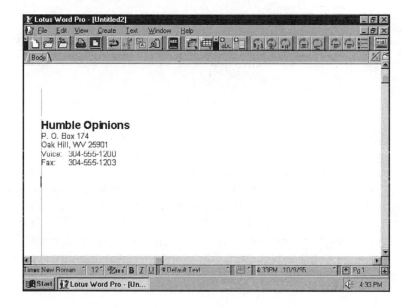

Fig. 15.10
After inserting a
glossary, you may
want to change
page or even text
formatting; you
can do so without
affecting the
original glossary.

II

Accelerating Your WP

Creating a Table of Contents

Creating a table of contents (TOC) for a document is easy in Word Pro because of the Table of Contents Assistant. The Table of Contents Assistant is a
dialog box that contains three tabs, each with instructions and options you
need to create a table of contents. When you're creating a table of contents,
you must make several decisions:

■ Decide whether to show or hide the page numbers and whether to
   right-align them.

■ Select a separator or leader (period, hyphen, or underscore) to use be-tween the table of contents entry and the page number. If you have many headings in the table of contents, visible separators help the viewer line up page numbers with appropriate headings.

■ Choose a location for the table of contents. You can place it at the be-ginning of the current document, at the beginning of a division or group, or at the insertion point.

▶ See "Creating and Using Divisions," p. 308

▶ See "Using Reference Tools," p. 321

■ You can also decide whether to place the table in a separate division. If you place the table in the same division as the document, the style of the table might not work—fonts, margins, alignment, and so on follow that of the document. Most times, you need to place the table in its own division so you can apply specific table of contents styles to the text.

> **Tip**
>
> If your document is a long one, use Word Pro's division feature to organize the docu-ment and then create a TOC across divisions and grouped divisions.

Creating Entries

You can create TOC entries by either using assigned paragraph styles or by marking the text you want to include in the contents list. When you create entries from styles, you can choose style names, such as Titles, Subheads, and so on as the entries in the TOC. Word Pro assembles all text assigned to those styles. Alternately, you can mark specific text, whether assigned as a style or not, to use as table of contents entries. The easiest method, (the one de-scribed here), is to use styles and the Table of Contents Assistant. If you want to mark entries throughout the text, see the section "Creating Index Entries" later in this chapter. The method for creating table of contents entries is the same.

Using the Table of Contents Assistant, Word Pro enables you to choose the styles you want to include from the document and to assign each style a TOC level. To use the Assistant to create the table of contents, follow these steps:

1. Place the insertion point anywhere in the document.

2. Choose Create, Other Document Part, Table of Contents. The Table of Contents Assistant appears (see fig. 15.11).

> **Note**
>
> Before creating the table of contents, make sure the titles and subheadings in the document appear the way you want them to look in the table of contents.

◀ See "Using Paragraph Styles," p. 102

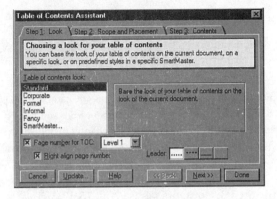

Fig. 15.11
Use the Table of Contents Assistant to quickly set up a table for your documents.

3. In the Step 1: Look tab, choose a style in the Table of Contents Look list. If you choose a SmartMaster, Word Pro displays a list of TOC SmartMasters from which you can choose to apply to just the table of contents.

> **Note**
>
> You can also change any of the default options: Page Number for TOC, Right Align Page Number, and the Leader type in the Step 1 tab.

4. Choose the Step 2: Scope and Placement tab (see fig. 15.12).

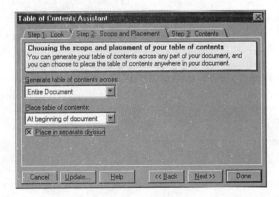

Fig. 15.12
Use the Scope and Placement tab to choose where to place the table of contents.

II

Accelerating Your WP

▶ See "Creating and Using Divisions," p. 308

5. In the Scope and Placement tab, choose whether to Generate the Table of Contents Across the entire document, grouped divisions, or only the current division.

In Place Table of Contents, choose one of the following: at the beginning of document, division, or group, or at the insertion point.

Choose to Place in Separate Division or not.

Note

When creating a table of contents, you can choose to place the table in a division or division group. Divisions are areas you can create in your documents that separate one part of the document from another. For example, chapter one might be in one division and chapter two in another division. Divisions make organizing and managing long documents possible.

---

6. Choose the Step 3: Contents tab (see fig. 15.13).

Fig. 15.13
Use the Contents tab to assign TOC levels to the styles in your document.

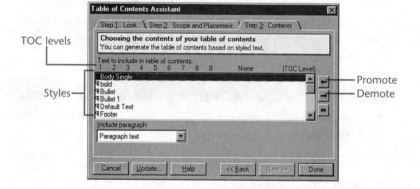

7. In the Contents tab, assign a TOC level to each style you want to use in the table of contents. Use the promote and demote arrows to move each selected style through the levels.

8. When you're finished, choose Done. Word Pro inserts the table of contents at the specified point. Figure 15.14 illustrates a completed table of contents.

▶ See "Editing Tables," p. 334

Note

Since Word Pro inserts the table of contents as a table, you can format and edit the contents as you would any table.

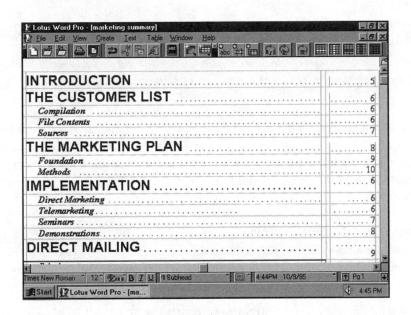

II

Accelerating Your WP

Fig. 15.14
The completed table of contents uses the same styles as the document uses.

Updating the Table of Contents

Whenever you edit your document's headings and subheadings, you'll want to update the table of contents to reflect the changes. You can quickly and easily update the table by following these steps:

1. Place the insertion point anywhere in the document.

2. Choose Create, Other Document Part, Table of Contents. The Table of Contents Assistant appears.

3. Accept or make any changes in the Look, Scope and Placement, and Contents tabs. Then choose the Update button. Word Pro updates the table of contents entries.

4. Choose Done when you are finished.

Creating an Index

Use an index to guide readers to specific topics and subjects in your document. You can create an index for one document or for multiple divisions, such as book chapters or report sections.

> **Tip**
>
> Word Pro's document division feature helps you manage and organize multiple documents, and you can create an index across documents using this feature.

To create an index, mark the entries in the document and then let Word Pro generate the index. Word Pro includes an index SmartMaster you can use to hold the index in a separate file, or you can use your document's styles and SmartMaster. Additionally, Word Pro uses an Index Assistant to make generating the index and choosing formatting options easier.

Creating Index Entries

You can mark any text in the document as an *index entry* (the page is marked and used when Word Pro generates the index). If you edit the text, the index mark moves with the marked text so the page number will always be correct.

When marking the index entry, you can enter the name you want to use for the entry in a primary field and a secondary field. The *primary field* holds general subjects whereas the *secondary field* holds more specific subjects. Suppose you enter Services for the primary field; you might enter such secondary fields as Printing, Composition, or Paste-up. Your primary index entry then, appears as Services with the secondary entries listed below it.

To mark index references in the text of your document, follow these steps:

1. Position the insertion point in the text you want to mark.

2. Choose <u>T</u>ext, Mar<u>k</u> Text As, <u>I</u>ndex Entry. The Mark Text bar appears (see fig. 15.15).

3. In the <u>P</u>rimary text box, enter the primary subject.

4. You can enter a secondary subject in the <u>S</u>econdary text box.

5. Choose <u>M</u>ark. The entry is added to the drop-down list. To view the entries, click the down arrow beside the Primary or Secondary text box.

6. Move the insertion point to the next spot in the text you want to mark. The Mark Text bar remains on-screen.

7. Mark all additional entries in the same way, selecting the text and following steps 2 through 6. If you choose to use the same primary entry, select it from the drop-down list box; then choose <u>M</u>ark. Alternatively, you can enter the text.

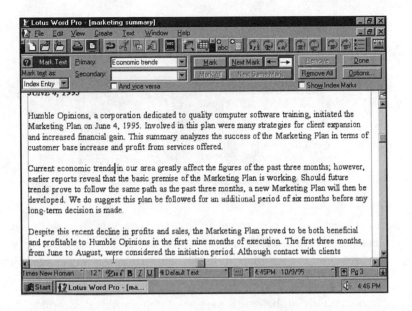

Fig. 15.15
Use the Mark Text
bar to enter index
entries.

Tip

Check the And Vice Versa option if you want both references to show as primary and secondary.

8. Choose the Options button to associate a page number or set any See Also options for the index. Choose OK to close the Index Mark Options dialog box.

9. Choose Done to close the Mark Text bar.

Generating the Index

After you mark the text for the index, you can tell Word Pro to generate the index. Word Pro creates the index using the Index Assistant and your guidance.

To generate an index after marking the index entries, follow these steps:

1. Choose Create, Other Document Part, Index. The Index Assistant appears (see fig. 15.16). You can also choose the Generate Index SmartIcon.

2. In the Step 1: Look tab, choose a look for the index. You can choose a SmartMaster if you want a specific look for the index.

Fig. 15.16
Use the Index Assistant to help set up and generate an index for your document.

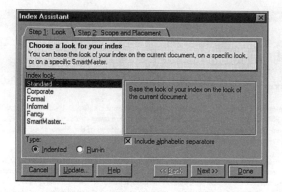

3. In the Type area, choose either an Indented or a Run-in index. *Indented* places the secondary entries on separate lines and spaces each entry 1/2-inch from the left margin. *Run-in* separates secondary entries only with a comma.

4. Choose Include Alphabetic Separators if you want A, B, C, and so on to head each index section.

5. Choose the Step 2: Scope and Placement tab (see fig. 15.17).

Fig. 15.17
Use the Scope and Placement tab to choose where the completed index will go.

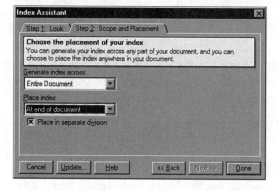

6. In the Scope and Placement tab, choose whether to Generate Index Across the entire document, grouped divisions, current division, or selected text.

7. Choose whether to Place Index at the end of the document, division, group, or section, or whether to place it at the insertion point.

8. Choose to Place in Separate Division so your index does not interfere with the document text.

9. Choose <u>D</u>one and Word Pro generates the index as shown in figure 15.18.

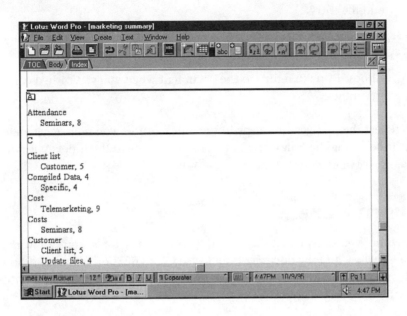

Fig. 15.18
Word Pro creates
the index using
the options and
formatting you
selected.

Modifying an Index

After you generate an index, you will likely want to make changes, additions, or deletions. Word Pro enables you to easily move from entry to entry, remove entries, and otherwise edit the index.

To modify an index, follow these steps:

1. Position the insertion point anywhere in the document.

2. Choose Text, Mar<u>k</u> Text As, <u>I</u>ndex Entry. The Mark Text bar appears.

3. Choose <u>N</u>ext Mark to move the insertion point to the next index entry in the document, moving one by one through the marked text.

Choose the left arrow and choose <u>N</u>ext Mark to move to the preceding index entry in the document.

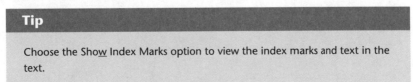

Tip

Choose the Sho<u>w</u> Index Marks option to view the index marks and text in the text.

II

Accelerating Your WP

4. To remove an entry, choose <u>R</u>emove when the text is displayed in the Pr<u>i</u>mary or <u>S</u>econdary text box. Word Pro removes the mark in the text and the entry.

5. To change an entry, type over the entry in the <u>P</u>rimary or <u>S</u>econdary text box and choose <u>M</u>ark.

6. Choose <u>D</u>one to return to the document when you've finished editing the entries.

To reflect the changes you made in the index entries, you must regenerate the index using the Index Assistant. Choose <u>U</u>pdate in the Index Assistant dialog box when you're done.

From Here...

Now that you know how to use Word Pro's reference tools, you can work more easily with long documents and Word Pro's division feature. Additionally, you can add charts and tables to your document. For more information, see the following chapters:

■ Chapter 16, "Managing Long Documents," shows you how to use Word Pro's features to create and format divisions in your documents to make them easier to organize and manage.

■ Chapter 17, "Working with Tables and Charts," explains how to create and edit tables, format tables, link and sort table data, and create and edit charts.

■ Chapter 22, "Desktop Publishing with Word Pro," shows you how to use design elements such as orientation, balance, and contrast to make your document look attractive and professional.

Chapter 16

Managing Long Documents

by Sue Plumley

Word Pro contains some special features that make creating and managing long documents easy and efficient. In Word Pro, you can create *divisions*—a document within a document—to help you visually organize the document parts, such as the chapters of a book or parts of a business report. Additionally, you can easily move and copy these divisions as well as apply specific formatting to each division.

Not only does Word Pro enable you to create and format divisions in a long document, but it gives you the capability to further separate the divisions into *sections*. Sections are parts of a document that you can manipulate and edit to further aid in organizing those long, complex documents.

Furthermore, you can create *master documents*. A master document is one file that contains many divisions and in each division is a part of your document. For example, a division may contain internal or external files, a table of contents or index, or other parts of your document. Use master documents to organize and administer your long documents.

In this chapter, you learn how to:

- Create divisions and sections
- Set division and section properties
- Rename and delete divisions and sections
- Create a master document
- Compile a table of contents and index across divisions

Understanding Divisions and Sections

When creating a long document, you'll want to organize the document so you can quickly move to certain areas of the document and move or format the document using the quickest and easiest method available. Word Pro supplies two features—divisions and sections—to help you organize and manage long documents.

Divisions enable you to identify parts of a document: introduction, goals, methods, and achievements in a business report, for example. A division can contain text, other divisions, external files (imported files), or sections. A division is a document within a document.

A section, on the other hand, is a part of a document. You might use sections in a business report, for example, in the introduction division. One section could contain a list of the company's officers and staff; another section could contain text describing the purpose of the report.

Note

Some procedures are the same for both divisions and sections, such as naming divider tabs. To avoid repetition, those procedures will be presented once in the following text covering divisions, along with a reference to the parallels when working with sections.

Using Divisions

Use divisions when working with a long, complex document that you want to separate into smaller, more easily handled portions. You can also use different SmartMasters for various sections of text in a division. Finally, use a division to designate an external file that you imported to the document.

Figure 16.1 illustrates a business report separated into several divisions.

Remember these points about divisions:

- Divisions always start on a new page.
- Each division uses its own SmartMaster.
- A division is a document with all document properties.
- Divisions can contain sections.
- A division can be an external file imported into the document.

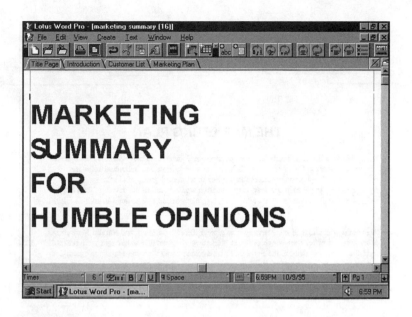

Fig. 16.1
Use divisions to separate a long document into smaller, more manageable documents.

Using Sections

Use sections when you want to use different page layouts on one page, such as margins or columns. Use a section when you want to change the format of one area of text but keep the same SmartMaster for the rest of the division. You may also want to use sections to quickly navigate your way to a part of the document.

Figure 16.2 illustrates the same business report as in figure 16.1, but with sections added to some of the divisions.

Remember these points when creating sections:

- A section can start anywhere on the page.

- A section can contain one page or many.

- More than one section can be on one page.

- A section is a part of a document, not a document by itself.

◀ See "Modifying SmartMasters," p. 247

◀ See "Creating a New Smart-Master," p. 261

◀ See "Setting Margins, Page Tabs, and Columns," p. 108

◀ See "Adding Borders, Lines, and Shading," p. 130

II

Accelerating Your WP

Fig. 16.2
Separate divisions into sections so that you can reformat or quickly access a part of the document.

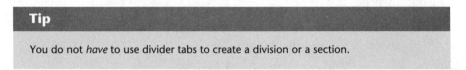

Using Divider Tabs

When you separate a document into divisions and/or sections, you can create divider tabs to help you structure and organize a document. After you create a section or division, you can name the divider tab to make it easy to find that area of the document.

> **Tip**
>
> You do not *have* to use divider tabs to create a division or a section.

If you want to use divider tabs, use them to quickly move through text and view the document organization at a glance. When you click a divider tab, that division comes to the foreground so that you can view its contents. Additionally, you can use divider tabs to quickly move a division and its text to another area of the document.

Creating and Using Divisions

You can create an unlimited number of divisions in a document, as long as your computer memory can handle it. You can even group, combine, and nest divisions to make document organization easier. Word Pro makes moving, formatting, and otherwise modifying divisions effective and useful.

You can create a division and enter or paste text and other elements into that division. Additionally, you can import an external file to a division. Each division is self-contained and uses its own SmartMaster.

> ### Tip
>
> When you import an external file, you create a division that contains the external file, thus creating a *master document*.

◀ See "Using Word Pro's SmartMasters," p. 242

▶ See "Using Master Documents," p. 318

Word Pro provides several tools that you can use to create and manage divisions. Before you create a division, take a look at figure 16.3. The figure shows three specific features that you can use to navigate divisions: Show/Hide Divisions button, Page Gauge, and the Next/Previous tab button.

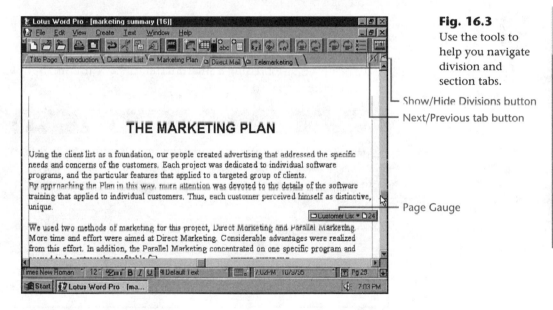

Fig. 16.3
Use the tools to help you navigate division and section tabs.

— Show/Hide Divisions button
— Next/Previous tab button

— Page Gauge

II

Accelerating Your WP

Creating Divisions

A Word Pro document starts with one division tab as the default, but you can easily add more. You can create a new division that's formatted like the original by right-clicking the division tab. A quick menu appears; choose Quick Division and Word Pro will insert the new division with its new tab.

If you want to create a new division using a different SmartMaster or by inserting a current Word Pro document, follow these steps:

1. Choose Create, Division. The Create Division dialog box appears (see fig. 16.4).

Fig. 16.4
Use the Create
Division dialog
box to control the
division that
you're inserting.

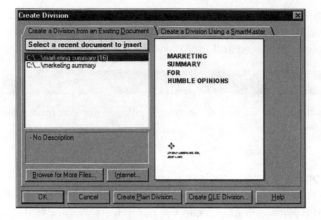

2. Choose one of the following tabs:

   ■ Create a division from an Existing Document. Select a Word Pro
   document to insert into the current document as a division.

   ■ Create a division Using a SmartMaster. Choose the SmartMaster
   from the displayed list.

> **Tip**
>
> In the Create Division dialog box, choose Create Plain Division if you prefer
> creating a new division that takes on the properties of the division pre-
> ceding it.

> **Note**
>
> You can, alternatively, create an OLE division and embed or link data to the
> new division.

▶ See "Using
Links," p. 523

3. Choose OK, and the Insert Division dialog box appears (see fig. 16.5).

4. Choose whether to insert the division After or Before the current division or at the Insertion point.

   Additionally, choose whether the selected file will be Inserted Into Current Document or Linked to External File. Choosing to link to an external file means that Word Pro will launch an external OLE application
   when you select the tab and you edit the external file in the source
   destination.

5. Choose OK, and Word Pro inserts the new division and tab.

After creating a division, you can name the tab, set division properties, and otherwise modify the division.

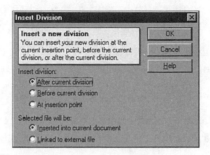

Fig. 16.5
In the Insert Division dialog box, you must choose where to place the division in the current document.

Naming and Renaming a Tab

Naming a division or section tab can be done in the same way, at any time. The name can be any length.

To name or rename a division tab, double-click the tab. The tab text becomes selected and you can enter new text. Press Enter when you're done.

Setting Division Properties

Division properties include the tab name, page style, starting point of the division, and the tab color. You can choose to save a division as a separate file. If you choose to import an external file, you also can pick document properties of the imported file.

To set division properties for a specific division, right-click the tab to display the quick menu. Choose Division Properties. The Divisions Properties dialog box appears as shown in figure 16.6.

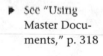

▶ See "Using Master Documents," p. 318

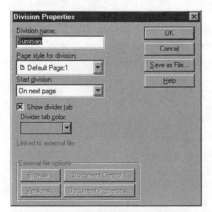

Fig. 16.6
Specify division properties using the Division Properties dialog box.

II

Accelerating Your WP

In the Division Properties dialog box, choose from the following options:

- *Division Name.* Change the tab's name if you want.

- *Page Style for Division.* Select a style from the list of page styles.

- *Start Division.* Choose which page to start the division: Within page, On Next page, On Odd page, or On Even page.

- *Show Divider Tab.* Choose whether to show or hide the tab for that specific division.

- *Divider Tab Color.* Choose a color for the tab from the palette.

- *Save as File.* Choose to place a copy of the division in a drive and directory as a saved file.

You can also choose certain options dealing with external files when you've linked files to a division. You can Browse for files, use Document Control and Document Properties features, and display and compare Versions when dealing with external files.

▶ See "Using Links," p. 523

▶ See "Consolidating Edits," p. 502

Choose OK to close the dialog box when you're done.

Moving Divisions

After you've created several divisions and organized your document, you may need to reorganize division tabs. When you move a division tab, you move all its contents with it. All other division and section tabs move to make room for the moved tab.

To move a division tab, click the tab to be moved and drag it to the right. You can move a tab only to the blank area at the end of all other tabs; you can't move a tab to the left of another tab.

Note

You can also move sections using the same procedure. However, you can move a section to any divider tab. In addition, if you move a section to a blank area on the division bar (the area that holds the tabs), you automatically create another division.

Deleting Divisions

You can easily delete a division and its contents. To delete a division tab, right-click the tab to display the quick menu. Choose Delete Division from the quick menu. You can also delete a section using the quick menu.

> **Caution**
>
> When you delete a division tab, you also delete all of its contents. The only way to retrieve the division tab and its contents is by choosing Edit, Undo.

Creating a Division within a Division

You can create a division within a division to further format and organize your long document. When you create a division within a division, all division rules still apply, such as separated SmartMasters, separate tabs, and so on.

To create a division within a division, select the division tab and right-click the mouse. From the quick menu, choose Group Tabs. Word Pro creates a new division so that the original division is the one within the new division. Figure 16.7 illustrates a group of division tabs.

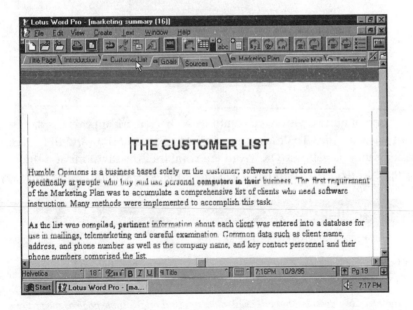

Fig. 16.7
You group divisions by placing one division within another.

II

Accelerating Your WP

You can collapse divisions within divisions (or sections within divisions) by clicking the minus sign on a tab. Collapsing the divisions hides those within the group. Clicking a plus sign expands the division or section group by one level.

Combining Divisions

You can combine two or more divisions or two or more sections. You can't, however, combine a division with a section. You can combine grouped divisions as well as single ones. Word Pro uses the division or section at the selection point as the first one to combine.

To combine two or more divisions, select one division that you want to combine and right-click the mouse. From the quick menu, choose Combine Divisions. The Combine Divisions dialog box appears (see fig. 16.8).

Note

When you combine two divisions, they use the same SmartMaster as the first selected division.

Fig. 16.8
Select the divisions that you want to combine in the Combine Divisions dialog box.

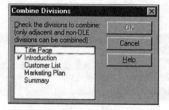

Select one or more divisions to combine. A check mark appears beside the tabs that you select. To deselect a tab, click it a second time and the check mark disappears. Choose OK. Word Pro combines the divisions and their contents into one division tab. The same applies for combining sections.

Troubleshooting

The page gauge is not showing on my screen.

Choose View, Set View Preferences. In the View Preferences dialog box, choose the Show tab and select Show Page Gauge.

I combined two divisions, but one division doesn't start on the same page as the first one ends on.

When you combine divisions, Word Pro does not remove the page break. You can delete the page break to combine the two on the same page.

I was renaming a division tab and I changed my mind.

While your insertion point is still within the division tab, you can press Esc to restore the original text. If you've already pressed Enter, double-click the tab and try again.

Creating and Using Sections

You can create sections within divisions for easier access to the text or for formatting purposes. Suppose that you have specific text within a division that you will often reference, such as a list or table. You can use section tabs to label the text and therefore move to each section of text quickly.

Additionally, you can change the page layout for a section by changing margins, columns, page tabs, and so on. Only the section changes; the rest of the SmartMaster in the division remains the same.

When working with sections, several procedures are the same as when working with divisions: moving, deleting, and combining sections.

Creating a Section

You create a section at the insertion point on a page within a division. Word Pro inserts a section divider to show where the section begins. The new section continues until you create another section. You can also create more than one section per page. After creating a section, you can format it.

Figure 16.9 illustrates a section marker on the page and the section divider tab.

◀ See "Moving Divisions," p. 312

◀ See "Deleting Divisions," p. 312

◀ See "Combining Divisions," p. 314

> **Tip**
>
> You can name a section tab just as you would a division tab.

If you delete the section divider on the page, the new section's formatting reverts to the previous section's formatting.

To create a section, follow these steps:

1. Position the insertion point where you want the new section to begin. Choose Create Section. The Create Section dialog box appears (see fig. 16.10).

2. In the Start section, choose from one of the following options:

   ■ *Within Page.* On the same page as the insertion point, at the insertion point.

   ■ *On Next Page.* On the page after the page containing the insertion point.

■ *On Odd Page.* On the next odd, or right-hand, page.

■ *On Even Page.* On the next even, or left-hand, page.

Fig. 16.9

When you insert a section, Word Pro creates a section tab and a section marker.

Section tab

Section marker

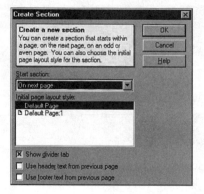

Fig. 16.10

Use the Create Section dialog box to specify where to start the section and to indicate the page layout.

3. In Initial Page Layout Style, select a style. Default Page style is always present; however, if you have saved other page styles, they will be listed as well.

4. Choose whether to show or hide the divider tab.

5. Choose whether to use the header and/or footer text from the previous page.

6. Choose OK to insert the section.

Word Pro inserts an icon to represent the new section; you can see the section marker in either Layout or Draft view (refer to fig. 16.9).

Formatting the Section

You can format the section any way that you want by using the Page Properties dialog box. You can change columns, margins, or tabs, add a different header or footer to the section, add lines and borders, or change the page in many other ways.

◀ See "Changing Margins, Columns, and Tabs," p. 108

Figure 16.11 illustrates two sections on one page of the division. The Introductory section is divided into two columns. The Calendar of Events section is one column and indents both the left and right margin by an extra half inch or so. This section makes the table and its paragraph stand out from the rest of the text.

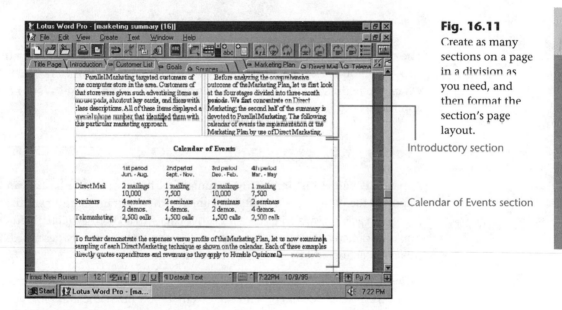

Fig. 16.11
Create as many sections on a page in a division as you need, and then format the section's page layout.

Introductory section

Calendar of Events section

II

Accelerating Your WP

Next, a third section resumes the page formatting of two columns with one inch left and right margins. The two-column format then continues if another section is created.

Tip

You can even save the page layout for the section as a page style and use it in other sections within the division.

Setting Section Properties

You can change the section properties—such as the section name, page style, and place to start the section—in the Section Properties dialog box.

To set section properties, position the insertion point in the section and right-click the section's tab. The quick menu appears. Choose Section Properties and the Section Properties dialog box appears, as shown in figure 16.12.

Fig. 16.12

Set properties such as the section name and style in the Section Properties dialog box.

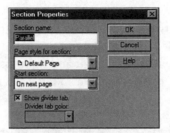

The options in the Section Properties dialog box are the same as those in the Create Section dialog box. Change any options that you want. Choose OK when you're finished with the Section Properties dialog box, and Word Pro applies any of the options you selected.

Using Master Documents

A master document is simply any document with a division containing an imported file. You create a master document when you import an external file—such as a spreadsheet, chart, or other data—to a Word Pro document. You also can create internal divisions and sections as previously described in this chapter and add those to the master document.

When you import an external file, Word Pro automatically creates a divider tab in the master document, and the external file's file name and path appear on the tab; if the file is located within the same folder, no path appears in the tab name. You can change the name of the divider tab if you like.

> **Tip**
>
> Each external file uses its own SmartMaster, but you can modify the file and formatting.

Figure 16.13 shows an imported 1-2-3 spreadsheet and its own divider tab.

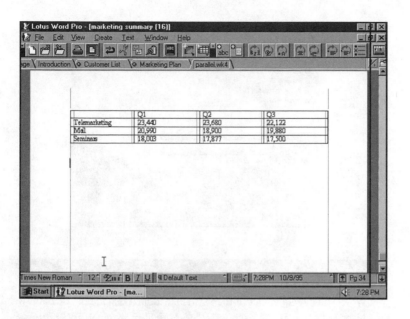

Fig. 16.13
Import files from other programs, such as 1-2-3 and Freelance Graphics, to add to your master document The spreadsheet's name—parallel.wk4—appears on this

Creating a Master Document

Creating a master document is simply a matter of importing a file. Word Pro automatically creates the file's division for you, and then you can format and modify the division any way that you want.

To create a master document, follow these steps:

1. Choose Create, Master Document. The Master Document dialog box appears (see fig. 16.14).

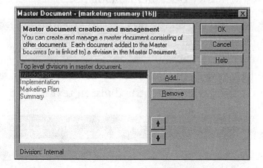

Fig. 16.14
Use the Master Document dialog box to import a file to a new division in a long document.

2. In the Top Level Divisions in Master Document list, a list of all divisions in the document thus far appears. Choose the Add button. The Browse dialog box appears as shown in figure 16.15.

Fig. 16.15
Select the drive, directory, and file that you want to import in the Browse dialog box.

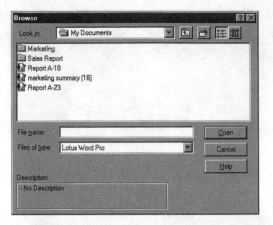

Tip

When you highlight a file in the Master Document dialog box, its status is identified either as internal or external. If the file is external, its file name and path are displayed.

---

3. In the Browse dialog box, choose the folder and then the File Name of the file that you want to import.

4. If the file is not a Word Pro file, choose the file type in Files of Type.

5. Choose Open to import the file. Word Pro adds the file to the list of divisions in the Master Document dialog box.

6. Choose OK to close the dialog box. Word Pro adds a new division and the imported file to your master document.

You can change the name of the tab, modify division properties, change SmartMasters, and otherwise modify the division text or data as you like.

Tip

Right-click an external file divider tab to display the Division Properties dialog box.

Removing an Imported File

You can remove any imported file from a master document using the Master Document dialog box.

To remove an imported file, choose <u>C</u>reate, <u>M</u>aster Document. In the Master Document dialog box, choose the division that you want to delete from the Top Level <u>D</u>ivisions in Master Document list box. Click the <u>R</u>emove button. The division and its contents disappear from the master document.

Troubleshooting

I've added many external files to my master document, but whenever I move from tab to tab to view the division contents, my computer moves very slowly.

The more division tabs and imported files you have in a document, the more system memory it takes to manage that master document. Try closing any other Windows applications that you might have open. If that doesn't help, you might consider dividing the master document into two separate files or obtaining more system memory (RAM).

Using Reference Tools

When you create a document using divisions or a master document, you can use Word Pro's reference tools—table of contents, index, and so on—across divisions and sections. You can, for example, create a book or report and compile a table of contents including all sections and divisions in the document.

Note

Marking and compiling a table of contents and an index are covered thoroughly in Chapter 15, "Using Reference Tools." This section covers only creating a table of contents and an index as it applies to divisions and sections.

Creating a Table of Contents

You can create a table of contents or index for just one division or for a group of divisions.

To create a table of contents for a long document, follow these steps:

1. In the long document, choose <u>C</u>reate, Other Document Part. From the secondary menu, choose <u>T</u>able of Contents. The Table of Contents Assistant appears.

2. In Step <u>1</u>: Look tab, choose a look for the table of contents.

◄ See "Creating a Table of Contents," p. 295

3. In Step <u>2</u>: Scope and Placement tab, click the down arrow in the <u>G</u>ener-
   ate Table Of Contents Across list box (see fig. 16.16). In the drop-down
   list, choose from the following options:

   ■ *Entire Document.* Compiles the table over all divisions and sections.

   ■ *Grouped Divisions.* Compiles the table over the selected group of
   divisions.

   ■ *Current Division.* Compiles the table over the current division
   only.

Fig. 16.16
Choose how much
of the document
you want to in-
clude in the table
of contents from
the Table of Con-
tents Assistant.

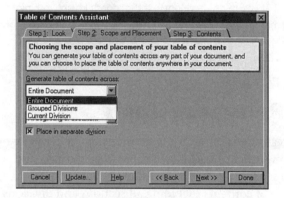

4. In the <u>P</u>lace Table of Contents drop-down list (located directly below
   the <u>G</u>enerate Table of Contents Across list box), choose from the following options:

   ■ *At Beginning of Document.* Places the table at the beginning of the
   entire document.

   ■ *At Beginning of Division.* Places the table at the front of the current
   division.

   ■ *At Beginning of Group.* Places the table in front of the first division
   of the group.

   ■ *At Insertion Point.* Places the table at the insertion point.

> **Tip**
>
> In the Step 2: Scope and Replacement tab, make sure that the Place in Separate Division option is selected so that the table doesn't interfere with the text in any other division.

5. Choose Next and select the styles that you want to use as table of contents levels in the Step 3: Contents tab.

6. Choose Done when you're finished, and Word Pro compiles the table of contents for you.

Creating an Index

Compiling an index for a long document or a master document is similar to compiling an index for any document. The differences are in where you place the index and in which divisions you choose to use for the index.

To compile an index, mark the index entries and then follow these steps:

◀ See "Creating an Index," p. 299

1. Choose Create, Other Document Part, Index. The Index Assistant dialog box appears.

2. In Step 1: Look tab, choose a look for the index.

3. Choose Next.

4. In Step 2: Scope and Placement tab, choose Generate Index Across and then select an option: Entire Document, Grouped Divisions, or Current Division.

5. In Place Index, choose where you want to locate the index from the following options: At End of Document, At End of Division, At End of Group, At End of Section, or At Insertion Point.

> **Tip**
>
> In Step 2: Scope and Placement tab, select the Place in Separate Division option so that the index doesn't interfere with the text in an existing division.

6. Choose Done; Word Pro compiles the index.

II

Accelerating Your WP

From Here...

Now that you know how to create divisions and sections in your documents, refer to the following chapters for other methods of organizing and managing documents:

- Chapter 8, "Marking and Searching Text," shows you how to use bookmarks to distinguish an area of the document, use find and replace for locating specific text or formatting, and use document-revision features to control others' use of the document.

- Chapter 14, "Outlining a Document," tells you how to create an outline, set outline style sequences, edit in outline mode, print an outline, and number paragraphs.

- Chapter 15, "Using Reference Tools," shows you how to create footnotes and endnotes, mark and compile a table of contents, and create an index for your documents.

Chapter 17

Working with Tables and Charts

by Sue Plumley

Word Pro tables give you great flexibility in working with words, numbers, and pictures. You can use data created in Word Pro or import data from other applications. Additionally, you can create formulas to calculate the contents of cells.

Another Word Pro feature, charting, adds to the long list of ways you can illustrate your documents and make them look more professional. Although Word Pro's charting feature is not as sophisticated as 1-2-3's, you still can create basic charts for your documents.

In this chapter, you learn how to:

■ Create tables and enter data

■ Insert columns and rows

■ Edit and format a table

■ Create and edit formulas in a table

■ Create a chart

Understanding Tables

To create an effective table, you must know the parts of a table. Tables are organized by *columns* and *rows*. Rows run horizontally and columns run vertically. Word Pro enables you to view the *table guides*—non-printing grids that form the rows and columns—and even apply lines to the grids, if you want.

> **Tip**
>
> To show or hide table guides, choose View, Set View Preferences, then choose the Show tab. Select or deselect Show Table Guides and choose OK.

You can also choose to show *headings*, which are the letters above the columns and the numbers to the left of the rows. In the View Preferences dialog box, choose Show Table Row/Col. Headings and choose OK. Table headings appear on-screen only when you're working in the table; headings do not print.

The intersection between a row and a column in a table is called a *cell*. Cells are the entry boxes in the table. A cell name includes the column letter followed by a row number, such as A1. Cells contain *cell markers* that help you select a cell or cells in the table. A cell marker appears only when you click in the cell; click the cell marker to select the entire cell and its contents. Figure 17.1 illustrates a table with the parts labeled.

Fig. 17.1

The table headings appear only when the insertion point is in the table.

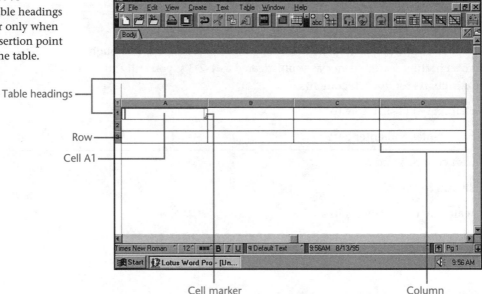

Table headings

Row

Cell A1

Cell marker

Column

Creating a Table

You can create a table on the page or in a frame. A table created on the page appears at the current insertion point; by default, Word Pro positions a table at the left margin. Any text at or below the insertion point is pushed below the inserted table. A table created in a frame appears wherever you position the frame. You can manipulate, edit, and format the frame the same way you can manipulate any other frame. Figure 17.2 illustrates two tables, one created on the page and the other created in a frame.

▶ See "Creating a Frame," p. 385

▶ See "Formatting Frames," p. 398

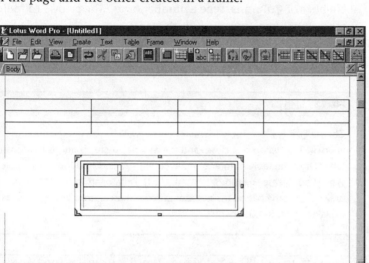

Fig. 17.2
The page table (top) looks similar to the frame table (bottom); however, the frame table uses two borders.

When you create or edit a table, Word Pro adds a Ta<u>b</u>le menu and table SmartIcons to help you work. Additionally, Word Pro includes a Table Cell and a Table Properties InfoBox you can use to complete your work. You can click the Cell InfoBox SmartIcon to open the Table Properties InfoBox. Using the Table Cell and Table Properties InfoBoxes is described later in this chapter.

To create a table, follow these steps:

1. Position the insertion point in a frame or on the page where you want to begin the table.

2. Choose <u>C</u>reate, <u>T</u>able. The Create Table dialog box appears (see fig. 17.3).

Fig. 17.3
In the Create Table dialog box, specify the number of columns and rows you want in the table.

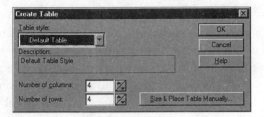

3. In Number of <u>C</u>olumns, type a number or use the arrows to indicate the number of columns you want in the table.

4. In Number of <u>R</u>ows, type a number or use the arrows to indicate the number of rows you want in the table.

> ### Note
>
> Choose <u>S</u>ize & Place Table Manually if you want to size and position the table yourself. The dialog box closes and the mouse pointer changes to a small table. Drag the table pointer to indicate the size and position of the table. When you release the mouse button, the table appears in the frame you have drawn. You can change the number of rows and columns at any time, as explained later in this chapter.

5. Choose OK to close the dialog box. Word Pro creates the table.

> ### Note
>
> To delete a table, position the insertion point in the table and choose Ta<u>b</u>le, <u>D</u>elete, <u>E</u>ntire Table.

Moving Around in a Table

When you work with a table, you can move around using the mouse or the keyboard. Using the mouse, you simply click the cell where you want to move, and the insertion point appears in that cell. However, if you're entering data, using the keyboard to move around may be easier. Table 17.1 describes ways to move around in a table using the keyboard.

Table 17.1 **Navigating a Table**	
Key	**Function**
Right arrow	Moves one character to the right or to the next column if no more characters exist in the current cell.
Left arrow	Moves one character to the left or to the preceding column.
Up arrow	Moves up to the previous row.
Down arrow	Moves down to the next row.
Tab	Moves to the next cell—as far as to the last column—and then to the first column of the next row.
Shift+Tab	Moves to the preceding cell and then to the far right column of the preceding row.
Home	Moves to the beginning of the cell contents.
End	Moves to the end of the cell contents.
Home, Home	Moves to the beginning of the row.
End, End	Moves to the end of the row.

Entering Data in a Table

You can enter data in a table by typing it or by importing data, pictures, or text from other applications. Figure 17.4 illustrates a table with text, numbers, and a graphic imported to a cell.

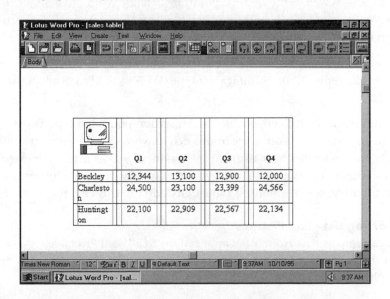

Fig. 17.4
Enter text, numbers, or import a file into a table you create in Word Pro.

Typing Text in a Table

To type text into a table, position the insertion point in a cell and begin typing. Word Pro automatically wraps the text as you type in a cell, enlarging the cell as needed. You can press Enter to enlarge a cell manually by one line; all cells in a row increase in height as you increase the height of any one cell in that row. To begin typing in another cell, move the insertion point and begin typing.

◀ See "Using Paragraph Styles," p. 102

The style of the text in a table is the Default Text style; however, you can choose any style or create a style of text for the table text. You use the same commands to choose and create styles for table text as you use for regular document text.

> **Tip**
>
> You can copy or cut and paste text from a document to a table the same way you do for any text; use tabs to separate columnar text before copying or cutting it from the document.

◀ See "Editing Text," p. 66

Entering and editing text in a table is similar to entering and editing text in your document.

Typing Numbers in a Table

Word Pro distinguishes between text and number cells automatically. A cell with letters or spaces is a *text cell*; a cell containing numbers is a *number cell*. In a number cell, you can insert operator signs, such as plus (+), minus (–), and so on—as well as the decimal point. By default, Word Pro adds a comma to separate thousands in your numbers. You can change the cell formatting, if you want, as described later in "Formatting Table Cells."

Word Pro displays text and numbers as left-aligned. It displays numbers without leading zeros. If, for example, you type 009.3, Word Pro displays the text as 9.3.

To enter numbers in a cell, position the insertion point and type as you would any text. After you move from a cell in which you've entered a number, Word Pro applies formatting to the number, such as the comma separating thousands, or other formatting you may specify. For more information on formatting, see "Formatting Table Cells" later in this chapter.

Importing Data and Pictures

You can import data from other applications to a Word Pro table, you can import a picture, or you can create a drawing with Word Pro's drawing applet and place that in a table.

To import a picture, position the insertion point and choose File, Import Picture. Select the file in the Import Picture dialog box and choose OK. You can crop a picture in the table by double-clicking the picture and then dragging the hand around in the cell until you see the picture you want.

▶ See "Importing and Exporting Text and Data Files," p. 513

To import a file from another application, position the insertion point in the table and then follow these steps:

1. Choose File, Import/Export.

2. In the Import or Export dialog box, choose Import Data from Another Application.

3. In Select Your Options, choose Import at the Current Insertion Point and then choose the Import button. The Open dialog box appears.

4. In the Open dialog box, select the file you want to import and choose OK. The data appears in the table; you may need to adjust the table formatting to fit the contents.

Troubleshooting

I created a table in a frame but It won't continue on the next page. Is there anything I can do?

You cannot continue a table in a frame on the next page; however, you can cut the table from the frame and paste it to the page. Page tables can continue on the next page; simply insert a page break in the table at the end of the page and continue it on the next page.

I can't add a tab to a table cell; do I have to use spaces?

No, you can add a tab. Press Ctrl+Alt+Shift+Tab to create a tab in a cell, then set the tab stop using the ruler if the default position is not appropriate for your text.

Selecting Tables and Contents

Select items in a table or table elements so you can edit and format them. Word Pro includes a couple of handy features that enable you to select columns, rows, cells, and data in a table.

You can use the mouse to select certain table items. Or you can choose the Table, Select command and select specific table contents or the entire table. Choose one of the following commands from the Select menu:

- *Cell Contents*. Selects the contents of the cell in which the insertion point appears.

- *Row Contents*. Selects the contents of the row in which the insertion point appears.

- *Column Contents*. Selects the contents of the column in which the insertion point appears.

- *Entire Table Contents*. Selects all table contents.

- *Cells*. Selects the cell in which the insertion point appears.

- *Entire Table*. Selects the table—contents and all.

To select one or more columns or rows, position the mouse pointer above the first column or in front of the first row you want to select until you see a small arrow. Click the arrow to select one row or column, or drag the arrow across several rows or columns to select them. Figure 17.5 shows a selected column.

Fig. 17.5
Slowly move the mouse around the top of the column until the small yellow arrow appears; then click to select the entire column.

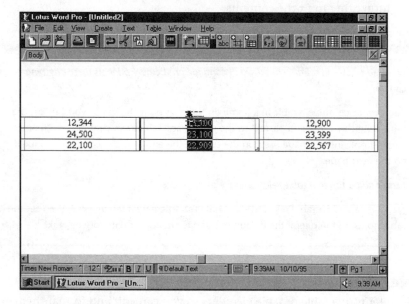

12,344	14,100	12,900
24,500	23,100	23,399
22,100	22,909	22,567

> **Tip**
>
> You can also use the cell marker to select one cell by clicking the cell marker.

To select text within a cell, drag the mouse over the text to highlight it; to select one cell, you can simply click the cell marker.

To select several cells (not necessarily an entire row or column), drag the mouse over the contents of the cells; thus selecting the contents and the cells. When you release the mouse button, the contents become selected. To deselect any selection, click the mouse anywhere in the table.

You can also use the following SmartIcons to select table parts:

 Select Row Contents

 Select Column Contents

 Select Entire Table

Using SmartFill

SmartFill is a procedure you follow to quickly fill cells in a table with a sequence of data. Word Pro fills the cells based on data and styles already in the table. If, for example, you enter A in a table, Word Pro can fill the following cells with B, C, D, E, and so on. You can also create sequences with numbers (use at least two numbers, such as 2, 4 or 12, 22), months, days, and so on.

You can view the SmartFill sequences already loaded into Word Pro by choosing File User Setup, SmartFill Setup. In the List Name drop-down box is a list of those sequences that Word Pro can follow; choose an item to see examples listed below the List Name text box (see fig. 17.6).

You can add new sequences by choosing the New List button. Enter the New List name and choose OK. Select the new name from the List Name drop-down list box, then choose the Add Item button to add items to the list. Enter each item's name in the New SmartFill Item text box and choose OK.

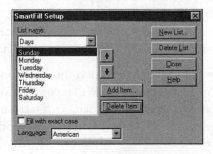

Fig. 17.6
Use the SmartFill Setup dialog box to add new items and lists.

> **Tip**
>
> You can create SmartFill sequences for company names, people, cities, products, or any other sequence you normally use as headings for tables.

> **Caution**
>
> Word Pro overwrites any data in a cell when you direct it to use SmartFill.

To use SmartFill, follow these steps:

1. Click the cell containing the first item in the sequence.

2. Hold down the Ctrl key, then click and drag the cell marker to select the cells you want to fill. The mouse pointer changes to a pointer with double arrows on the right and the bottom.

3. Release the mouse button and SmartFill completes the series.

Editing Tables

◀ See "Editing Text," p. 66

Editing tables and table data is quick and easy in Word Pro. Familiar editing techniques—such as cutting, copying, moving, and deleting text—apply to table text just like any other text in a document. Some editing commands are specific to tables, such as inserting or deleting columns and rows and adjusting column width and row height. Word Pro's editing techniques save you time and energy when working with tables.

Cutting, Copying, and Pasting

You can cut and copy table data the way you cut and copy other data. Select the text in one cell or in a range of cells and choose Edit, Cut or Edit, Copy; or you can click either the Cut or Copy SmartIcon. You can cut or copy text, numbers, pictures, formulas, or anything else you can place in a table cell.

To paste table data or another item, position the insertion point and choose Edit, Paste, or click the Paste SmartIcon. When you paste table data, such as numbers or text, Word Pro separates the data with tabs and adds a carriage return at the end of each row except the last; the insertion point appears at the end of the last row.

Moving Data with Drag and Drop

You can use drag-and-drop editing to move data from one cell or several cells to other cells in a table, or even to another position on the page. To use drag and drop, select the data, position the mouse over the selected data until the hand appears, then drag the data to a new position. When you release the mouse button, the data drops into the cell, overwriting any previous data in the cell.

You can also move a column or row using the drag-and-drop feature. Position the mouse pointer above or below the column or row so that the up/down or left/right arrow appears. Click and move the arrow over the column or row until the hand appears, then drag the column or row to the new position.

To *copy* a row or column instead of moving it, press and hold the Ctrl key before dragging the hand over the row or column.

Inserting and Removing Columns and Rows

You may often discover one too many rows or one too few columns in a table you're working on. You can easily add or remove rows and columns in Word Pro's tables.

Inserting Rows and Columns

To insert a new row or column, click the point in the table after which you want to insert the row or column. Choose Table, Insert, and then choose either Row or Column. The row or column inserts in the table. Alternatively, you can click the Insert Row in Table or Insert Column in Table SmartIcon.

To insert more than one row or column at a time, follow these directions:

1. Position the insertion point in the row or column after which you want to insert rows or columns, then choose Table, Insert, Row/Column. The Insert Row/Column dialog box appears (see fig. 17.7).

Fig. 17.7
Use the Insert Row/Column dialog box to insert more than one row or column at a time.

2. In Insert, choose Column or Row.

3. In the Number to Insert text box, enter the number of rows or columns.

4. In the Insert New Row/Column area, choose to insert the rows or columns Before or After the cell in which the insertion point currently appears.

5. Click OK to insert the rows or columns.

> ### Tip
>
> You can choose to Insert a Row or Insert a Column from the Table quick menu; access the Table quick menu by right-clicking the mouse on the table.

Removing Rows and Columns

To remove a row or column from the table, position the insertion point in the row or column. Choose Table, Delete, Row or Column. To delete more than one row or column, use the selection arrow to select the rows or columns. Then choose Table, Delete. Alternatively, you can select the row or column you want to delete and click the Delete Selected Rows or Delete Selected Columns SmartIcon. Word Pro deletes the selected row or column.

> ### Tip
>
> You can choose to Delete Row/Column from the Table quick menu; access the Table quick menu by right-clicking the mouse on the table.

Adjusting Column Width and Row Height

▶ See "Formatting Frames,"
p. 398

Just as it does for frames and text, Word Pro includes InfoBoxes that help you to format and edit tables and cells. Use the Table Cell Properties InfoBox to adjust the column width and row height of your table.

> ### Tip
>
> To display the InfoBox, right-click the table and choose Cell Properties from the quick menu.

To change the size of a row or column and to access the Table Cell Properties InfoBox, follow these steps:

1. With the row or column selected, choose Ta_b_le, Si_z_e Row/Column. The Table Cell Properties InfoBox appears. Choose the Size and Margins tab (see fig. 17.8).

Tip

You can adjust the size of a column or row by positioning the mouse over any column or row line until you see a double-headed arrow. Drag the arrow and the guide to adjust the size.

Size and Margins tab ———

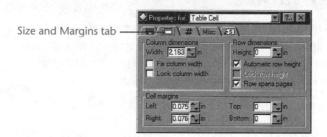

Fig. 17.8
Use the Table Cell Properties InfoBox to set column and row dimensions.

2. In the Column Dimensions box, type the Width in the text box or use the spinner arrows to select the width; when you change the column width, the table column changes on-screen.

3. In the Row Dimensions box, type the Height in the text box, or use the spinner arrows to select the height.

4. Choose any other options in the Size and Margins tab, as described in table 17.2.

Table 17.2   Size and Margin Options

Option	Description
Fix Column Width	Freezes column guides so you cannot change the column size.
Lock Column Width	Sets the column width to the measurement you specify; widths do not adjust to reach from margin to margin as they would if this option were not selected.
Automatic Row Height	Sets height to text height.

(continues)

Table 17.2 Continued	
Option	**Description**
Lock Row Height	Sets row height to a specific measurement; you cannot use drag and drop to change row sizes.
Row Spans Pages	For page tables only, enables the row and data to move to the next page if necessary.
Cell Margins	Sets space between the cell contents and the cell borders; set Left, Right, Top, and Bottom.

Formatting Tables

Word Pro enables you to format a table by adding lines and colors, styles, text wrap, and so on that apply to the entire table rather than just one cell. You can use two InfoBoxes for tables: Table Properties and Table Cell Properties. To format a table, use the Table Properties InfoBox.

To access the Table Properties InfoBox, choose Table, Table Properties.

Setting Lines and Colors

You can set lines and borders for the entire table, as well as background, colors, and shadows, in the Lines and Colors tab of the Table Properties InfoBox. Figure 17.9 shows the Lines and Colors tab.

Fig. 17.9
The Lines and Colors tab offers great variety in line style, width, and colors.

Lines and Colors tab —

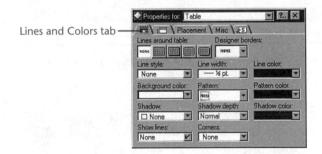

Table 17.3 describes the options in the Lines and Colors tab.

Table 17.3 Line and Color Options	
Option	**Description**
Lines around Table	Choose from four border designs: rectangle, rectangle with shadow, rounded rectangle, or rounded rectangle with shadow. All include lines around all cells. You can also choose None.
Designer Borders	Choose from twelve fancy table borders with no lines around the cell.
Line Style	Apply solid, double, dashed, zigzagged, and other lines for the border.
Line Width	Select from 1/4-pt. to 8-pt. line border width.
Line Color	Choose any color on the palette for the border.
Background Color	Choose any color on the palette for the entire table background. (Be careful when choosing a pattern or solid color for a table; too dark a color or pattern may hide the table contents.)
Pattern	Choose from stripes, dots, or other patterns to place in the background of the table.
Pattern Color	Choose a color for the stripes, dots, and so on in the pattern.
Shadow	Choose whether the table shadow is on the top-right, bottom-right, top-left, or bottom-left.
Shadow Depth	Select a Shallow, Normal, Deep, or Other shadow depth; if you choose Other, set the depth in the Shadow Depth dialog box.
Shadow Color	Choose the color for the shadow.
Show Lines	Choose to show all lines or only the left, right, top, and/or bottom lines of the border.
Corners	Select the amount of corner roundness for the table border if you chose to use rounded corners.

Setting the Table Margins

Use the Size and Margins tab of the Table Properties InfoBox to set table margins. The margins you set appear on all sides between the table text and the table border; alternatively, you can set each individual margin. Figure 17.10 shows options in the Size and Margins tab and margins in the sample table.

Fig. 17.10
Set all margins the
same or choose
Margin Options
to set them
individually.

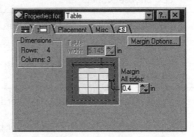

To set margins around the table, type the amount of margin space you want in the Margin All Sides text box. If you prefer to set each margin individually, click the Margin Options button. In the Margin Options dialog box, type the amount of margin space you want in the Top, Left, Bottom, and/or Right text boxes. Click OK to close the dialog box and return to the InfoBox.

Setting Alignment and Wrap

Use the Placement tab of the Table Properties InfoBox to set table alignment and text wrap options. Additionally, you can choose to anchor the table. *Anchoring* the table means to attach it to a specific point in the text or on the page so the table does not move, even if the text around it does move. Figure 17.11 shows the Placement tab and table 17.4 explains the Placement options.

Fig. 17.11
The controls in
the Placement tab
enable you to
position the table
on the page to suit
your document.

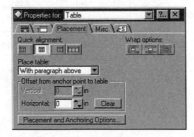

Table 17.4 Placement Options	
Option	**Description**
Quick Alignment	Positions the table in relation to the left and right margins; the first button aligns the table to the left margin, the second button centers it, the third button aligns it to the right margin, and the fourth button spans the table from the left margin to the right.
Wrap Options	Wraps the surrounding text around the table; the first button wraps on one side only, the second button wraps top and bottom (no sides), and the third button doesn't wrap but runs the text through the table.
Place Table	Indicates how the table is anchored and placed: With Paragraph Above, On All Pages, On Left/Right Pages, In Text, Same Page As Text, On Current Page, or In Text-Vertical.
Offset from Anchor Point to Table	Indicates the amount of space to compensate vertically or horizontally.
Placement and Anchoring Options	Enable you to click the area on a figure of the page to place and anchor the table.

Setting Miscellaneous Options

The Misc tab of the Table Properties InfoBox offers cell and table protection. Figure 17.12 shows the options in the Misc tab of the InfoBox.

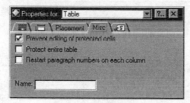

Fig. 17.12
Protect cells or the entire table using the Misc tab.

To protect the table, click the Protect Entire Table option in the Misc tab. Alternatively, you can prevent editing of specific cells by first selecting the cells before you open the Table Properties InfoBox. Then in the Misc tab, click the Prevent Editing of Protected Cells option.

Using Table Styles

You can use *table styles* to format table size, positioning, lines, colors, margins, and so on, and *table cell styles* to format the cell properties. You create and redefine styles in the Style tab of the Table or Table Cell Properties InfoBox. Figure 17.13 shows the Style tab of the Table Properties InfoBox.

Fig. 17.13
Create styles to use in your tables so you need to format a table only one time.

Style tab

◄ See "Using Paragraph Styles," p. 102

◄ See "Managing Styles," p. 257

To create a new table style, follow these steps:

1. Select the formatted table.

2. Right-click the table to reveal the quick menu and choose Table Properties. The Table Properties InfoBox appears.

3. In the Style tab of the Table Properties InfoBox, click Create Style.

4. In the Create Style dialog box, type the Style Name to represent the table. Enter a Description, if you want.

5. Choose the Hierarchy command button. The Style Hierarchy Definition dialog box appears (see fig. 17.14).

Fig. 17.14
Choose specific table properties to include in the style using the Style Hierarchy Definition dialog box.

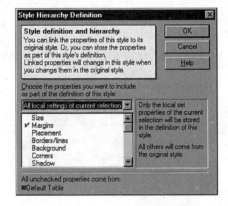

6. In the Choose the Properties You Want... list box, select the formatted properties you want to include with the saved styles.

7. Click OK to return to the Create Style dialog box.

8. Click OK to accept the new style. The style now appears in the Style list in the Style tab of the Table Properties InfoBox.

To use the style, select any table in your document and double-click the style from the Style list in the Style tab. The properties are then assigned to the selected table.

Formatting Table Cells

The Table Cell Properties InfoBox offers several options you can use to format table cells. The Lines and Colors tab, for example, is similar to the Lines and Colors tab of the Table Properties InfoBox. The only difference is in the line options. Additionally, the table cell styles work similarly to the table styles. To access the Table Cell Properties InfoBox, right-click any table cell and choose Cell Properties from the quick menu.

> **Note**
>
> For more information about the Style tab, see the previous section, "Using Table Styles." For more information about the Misc tab, refer to the section "Setting Miscellaneous Text Options" in Chapter 20, "Using Advanced Frame Techniques."

Adding Lines around Cells

The Lines and Colors tab of the Table Cell Properties InfoBox is very similar to the same tab in the Table Properties InfoBox. You can choose from lists of line styles, line widths, background color, line color, and so on. Figure 17.15 illustrates the Lines and Colors tab.

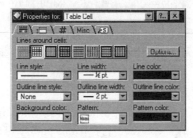

Fig. 17.15
Use the Lines and Colors tab of the Table Cell Properties InfoBox to apply lines and colors to individual or selected cells.

The lines and colors you select in the Table Cell Properties InfoBox apply only to selected cells, not to the entire table. To apply lines and colors to selected cells, follow these steps:

1. Select the cell or cells to format.

2. Choose from the following Lines around Cells options: No Lines, Lines Inside and Outside Selected Cells, Outline Only, Bold Outline and Lighter Inside Lines, Horizontal Lines Only, Vertical Lines Only, Horizontal Lines Plus Bold Outline, or Vertical Lines Plus Bold Outline. To assign other outline options, click the Options button.

3. Make any other selections in the tab as described in the earlier section, "Setting Lines and Colors."

Formatting Cell Contents

You can format cells to display the contents in specific ways, such as currency, percentages, text, and so on. Use the Format tab of the Table Cell Properties InfoBox to format cell contents. Figure 17.16 shows the Format tab.

Fig. 17.16
Format cell contents to display currency, percentages, or whatever type of data you want.

Format tab

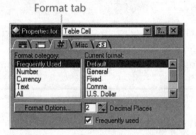

> **Tip**
>
> If you want to add a format to the Frequently Used list so it's easier to find, select the format and then click the Frequently Used option at the bottom of the Format tab.

To format cell contents, select the contents of the cells and choose the Format tab of the Table Cell Properties InfoBox. In the Format Category, choose from Frequently Used, Number, Currency, Text, or All.

In the Current Format list box, a list of related formats appears; for example, if you choose Number as the category, formats such as Fixed, Comma, Percent, and Scientific appear. Select the format you want and then select the number of Decimal Places, if applicable.

Using Formulas in Tables

> **Tip**
>
> To view column and row headings so you can easily identify addresses, choose <u>V</u>iew, Set <u>V</u>iew Preferences. Choose the Sho<u>w</u> tab and then choose Show Ta<u>b</u>le Row/Col. Headings and click OK.

In tables, you can use formulas that add, subtract, multiply, and use sums and percents for numbers. Word Pro performs the calculation and enters the results into the formula cell. When using formulas in cells, you must use addresses to refer to the cells. A *cell address* consists of the column letter plus the row number, such as A1 or B4.

Creating Formulas

The formulas you use are similar to those used in common spreadsheet programs. Any simple or common formula you use in 1-2-3, for example, can be used in Word Pro. You can, for example, choose a Sum @function that looks like this: @SUM(B2..B4). The SUM @function adds cells B2 through B4; the two periods indicate a range. An averaging formula may look like this: @AVG(B4..D4). Place the formula in the cell in which you want the answer to appear. If you change any figures in the range, the answer automatically changes as well.

To insert formulas in a table, follow these steps:

1. Position the insertion point in the cell where you want to place the formula.

2. Choose Table, Insert Formula. The Insert Formula dialog box appears (see fig. 17.17).

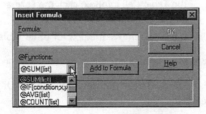

Fig. 17.17
Insert formulas in tables to perform your calculations automatically.

3. Enter the formula you want in the <u>F</u>ormula text box, or select a formula from the @<u>F</u>unctions drop-down list.

4. If you choose from the @Functions drop-down list, you must modify the formula by adding cell addresses. Click the Add to Formula button. The selected formula now appears in the Formula text box.

5. Type the cell range or other values to the formula in place of the word *list*, and click OK. The result appears in the selected cell.

Editing Formulas

You sometimes may need to edit the formulas in your table. You can easily edit any formula by right-clicking the formula's cell. From the quick menu, choose Edit Formula. The Insert Formula dialog box appears, which enables you to edit the formula. (An alternative is to click the Edit Formula in Table Cell SmartIcon to display the Insert Formula dialog box.)

Using SmartSum

SmartSum is a shortcut for adding the numbers in a row or a column. You can quickly and easily insert the formula and total the results. To use SmartSum, select the cell where you want the result to appear. Choose Table, Insert SmartSum, and then choose either Row or Column. Word Pro assumes the values you want to add are those in succession preceding the selected cell.

> ### Troubleshooting
>
> *I have a formula in a table cell but the only result I get is REF. What am I doing wrong?*
>
> REF stands for reference; you've referred to a number cell in the formula and Word Pro cannot understand the contents of the cell. Check all numbers in the referenced cells and try again. You may need to change the referenced cells or change the formula.
>
> *I want to use a specific symbol before all the numbers in my table, but I can't find that symbol in the list of formats. Is there anything I can do?*
>
> Yes, in the Format tab of the Table Cell InfoBox, click the Format Options button; enter the text before or after and then choose OK. Later, you can choose the Reset button in that same dialog box to remove the text for other tables.
>
> *I've anchored my table to some unknown text that I can't find. How can I unanchor it?*
>
> In the Table Properties InfoBox, choose the Placement tab. In Offset from Anchor Point to Table, choose Clear.

Charting with Word Pro

Word Pro includes a charting feature that enables you to create simple charts to enhance your documents. You can choose the chart type, add a legend and grid, change some chart types to three-dimensional, and apply various colors to the data series markers (the columns in a column chart or the slices in a pie chart, for example).

> **Tip**
>
> If you want to create a chart using data from a table or spreadsheet, copy the data to the Clipboard. When you choose to create a chart, Word Pro then enables you to paste the copied data.

To create a chart, follow these steps:

1. Create a frame the size of the chart and choose <u>C</u>reate, <u>C</u>hart. Word Pro displays the Create Chart dialog box (see fig. 17.18).

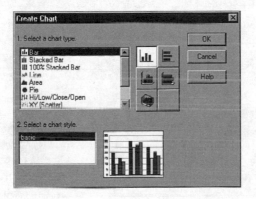

Fig. 17.18
Choose your chart type and style before entering the data.

Accelerating Your WP

2. In list 1, choose a chart type from the following types:

   ■ *Bar, Stacked Bar,* or *100% Stacked Bar.* Represents data by the height or length of each bar; this type of chart is valuable for comparing one item to another or comparing different items over a period of time.

   ■ *Line* or *Area.* Consists of a series of points that are connected by a line or shaded area; the movement of the line or area indicates a trend over a period of time.

■ *Pie.* Consists of a round, pie shape with different colored wedges; each piece or wedge shows a data segment and its relationship to other parts and to the whole.

■ *Hi/Low/Close/Open.* Used to express a range of values for a single item in a particular time period, such as stock market information, currency, weather.

■ *XY (Scatter).* Shows trends or patterns and how the variables affect each other using lines or data points; useful for developing a conclusion to the relationship of two or more variables.

After selecting a chart type, to the right of the chart type list, choose a button that best describes the view you want of the chart.

3. In list 2, choose a chart style; a sample appears in the preview box next to the list.

4. Choose OK. The Edit Data dialog box appears (see fig. 17.19).

Fig. 17.19
Entering data in the Edit Data dialog box is similar to entering data in a spreadsheet application.

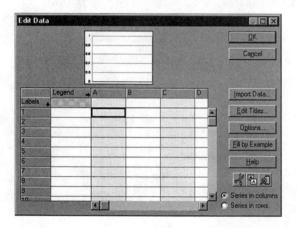

5. Type the labels and data in the worksheet or choose the Import Data button to import data from any file or application; import data from a spreadsheet application or a table. As you enter data, notice data is added to the sample chart at the top of the dialog box.

6. Choose Edit Titles to enter a chart title, axis titles, or notes. Choose Edit Data to return to the worksheet.

7. Choose OK to close the dialog box and create the chart.

To edit the chart at any time, double-click the chart; the Properties InfoBox appears. In the Properties InfoBox, choose the down arrow beside Properties to select from the following properties to edit: chart, title, legend, axes, series, notes, plot, labels, or table. Each property displays different tabs from which to choose, such as Fonts, Lines and Colors, Style, Format, and so on; each tab is similar to those you've worked with in the Table and Table Cells Properties InfoBoxes.

From Here...

Now that you understand tables, you can move on to other Word Pro features that can help you create and format your documents. Take a look at the following chapters:

- Chapter 19, "Using Frames," shows you how to create and edit a frame as well as how to fill a frame with text and graphics. You can even place a table within a frame for ease of movement and use.

- Chapter 21, "Using Draw," shows you how to use Word Pro's drawing applet to create objects, edit drawings and clip art, work with text in a drawing, and import objects to a drawing.

- Chapter 22, "Desktop Publishing with Word Pro," teaches you to use design strategies when planning and creating documents so they are readable and interesting. Additionally, this chapter explains the design elements and how to organize an attractive page.

II

Accelerating Your WP

Chapter 18

Merging Data

by Lisa Bucki

Before automation, if you wanted to send a personalized form letter to a list of people, you had to type every letter individually. Most of the information in each letter was the same, but each person's name and address—and perhaps other information, such as specific information about the product the person purchased—needed to be changed for each letter.

Merges eliminate much of the unnecessary labor in this process. In a Word Pro merge, you create a *merge document* with the information that is the same in each letter. You insert special codes in the merge document to tell Word Pro where the variable information (data) belongs. Later, when you tell Word Pro to perform the merge, the program uses these special codes to insert the data—customizing each individual letter.

Merges are appropriate for more than just letters. Any time you want to create a standard document with data that varies, you should consider using a merge. You can merge to create mailing labels, contracts, proposals, and many other kinds of documents, as well as letters.

In this chapter, you learn how to:

- Use Word Pro's automated merge procedure to create merge data files to hold the names, addresses, and other information you want to merge

- Create the merge document to accept your merge data, and specify where to insert the merge data

- Combine merge documents and data files to create finished documents

- Merge only the records you select in your data file

Understanding Merge

A merge combines changing information with information that has not changed. It combines variable text and a document with fixed text and formatting to produce a set of finished documents.

Word Pro has always had the capacity to merge data. In earlier versions, however, you had to set up the merge document and data file manually. The previous version of Word Pro (called Ami Pro) added an easy-to-use, automated procedure for creating both data files and merge documents. Word Pro's new Merge Assistant streamlines the process even further. The Merge Assistant dialog box, shown in figure 18.1, walks you through the entire process of compiling your merge data, creating the merge document, and performing and printing the final merge.

Fig. 18.1
The Merge Assistant dialog box walks you through the process of creating merge data files and document files.

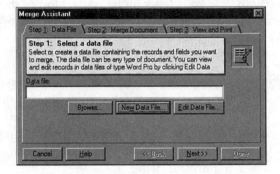

You start a merge by creating or selecting two documents. One document contains *data*. Data, as the term is used in Word Pro merge operations, is information that varies in each finished document—such as the names and addresses of people to whom a form letter will be sent. Word Pro calls the specially formatted document containing this data the *data file*. You can also use data from a database management program (such as dBASE) or from a spreadsheet (such as Excel or Lotus 1-2-3). If you use a database or spreadsheet as your source of data, however, you don't need an Word Pro data file. The database or spreadsheet file serves as the data file.

Word Pro organizes each data file into *fields*. Each field contains one type of information. In a list of customers, for example, you may have a last name field, a first name field, a street address field, and so on.

The second document contains fixed information—information that is the same in every finished document—as well as the information you merge with the fixed text. Fixed information usually includes standard text (such as the text of a form letter), the formatting, and any graphic elements you specify.

The document with the fixed information is the *merge document.* The merge document includes not only the standard text and formatting codes, but also special codes called *merge fields.* The merge fields tell Word Pro where in the finished document to insert the data from each field.

After you create these two documents, you tell Word Pro to merge the documents. Word Pro responds by creating a set of finished documents. For example, if you have ten records in the data file, Word Pro creates ten finished documents. Each finished document contains the following:

- The standard text from the merge document

- The formatting from the merge document

- The data pertaining to one item, or *record*, from the data file list (if the list represents customers, for example, each finished document includes the name, address, and any other fields with data for one customer or record)

◀ See "Editing Text," p. 66

◀ See "Formatting Text," p. 79

You must create or select the data file first to set up the merge, because you use the fields in the data file to create the merge document. You can also insert the merge fields in an existing document you select. Producing a simple merge requires three basic steps:

1. Create the data document or choose an existing data document.

2. Create or select the merge document and insert merge fields into it.

3. Instruct Word Pro to merge the two documents and print the resulting documents.

To begin the merge process, you open the Text menu and choose Merge. Word Pro displays the Merge Assistant dialog box (refer to fig. 18.1). Notice that the three tabs in this dialog box correspond to the three steps to create a merge. Word Pro keeps track of where you are in the merge process, and the selected tab in the Merge Assistant dialog box reflects the step you need to complete next.

II

Accelerating Your WP

Tip

If you want to create a brand new merge document, make sure that you create a new document and select a style sheet for it before you display the Merge Assistant dialog box.

Word Pro leads you through each of the steps in the merge process and the Merge Assistant dialog box, as described in the next few sections in this chapter. You can use the Back and Next buttons or click a particular tab to move to a different step in the merge process. To close the Merge Assistant dialog box without finishing the merge, click the Cancel button. To finish the merge from any tab, click the Done button.

Creating a Merge Data File

The first step in performing a merge operation is to create the data file—the file into which you insert the variable information. (To use an existing data file, see the section later in this chapter called "Using an Existing Data File.") This process involves two major steps: defining the names of the fields, and entering the data for each *record* (all the fields for one single entry, such as one customer).

For maximum flexibility in merging and sorting data, break down the data into fields that are as specific as possible; you'll use the field names later to tie the data to the merge document. For example, create separate fields for the first and last name rather than using one field for the whole name (in which case, you won't be able to sort by the last name only). Also be sure to include a field for every possible item of data. If some addresses fit on one line and others require two lines, for example, define two fields—*Address 1* and *Address 2*. Make field names long enough to be descriptive, but not overly long. For a last name field, *LN* is probably too cryptic, and *Last name of the client* too long. *Last Name* and *Last* are good compromises for the field name.

To create a new merge data file, follow these steps:

1. Open the Text menu and choose the Merge command. Or, if you've added it to the current iconbar, click the Merge Assistant SmartIcon (it looks like a yellow traffic merge sign). The Merge Assistant dialog box appears (refer to fig. 18.1).

2. Make sure the Step 1: Data File tab is selected. If not, click to select that tab.

3. Click the New Data File button. Word Pro displays the Create Data File dialog box (see fig. 18.2). Because you haven't defined field names for this data file, the Fields for New Data File area is blank. The cursor is in the Field Name text box; Word Pro is waiting for you to type a field name.

Enter a field name here

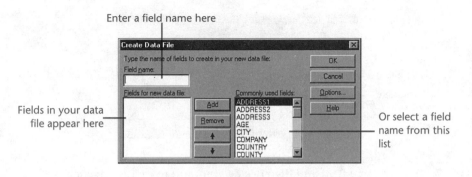

Fields in your data
file appear here

Or select a field
name from this
list

Fig. 18.2
Use the Create
Data File dialog
box to create the
fields for your data
file; Word Pro even
offers a list of
common fields
you can use.

4. If you want to use one of the fields Word Pro suggests, scroll through
   the Commonly Used Fields list and click the name of the field you
   want. Otherwise, type the name of the first field in the Field Name text
   box. You can use letters, numbers, and spaces, but the first character
   must be a letter or an underscore character. (Capitalization doesn't
   matter.)

> **Note**
>
> You can enter field names in any order in the data file. You should include a
> field to enable you to track the order in which you enter the records. If the
> data file is a customer address list, for example, you may want to include a
> Customer Number field. When you enter the records for the data file, you
> would enter **001** in the Customer Number field for the first customer record
> you enter, **002** for the second customer, and so on. Whenever you want to
> restore the records to the original order, you can sort by the Customer Num-
> ber field.

5. After you select or type the field name, click the Add button. Word Pro
   moves the field name you selected or typed to the Fields for New Data
   File list box. It also clears the Field Name text box to prepare it for the
   next field name.

6. Repeat steps 4 and 5 to add the rest of the fields. After you finish entering the fields, the dialog box may resemble figure 18.3. Because the
   example contains more fields than can fit in the Fields for New Data
   File list box, you can scroll through the list to find a field to select.

II

Accelerating Your WP

Fig. 18.3

After you've added fields to your data file, you can change a field's position or delete a field.

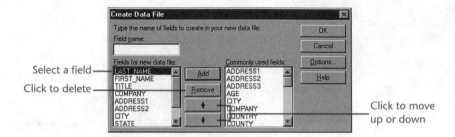

Select a field

Click to delete

Click to move up or down

7. If you enter a field and then decide you want to remove it, click the field to select it in the Fields for New Data File list box. Then click the Remove button. The field disappears from the list.

> **Tip**
>
> To edit a field name, you can delete the field and then retype the field name as you want it to appear.

8. The order of fields in the data file doesn't really matter because you can use the data in any order in the merge document. You may want to keep fields in a certain order, however, to make data entry more convenient. If you're creating a data file for your phone list, for example, you may want the *Work Phone* and *Fax Number* fields to be close together. Word Pro uses the first field on the list to help you identify data as you enter records (more on this shortly).

   To change the position of a field in the Fields for new data file list, click the field you want to move to select it in the list. Then click the large up-arrow or down-arrow button. Each time you click the arrow button, the field name moves up or down one position in the list box.

At this point, the data file isn't finished. You may want to specify *delimiters* for your data file. And you'll definitely need to enter the data for each record into your data file. You continue on to each of these operations directly from the Create Data File dialog box (without closing it first). Read the next two sections to learn how to perform each of these operations.

Specifying Field and Record Delimiters

By default, Word Pro uses the tilde (~) and the vertical bar (|) as *delimiters* in data files. Delimiters tell Word Pro where one field ends and the next field begins, and where one record ends and the next record begins. You don't need to know much about delimiters unless you plan to edit the data file directly (a practice that isn't recommended). However, you need to make sure that Word Pro's delimiter characters are different from characters appearing in your data. In other words, if there's any chance that some of your field entries will contain a tilde (~) or vertical bar (|), you must specify other characters as delimiters. If neither of these characters exists in the data, you can skip ahead to the next section.

> **Caution**
>
> The field delimiter and record delimiter characters cannot be the same.

To change the delimiter characters, follow these steps:

1. In the Create Data File dialog box (refer to fig. 18.3), click the Options button. The Data File Options dialog box appears (see fig. 18.4).

Fig. 18.4
Use the Data File Options dialog box to change the delimiters for fields and records.

2. To change the Field Delimiter, click the down arrow beside the text box to display a drop-down list of delimiter choices. Scroll to display the character you want, and then click to select it, which closes the list.

3. To change the Record Delimiter, click the down arrow beside text box to display a drop-down list of delimiter choices. Scroll to display the character you want, and then click to select it, which closes the list.

4. After you define the delimiters, choose OK or press Enter to close the Data File Options dialog box and return to the Create Data File dialog box.

At this point, you should be ready to begin entering the data for your data file. Continue on to the next section to learn how to do so.

Creating Data and Saving the Data File

After you set up the fields for your data file, you need to finish creating the data file by entering the data for each record into the fields and then saving your data file. After you've created the fields you want in the Create Data File dialog box, click the OK button to begin entering data. The Edit Data File dialog box appears, as shown in figure 18.5.

Fig. 18.5
Enter information
into the fields for
each record in the
Edit Data File
dialog box.

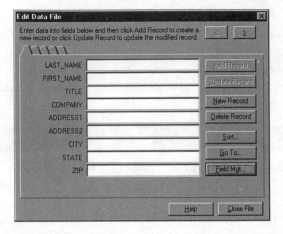

Notice that the Edit Data File dialog box looks like a series of tabbed Rolodex cards. On the top card, you can see the field names you created earlier. All you can see of the cards behind the first card is a set of blank tabs. Each tab represents one record in a data file; because you haven't entered any data, all the tabs are blank. Each tab displays the field names you specified earlier. If all the fields fit on a single card, all of them appear. If more fields exist than space on the card, the field names continue on subsequent pages of the card.

To enter data in the fields on the card, type the entry for the first field in the first text box. For example, if you're creating a contact list, type the first person's first name in the First_Name text box (see fig. 18.6).

Fig. 18.6
Type the data for
each field in a
record in the field
text boxes.

Type an entry,
and then tab to
the next field

Click to add the
record to the
data file

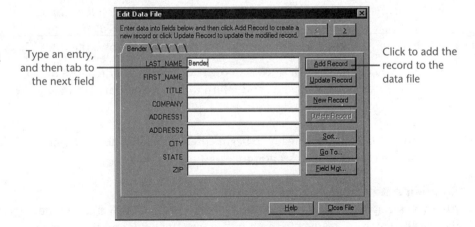

To move to the next field, press Tab or click in the text box for the field. To move back to a previous field, press Shift+Tab. Continue moving from field to field and entering data. Leave a field blank if the record contains no data of that type; for example, if a person in a contact list you're creating is a casual acquaintance for whom you don't want to use a job title, leave the Title field blank.

> **Tip**
>
> If your card contains more than one page, you can move to the second page of the card by clicking the Scroll Fields Up and Scroll Fields Down arrows.

After you enter data in the last field on the last page of the tab, click the <u>A</u>dd Record button. Word Pro "files" the card you just completed. To create a new record, click the <u>N</u>ew Record button. Notice that the first record moves behind the new (blank) record. The tab for the record you added shows the text you entered into the first field for that record; because the Last_Name field appears first for each record, the tab for the record just added displays "Bender" to identify the record. Enter the field text for new records in the same way that you entered the first record (see fig. 18.7).

The tab for each added record shows the first field

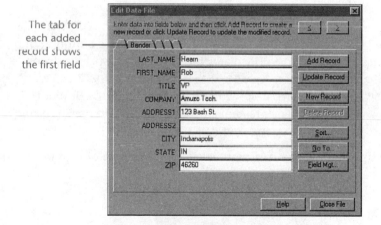

Fig. 18.7
With one record added to your data file, you're ready to begin making the entries for another record.

Troubleshooting

I entered information in a field in the Edit Data File dialog box, but the entry is too long to fit in the field. Did I lose part of the entry?

Don't worry. The data file contains the entire field entry, even though you cannot view the entire name at one time on the card. To see the rest of the field entry, click in the field text box and then press the right-arrow and left-arrow keys as needed.

After you enter a few records in the data file, you may want to move around in the data file to insert records, edit existing records, or delete records. You can move around in a data file, one record at a time, by clicking the left- or right-arrow button in the upper right area of the Edit Data File dialog box. You can go directly to a specific record by clicking the record's tab.

By default, Word Pro inserts new records at the beginning of the data file. Word Pro displays a blank record. Complete the record and click the Add Record button. The new record is added at the beginning of the file.

To delete a record, click its tab to select it, then click the Delete Record button. To change an existing record, display the record, make the changes, and click the Update Record button. Word Pro replaces the existing record in the data file with the revised record.

When you're finished adding records to your data file, close the Edit Data File dialog box and save your data file. To do so, click the Close File button in the lower left corner of the Edit Data File dialog box. Word Pro displays a dialog box asking whether you want to save the data file (see fig. 18.8). Click Yes. The Save As dialog box appears. If needed, use the Save In list to tell Word Pro where to save the file, then enter a name for the data file in the File Name text box. Click Save to finish saving your data file.

Word Pro returns to the Merge Assistant dialog box. The name of your newly saved data file appears in the Data File text box (see fig. 18.9).

Fig. 18.8
Saving your new data file.

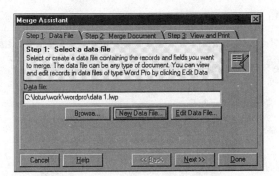

Fig. 18.9
The Merge
Assistant dialog
box displays the
name of the data
file you've just
created and saved.

Editing Data Files

While you're working in the Edit Data File dialog box, you can perform several operations in addition to the basics of adding and editing records. You can sort the data file records, go directly to a particular record, or even change the arrangement of the fields.

Even if you go on to the next step in merging (creating the merge document), you always can come back to the data file and add, delete, or change records by clicking the Edit Data File button in the Step 1: Data File tab of the Merge Assistant dialog box. The Merge Assistant displays the Edit Data File dialog box with the tabs for your data file records.

The next three sections describe how to use the sorting, Go To, and field editing features of the Edit Data File dialog box.

Sorting Data

You can sort the records in a data file. You can sort on any field, in ascending order (A to Z and 1 to 9) or descending order (Z to A and 9 to 1). If the data includes numbers, you can also sort numerically or alphanumerically.

Suppose that the following numbers are in the data file: 10, 22, 3, 20, 1, 12, 11, 21, and 2. *Numeric sorts* look at each set of digits as a numeric quantity. With a numeric sort, Word Pro sorts the numbers in numeric sequence: 1, 2, 3, 10, 11, 12, 20, 21, 22. *Alphanumeric sorts* look at each digit as an individual character. With an alphanumeric sort, Word Pro produces the sequence 1, 10, 11, 12, 2, 20, 21, 22, 3. Usually, you sort numeric data (such as ZIP codes) numerically.

To sort the data file, follow these steps:

1. Display the Edit Data File dialog box, if it's not already displayed.

2. Click the Sort button. The Sort Records dialog box appears (see fig. 18.10).

Fig. 18.10
The Sort Records dialog box enables you to decide what order to display records in to determine the order in which the records are merged.

3. To select the field you want to sort, click the down-arrow button at the right of the Sort by Field text box to display a drop-down list of fields. Click the field you want to select it, which closes the list.

4. The default sort type is Alphanumeric. To sort numerically, click the Numeric option button.

5. The default sort order is Ascending. To sort in descending order, click the Descending option button.

6. When the options are set correctly, click OK. Word Pro sorts the data file.

When you sort the data file, Word Pro displays on the tabs of the cards the first few characters of the field on which you sorted. If you sort by Last Name, for example, the cards appear as shown in figure 18.11. If you sort by a field other than the first, you can redisplay the first field in the tabs by sorting the data file by the first field.

Fig. 18.11
The data file tabs display the sorted field entries.

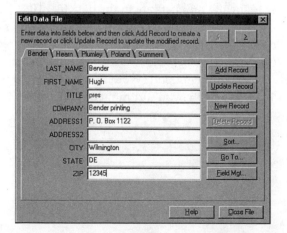

This automated sort procedure enables you to perform simple sorts, such as sorts on a single field. If you need to perform a multilevel sort, sort the least important field first, then sort the next most significant field. Continue until you have sorted all the relevant fields. If you want to sort clients by company, last name, and first name, for example, sort by the least important field—first name. Then sort by the next most important field—last name. Finally, sort by the most important field—company.

Go To a Record

To go directly to a record that doesn't appear in the Edit Data File dialog box, search for the record by clicking the <u>G</u>o To button. Word Pro displays the Go To Record dialog box (see fig. 18.12).

Fig. 18.12
Go to any record or the first or last record in your data file.

This dialog box contains three options: <u>S</u>pecific Record, <u>F</u>irst Record, and <u>L</u>ast Record. <u>F</u>irst Record and <u>L</u>ast Record go to the first and last record, respectively. The <u>S</u>pecific Record option searches for a record with field contents matching the field contents you specify.

To search for a record in a particular field matching the contents you specify, click the down arrow to display the <u>S</u>pecific Record drop-down list. In the list, click the name of the field that holds the contents you want to display. Clicking selects the field name and closes the list. Then type the contents you want to match in the text box to the right of the drop-down list. If you are looking for a record with the last name *Meyerson*, for example, just type **Meyerson** in the text box (capitalization doesn't matter). Click OK. If a matching record exists, Word Pro displays its tab; otherwise, Word Pro displays a dialog box indicating that no match exists.

Keep in mind the following points:

■ By default, Word Pro matches only complete words. (The word doesn't need to be the first word in the field; however, it must be a complete word.) Word Pro doesn't find *Meyerson* if you type **Meyer**. To search for a complete word, using only part of the word in the search, type the part of the word for which you want to search, and then add an asterisk (*). The asterisk matches any group of letters; *Meyer** matches Meyer, Meyerson, and Meyersen.

■ Word Pro always searches from the top tab and therefore always finds the first record that matches the search. If you have two Smith records, for example, Word Pro always finds the first one. The only way to find the second Smith is to search on some unique field, such as a Social Security number.

To go to the first or last record in the data file, select the First Record or Last Record option, and then click the OK button.

Changing Fields

When you're entering data, you may realize that you forgot to define a field that you need, or you may decide you need to delete or move a field. You can make changes to your data file fields by starting from the Edit Data File dialog box. To make changes to your data file fields, follow these steps:

1. Click the Field Mgt button in the Edit Data File dialog box. The Create Data File dialog box appears (see fig. 18.13).

Fig. 18.13
The Create Data File dialog box enables you to make changes to your data file fields.

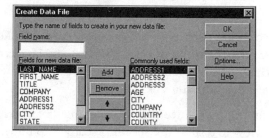

2. In the Fields For New Data File list box, select the field you want to work with. If you're inserting a new field, it will appear at the end of the list.

3. Depending on whether you're moving, renaming, or deleting the field, use one of the following actions:

   ■ Click the Remove button to delete the selected field.

   ■ To move the selected field up or down in the list of fields, click either the up- or down-arrow button next to the Fields For New Data File list box.

■ To add a field, type the name of the new field you're adding in the Field Name text box. (Alternatively, you can click a field in the list of suggested fields at the right side of the dialog box.) Click the Add button.

4. Click OK. Word Pro returns to the Edit Data File dialog box, displaying your field name changes.

In the Edit Data File dialog box, Word Pro updates all the tabs to reflect the data file changes you've made. If you made a field name change, that change appears on all the tabs. If you deleted a field, the field and the contents you entered are removed from all the tabs. If you added a new field, it appears on each of the tabs as a blank field text box, ready to accept new data.

Using an Existing Data File

Keeping data in a Word Pro data file document and using that data in merges is a satisfactory solution if your data management needs are relatively simple. However, dedicated database and spreadsheet programs have much richer capabilities for managing data. But these applications can't compare with Word Pro when combining data with standard text and presenting the combined information in a nicely formatted style.

Fortunately, Word Pro enables you to use its own data files plus the following types of files (created by many of the most popular database and spreadsheet programs) as data files for a Word Pro merge:

1-2-3 (through Release 5 for DOS and Windows)

Ami Pro

MS Word for Windows 1, 2, and 6

Comma-delimited or fixed-length ASCII

dBASE II, III, and IV

Data Interchange Format (DIF)

Microsoft Excel (through version 5.0)

Lotus Organizer lists

You don't have to convert the files or import them into Word Pro. You simply tell Word Pro what kind of file you're using, and then set up the merge as usual.

> **Note**
>
> If you have data in an application not listed in this section, you may be able to import the data into a Word Pro table and then use the table as your data file. See Chapter 25, "Importing, Exporting, and Linking Files," for information on importing data into Word Pro.

To use an external data file, Word Pro must have field names for the data in that file. For some formats, you may need to supply a *description file* that tells Word Pro what kind of file is being used and the names of the fields in that file.

In many cases, Word Pro can determine the field names. If the external file is a database file from dBASE, Word Pro uses the field names stored in that file; you don't need a description file. If the external file is a spreadsheet file or an ASCII file, and the first record in the file contains the field names, you can tell Word Pro to use the first record as the description file.

To use another data file, in the Step 1: Data File tab of the Merge Assistant, click the Browse button. In the Files of Type list box, click the kind of data file you want to use (see fig. 18.14) to select that type, and then close the list. Change to the drive or directory in which your file is stored. Click the name of the file you want to use in the Look in list box, then click Open.

Fig. 18.14
Select a data file type, and then select the data file itself.

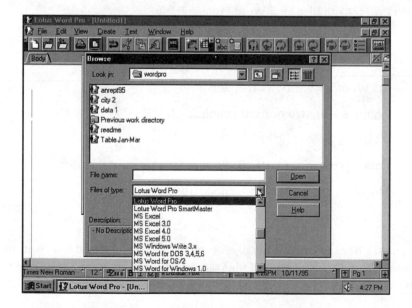

Using a Word Pro Table for Data

You can use a Word Pro table as your data file. When you use a table, each *row* of the table represents one record and each *column* represents one field. You don't supply delimiters if you use a table—Word Pro uses the table formatting to organize the document into records and fields. You must supply field names, however, by entering the field names in the top row in the table. The first record appears in the second row of the table.

◀ See "Creating Tables," p. 327

> **Caution**
>
> When you use a Word Pro table as a data file, the table must begin on the first page of the first division of the document and must be the only contents of the division.

To use a table as a merge data file, create the table, enter the field names, enter the data, and save the file. Click the <u>B</u>rowse button in the Merge Assistant dialog box to select the Word Pro file that contains the table. Keep in mind the following conditions:

- You can use a page table or a frame table. *Page tables* enable you to enter as many records as you want. *Frame tables* restrict you to the number of records that fit on a single page.

- Word Pro considers each table column a field.

- If the table contains blank rows, Word Pro ignores them.

- You can increase or decrease the columns or the rows later.

- When Word Pro reads the data in the table during the merge, any formatting specified in the table is ignored.

- The first row of the table must contain field names, one field name per column. The field names can wrap to more than one line if necessary.

- Type the data beginning in the second row. Put each record on a separate row, with the record fields in the appropriate columns. Data can wrap to more than one line if necessary.

Creating the Merge Document

When you finish creating the data file (or selecting one you've previously created), you are ready for the second major step in merge operations: creating the merge document (the file that contains the standard information and formatting). To begin the process, click the Step <u>2</u>: Merge Document tab, or click the <u>N</u>ext button in the Merge Assistant dialog box. Figure 18.15 shows the contents of this tab.

Fig. 18.15

The second tab in the Merge Assistant dialog box enables you to specify and set up the merge document.

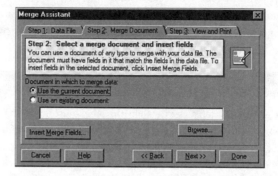

Creating the merge document involves two major steps:

1. Specify whether to use the current file or a previously saved file as the basis for the merge document.

2. Insert the merge fields into the document, create or edit the document's fixed text, and format the text in the merge document.

The next two sections provide the details for creating and setting up the merge document. If you have a merge document format you use often, enter the standard information, formatting, and merge fields; then save the document as a SmartMaster with contents. Chapter 12, "Working with SmartMasters," offers information on saving new style sheets.

Assigning the Merge Document

In the second tab of the Merge Assistant dialog box (refer to fig. 18.15), Word Pro enables you to specify the document in which to merge data. By default, the Use the <u>C</u>urrent Document (Untitled) option button is selected. If you want to use the current document, simply proceed to the next section to begin inserting the merge fields and fine-tuning the merge document text.

If, on the other hand, you want to use a Word Pro document that you previously saved as the merge document, click the Use an E<u>x</u>isting Document option button. Then click the <u>B</u>rowse button to display the Browse dialog box. Navigate to the location where you saved the file you want. Click the desired file in the Look <u>I</u>n list, and then click <u>O</u>pen. The Browse dialog box closes, and the Step <u>2</u>: Merge Document tab displays the name of the file you selected.

At this point, you're ready to insert the merge fields in the merge document.

Inserting Merge Fields

After you've specified the merge document in the Step <u>2</u>: Merge Document tab of the Merge Assistant dialog box, click the Insert <u>M</u>erge Fields button.

If you selected a data file that's in a format other than Word Pro data, Word Pro displays the Merge Data File Fields dialog box. If the first record (for example, the first spreadsheet row) in the data file contains the names of the fields, simply click OK to accept the default option (Field Names in the first record of the data file). Otherwise, use the Create Description File button to create a description file, then specify the field names and click OK. Or use the Field Names Listed In option button plus the <u>B</u>rowse button to specify a description file. After you finish this process, close the Merge Data File Fields dialog box by clicking OK, and proceed with the rest of the merge operation.

Word Pro closes the Merge Assistant dialog box and displays the merge document with the modeless Merge bar at the top of the screen (see fig. 18.16).

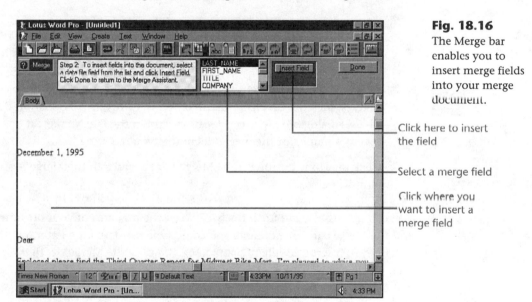

Fig. 18.16
The Merge bar enables you to insert merge fields into your merge document.

Click here to insert the field

Select a merge field

Click where you want to insert a merge field

To insert merge fields in the document, follow these steps:

1. If you're working in a new document, begin typing text in the document.

2. Click to position the insertion point where you want to insert a merge field.

> **Tip**
>
> You can use a merge field more than once in a merge document. For example, you can use a First_Name field in both the address portion and salutation of a letter.

3. Scroll through the list of merge fields in the Merge bar. Word Pro lists the field names in the order you specified in the Create Data File dialog box. Any spaces used in the field names have been replaced by underscores in the Insert Merge Field dialog box. Click the name of the merge field you want to insert.

4. Click the Insert Field button on the Merge bar. Word Pro inserts the specified field in the document. The field name appears in the document between angle brackets (<>).

5. Continue typing and editing text. Repeat steps 2–4 to insert merge fields wherever you want.

6. Apply any formatting you want to the fixed text and the merge fields.

7. Save the merge document. To do so, open the File menu and choose Save, or click the Save File SmartIcon on the Universal iconbar. In the Save As dialog box, specify a location, and in the File Name text box, specify a name, for the merge document you're saving.

8. Click the Done button on the Merge bar to return to the Merge Assistant dialog box.

You can move back and forth freely between the text area of your document and the Merge bar. For example, you could type the date for a letter, use the Enter key to insert a couple of blank lines, then use the Merge bar to insert a merge field. Figure 18.17 shows an example letter merge document with several fields inserted.

You can perform several operations on the merge fields you insert in a document before clicking the Done button to return to the Merge Assistant dialog box. First, select the entire merge field (including the angle brackets) by dragging over it. Then, perform any of the following operations as needed:

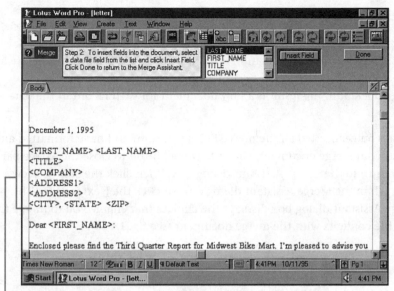

Fig. 18.17
A letter set up for
a merge.

Merge fields

■ Click the Cut SmartIcon on the Universal iconbar to cut the selected
field from the text.

■ Click the Copy SmartIcon on the Universal iconbar to copy the selected
field.

■ Position the insertion point, and then click the Paste SmartIcon on the
Universal iconbar to paste a previously cut or copied field.

> **Caution**
>
> You can undo a merge field cut or delete operation; Word Pro restores the
> merge field.

■ You can enhance the appearance of the text that appears in the merge
fields (by making it boldface or underlining it, for example). Apply the
enhancements from the Text menu (or using the CycleKeys or formatting Cycle SmartIcons on the Text iconbar) to the merge fields in the
merge document. When Word Pro merges data into the standard document, the text appears with the enhancements you applied to the
merge fields.

◀ See "Changing
Character
Formatting,"
p. 79

II

Accelerating Your WP

Merging Documents

After you finish the data file and the merge document, most of the work is done. The actual merge operation is a simple procedure that can generate a large volume of personalized documents quickly. When you perform the merge operation, the result is a new document for each record in the data file.

When you've inserted all the merge fields you want and have formatted and edited your merge document, click the Done button to close the Merge bar and return to the Merge Assistant dialog box. Then click the Step 3: View Print tab in the Merge Assistant dialog box, or click the Next button. The Merge Assistant dialog box displays the choices that enable you to merge the data file contents with the merge document (see fig. 18.18).

Fig. 18.18
The final tab in the Merge Assistant dialog box presents options that enable you to complete the merge.

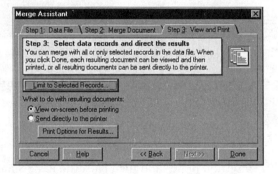

To merge all the records with the merge document and send the merged pages directly to the printer, click the Send Directly to the Printer option, and then click the Done button to print the merge.

The safer option, which is also the default, is to use the View On-Screen Before Printing option and click the Done button. Viewing the merged information on-screen gives you the opportunity to check for errors before printing. After you select the View On-Screen Before Printing option and click the Done button, Word Pro displays the Merge bar on-screen again with some slightly different options (see fig. 18.19). In addition, the first merged document (for the first record in your data file) appears on-screen.

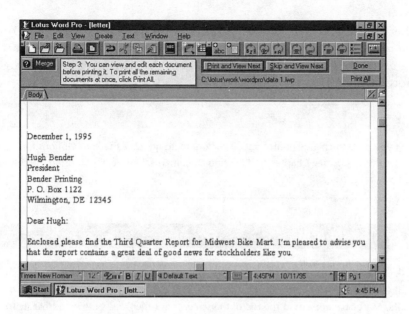

Fig. 18.19
The Merge bar
enables you to
review and print
merged data.

The Merge bar offers options for reviewing and printing one or all of the merged documents. (There's a merged document for each record in the data file that you merged.) Choose one of the following options from the Merge bar:

- Click the Print and View Next button to print the document for the current record and review the next document on-screen. Repeatedly selecting this option enables you to review and print the document for each record.

- Click the Skip and View Next button if you don't want to print the displayed document. Word Pro shows the next document.

- Choose the Print All button if the first merged letter appears to be correct and you want to print the rest of the letters without reviewing them.

- Click the Done button to close the Merge bar and discontinue or finish printing. If you noticed a general problem (for example, a field in the wrong place) with the merged document, redisplay the Merge Assistant dialog box, select the second tab, and click the Insert Merge Fields button to return to editing the merge document.

After the merge is complete, Word Pro redisplays the merge document. You can resave it at this point if needed. If you later want to rerun the merge with the existing files, open the Text menu, choose Merge, and repeat the merge procedure.

Note

If you need to change printer options before merging, click the Print Options for Results button. See Chapter 10, "Printing Documents," for details on using the dialog box that appears.

Troubleshooting

I accidentally clicked the Done button before I finished the merge. Do I have to start over?

If you choose Done in the Merge Assistant dialog box, the dialog box disappears. If the Merge bar appears at the top of the screen, click the Done button to close it. To continue the merge, you must open the Text menu and choose Merge. You may or may not have to reselect the data file and merge document.

Merging Selected Records

The standard merge just described in this chapter creates one finished document for each record in the data file. Sometimes you may want to merge selectively, skipping some records in the data file, depending on what those records contain.

Suppose that you have a standard mailing list containing the addresses of customers from many different states. You are located in New Jersey. You want to send a notice to your out-of-state customers (those whose address isn't New Jersey) regarding sales tax. Or perhaps you want to send an executive-level briefing only to customers with the title of President; or only to customers with ZIP codes between 53000 and 53999; or only to customers with addresses in Madison or Milwaukee.

You can merge records selectively by clicking the Limit to Selected Records button on the third tab of the Merge Assistant dialog box. When you click this button, Word Pro displays the Merge Records dialog box (see fig. 18.20).

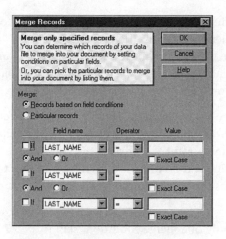

Fig. 18.20
Use the Merge
Records dialog box
to select only
certain records for
merging.

The Merge Records dialog box enables you to select records based on merge conditions or particular records. The default is to specify records by merge conditions. Using this method, you give Word Pro one or more conditions, and Word Pro merges only those records that meet the conditions. For example, let's say you want to mail a letter to customers in every state but New Jersey. You would want Word Pro to merge those records where the State field value (contents you entered) *is not equal to* (!=) New Jersey. In this case, the full condition expression is: STATE != NJ.

To set up a merge condition, leave the Records Based on Field Conditions option button in the Merge Records dialog box selected. Then specify a field name, a value, and an operator using the following steps:

1. Click to select the first If check box.

2. Click the down arrow beside the first Field Name drop-down list to display the names of the fields in your data file. Click a field name to select it and close the list. (Obviously, the field name must have been defined in the data file for the merge. For example, to select certain states, you must have created a State field.)

3. Click the down arrow beside the first Operator drop-down list to display the operator choices. The *operator* tells Word Pro what relationship to find between each record and value. (For example, you could choose the *!=* or *not equal to* operator). Table 18.1 describes each of the operators. Click one of the operators in the list to select it, which closes the list.

4. Click in the first Value text box and type the value for the field you specified earlier. The *value* is the contents of the field that Word Pro uses to decide whether to merge the record. (For example, you could enter **NJ**, the abbreviation for New Jersey, to complete the expression State != NJ, or *State is not equal to New Jersey*.)

   You must type a text value exactly as it appears in the data file. If you want Word Pro to match capitalization, type the value entry with the capitalization you want and click to turn on the Exact Case check box below the Value text box. With this check box selected, if you type **new jersey** as the value, Word Pro doesn't select a record where the value is New Jersey.

5. If you need only one merge condition, skip to step 7. Otherwise, click to select the And or the Or option button below the first Field Name text box. The option buttons are connectors that enable you to specify how merge conditions work together. The And connector means Word Pro merges only those records that match all the merge conditions you specify; the Or connector means Word Pro merges those records that match any one of the merge condition expressions you set up in the dialog box.

   For example, if you want Word Pro to merge all records except for cus-tomers residing in Newark, NJ, you would set up the expression State != NJ in the first set of expression boxes, leave the And option button selected, and set up the expression City != Newark in the second set of expression boxes.

6. Using the techniques outlined in steps 2–5, enter the second merge condition in the second set of expression boxes. If necessary, enter a third merge condition expression in the third set of boxes. Make sure that the correct connecting word, And or Or, is selected to connect each pair of conditions.

7. After you finish specifying merge conditions, click OK to return to the Merge Assistant dialog box.

8. Proceed with the merge.

As mentioned earlier in this section, the Merge Records dialog box also en-ables you to select specific records for merging. To use this method, select the Particular Records option in the Merge Records dialog box. The dialog box contents change, as shown in figure 18.21.

Table 18.1   Operators in the Merge Records Dialog Box

Operator	Purpose
= (equal to)	Merges records where the designated field in the record is equal to the value typed in the Value text box.
< (less than)	Merges records where the designated field in the record is less than the value typed in the Value text box.
> (greater than)	Merges records where the designated field in the record is greater than the value typed in the Value text box.
!= (not equal to)	Merges records where the designated field in the record *is not* equal to the value typed in the Value text box.
<= (less than or equal to)	Merges records where the designated field in the record is less than or equal to the value typed in the Value text box.
>= (greater than or equal to)	Merges records where the designated field in the record is greater than or equal to the value typed in the Value text box.

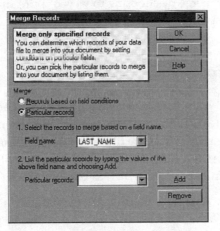

Fig. 18.21

Select particular records to use rather than specifying merge conditions.

In this method, you select a particular field and then tell Word Pro to merge records having particular entries in that field. Word Pro then merges the records you specified. Use these steps to specify matching records to merge:

1. Click the down arrow to display the Field Name drop-down list. Scroll through the list, and then click the name of the field you want to use to

select the merge records. (For example, you could choose the State field if it exists in your data file.)

2. Click in the Particular Records text box. Enter the field value for the records you want to merge. (For example, if you chose *State* for the field, you could enter **New Jersey** here.)

3. Click the Add button to add the record to the list.

4. Repeat steps 2 and 3 to have Word Pro merge records with other values for the specified field.

> **Tip**
>
> To delete a field value that you've added, click the drop-down arrow to display the Particular Records list box, click a value to select it, and then click the Remove button.

5. Repeat steps 1–4 as many times as needed to have Word Pro merge records based on the contents in other fields.

6. Click the OK button to return to the Merge Assistant dialog box.

7. Complete the merge by choosing to view or print in the Step 3 tab of the Merge Assistant dialog box.

From Here...

In this chapter, you learned how to create multiple similar documents by merging data with text. You use merges to create documents that combine standard information from a merge file with variable information from a data file. The data file can be a specially formatted Word Pro file, a Word Pro table, or an external file from a program such as Excel or dBASE.

You can attractively format, print, and otherwise dress up your merge documents with all the Word Pro features that are available to you. To learn more about techniques you can use to enhance and work with your merge documents, refer to these chapters:

■ Chapter 4, "Formatting Text," explains how you can choose new fonts and attributes (bold, underline, and the like) to text. It also explains how to format paragraphs.

■ Chapter 10, "Printing Documents," explains how to print and set printing options. It also explains how to print envelopes, which you may need to mail your merged documents.

■ Chapter 19, "Using Frames," introduces how you can use frames to arrange text and graphics for more attractive document layout.

■ Chapter 21, "Using Draw," teaches you how to use the tools on the Drawing Actions iconbar to create your own custom illustrations for your documents.

II

Accelerating Your WP

Part III

Producing Professional Output with Word Pro

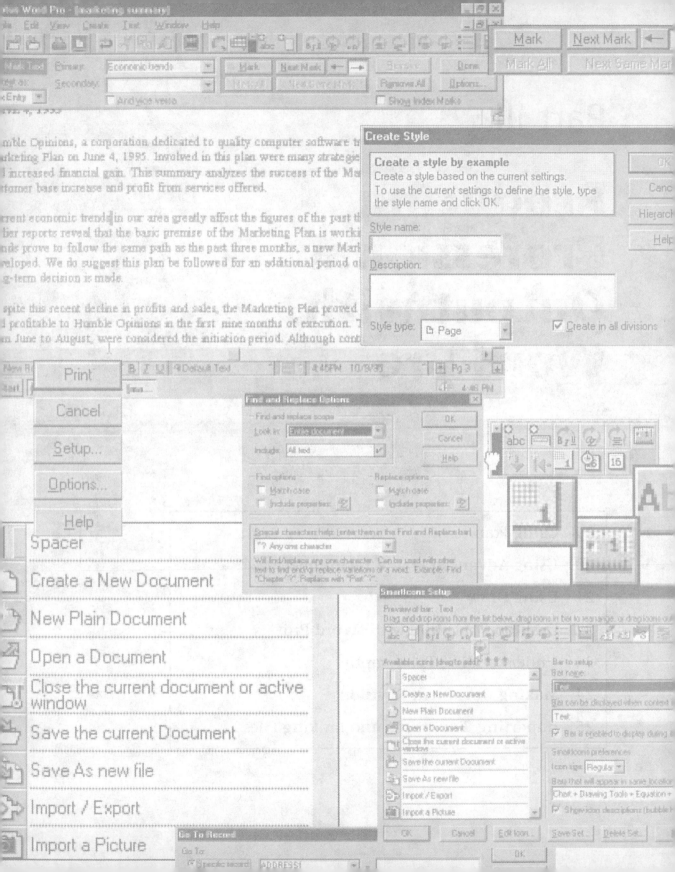

Chapter 19

Using Frames

by Sue Plumley

Frames are often an "ah-ha" experience—a breakthrough discovery for people who are used to character-based programs. Frames provide a logical way to insert special text or graphics into a document and help to organize text on the page. Frames also contribute to the appearance of your document by adding lines, patterns, screens, colors, and borders. You can use frames to hold headers and footers, mastheads, tables of contents, headings, or forms. You can use frames to display clip art, scanned halftones, drawings, tables, and spreadsheets. In this version of Word Pro, you can even use a frame to hold a frame to hold another frame.

When you create a Word Pro frame, you see exactly how it will print as you create and format it. Additionally, a frame's flexibility is a big bonus; you decide how the text wraps around the frame, and Word Pro adjusts the text if you move the frame. You choose how to format a frame's margins, lines, background, and size. You can also decide how text or graphics in the frame are formatted and placed. After creating the perfect frame, you can save it as a style and use that style over and over again in your document.

In this chapter, you learn to create frames and use them successfully in your documents. Additionally, you learn how to:

- Select frames
- Size frames
- Copy and move frames
- Enter text in a frame
- Use graphics in a frame
- Nest frames

Understanding Frames

A *frame* is a rectangle you can add to your document to hold text, graphics, tables, and so on. You use a frame to vary the layout and design of the page. You can add one or many frames to the page, each frame holding different elements. Additionally, you can place the frames anywhere on the page, including the header or footer area and the margins. You can also place frames inside other frames, and you can overlap frames.

When placing text in a frame, you can create columns, tabs, or tables in the frame to organize the text. You can set margins in a frame to separate the text from the border, as well. Word Pro enables you to easily format any text in a frame and switch between formatting the frame text and the frame properties using the same InfoBox. Finally, you can choose how to wrap the text outside a frame so the design and layout of the page are just how you want them.

Formatting frames includes many options. Frames you create in Word Pro can have various line thicknesses, colors, and styles around the border. Frames can also have background colors, patterns, or screens to enhance them. You can size a frame, move it, copy it, or delete it. You can even anchor a frame so it remains in a specific place in relation to the text.

After you format a frame to use in your document, Word Pro enables you to save the frame format: border style, line thickness, background, margins, text wrap, and so on, to use over and over again in your document, just as you would use paragraph styles. Figure 19.1 illustrates a newsletter page using a variety of frames to organize the text.

Fig. 19.1
Use frames in a document to add pizzazz and to organize page elements.

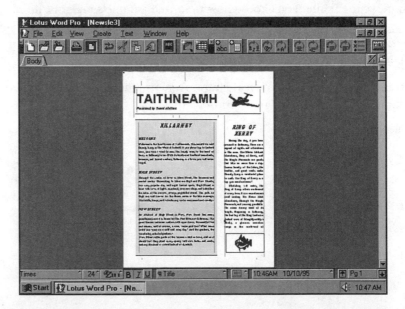

Creating a Frame

When creating a frame, you must use layout mode instead of draft mode. You cannot see frames in draft mode. To determine which mode you are using, choose <u>V</u>iew. A check mark appears next to the current mode. To switch to layout mode, choose <u>L</u>ayout.

You can create a frame in one of two ways: using the mouse to manually draw the frame, or by specifying the dimensions and position in the Create Frame dialog box and letting Word Pro draw the frame for you.

Using Exact Measurements to Create a Frame

Creating a frame using exact measurements enables you to specify the height and width of the frame. You might use this feature when placing a graphic that must be a specific size or when creating a border for a sized photograph, for example.

To create a frame using exact measurements, follow these steps:

▶ See "Format-
ting Frames,"
p. 398

1. Choose <u>C</u>reate, <u>F</u>rame. The Create Frame dialog box appears (see fig. 19.2).

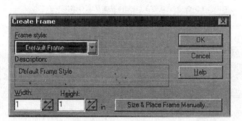

Fig. 19.2
Use the Create Frame dialog box to specify exact frame measurements.

2. In the <u>W</u>idth and H<u>e</u>ight text boxes, enter the appropriate frame measurements; the default unit is inches. You can either type the number in or use the arrows.

> **Tip**
>
> You can change the unit of measurement by choosing <u>F</u>ile, <u>U</u>ser Setup, Word Pro <u>P</u>references and choosing the <u>G</u>eneral tab.

> **Note**
>
> You can, alternatively, click the <u>S</u>ize & Place Frame Manually button to close the dialog box and draw a frame with the mouse.

3. Click OK. Word Pro automatically places the sized frame in the top left corner of the document.

Using the Mouse to Create a Frame

Use the mouse to create a frame when you want to draw a frame quickly and easily. You can click and drag the mouse to the appropriate size and in the correct location. The easiest method of creating a frame is to use the Create a Frame SmartIcon on the Universal iconbar.

To create a frame using the mouse, click the Create a Frame SmartIcon. The mouse pointer changes to a frame icon. Position the frame icon where you want the upper-left corner of the finished frame to appear, then click and drag the frame icon to the location where you want the opposite corner to appear. As you drag, a rectangle representing the frame's size and shape appears (see fig. 19.3).

Note

If you choose the Size & Place Frame Manually option in the Create Frame dialog box, the mouse changes to the same frame icon when the dialog box closes. You can then use the frame icon to draw a frame in your document.

Fig. 19.3
Create a frame manually by drawing it on-screen with the frame icon.

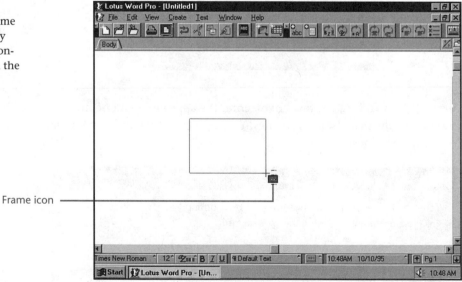

Frame icon

When you release the mouse button, the frame appears with corner and side handles, a border frame, and a blinking cursor inside the frame. The new frame takes on the default frame style. Frame SmartIcons and a special Frame menu you can use to format and manipulate the frame also appear on-screen. Figure 19.4 shows the resulting frame.

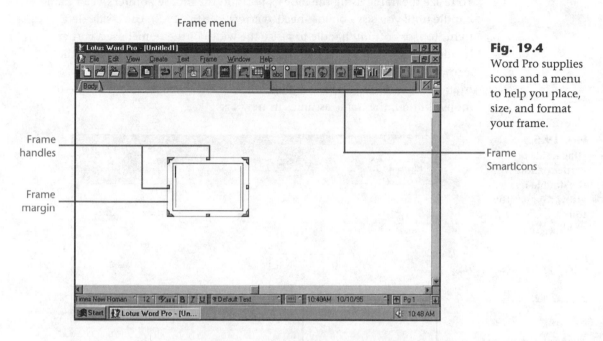

Fig. 19.4
Word Pro supplies icons and a menu to help you place, size, and format your frame.

Editing a Frame

After you create a frame, you can easily move it to a new location and even resize it; you can also copy and paste frames within your document. Before you can manipulate a frame, however, you must learn to select and then deselect it.

Selecting and Deselecting a Frame

To select a frame, move the mouse pointer anywhere within the borders of the frame and click. The frame's handles appear when it's selected. You can manipulate a selected frame by moving, resizing, copying, or deleting it.

To deselect the frame, move the mouse pointer anywhere outside of the frame and click. The handles disappear, indicating the frame is no longer selected.

III

Professional Output

Sizing a Frame

You can change the size of the frame quickly and easily with the mouse using the frame's handles. You can also resize a frame by specifying an exact height and width.

To resize the frame using the mouse, position the mouse pointer over a frame handle until you see a double-headed arrow (see fig. 19.5). Use a side (left, right, top, or bottom) handle to resize the width of the frame; use a corner handle to resize the width and height at the same time. Click and drag the arrow toward the center of the frame to make the frame smaller or away from the center of the frame to make the frame larger. When you release the mouse button, the frame assumes its new size.

Fig. 19.5
Drag a side or corner handle with the double-headed arrow to resize the frame.

Double-headed arrow

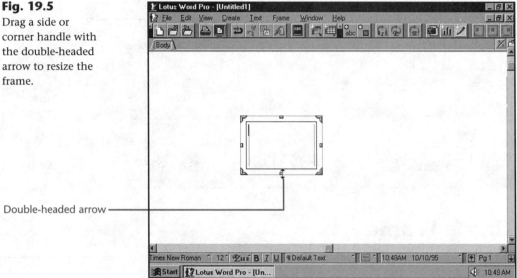

To resize the frame using exact measurements, follow these steps:

1. Right-click the frame to display the quick menu and choose Frame Properties. The Frame Properties InfoBox appears (see fig. 19.6).

Fig. 19.6
You can use the Properties InfoBox to resize the frame.

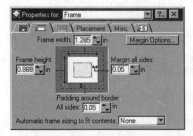

2. Choose the Size tab (the tab with the red lines measuring the white frame). In the Frame Width text box, enter the exact measurement (in inches), then enter the height in the Frame Height text box. The frame changes size on-screen.

3. You can either close the Frame Properties InfoBox or leave it open for later use. To close the Properties InfoBox, double-click the Control menu or click the Close button.

Note

If you want the frame to fit the entire page, choose Frame, Alignment, Span Margin to Margin and then choose Frame, Alignment, Span Top to Bottom. These options are only available if the frame placement is set to On Current Page, On Left/Right Pages, and With Paragraph Above.

Copying a Frame

You can insert a copy of an existing frame on the same page of the document, on a different page, or even in another document by copying and pasting the frame. To copy a frame, follow these steps:

1. Select the frame.

2. Choose Edit, Copy or click the Copy SmartIcon.

3. Move to the appropriate page or document.

4. Choose Edit, Paste or click the Paste SmartIcon. Move the copied frame if necessary.

Moving a Frame

You can move a frame to a new position on the same page using the mouse. You can also move a frame to another page or document using the Edit menu.

To move a frame using the mouse, select the frame. Position the mouse pointer over one border of the frame until you see the hand. Click and drag the mouse, and the hand looks as if it closes. Then drag the frame to a new position.

To move the frame to another page or document, follow these steps:

1. Select the frame.

2. Choose Edit, Cut or click the Cut SmartIcon.

3. Go to the page or document you want to move the frame to.

4. Choose Edit, Paste or click the Paste SmartIcon.

Deleting a Frame

You can delete a frame easily but keep in mind that when you delete a frame, you also delete its contents. To delete a frame, select the frame border by clicking the hand on the border. The border changes to a thick line (see fig. 19.7). Simply press the Delete key.

Fig. 19.7
Select the frame's border to delete the frame.

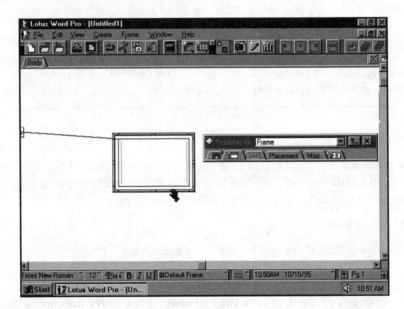

Alternatively, you can select the frame and choose Frame, Delete Frame. Word Pro removes the frame from the screen.

Troubleshooting

I was creating a frame, and I accidentally let go of the mouse; now the frame is too small to use. What do I do?

When you let go of the mouse, the frame was created and automatically selected. As long as the frame is selected—indicated by the handles—you can either resize it by grabbing one of the handles with the mouse and dragging, or you can simply press the Esc key, then press the Delete key and try again.

When I try to move my frame, it doesn't budge.

Make sure you drag the frame's border instead of trying to drag from the center of the frame. Position the mouse over the border until you see the grabber hand; then click and drag the frame.

I moved the pointer to the frame's border to move the frame, but I can't get the hand. All I get is the double-headed arrow.

When the pointer is over a handle, it changes to a double-headed arrow. Move the mouse to a part of the border where there is no handle. When the pointer is on the border, it changes to the hand.

Filling a Frame

Word Pro's frames can hold text, graphics, tables, spreadsheets, equations, drawings, and more. You can even place frames in frames in frames in Word Pro. Additionally, Word Pro enables you to manipulate text and graphics within a frame, which makes the frame feature all the more flexible and powerful.

◄ See "Creating Tables," p. 327

▶ See "Creating a Drawing," p. 426

Figure 19.8 illustrates a second newsletter design that uses frames to separate text, present a picture, and emphasize a story. In addition, the frame makes it possible for the nameplate to span two columns of text. A frame holds the nameplate and a *nested* frame—a frame within a frame—holds the graphic. One other frame holds the story titled "Killarney."

Fig. 19.8
Use frames to organize the text and create an interesting layout.

III

Professional Output

Using Text in Frames

You enter and edit text in frames just as you would elsewhere in your document. Selecting, copying and pasting, formatting, as well as other techniques you use with text also apply to using text in a frame. You can even open another document in a frame.

◀ See "Placing Text in a Document," p. 58

▶ See "Formatting Frames," p. 398

To enter text into a frame, move the insertion point to the frame and click. The selection handles appear, and the blinking cursor appears within the frame. Type the desired text. When you're finished entering the text, click the mouse outside of the frame.

To insert another document in a frame, click the frame to select it. Choose File, Open and select the document you want to insert into the frame.

◀ See "Changing Character Formatting," p. 79

◀ See "Using Paragraph Styles," p. 102

If the text you entered into the frame does not fit in the frame, the text is hidden. You can enlarge the frame to display hidden text. Similarly, if you reduce the frame's size, you hide some of the text in the frame.

> **Tip**
>
> You can format the text in a frame using the Text menu, the Status bar, the SmartIcons, or the Styles list box.

Using Graphics in a Frame

You can insert any graphic in a frame: pictures, clip art, tables, drawings, and so on. Any graphic you can insert into your document, in fact, can be inserted into a frame. By using frames to contain graphics, you can more easily size and move the graphic.

> **Note**
>
> Other chapters in this book provide detailed information for using frames with specific graphics. Chapter 21, "Using Draw," shows how to create a drawing in a frame. Chapter 17, "Working with Tables and Charts," shows you how to create a table in a frame.

To insert a graphic into a frame, select the frame and choose the command to create the graphic—Create, Table, for example, or Create, Drawing.

To insert a picture into a frame, follow these steps:

1. Select the frame and choose File, Import Picture. The Import Picture dialog box appears (see fig. 19.9).

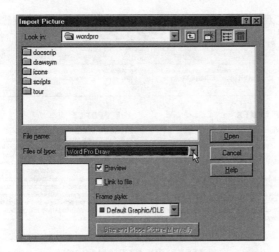

Fig. 19.9
Import a TIFF,
PCX, or other file
type into the
frame.

2. In the Files of Type list box, select the type of file you want to import.
   The following table describes the available file types.

File Extension	File Type
BMP	Windows Bitmap
SDW	Word Pro Draw
TIF	Tagged Image File Format
WMF, EMF	Windows Metafile
TEX	Equations
PCX	PC Paintbrush
WPG	DrawPerfect 1 and 2
JPG	JEPG

3. Choose the appropriate drive and folder.

4. Select the File Name and click Open. Word Pro imports the picture to
   the frame (see fig. 19.10).

Fig. 19.10
Importing a
picture file to a
frame makes your
documents more
attractive.

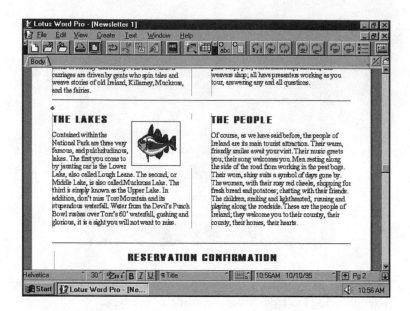

> **Note**
>
> You can *crop* a picture—or cut some of the picture away—by double-clicking the picture and dragging the left hand around in the frame. As you drag the hand, the picture moves within the frame and the frame sides hide part of the picture. Click outside the frame to complete the crop.

▶ See "Formatting Frames," p. 398

If you resize a frame containing a picture, you also resize the picture, unless you format the frame using the Graphics Scaling feature described in the Chapter 20, "Using Advanced Frame Techniques."

From Here...

Now that you know how to create and edit frames, you can learn to format frames and use frames for more advanced purposes. See the following chapters for more information about frames:

■ Chapter 20, "Using Advanced Frame Techniques," shows you how to change frame margins; add columns and tabs to a frame; create lines, borders, and shadows; wrap text around a frame; anchor a frame; and scale graphics within a frame. You also learn how to work with multiple frames in your document.

■ Chapter 21, "Using Draw," teaches you to use the Word Pro Draw feature. You can learn to create a drawing within a frame and then edit the drawing, format the drawing objects, add drawing text, and even import objects into the drawing.

■ Chapter 22, "Desktop Publishing with Word Pro," takes the use of frames even further by showing you how to design documents with consistency and emphasis, and how to use design elements to create balanced and interesting pages. Frames are an important component of designing a desktop-published page.

III

Professional Output

Chapter 20

Using Advanced Frame Techniques

by Sue Plumley

Frames supply a document with exciting possibilities for an attractive and interesting page layout. You can use frames to artfully design a page of text and graphics, vary placement and presentation, or simply make document creation easier.

Frames make your document creation easier by enabling you to enter text and graphics and then move the frames around on the page until everything fits. Additionally, Word Pro's frame features let you add a variety of borders, shadows, screens, and colors to a frame to make your document exciting. Using other frame control features makes Word Pro's frames powerful as well as utilitarian.

Another important frame feature is frame styles. You can create the perfect frame design by choosing borders, shadows, margins, and so on and then save that frame as a style. Use a frame style throughout the document without formatting it over and over again. Using frame styles guarantees consistency in a document and makes your life easier.

In this chapter, you learn how to:

- Adjust frame margins
- Set columns and tabs
- Add lines, shadows, and backgrounds
- Wrap text around frames
- Work with multiple frames
- Use frame styles

Formatting Frames

You can modify the appearance and layout of a frame by changing its margins, setting columns, selecting line and background styles, and so on. To format frames, you can use the Frame menu or the Frame Properties InfoBox (see fig. 20.1). Using the Frame Properties InfoBox may be the most beneficial method of formatting a frame because you see the changes on-screen as you make them. Additionally, the InfoBox enables you to make many different modifications all in one InfoBox.

Fig. 20.1
Use the Frame Properties InfoBox to format the frames in your document.

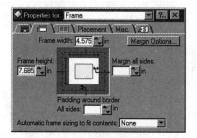

See "Creating a Frame," p. 385

You can access the Frame Properties InfoBox in any of the following ways, after selecting the frame:

- Right-click a frame and choose Frame Properties from the quick menu.

- Choose Frame, Frame Properties.

- Click the Frame InfoBox SmartIcon.

Changing Margins

The frame margin is the space between the frame's edge and whatever is inside the frame—text, graphics, and so on. You can use margins to keep text or graphics from touching a frame border. Similarly, you use the frame margin *padding*—the space between a frame's border and the text outside the frame—to separate the frame border from the text in your document.

You can set all of the margins for a frame at one time or set each margin individually. Likewise, you can set the padding for all sides the same or each side can be set to a different measurement.

> **Note**
>
> You can also set the frame margins using the ruler in a similar method to setting page margins. Select the frame and position the mouse pointer over the end of the frame ruler—the line that separates the frame ruler from the normal ruler. Drag the mouse to change the margins.

Setting All Margins and Padding

In the Frame Properties InfoBox, you can quickly set the margins of a frame so that all sides are the same. Similarly, you can set the padding for all sides at the same time. To set the margins and padding for a frame, follow these steps:

1. In the Frame Properties InfoBox, select the Position tab.

2. In Margin All Sides, enter a measurement in inches for the margins or use the arrows to enter the number.

3. In Padding Around Border All Sides, enter a measurement in inches or use the arrows to enter the number.

Figure 20.2 shows the Frame Properties InfoBox, Position tab, set to .25 inches for margin and padding. The frame illustrates the padding and margin.

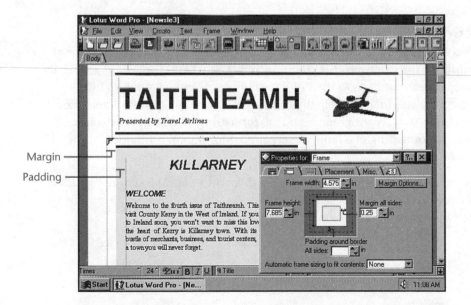

Fig. 20.2
Set all sides of the margins and padding at the same time in the Frame Properties box.

Setting Individual Margins and Padding

You can also set each side of a frame to a different margin or padding using the Frame Properties InfoBox. To individually set margins and padding, follow these steps:

1. In the Frame Properties InfoBox, choose the Position tab.

2. Choose the Margin Options button. The Margin Options dialog box appears (see fig. 20.3).

Fig. 20.3
Set individual margins in the Margin Options dialog box.

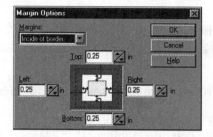

3. In Margins, choose either Inside of Border (margins) or Outside of Border (padding).

4. Enter the measurement, in inches, you want for the Top, Left, Bottom, and Right.

5. Choose OK to return to the Properties InfoBox. The changes take place in the frame.

Adding Columns

◄ See "Setting Margins, Page Tabs, and Colums" p. 108

You can format a frame to hold columns of text by choosing the number of columns, space between the columns, and even whether you want a vertical line between columns in the Columns tab of the Frame Properties InfoBox. You can also set tabs to help divide the text in a frame. Use the Frame Properties InfoBox to set the column and tab formatting of a frame. The column and tab formatting of a frame is very similar to column formatting of the page.

Set columns the same way that you set them on a page. Make sure you allow for adequate gutter space—the space between the columns. To set columns within a frame, follow these steps:

1. In the Frame Properties InfoBox, choose the Columns tab (see fig. 20.4).

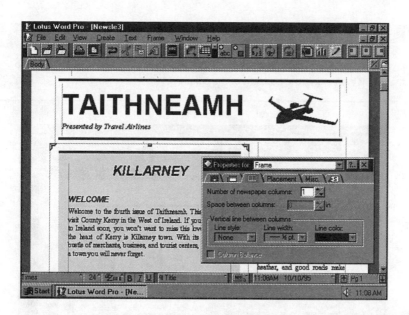

Fig. 20.4
Use the Columns
tab to choose
the number of
columns and
the separators.

> **Tip**
>
> You can set columns in a frame and then add text or you can enter the text and then set the columns.

2. In Number of Newspaper Columns, enter a number or use the spinner arrows to enter the number.

3. In Space Between Columns, either accept the measurement Word Pro set or enter your own measurement.

> **Tip**
>
> If you use a vertical line in the gutter or space between columns, increase the space to at least .25 inch so that the line and text have room to breathe.

4. Optionally, add a vertical line between the columns by choosing a Line Style, a Line Width, and a Line Color.

5. If you want the columns to be balanced, select that option. Figure 20.5 illustrates a frame divided into two columns with a .35-inch space between the columns and a vertical line in the gutter.

> **Note**
>
> If you choose balanced columns, the text in the columns in the frame will adjust so the text is even along the bottoms of the columns.

Fig. 20.5
Divide text in a frame into two or more columns for interest and easier reading.

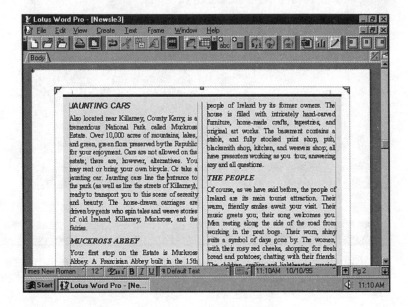

Setting Miscellaneous Text Options

The Misc tab of the Frame Properties InfoBox offers some interesting options for formatting the text in your frames. You can set tab stops, vertically align the text, rotate the text in a frame, apply a default paragraph style to the text in a frame, and protect a frame from being changed. Figure 20.6 shows the Misc tab of the Frame Properties InfoBox.

Tab Settings

Set tab stops for a frame using the Misc tab of the Frame Properties InfoBox. In Tab Settings, choose to space tab stops evenly, from the Left Edge, from the Right Edge, Custom tab settings, or None. If you choose the Custom settings, Word Pro displays the Set Tabs on Ruler dialog box, and you use the ruler as you would when setting tabs on the page.

In the Tab Settings text box, enter the measurement for the tab stops. For example, you can choose to evenly space tabs every .25 inch. The Set Tabs button in Tab Settings also displays the Set Tabs on Ruler dialog box.

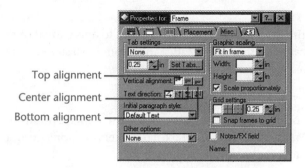

Fig. 20.6
The Misc tab of the Frame Properties InfoBox enables you to set tabs, vertical text alignment, text rotation, and more.

Top alignment

Center alignment

Bottom alignment

Vertical Alignment

Vertical alignment designates whether to align the text in the frame at the top (first button), in the middle (second button), or at the bottom of the frame (third button). Use this option, for example, when you want to vertically center a headline in a frame.

Text Direction

Text Direction controls the rotation of the text in a frame. If you rotate one line of text, you rotate all of the text in the frame. The first button is normal text, the second represents a 90-degree rotation, the third is rotated 180 degrees (or upside down), and the fourth represents 270 degrees rotation. Figure 20.7 illustrates the text rotation.

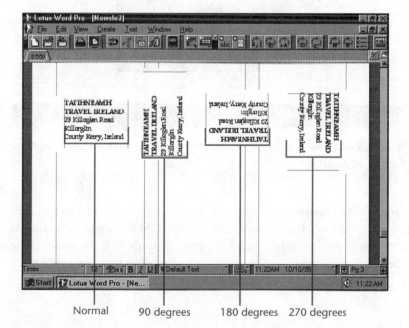

Fig. 20.7
Rotate text in a frame for special headline effects.

Normal   90 degrees   180 degrees   270 degrees

Default Paragraph Styles

◀ See "Creating Styles," p. 254

Choose a style from the Initial Paragraph Style list box to apply to all of the text in a frame. You can choose from any style in the SmartMaster you are using, even from styles you've created yourself.

Frame Protection

To protect a frame's contents from being altered, choose Other Options, Protect Frame from the Frame Properties InfoBox. To cancel the protection, select the option again to remove the check mark.

Adding Lines, Borders, and Drop Shadows

You can add a variety of lines and borders to your frames by choosing the line style, line width, and line color on the Lines and Colors tab. Alternatively, you can choose a designer border to apply to a frame.

Lines and Borders

To add a line or border to the frame, choose the Lines and Colors tab in the Frame Properties InfoBox (see fig. 20.8).

Fig. 20.8
Choose lines and shading to apply to the frame in the Frame Properties InfoBox.

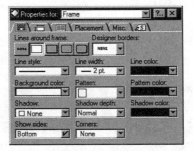

Tip

You can choose how rounded the corners of the Lines around Frame are from the Corners drop-down list.

In Lines around Frame, select the type of border you want: rectangle, rectangle with shadow, rounded rectangle, or rounded rectangle with shadow. Alternatively, you can select None or Designer Borders. If you select Designer Borders, a drop-down box of thirteen custom borders you can apply to the frame appears.

In Line Style, choose from straight, zigzagged, dashed, doubled, and many other styles of lines. Choose a Line Width from 1/2 point to 8 points and choose a Line Color from the palette of available colors. As you make each selection, the change is automatically made to the frame. You can also choose Other in the Line Width drop-down list and set the line width to a custom size.

If you prefer to place lines on the left and right or top and right of a frame, you can choose Show Sides and select from the following in the drop-down list: None, All Sides, Left, Right, Top, Bottom. Each option you choose displays a check mark beside it; you can select one or all sides in this option.

> **Tip**
>
> If you select a line style, you cannot use a designer border.

Drop Shadows

If you chose a border with a drop shadow, you can choose the Shadow placement, depth, and color. In Shadow, choose the placement of the shadow by selecting Top Left, Top Right, Bottom Left, or Bottom Right.

In Shadow Depth, choose from Normal, Shallow, Deep, or Other. If you choose Other, you can set the Shadow Depth in the Shadow Depth dialog box. You can also choose a color for the shadow other than the default black. Click Shadow Color to display the color palette and choose a color.

Adding Backgrounds

You can add a background color, screen, or pattern to your frame. The background can stand on its own or be paired with a line around the frame or designer border. Gray- or pastel-colored screens attract attention and if light enough, enable text to be read in the frame. Patterns, whether black and white or color, make interesting borders or backgrounds for heavy, black graphic images (see fig. 20.9).

> **Tip**
>
> Be careful when adding a background to a frame that contains text; too dark of a color or too much of a pattern may make it hard to read the text in the frame.

Professional Output

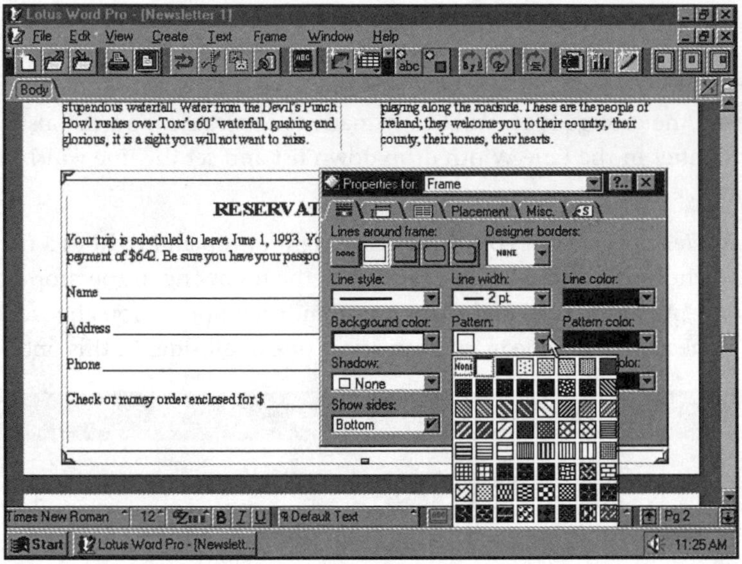

Fig. 20.9
Choose a pattern
from the Lines and
Colors tab of the
Frame Properties
InfoBox to apply
to the background
of a frame.

▶ See "Using
Design Ele-
ments," p. 455

To add a background to a frame, open the Frame Properties InfoBox and
choose the Lines and Colors tab. In Background Color, pick a solid or
screened color from the palette. Additionally, choose Pattern and select from
dots, stripes, bricks, graded screens, and so on to apply to the background of
the frame. The default color for Pattern is black and white; however, you can
choose Pattern Color to add color to the pattern.

Using Graphics Scaling and Image Properties

Graphics scaling refers to how the graphic image fits into the frame. You can,
for example, make the graphic fit the size and shape of the frame, which
creates an interesting effect in some cases. You might fit a tall building into a
frame that's wider than it is tall. The building would then change shape to
match the frame. Alternatively, you can make the graphic fit proportionately
into a frame, no matter the size or shape of the frame.

Image properties refer to the brightness and sharpness of a graphic. You can
adjust the contrast or enhance the edges of an image as well. Image properties work best with halftone or screened images although you can apply these
effects to line images.

Note

Halftone and screened images are created by patterns of gray dots, like the product
you get when you've scanned a photograph. Line images differ in that they are only
black lines or shapes on white, no grays.

Graphics Scaling

Access the Graphic Scaling option in the Misc tab of the Frame Properties InfoBox (see fig. 20.10). Alternatively, you can click the Scale a Picture SmartIcon. The graphic in the figure is scaled proportionately.

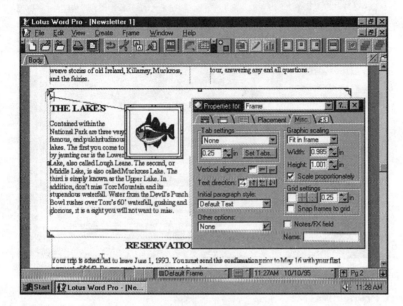

Fig. 20.10
Use the Graphic Scaling option in the Misc tab to alter your graphic images.

In the Graphic Scaling area of the tab, you can choose to scale the image in a variety of ways, as described in table 20.1. Additionally, you can enter a Width and Height of your own to use for the graphic.

Table 20.1   Graphic Scaling Options

Option	Description
Original Size	Changes the graphic to its original size, regardless of the size of the frame. If the graphic is larger than the frame, only a part of the graphic shows.
Fit in Frame	Changes the image to fit the frame; so if your frame is 2.5 inches wide and the image is 3 inches wide, the image is made to fit the 2.5-inch frame.
Percentage	Increases or decreases the size of the graphic to the desired proportion; default value is 100%.
Custom	Increases or decreases the size of the graphic to the height and width you indicate.
Scale Proportionately	Keeps the size of the graphic proportionate within the frame.

Figure 20.11 shows a graphic image scaled to fit in the frame. The distortion creates an interesting effect that could be used as a logo.

Fig. 20.11
You can choose to distort a graphic by deselecting the Scale Proportionately option in the Misc tab and choosing Fit in Frame.

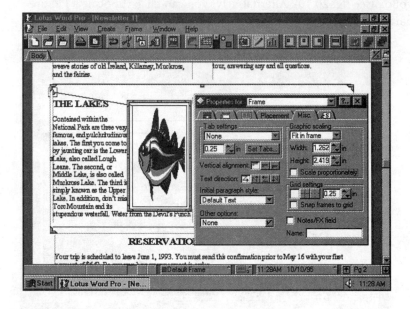

Image Properties

You can adjust the image properties of both line and screened graphics. Line graphics are those you might create in a drawing program, whereas screened images are, for example, scanned photographs.

▶ See "Working with Images," p. 520

To access the Image Properties dialog box, double-click the image to select it and then right-click the image and choose Image Properties from the quick menu. The Image Properties dialog box appears (see fig. 20.12). Figure 20.13 shows an image that has been enhanced using the options in the Image Properties dialog box.

Table 20.2 describes the options in the dialog box.

Table 20.2 Image Properties Options	
Option	**Description**
Brightness	Adjusts the brightness of an image from dark to light; the default is 50, although you can change the number from 0 (black) to 100 (white).
Contrast	Adjusts the contrast between lights and darks in the graphic; 0 equals all gray and 100 equals the greatest contrast between light and dark. The default is 50.

Option	Description
Edge Enhancement	Sharpens the line between dark and light. 0, the default, makes for fuzzy lines, whereas 100 makes the contrasting line sharper.
Smoothing	Softens lines and transitions by making lines blurry. 0, the default, means sharper lines, and 100 means very blurry lines.

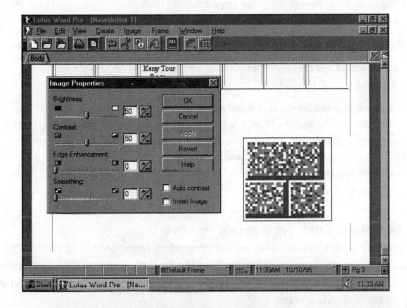

Fig. 20.12
The Image Properties dialog box and a graphic image before adjustments are made.

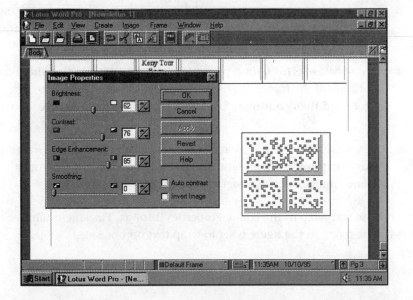

Fig. 20.13
This graphic image has been changed to create a softer image; see the settings in the Image Properties dialog box.

> **Troubleshooting**
>
> *I try to move the frame, but I end up moving the graphic within the frame. What am I doing wrong?*
>
> If you double-click the image before trying to move it, you only succeed at cropping the image—moving the image around within the frame. To move the frame, click the border of the frame to select it and then drag the frame to its new location.
>
> *I was playing around with the Image Properties, but I really don't like anything I did. How can I get back to my original?*
>
> Right-click the graphic and choose <u>R</u>evert.
>
> *I double-clicked and then right-clicked the graphic, but <u>I</u>mage Properties is not on my quick menu.*
>
> The image may not be the kind Word Pro accepts for image processing. When you double-click the image, the Word Pro Draw program may appear, or the crop (left) hand may appear for you to move the image around in the frame. If the Image Properties dialog box does not appear, try saving the image in TIFF format in its original program.

Wrapping Text Around a Frame

Word Pro enables you to treat the text outside a frame in any of three ways. You can make the text on the outside of the frame more readable by directing the text flow, or wrap, around the frame. You can choose to wrap the text in any of the following ways:

- *One side*. Use this option to wrap the text around one side of the frame. Text does not wrap on both sides of a frame. This option works particularly well with text in columns.

- *Top and bottom*. This option prevents text from appearing on the right or left side of the frame. Text skips from the top of the frame to the bottom and then continues. Use this option with text in two or more columns.

- *Through the frame*. This option flows text directly through the frame as though no frame were present. This is a good choice for applying a screened image, such as a logo, in the background of the text.

You choose text wrap in the Frame Properties InfoBox, Placement tab (see fig. 20.14). The frame in the figure is set to wrap text on one side.

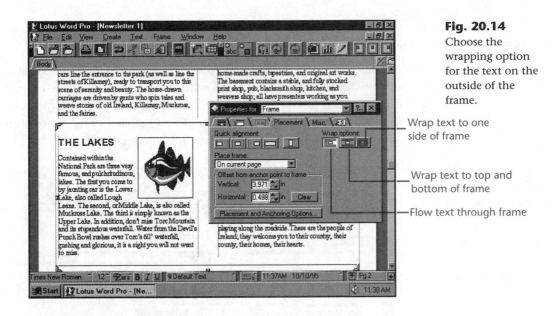

Fig. 20.14
Choose the wrapping option for the text on the outside of the frame.

Wrap text to one side of frame

Wrap text to top and bottom of frame

Flow text through frame

Figure 20.15 illustrates the frame with the text wrapped from top to bottom.

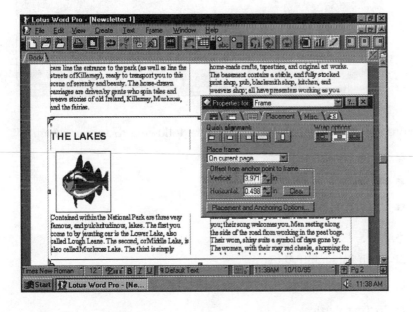

Fig. 20.15
Choose the text wrap that fits the text, frame, and page design of your document.

III

Professional Output

Anchoring Frames

Word Pro anchors your frames, by default, to the top left corner of the page or frame in which you place the frame. When you select a frame so that the thick border around the frame appears, a line connects the frame to its anchor. The easiest method of moving the anchor is to select and drag the anchor to a new spot using the mouse pointer.

You can, alternatively, choose where to anchor or place the frame so that the frame moves with its text references or remains on the current page using the Frame Properties InfoBox. In addition to choosing an anchor, you can enter an offset measurement to place the frame. To set the anchoring options, use the Placement tab in the Frame Properties InfoBox (see fig. 20.16).

Fig. 20.16
Set anchoring options to indicate exactly where the frame should appear.

Anchor and line

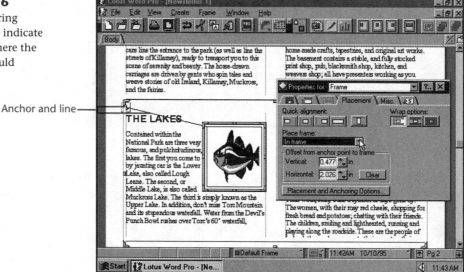

Word Pro enables you to choose from the following to anchor a frame:

- Same Page as Text
- On All Pages
- On Left/Right Pages
- In Text
- With Paragraph Above
- On Current Page
- In Text-Vertical

In addition to choosing a placement for the frame, you can set a Vertical and Horizontal in Offsets from Anchor Point to Frame. When you enter a vertical or horizontal offset, you move the frame on the page. The frame then remains at that location until you change the offset measurement. You can click the Clear Offsets button in Offset from Anchor Point to Frame to clear the offsets and begin again. When you clear the offsets, the frame moves to the top left corner of the page.

You can also use the Placement and Anchoring Options button to access more direct control over anchoring your frame. When you click the button in the Placement tab, the Placement Options dialog box appears (see fig. 20.17).

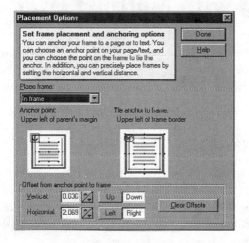

Fig. 20.17
Using the Placement Options dialog box, you can indicate the frame placement on the displayed graphic instead of entering measurements.

Using the graphics in the Placement Options dialog box, you can click the mouse pointer on the corresponding area of the page that you want to anchor the frame. To anchor the frame, follow these steps:

1. In the Placement Options dialog box, choose a frame placement in the Place Frame drop-down list.

2. In Anchor Point, choose the position on the page for the frame by clicking an area on the page. The anchor in the graphic moves to the new location.

3. In Tie Anchor to Frame, click an area in the frame to tie the anchor to; the graphic moves to that area.

4. If you want to use exact measurements, enter them in the Offset from Anchor Point to Frame text boxes.

> **Tip**
>
> The choices you make in the Placement Options dialog box appear on-screen as you make them. Before using anchoring options, choose the full page view so you can see where the frame is placed as you change options.

5. When you are finished placing the frame and anchoring it, choose Done to close the Placement Options dialog box.

Working with Multiple Frames

Most of your documents will have more than one frame. Some frames will contain text, others graphics or tables, and so on. When you have more than one frame in a document, you can select multiple frames and work with them as a group instead of performing actions on one frame at a time.

In Word Pro, you can group frames together so that you can resize, copy, or delete them. You can also align frames, layer frames, and repeat a frame on every page of the document.

Before you can work with multiple frames, you must learn to select them. To select multiple frames, select the first frame by clicking its border. Press and hold the Shift key while clicking the borders of the other frames you want to select. To deselect one frame from a group of selected ones, hold the Shift key and click the frame you want to deselect.

Aligning Frames

Aligning frames in Word Pro is easy. Suppose you want to line up all frames on a page along the left margin. You can do it with a quick click of the mouse. You can alternatively align frames right or center.

To align frames, select a frame and display the Frame Properties InfoBox. Choose the Placement tab and click the appropriate alignment in the Quick Alignment area (see fig. 20.18). Select the next frame and choose the appropriate alignment. Alternatively, you can select the frames and click the Frame Left Align or Frame Center Align SmartIcons.

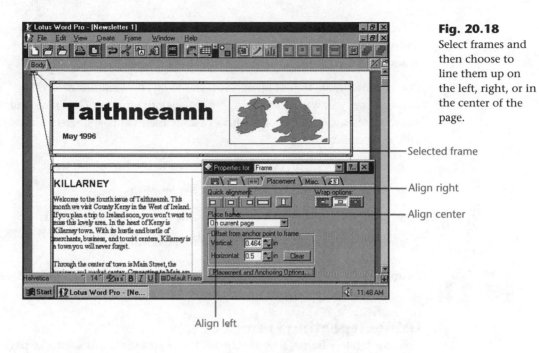

Fig. 20.18
Select frames and
then choose to
line them up on
the left, right, or in
the center of the
page.

Selected frame

Align right

Align center

Align left

Grouping Frames

You can perform actions—such as copying, deleting, and moving—to a group
of frames just as you do to one frame. You can also format any individual
frame in the group as well as add text or graphics to an individual group.

To group frames, select the frames and choose Frame, Group. A rectangular
border surrounds the grouped frames; the rectangular border indicates the
frames in the group but is not a frame in itself. To ungroup frames, select the
group and choose Frame, Group; the check mark disappears from the Group
command. Alternatively, you can click the Group/Ungroup SmartIcon.

Layering Frames

You can create any number of frames in a document and then layer, or overlap, the frames. You might layer frames to create an interesting graphic design or so you can add a text frame to a graphic frame, for example. When
you layer frames, Word Pro supplies a method of selecting and manipulating
the layered frames for easier access to them.

To layer frames, create as many frames as you want. You can draw each frame
on top of the other or you can draw them separately and then drag a frame
over the top of the next. The layer is created in the order you draw the
frames. The first frame you draw, for example, is on the bottom layer and the
last frame you draw is on the top layer.

III

Professional Output

To access frames in the layers, hold Alt and click the frame on top. Each layered frame comes to the top of the stack one at a time, as you click the mouse.

You can also move frames up or down in the layers of frames. Select the frame border you want to move and right-click the mouse. The Frame quick menu appears. Choose Priority and a cascade menu appears. Select one of the following commands:

- *Bring to Front.* Moves the selected frame to the top of the stack.

- *Bring Forward One.* Moves the selected frame up one.

- *Send to Back.* Moves the selected frame to the back of the stack.

- *Send Back One.* Moves the selected frame down one.

  As an alternative to choosing Priority, you can click the Send Frame to Back or the Bring Frame to Front SmartIcons to move the selected frame.

Using Repeating Frames

You can create a frame, format it, place it in a specific position on the page, fill it with text or graphics like a logo, and then repeat that frame on every page of your document.

To repeat a frame, select the frame and open the Frame Properties InfoBox. Choose the Placement tab, and in Place Frame, choose On All Pages. The frame repeats on all of your pages.

Using Frame Styles

 One of the greatest features of Word Pro is frame styles. You can now create a frame and format it with lines, shadows, margins, anchoring, text wrap, and so on, and save the frame and its formatting as a style to use over and over again in your document. Think of the time you'll save.

Use the Style tab of the Frame Properties InfoBox to create, edit, and manage frame styles (see fig. 20.19). Begin by creating a frame with all of the properties you want to apply to the style.

Creating a Style

To create a frame style, you must first create the frame. Format the frame any way you want using the Frame Properties InfoBox or the Frame menu. When you've completed the frame and it's exactly as you want it, you're ready to create the style.

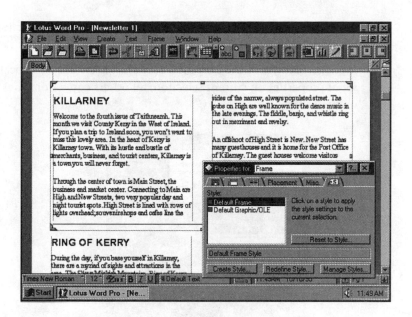

Fig. 20.19
The frame style in this figure has two columns with a .5-inch space between the columns, a 1/2-point line along the top and bottom of the frame, and a .125-inch margin at the top.

To create the style, follow these steps:

1. In the Style tab of the Frame Properties InfoBox, choose the Create Style button. The Create Style dialog box appears (see fig. 20.20).

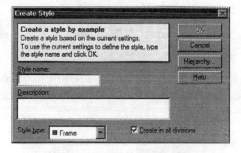

Fig. 20.20
Create a frame style to save time and energy.

2. In Style Name, enter a name describing the frame style.

3. In Description, enter a description of the frame style if you want.

4. Choose the Hierarchy button. The Style Hierarchy Definition dialog box appears (see fig. 20.21).

5. In Choose the Properties You Want To Include as Part of the Definition of This Style, select from one of the following options:

   ■ *Specific Properties*. Selects only the marked properties of the current selection and all other properties of the original style.

■ All Properties. Selects all of the properties of the current selection, but none of the properties of the original style.

■ All Local Settings of the Current Selection. Selects only the local set of properties on current selection; all others come from the original style.

Fig. 20.21
You can choose the frame formatting you want to include in the style.

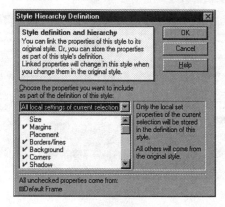

6. If you choose Specific Properties, you can select the properties you want to include from the list. Those properties with a check mark are selected. Click a property to select it and add a check mark, or click a property to deselect it and remove the check mark.

7. When done, choose OK to close the dialog box and return to the Create Style dialog box.

8. Choose OK to close the dialog box and return to the document. The new frame name is added to the Style list in the Frame Properties InfoBox (see fig. 20.22).

Fig. 20.22
Create new styles and add the style names to the Style list in the Frame Properties InfoBox.

Using a Style

You can apply a style you create to any style in a document. To use the style, select a frame and select the style from the Style list in the Frame Properties InfoBox. Word Pro assigns the selected style elements to the frame.

Redefine a Style

Redefine a style by changing the properties you want to include as part of the style—margins, borders, corners, and so on. You can redefine a style at any time by choosing Redefine Style in the Style tab of the Frame Properties InfoBox. The Redefine Style dialog box looks just like the Create Style dialog box and works the same way.

To redefine a style, choose the Redefine Style button in the Style tab. The Redefine Style dialog box appears. Choose the Hierarchy button. The Style Hierarchy Definition dialog box appears; in this dialog box, choose the properties you want to include and exclude in the style. Choose OK to close the dialog box and OK again to close the Redefine Style dialog box.

Managing Styles

You can manage frame styles, deleting and renaming styles you've created. Probably more importantly, you can use the Manage Styles feature to copy a frame style from one document to another. The capability to copy a style means you can create your favorite styles and then use them over and over in any Word Pro document.

To manage styles, follow these steps:

1. Choose the Style tab in the Frame Properties InfoBox.

2. Choose Manage Styles. The Manage Styles dialog box appears (see fig. 20.23).

Fig. 20.23
You can manage frame styles as easily as you can manage text styles.

3. In the Style Name list box, select the style name of the frame you created. The frame styles are listed after the text styles.

◀ See "Using Paragraph Styles," p. 102

4. Choose Rename to change the name of the style; the Rename Style dialog box appears. Enter a new name in the To text box and then choose OK.

5. Choose <u>D</u>elete to delete the style from the list. Choose <u>Y</u>es in the confirmation dialog box and the style is deleted.

6. Choose the Copy <u>F</u>rom button to copy the style to another document. The Copy Styles From dialog box appears (see fig. 20.24).

Fig. 20.24
Copy styles from
other documents
or from within the
current document.

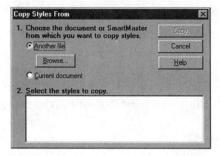

Choose <u>A</u>nother File to indicate the file from which the style will be copied. Alternatively, choose <u>C</u>urrent Document if the style is in the current document.

In number 2, <u>S</u>elect the Styles to Copy, click the frame styles you want to copy from another document.

Choose Copy. The files are added to the Style list in the Frame Properties InfoBox and Word Pro returns to the Manage Styles dialog box. Choose <u>C</u>lose to close the Manage Styles dialog box.

Troubleshooting

I redefined a frame style and now all of my frames are changed. I only wanted to change the one frame. What can I do?

When you redefine a frame style, all frames using that style are also redefined. Instead of redefining the style, you should first create a new style based on the old. Give a frame formatted with the old style a new style name and then redefine that style.

I want all my frames to stretch from the top margin to the bottom margin, but I can only align them along the top or along the bottom using the Quick Alignment buttons in the Placement tab. How can I align them both ways and make sure they are all the same size quickly and easily?

In the Placement tab beside the Quick Alignment buttons are two Span buttons. The first is the Span Margin to Margin button (left to right margins) and the second is the Span Top to Bottom (margins) button. Click a Span button and the selected frames stretch to align both at the top and bottom or at the left and right.

From Here...

Now that you can format frames and work with multiple frames, you're ready to use frames with other Word Pro features. For more information about using frames, see the following chapter:

■ Chapter 21, "Using Draw," shows you how to create and edit a drawing, format objects, work with multiple objects as well as text, and how to import objects to the drawing applet.

Chapter 21

Using Draw

by Sue Plumley

Word Pro comes with a fully equipped Draw feature, also called an *applet*—a feature so function-rich that it borders on being an application. You use this feature to create or modify pictures in Word Pro. You can create nearly any shape or drawing, modify line thickness and color, add color to the background of a drawing, and add text to the drawing.

Word Pro also enables you to select, copy, and move the objects you've drawn as well as rotate and flip objects for more variety in your drawings. Word Pro supplies drawing tools to help you quickly and efficiently create and modify your drawings. When you combine the power of frames with the power of drawing, you have a capability unmatched by any other word processing software currently on the market.

In this chapter, you learn how to:

- ■ Create and edit drawings
- ■ Format objects
- ■ Work with multiple objects
- ■ Work with text in a drawing
- ■ Rotate, flip, and align objects

Starting Draw

To create a drawing, you must use a frame. If you don't create a frame before starting Draw, Word Pro creates the frame for you. You cannot create a drawing in a text frame or in a frame containing a non-Draw object, such as a table or chart. If Word Pro creates the frame, it uses the current settings in

◄ See "Editing a Frame," p. 387 the Create Frame dialog box. You can resize and move the frame at any time using the Frame Properties InfoBox if you want.

 To start the Draw feature, choose Create, Drawing. Alternatively, click the Create a Drawing SmartIcon. Word Pro creates a frame to hold the drawing and then displays the two Draw iconbars and the Draw menu (see fig. 21.1).

Fig. 21.1
Use the Draw icons to create and manipulate objects.

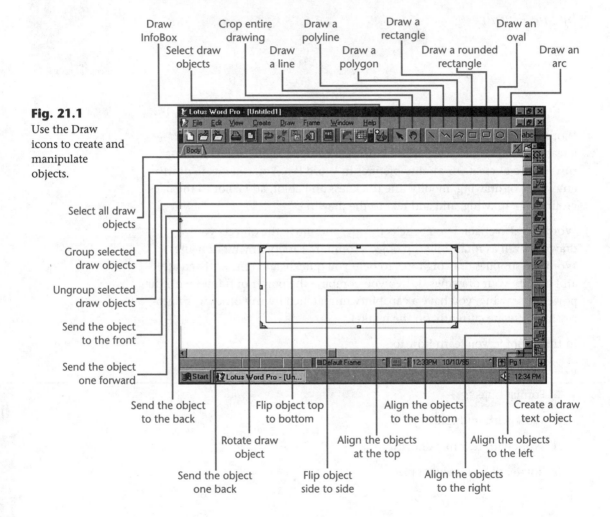

Draw InfoBox

Select draw objects

Crop entire drawing

Draw a line

Draw a polyline

Draw a polygon

Draw a rectangle

Draw a rounded rectangle

Draw an oval

Draw an arc

Select all draw objects

Group selected draw objects

Ungroup selected draw objects

Send the object to the front

Send the object one forward

Send the object to the back

Send the object one back

Rotate draw object

Flip object top to bottom

Flip object side to side

Align the objects at the top

Align the objects to the bottom

Align the objects to the right

Align the objects to the left

Create a draw text object

Table 21.1 describes the tools in the Draw iconbars.

Table 21.1 Drawing Tools	
Tool	**Description**
Draw InfoBox	Displays the Draw Properties InfoBox in which you can change line style, thickness, color, and so on.
Select all draw objects	Selects or deselects all objects in the frame.
Group selected draw objects	Groups all selected objects in the frame.
Ungroup selected draw objects	Ungroups the selected objects.
Send the object to the front	Brings the selected object to the front of all other objects in the frame.
Send the object one forward	Brings the selected object up one layer in the stack of objects.
Send the object to the back	Sends the selected object to the back of all other objects.
Send the object one back	Sends the selected object back one layer in the stack of objects.
Rotate the draw object	Rotates the selected object clockwise with each click of the mouse.
Flip the object top to bottom	Flips the selected object by swapping top and bottom.
Flip the object side to side	Flips the selected object by swapping left and right sides.
Align the objects at the top	Aligns the selected objects along their top edges.
Align the objects to the bottom	Aligns the selected objects along their bottom edges.
Align the objects to the right	Aligns the selected objects along their right edges.
Align the objects to the left	Aligns the selected objects along their left edges.
Select the draw objects	Selects the object by clicking the object or by using the tool to draw a rectangle around the object; also sizes objects by dragging selection handles.
Crop the entire drawing	Moves the objects around inside the frame and crops, or hides, part of the image beyond the frame borders.

III

Professional Output

(continues)

Table 21.1 Continued	
Tool	**Description**
Draw a line	Draws a straight line when you drag the mouse pointer; draws the line at a 45-degree angle if you hold down Shift while dragging the mouse pointer.
Draw a polyline	Draws a line that connects two points. Draws multiple connected lines if you click the tool at every direction change inside the frame; double-click to end line.
Draw a polygon	Draws a polygon when you click at each point where you want a corner of the polygon to be; double-click to end line. The shape automatically closes when you double-click.
Draw a rectangle	Draws a rectangle; draws a square if you hold down Shift as you draw.
Draw a rounded rectangle	Draws a rectangle with rounded corners; draws a square with rounded corners if you hold down Shift as you draw.
Draw an oval	Draws an oval; draws a circle if you hold down Shift as you draw.
Draw an arc	Draws a parabolic arc.
Create a draw text object	Enables you to type text as part of the drawing.

◄ See "Under-
standing
Frames," p. 384

If you click outside the drawing frame, Word Pro closes the Draw feature by deselecting the frame and hiding the Draw iconbars. To start Draw again, double-click the drawing frame.

Creating a Drawing

On the Draw screen, Word Pro displays Draw icons that you use to produce basic lines and shapes, such as rectangles, ovals, and so on. Any one line or shape you create is called an *object* in Word Pro. A drawing can consist of one object or a combination of objects.

After creating a drawing, you can select objects to modify, move, copy, and so on. You can select just one object or several in a drawing.

Using the Draw Tools

To use the Draw tools, you first click an icon that represents the object you want to draw. Then you click and drag the mouse pointer in the frame to draw the object. Refer to table 21.1 for the basic use of each tool. You can use the following steps to draw any shape or line in Draw. This example is for a rectangle:

1. Create a drawing frame or let Word Pro create the frame for you. Choose Create, Drawing, and the drawing tools appear.

2. Click the Create Rectangle icon and move the mouse pointer to the frame. The mouse pointer changes to a cross.

3. Position the cross in the frame at the point where you want the top left corner of the rectangle.

4. Drag the cross to the point where you want the bottom right corner of the rectangle and release the mouse button. Word Pro draws the rectangle, and the mouse pointer remains in the shape of a cross (see fig. 21.2).

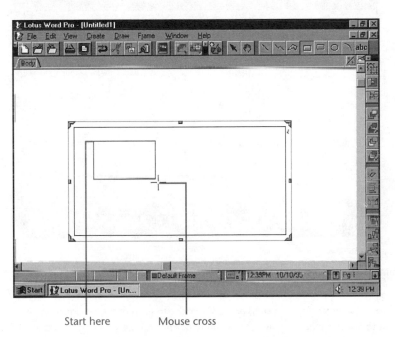

Start here   Mouse cross

Fig. 21.2
Draw a rectangle using the Create Rectangle tool.

5. Click the Selection tool to change the mouse back to its pointer shape.

> **Note**
>
> When creating a drawing, you may need to change views of the screen. Try using a 200% view or even creating your own custom view so you can better see the objects you're creating.

◄ See "Using Zoom," p. 143

III

Selecting and Deselecting Objects

When you finish drawing a shape or line, you can select that object to manipulate. You can resize, copy, cut, delete, or move a selected object, and you can manipulate more than one object at a time as well.

To select a drawn object, follow these steps:

1. Click the Select Draw Objects tool to change the mouse to a pointer.

2. Click the pointer on a line or inside a shape to select it. The object appears with *handles*, small black boxes, on the ends of the lines or evenly spaced on the sides of shapes. Figure 21.3 shows a selected rectangle.

Fig. 21.3
Select an object by clicking the Select Draw Objects tool on the object.

Handles—

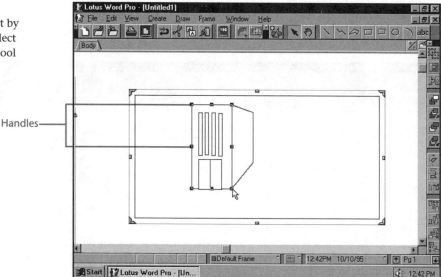

Note

If you have objects that overlap or are very close to each other, you may find it difficult to select the object you want. If you're having trouble selecting the object, hold down the Ctrl key while you select the object; this helps you zero in on the object you want.

To select multiple objects, click the first object, hold down the Shift key, and then select each additional object you want to select. You can also use the Selection tool to draw a dashed rectangle around one object or a group of objects. All objects included in the rectangle become selected. If you want to select all objects, click the Select All SmartIcon. To deselect all objects, click anywhere in the drawing frame.

Editing a Drawing

Editing in Draw isn't much different from editing in Word Pro. You select the objects you want to edit; then you edit the objects using the Draw Properties InfoBox, menus, or SmartIcons.

Edit objects in a drawing by moving or copying them just as you move or copy text or frames. Additionally, you can resize objects in the drawing.

Moving and Copying Objects

To move or copy an object, select the object or objects you want to edit. Choose Edit, Cut to remove the object and copy it to the Clipboard, or choose Edit, Copy to duplicate the object. Alternatively, you can click the Cut or Copy SmartIcon.

To move or copy the object to another frame or document, position the insertion point in the new location; choose Edit, Paste. Alternatively, click the Paste SmartIcon after positioning the insertion point.

To move an object within the drawing frame, select the object and drag it to the new location within the frame. If you have copied the object, choose to paste it; the copy is pasted on top of the original object. You can then drag the copied object to a new location.

Resizing Objects

When you select an object, handles appear around the edges of a shape or on the ends of a line. Use these handles to resize the object.

> **Tip**
>
> When resizing rectangles, use a corner handle to resize two sides at the same time.

To resize an object, select it and then position the mouse pointer over one of the handles. Drag the handle toward the center of the object to reduce the size or away from the center of the object to enlarge the size.

III

Professional Output

Troubleshooting

I accidentally clicked outside the drawing frame. How can I get back into the drawing?

Double-click the drawing frame; the Draw iconbars and menu appear.

I held the Shift key while selecting several objects, but when I deleted the objects, one that should not have been selected was deleted as well.

You may have included the object without knowing it. Always click the first object before pressing the Shift key to ensure you don't include an unwanted object. You can choose Edit, Undo to reverse the deletion and then try selecting the objects again.

I selected several objects, but I can't move them together; I have to move each one separately. Is there a better way?

Yes, select the objects and group them by clicking the Group SmartIcon. You can manipulate and format grouped objects as if they were one.

Formatting Objects

Word Pro enables you to select a line or shape and change the line and fill styles for that object. You can, for example, choose to make a line 1/4 point or 4 points. Additionally, you can choose a solid color as a fill for a shape or you can choose a pattern of two colors.

 You use the Draw Properties InfoBox to select line and fill options for your drawing objects (see fig. 21.4). To display the Draw Properties InfoBox, right-click the drawing object to display the quick menu. Choose Draw Properties. Alternatively, click the Draw Properties SmartIcon.

Applying Line Style

Line styles range between dashed and solid, very thin (3/4 point) to very thick (8 points). To apply a line style, select the object or objects in the drawing. In the Draw Properties InfoBox, click the arrow in the Line Style list box.

Fig. 21.4
Choose a line style and fill to format your objects.

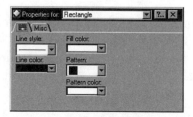

A drop-down list of over ten line styles appears. Select the line style you want to use for the selected object.

Applying Fill

If you create a closed shape—such as a rectangle or oval—you can apply a fill color or pattern to the shape. Select the shape and then in the Draw Properties InfoBox, click the Fill Color list box. A palette of available colors appears; select the color you want to apply.

Alternatively, you can apply a pattern to a shape by clicking the Pattern list box and selecting a pattern you like. Click the Pattern Color list box to select a color.

Extracting a Line Style and Fill

When formatting line style and fill, you may create a line or pattern you particularly like and want to use again in your drawing. You can extract a line style and fill from one object to another to save time in formatting and provide consistency in your drawing.

To extract a line style or fill, select the object containing the line or fill you want to use. Choose Draw, Extract Properties or click the Extract Line & Fill SmartIcon.

Applying Current Line Style and Fill

You may want to apply the current line style and fill pattern to selected objects—perhaps you have created an object using a previous line style and fill, and now you want to change the line and fill to the current line style and fill. Current is the line style of the selected line.

To apply the current line style and fill to an object, select the object and click the Apply Line & Fill SmartIcon.

Working with Multiple Objects

Working in Draw is much easier if you group objects together before you work with them. You treat grouped objects as if they were one. You can perform any action—copying, deleting, moving, and so on—on the group, just as you do on a single object.

Another handy feature of Draw is layering objects. You can place one object on top of another, somewhat like a stack of cards. Then you can move any object through the stack so that you can format it or change the appearance of the objects.

Grouping Objects

You might want to group objects to make formatting—applying line style or fill, for example— faster and easier or to move or delete several objects at the same time. Before grouping objects, you must first select each object. If you want, you can select and group several different sets of objects for easier manipulation in your drawing.

To group objects together, follow these steps:

1. Select the objects you want to group.

2. Click the Group SmartIcon. The objects are grouped, indicated by one set of handles surrounding all the objects (see fig. 21.5).

Fig. 21.5
Eight objects form a group surrounded by one set of selection handles; other objects are not included in the group.

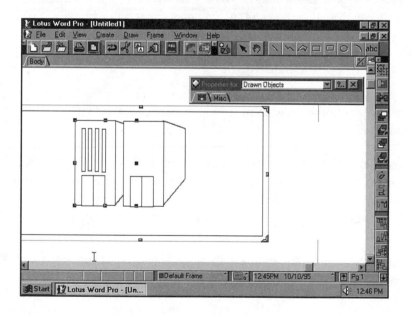

To ungroup a group of objects, select the group by clicking one of the objects, and then click the Ungroup SmartIcon.

Layering Objects

When drawing, you can place objects on top of other objects. Sometimes one object may hide another object entirely. Unless you change the order, the most recently drawn object appears on top of the stack. Use object layering to create perspective, or depth, in a drawing, for example.

After drawing several layered objects, you may decide that you want to change the order of the objects. You can bring an object to the front of the stack or send it to the back. You can even select an object and move it one layer forward or back. Figure 21.6 shows objects layered, with the object in the back selected.

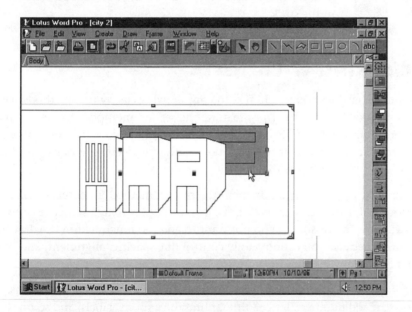

Fig. 21.6
When working with layers of objects, you can select the object at the bottom of the stack to edit, copy, or move.

> **Tip**
>
> To select an object hidden by other objects, hold down the Ctrl key while clicking the top object. Selection handles appear for each object in the stack one at a time with each click.

To change the priority—the object's place in the stack—select the object and right-click the object to display the quick menu. Choose Priority. From the Priority menu, choose one of the following: Bring to Front, Bring Forward One, Send to Back, or Send Back One. The descriptions of the menu choices match those of the following SmartIcons.

As an alternative, you can change the object's priority by clicking one of the following SmartIcons:

 Send object to the front. Moves the selected object to the front of all objects in the drawing frame.

 Send object one forward. Moves the selected object up one layer in the stack.

 Send object to the back. Moves the selected object to the back of all objects in the drawing frame.

 Send object one back. Moves the selected object back one layer in the stack.

Working with Text

Word Pro enables you to add text to your drawings using two methods. The first method is to use the Draw feature; the second method is to use a transparent frame that contains only text. If you want to add a great deal of text (more than a sentence or two), the best method is to create a transparent text frame to place on top of the drawing frame.

◀ See "Creating a Frame," p. 385

◀ See "Filling a Frame," p. 391

Adding text to the drawing frame is the perfect method for entering a small amount of text, such as a few words, logo or display text, a sentence or two, and so on. The reason you do not want to add too much text in the drawing frame is because you cannot easily control line spacing, alignment, and other text formatting features in Draw.

Adding text to the drawing frame is useful, however, in several situations. You can add numbers, letters, titles, phrases, captions, labels, and so on to your drawings, while ensuring the text remains with the drawing.

Text in the Draw feature is referred to as an object, just like a rectangle or line. Each line of text is a separate object, making it difficult to work with large bodies of text. You can use drawing features, such as rotating, grouping, and layering, to format and design with the text objects.

Creating Text in Draw

Each line of text (a line of text is created when you press Enter) is a separate object in the Draw feature. You have the option of moving, cutting, copying, and editing the line of text separately from any other text or graphic object in the drawing. However, you *must* format, align, and space the line of text separately from other objects in the drawing.

To create a text object in a drawing, click the Create Text SmartIcon. Move the mouse pointer into the draw frame and click the mouse button one time to position the cursor at the point where you want the text to begin. Type the text as you normally do.

To edit the text, use the Backspace and Delete keys. You can position the insertion point within the text anytime to delete or add text.

> **Note**
>
> To align the text (center, left, or right), click the Select Draw Objects tool, then click the text block. Handles appear (as with a drawing object). You move the text object to align it.

Formatting Text

When using the Draw feature in Word Pro, you cannot select text by dragging the cursor across it, as with normal text. In drawing, selecting the text means using the Selection tool to click the text object like any other object in the drawing frame. When selecting the text object in this manner, the text object can be treated like any other Draw object (moved, copied, deleted, and so on). To apply formatting, such as typeface, size, and style, you select the text object first and then apply the formatting.

> **Tip**
>
> You can also format drawing text by first clicking the insertion point in the text object, choosing the typeface, size, and style of the text, and then typing the text.

To format drawing text, follow these steps:

1. Type the text and then click the Select Draw Objects tool.

2. Select the text object by clicking it.

> **Tip**
>
> You can also boldface or italicize type in the text object by using the SmartIcons or the keyboard shortcuts (press Ctrl+B for bold or Ctrl+I for italic).

3. Choose the font, text size, and color by clicking the Font, Size, and Color buttons on the status bar and choosing the options you want.

You can apply other text attributes from the Draw Text Properties InfoBox. Right-click the text object and choose _D_raw Properties. Figure 21.7 shows selected text and the Draw Text Properties InfoBox.

Fig. 21.7
Format selected
text objects using
the Draw Text
Properties
InfoBox.

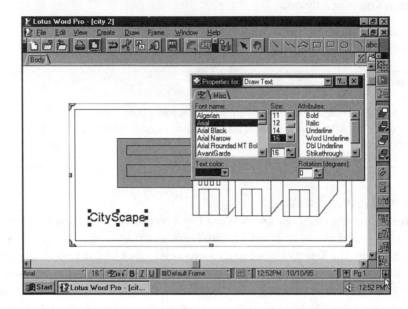

4. Align the formatted text by dragging the selected text block to a new position.

Using Advanced Drawing Techniques

You can select any drawing or text object in a drawing frame and perform various drawing techniques to help produce the results you want in your drawing. You can rotate objects, flip objects top to bottom and side to side, and align objects in a drawing. You can perform any of these techniques on a single object or group of objects.

Rotating Objects

You can easily rotate an object manually using the rotation arrows all objects have. To display the rotation arrows, double-click the object or group. Figure 21.8 shows the rotation arrows and the center point of the object group.

To rotate the object, drag any of the rotation arrows with the Selection tool. As you drag, a dashed outline of the object rotates with the arrow to indicate the amount of rotation. When you release the mouse button, the object appears in its new position.

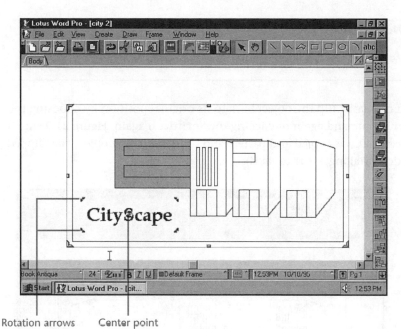

Rotation arrows   Center point

Fig. 21.8
Double-click an
object to display
its rotation arrows
and its center
point.

The center point of the object indicates the point around which the object rotates (like the center of a pinwheel). If you click and drag the center point to a different location and then drag a rotation arrow, the object's rotation is different. To learn how to control the center point, experiment with moving it around within an object. To return to the original center point, click inside the drawing frame but outside the object. Then double-click the object again.

You can also rotate an object a few degrees at a time by clicking the Rotate SmartIcon. Each time you click the icon, the object rotates a few degrees clockwise. You can turn rotation to counterclockwise through the Draw Properties InfoBox.

Flipping Objects

You can flip objects top to bottom and side to side to help create and organize your drawing. Use the Draw menu or the SmartIcons to flip your drawing.

To flip from top to bottom, select the object or group of objects and choose Draw, Flip, Top to Bottom. Alternatively, click the Flip Object Top to Bottom SmartIcon.

To flip an object side to side, select the object or group of objects and choose Draw, Flip, Side to Side. Alternatively, click the Flip Object Side to Side SmartIcon.

III

Professional Output

> **Note**
>
> You cannot flip text objects, but you can rotate them.

You can easily flip the object back to its original position by choosing the menu command again or clicking the SmartIcon again. Figure 21.9 shows an object that was copied and pasted, and then the pasted object was flipped vertically (along a vertical axis).

Fig. 21.9
Select an object and flip it to add variety or to enhance the design in your drawings.

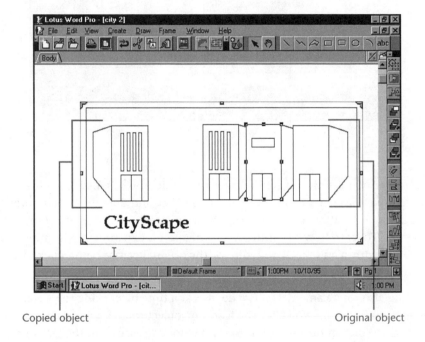

Copied object   Original object

Aligning Objects

Word Pro enables you to align drawn objects to save time and to give your drawings a more professional look. You can align objects along their top, bottom, left, or right edges using the Draw menu or the SmartIcons.

To align several objects in your drawing, select the objects and choose Draw, Align, and Top, Bottom, Left, or Right. Alternatively, choose one of the following SmartIcons:

   Align the objects at the top

   Align the objects to the bottom

Align the objects to the left

    Align the objects to the right

Figure 21.10 shows one use for aligning objects. The rectangles in the organizational chart are copied so they all are the same size; however, instead of wasting time trying to align the rectangles manually, select the rectangles on any row and click the Align the Objects At the Top SmartIcon.

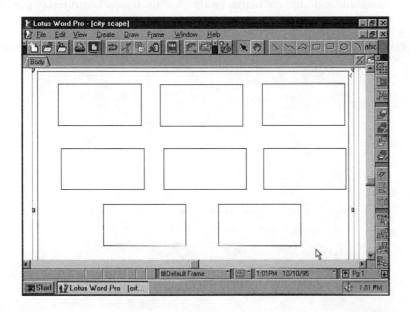

Fig. 21.10
Select objects and choose to align them along their top, bottom, left, or right edges; these objects are aligned along the top.

Note

You may prefer to use the grid to align objects manually. You can show the grid by opening the Draw Properties InfoBox and selecting the grid type you want. Additionally, you can show the grid settings and choose to snap to grid using the Draw, Grid menu commands. The grid is an invisible pattern of horizontal and vertical lines that acts like a magnet by aligning the objects you draw or move.

III

Professional Output

From Here...

You've learned to create drawings and modify drawings in Word Pro. Now you can apply some of that knowledge to making your documents look attractive and professional. See the following chapters for more information:

- Chapter 20, "Using Advanced Frame Techniques," gives you information about formatting frames and using frame styles. Additionally, this chapter shows you how to work with multiple frames.

- Chapter 22, "Desktop Publishing with Word Pro," introduces desktop publishing, design elements, and design strategies. Learn to lay out an eye-catching document to use in your business.

- Chapter 25, "Importing, Exporting, and Linking Files," describes how to import graphics and edit them.

Chapter 22

Desktop Publishing with Word Pro

by Sue Plumley

You can use Word Pro to create simple letters and memos, check spelling, print envelopes, and perform basic everyday word processing tasks. You can also use Word Pro to perform true desktop publishing tasks such as produce professional-looking newsletters complete with pictures, columns, mastheads, and so on; create multiple-page reports with charts and graphs; and generate a complete advertising campaign with newspaper ads, flyers, and brochures.

> **Note**
>
> The content and form of documents such as flyers, brochures, and forms are described later in this chapter.

Desktop publishing is using your computer and software to create formatted, professional-looking documents, such as newsletters, brochures, flyers, and the like. Anyone can produce a formatted document; however, creating a formatted document that is attractive, easy to read, and professional looking takes some work.

Word Pro provides the tools necessary for desktop publishing: font and paragraph formatting capability, frame and table creation, use of SmartMasters, and style creation and modification to name only a few. In addition to the tools, however, you must also understand what it takes to make an attractive document—design elements and strategies.

Producing attractive documents means using certain design strategies, such as planning the document before creating it. You must plan for the amount of text and the type of graphics you want to use, then you can decide how to arrange the elements on the page. Additionally, you'll want to choose the right document type for the job, the number of pages, and so on.

Certain design elements must be considered when producing a professional-looking document. You need to consider, for example, which page orientation would look best with your text and graphics, how many columns to use, and how to arrange the text on the page. This chapter shows you how to plan your document and how to incorporate the design elements to create a successful desktop-published document.

In this chapter, you learn how to:

- Plan design strategies
- Maintain consistency within the document
- Use design elements to enhance the page

Introducing Desktop Publishing

Personal computers are capable of performing page layout and design tasks that were once only attempted in print shops by conventional typesetters. The ability to write a document and design it completely on your own saves the desktop publisher time, money, and effort. The benefits of doing your own page layout become apparent as you learn more about Word Pro and its special features. This section discusses some of those features and how you can benefit from desktop publishing with Word Pro.

What is Desktop Publishing?

In desktop publishing, you use the personal computer to create a formatted document, usually for widespread distribution. The personal computer includes the software program used for formatting the page. Word Pro is a powerful tool for page formatting. In addition to Word Pro's word processing capabilities, the program includes drawing, charting, and table features that contribute to a well-formatted document.

◀ See "Creating a Frame," p. 385

◀ See "Creating a Drawing," p. 426

Other programs, such as spreadsheet, database, scanning, and so on, can also combine with Word Pro for a comprehensive and effective end result. Desktop publishing includes all elements, applications, and tools necessary to produce a document that provides the reader with good-looking, high-quality output.

Benefiting from Desktop Publishing

The obvious benefit of desktop publishing is the professional-looking document you produce. In addition, desktop publishing with Word Pro affords you many other advantages, such as saving you time and money, allowing you more control over your documents, and letting you integrate other software programs to produce more comprehensive documents.

You save time and money by formatting your own documents. You don't need to travel back and forth to a print shop or professional typesetter; you don't waste time correcting someone else's mistakes or explaining what you want. You don't need to wait for the print shop to call you with the proof or work around typesetting schedules. By producing your own page layout, you don't have to pay for professional typesetting.

Formatting your own documents gives you control over your document. You can experiment with various type and graphic elements to see what looks best. You can edit or add text at the last minute, update a spreadsheet or chart, or change dates and times in a flyer or program. Finally, you don't need to wait for the print shop to complete your changes or pay for alterations to the original documents.

> **Tip**
>
> Consider personalizing some documents by adding a customer's name or other pertinent information in the text.

Another advantage of doing your own page layout is that you can use other software programs to enhance your documents. You can add a spreadsheet or scanned art to your document, then modify the document to suit your purpose. Using your own applications and data means more efficient and effective documents.

Word Pro Features for Desktop Publishing

Word Pro is a word processing package with features that expedite day-to-day chores, such as typing and editing documents, spell and grammar checking, performing mail merge, and so on. Word Pro is also a powerful tool to use for page layout and design. You can easily produce attractive designs by using Word Pro features, such as the frame feature, SmartMasters, and styles.

▶ See "Importing and Exporting Text and Data Files," p. 513

With frames, you can add special text, graphic images, tables, spreadsheets, and so on. You can add a drawing, chart, or equation in a frame. Frames

◀ See "Formatting Frames," p. 398

III

Professional Output

make page layout easy by enabling you to divide and organize the text and pictures. Additionally, frames can make the page attractive with added options such as borders, lines, and shading.

Another feature well suited to desktop publishing is Word Pro's SmartMaster style sheets. The SmartMasters were created by professionals who use the design elements consistently and deliberately to give you a library of integrated styles. If you use a SmartMaster as a base for your document, the document will look professional and attractive.

◀ See "Using Word Pro's SmartMasters," p. 242

Additionally, you can create your own SmartMasters and styles and save the page and paragraph formatting for use in other documents. Using similar formats adds consistency to your company's documents and makes them easily recognizable to your customers.

Suppose, for example, you create a company newsletter that you mail to customers each month. By saving the original paragraph and page settings, text styles, and so on in a SmartMaster, you have a base from which to begin each month's newsletter. Each month's newsletter is formatted similarly to the last, thus guaranteeing consistency.

◀ See "Modifying SmartMasters," p. 247

Word Pro has many more features, covered in the rest of this book, that make the software perfect for desktop publishing—including drawing, charting, graphics control, and column control. Word Pro may be the most valuable tool you use in formatting and designing your business documents.

Using Design Strategies

Creating a successful design involves many steps. Because each step builds on the last, the first step is the most important: planning and preparing your design for a specific purpose. The main purpose of all printed material is to convey a message to the reader. Likewise, the main purpose of design is to convey its own message—a message that attracts the reader's attention and persuades the reader to pick up and read the printed material.

This section helps you define the purpose of your document, gives you hints to plan your piece, and includes ways to create consistency in a document and add emphasis for interest.

Planning the Document

Planning your document includes writing and organizing the text and graphics (called the *copy*), selecting the format, and determining the document's size. Each decision you make depends on the purpose of your document. If you're announcing a sale, for example, you want to include the word "Sale" in the document, adding prices, discounts, and so on. You also want to announce the sale on a sheet of paper large enough to be seen and in a suitable format, such as a flyer, and in a type size large enough to be noticed. How you distribute the flyer depends on your audience. The decisions you make when planning your document determine its success or failure.

Purpose

When planning a document for publication, you need to know the specific purpose of that document. What do you want to achieve? Who is your audience? What do you want to communicate? Answers to these questions help you define the purpose of your document.

What do you want to achieve with your document? Are you selling a new product? Are you having a sale? Are you informing employees of new benefits? What do you want to communicate? Deciding the desired results helps you determine purpose.

Who is your intended audience? Who are you trying to reach: customers or prospective customers; fellow employees; your boss? Are you trying to reach a group of professionals or the general public? Are your readers men or women, young or old, rich or poor? You cannot successfully communicate with readers unless you know who they are. Each audience has its own communication needs. The more you know about your readers, the easier it is to plan and prepare the appropriate design for your document. Answer these questions, and your document will have a successful purpose.

Content

When writing and organizing the text and graphics for your document, keep your purpose in mind. Organize the main topics and subtopics first, then form them into well-written, interesting copy. The main topics, or heads, of the document should pique the reader's interest and persuade him or her to read the text. Any added graphic images, such as charts, drawings, or photos, should contribute to gaining the reader's interest. Remember that everything—heads, body text, images, and design—must support the message and interest the reader.

Document Format

The format, or type, of document you use—flyer, brochure, letter, newsletter, report, and so on—depends on the purpose of the document, the document's size, and its method of distribution. If the method of distribution is the mail, for example, the document must conform to postal regulations for size, shape, and weight of mailable pieces.

The size of a particular document depends on the amount of copy, the format, the quantity printed, and the method of distribution. Most document types conform to common sizes used in the printing industry. When you stray from these common sizes, you must pay more for paper, printing, and mailing. Naturally, if you produce a document on your printer, you must also conform to your printer's size limits. Common sizes and document types are listed in the section "Types of Documents" later in this chapter.

Maintaining Consistency

First impressions are critical in a printed document. If the document doesn't impress a reader at first glance, the reader ignores it. *Consistency* can help you create a positive first impression. A consistent page is clear, organized, and simple. Consistency in design and typography is vital to the success of any document. Proper use of the design elements, such as balance, margins, columns, rules, and shading promote consistency.

Balancing, or distributing, the type and design elements on the page creates a pleasing typeset piece. Keeping individual pages balanced throughout the document, for example, by using the same number of columns and the same margin widths, enhances consistency. The section "Using Design Elements" later in this chapter explains these design elements and how to keep them consistent.

> **Tip**
>
> Create consistency with frames by using styles to make all frames modeled after one formatted frame; do the same thing with text styles.

◀ See "Creating Styles," p. 254

◀ See "Using Frame Styles," p. 416

You can also achieve consistency by repeating design and type elements. To create consistency, for example, you can use the same size lines above all heads or end each section with the company logo, or you can use the same size and style of heads throughout the document. Figure 22.1 shows consistency in an advertisement. Notice the typeface, type size, margins, and graphic lines. Figure 22.2 shows the same advertisement with much less consistency.

===============================

GAN ANIN
RECORDS AND TAPES

Music For The World!

IRISH	BLUES
ENGLISH	EARLY JAZZ
WELSH	CLASSIC FOLK
SCOTTISH	COUNTRY
AFRICAN	FOLK ROCK
REGGAE	CALYPSO
SALSA	SOCA
CUBAN	GOSPEL
CHINESE	APPALACHIAN

4714 N. ALVIS STREET, CHARLESTON, WV 25303
CALL TODAY TOLL FREE
1-800-011-2345

===============================

Fig. 22.1
This consistency was created by repeating and balancing elements.

Adding Emphasis

As mentioned earlier, first impressions influence a reader. You can generate a favorable first impression by using design elements consistently. Another tool you can use to create a good first impression is *emphasis*.

Use emphasis to attract attention and add pizzazz to your document. You can emphasize a subject in a variety of ways. Use a graphic element such as a double line to frame a figure, for example; or a fancy typeface to make important text stand out. Shading or color within a frame attracts the eye just as a series of vertical or horizontal lines can lead the eye to a specific point in the document.

Fig. 22.2
Too many varying
elements cause
this advertisement
to be inconsistent.

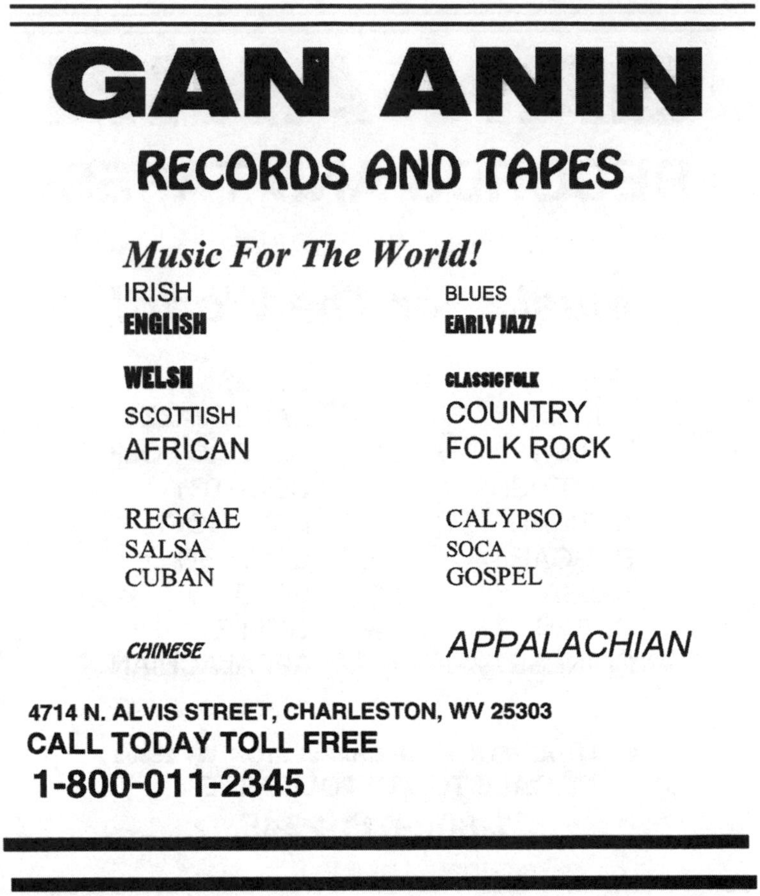

GAN ANIN
RECORDS AND TAPES

Music For The World!

IRISH	BLUES
ENGLISH	**EARLY JAZZ**
WELSH	**CLASSIC FOLK**
SCOTTISH	COUNTRY
AFRICAN	FOLK ROCK
REGGAE	CALYPSO
SALSA	SOCA
CUBAN	GOSPEL
CHINESE	*APPALACHIAN*

4714 N. ALVIS STREET, CHARLESTON, WV 25303
CALL TODAY TOLL FREE
1-800-011-2345

Tip

▶ See "Formatting Text," p. 464

You can use large 60- or 72-point type to add emphasis, as well as bold text, bullets, and numbered lists.

It is just as important to know when *not* to use emphasis as it is to know when to use it. Too much emphasis in a document creates disorder and clutter. The reader might not understand the important information because everything stands out. Figure 22.3, for example, shows a flyer with the proper amount of emphasis added. Figure 22.4 demonstrates the misuse of emphasis in the same flyer. Remember to add emphasis to only one idea or topic per page of your document.

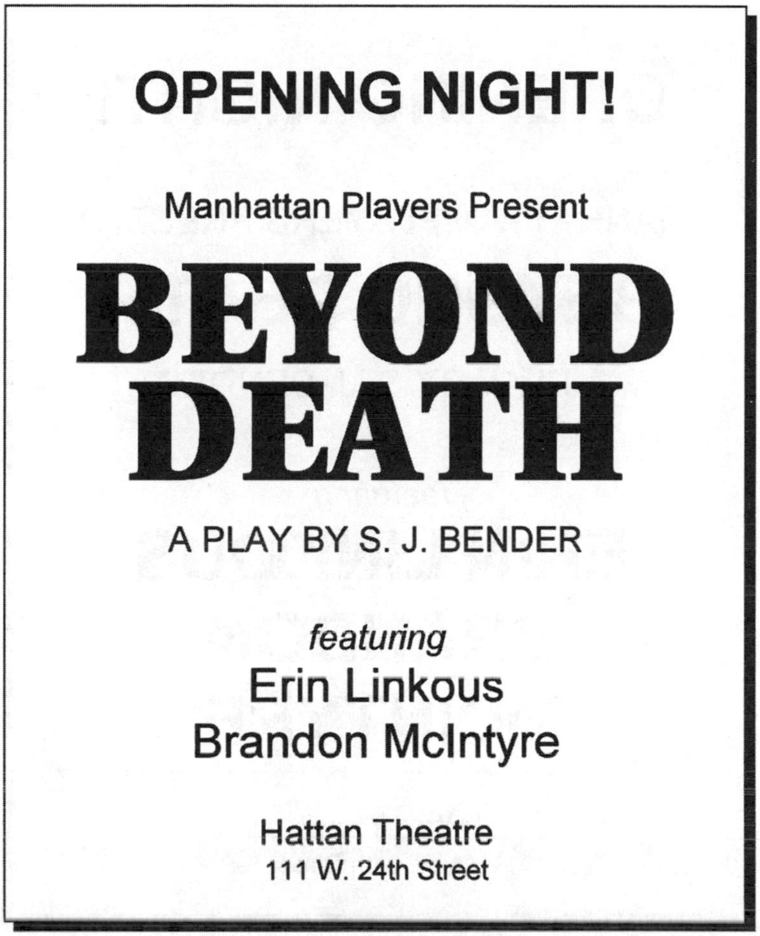

OPENING NIGHT!

Manhattan Players Present

BEYOND DEATH

A PLAY BY S. J. BENDER

featuring
Erin Linkous
Brandon McIntyre

Hattan Theatre
111 W. 24th Street

Fig. 22.3
When you emphasize just one element on a page, it really stands out.

Troubleshooting

My document looks too crowded with too many fonts, lines, shaded areas, and so on. What can I do to make it look better?

For the most successful document, the one that is read more frequently, keep it simple. Too many different fonts or too many graphics confuse the reader and create a busy page. The reader might decide it's too much trouble to read your document. Tone it down; keep it simple.

I have more text than will fit in the size document I've chosen. What can I do to fit it all in?

Don't crowd the text; crowded text is difficult to read. Instead, cut some text. Cut out anything that does not support the purpose. Reduce sentences to catchy phrases and phrases to single words that deliver impact.

OPENING NIGHT!

MANHATTAN PLAYERS PRESENT

BEYOND DEATH

A PLAY BY S. J. BENDER

featuring

ERIN LINKOUS
BRANDON
MCINTYRE

Hattan Theatre
111 W. 24th Street

Types of Documents

You can create numerous types of documents, such as brochures, newsletters, books, forms, magazines, and programs—the variety is endless. Each type of document uses common sizes and layouts, although some variation adds interest to the designs.

The following section describes some of the most common kinds of documents and sizes. Some sample layouts in the form of thumbnail sketches are included. *Thumbnails* are small drawings placed where the text and graphics fit onto the page. Thumbnails are used for design and not for actual text or details.

Creating a Flyer

A *flyer* is a quick-sell advertisement designed to announce, introduce, or re-mind. A flyer briefly describes sales, grand openings, new products, and so on.

Use a flyer to attract immediate attention and get the point across quickly. When you design the flyer, use a short, hard-sell technique that includes a list of products, items, or services, or a short list of dates, times, and places. Use no unnecessary explanations, but do use descriptive adjectives. Figure 22.5 shows a sample layout for a flyer; use heads and subheads, a picture, and a small amount of body text. *Body text* is the majority of your text, usually sized at 10- or 12-point.

◀ See "Changing Character For-matting," p. 79

▶ See "Formatting Text," p. 464

Fig. 22.5
A flyer should be laid out on one page, using pictures, heads, and just a small amount of body text.

You can print a flyer on one side of paper, one column or two, with large typefaces and perhaps bulleted lists. Common flyer sizes, in *portrait* (vertical) or *landscape* (horizontal) orientation, include 5 1/2 by 8 1/2 inches, 8 1/2 by 11 inches, or 8 1/2 by 14 inches.

Using Brochures

A *brochure* explains, instructs, details, or informs; therefore, the customer will keep this document for future reference. A brochure might include a list and description of products, a detailed explanation of services, or a price list.

Design the cover (page 1 or the front panel—whatever is appropriate for the document) for soft-sell to gently invite the reader to open and read the contents. Inside the document, describe the details of the service or product,

III

Professional Output

perhaps with art, logos, or pictures. Titles, heads, subheads, and captions accompany body text in a brochure. The back panel or page contains summary points in a bulleted or numbered list, return address, logo, and often a mailing panel. A logical development of ideas leads the eye through the brochure, starting with the front panel or cover, continuing through the inside, and finishing with the back panel.

◀ See "Changing Paragraph Formatting," p. 88

Figure 22.6 shows a sample layout for the outside panels of a six-panel brochure. A graphic image is used on panel 1 (the right panel) with several large headlines. The middle panel (panel 6) is for mailing, and panel 5 (to the far left) contains a summary and the company's address.

Fig. 22.6
The outside panels of a six-panel brochure; the layout should make you want to read the inside as well.

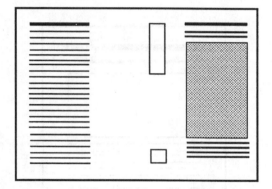

> **Tip**
>
> Word Pro enables you to rotate text using drawing text in a frame.

Brochures are usually printed in landscape mode (11 by 8 1/2 inches for three columns or 14 by 8 1/2 inches for four columns). A brochure can also be in portrait mode (11 by 17 inches folded to 8 1/2 by 11 inches; or 8 1/2 by 11 inches folded to 5 1/2 by 8 1/2 inches). The layout in figure 22.7 is for a landscape 8 1/2 by 11 inches in three columns, illustrating the inside three panels of a six-panel brochure.

Producing Newsletters

Newsletters come in many sizes, shapes, and designs. A newsletter generally has from 1 to 16 pages with one to four columns per page, in either portrait or landscape orientation (portrait is the most common).

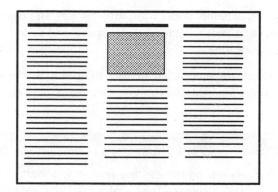

Fig. 22.7
Use the inside of
the brochure to
describe products
or services.

Newsletters can explain, inform, announce, introduce, repeat—just about anything. Some companies use newsletters to inform clients or employees; many companies use newsletters to sell products and services. Some companies even make a business of selling informational newsletters.

The first page of a newsletter contains a *nameplate*. A nameplate is an identifier for the newsletter that consists of the name of the newsletter or the company's name, a catchy phrase, and perhaps a graphics image. Any text in the nameplate is usually in a different typeface than the body text and the heads. You can create a nameplate in Word Pro, in a paint program, or an artist can hand draw a nameplate for your newsletter. The type can be stretched, condensed, slanted, vertical, on an arc, or changed in any way that makes it stand out.

Headers or footers provide consistency within a newsletter and add a professional touch. Never, however, place a header or footer on the first page of the newsletter. Start page numbering and headers/footers on page two and continue throughout the document. In addition to a page number, you might want to add the publication's name, the date, the volume, or the issue number in a header or footer.

◀ See "Adding
Headers and
Footers," p. 120

◀ See "Working
with Text,"
p. 434

If you send a newsletter by mail, you will want to include a mailing panel, on the last page of the document, that contains your return address, postage permit, and a place for mailing labels.

> **Caution**
>
> Be sure the postage permit follows U.S. Postal Service regulations governing the exact placement, wording, and punctuation. Check with your Postmaster.

The most important design point of a newsletter is consistency within an issue and between issues. Individual page layouts differ from issue to issue, but the nameplate, dateline, publication information, and design elements (column number and width, balance, gutter space, and so on) should remain nearly the same each time.

Type styles, spacing, and graphic elements also need to be the same between issues. Use Word Pro SmartMasters and/or styles to achieve consistency between issues.

Tip

Tie all company documents together—so they are easily recognizable—by maintaining consistency between documents. Use the same type styles, add the company's logo, or use the same colors of ink and paper.

◀ See "Setting Page Size and Orientation," p. 106

Popular sizes for newsletters are 8 1/2 by 11 inches, printed on both sides; 11 by 17 inches, folded to 8 1/2 by 11 inches or smaller, for mailing; or 22 inches by 17 inches, printed on both sides, folded to 11 by 17 and then to 8 1/2 by 11 inches (see fig. 22.8).

Fig. 22.8
One side of a 22- by-17-inch newsletter uses mirrored balance of columns.

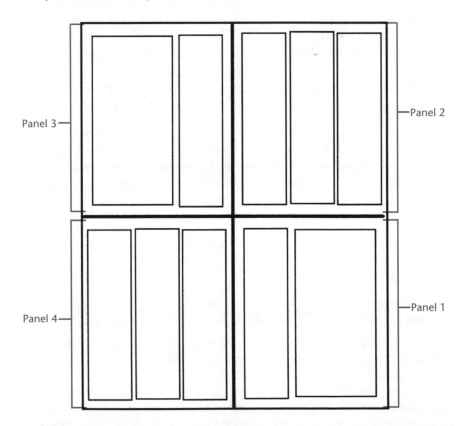

Panel 3

Panel 2

Panel 4

Panel 1

Using Design Elements

After you choose the purpose and type of document you want to use, your next step is to choose the document design. The document design includes *design elements*: size, shape, format, and layout. These and other elements help make a document attractive, practical, and effective. The primary purpose of any document is to communicate a message to readers, so effective use of basic design elements can help you accomplish this task. In this section, you learn about using the elements of design to produce professional-looking documents.

Choosing Page Orientation

A basic element of design is the *page orientation* of the document: portrait or landscape. Each orientation has specific uses, and each employs the design elements in certain ways. Which orientation you choose depends on the purpose of your document and the size and shape of your copy. Determine how much copy you have and how the information flows on the pages. Is the copy in short lists that you can include in a narrow column, or is it in long paragraphs that need wide columns? Is the art horizontal or vertical? Can the text fit the same orientation as the artwork? If so, mirror, or reflect, this orientation with the page.

Although *portrait* orientation is vertical, it's measured by width first and then height (8 1/2 by 11 inches, for example). Lists of words or short sentences, graphics or photos that are taller than they are wide, shorter headlines, and multiple subheads fit portrait orientation. You can use large amounts of text in portrait orientation if you use two or three columns to divide the page.

◀ See "Setting Page Size and Orientation," p. 106

> **Tip**
>
> Usually, you produce letters, newsletters, resumes, and reports in portrait orientation. Flyers and books can be portrait-oriented, as well.

Landscape orientation is also measured by width first and then height (11 by 8 1/2 inches). Long headlines, wide graphics or photos, and more pictures than text work well with this orientation. This mode is also well suited for spreadsheets, tables, charts, flyers, brochures, envelopes, programs, some forms, and books.

Balancing Design Elements

Text and graphics must *balance* on the page to create an attractive document; one element cannot dominate the other. A well-balanced page of text and

III

Professional Output

graphics attracts readers to the document and leads them through the text in logical steps. A balanced document also helps readers mentally organize the information after one reading, which helps the reader retain the information longer. Page layout uses three major kinds of balance: symmetrical, asymmetrical, and modular. Staying with one kind of balance throughout the document avoids confusion for the reader.

Consider the text as the gray of the page (a page of nothing but text gives the impression of being gray). Graphics, art, photos, and illustrations are gray if they are light, but black if they are very dark; thus black objects have more weight than gray or white space. Measure the page's white space in the margins, gutter space, the area around headlines and graphics, and even within the text (line and paragraph spacing, for example). By balancing the grays, blacks, and whites on a page, you end up balancing the actual text, graphics, and white space.

Using Symmetrical Balance

Symmetrical balance is the equal distribution of the text, graphics, and white space on a page. *White space* is any area free of text and graphics, such as margins, gutters, and so on. Size, form, and arrangement of page elements correspond on opposite sides of a point (usually the center). What you see on one side of the center guide is replicated on the opposite side. Figure 22.9 shows two examples of symmetrical balance; the center guide on both is the gutter space between the columns.

Fig. 22.9
Symmetrical balance in either portrait (left) or landscape orientation provides an even, formal look to the page.

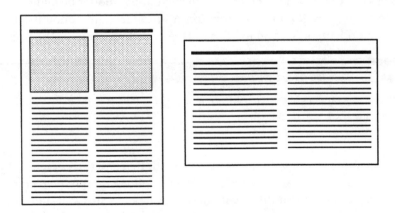

Symmetrical balance is a division of the visual weight on the page; the text and graphics are exactly the same on either side of the center guide. Symmetrical balance is a formal, sophisticated, even balance that gives consistency to a document.

Tip

Right- and left-aligned body text provides more white space than justified text.

Using Asymmetrical Balance

With *asymmetrical balance*, the elements on either side of the center guide don't exactly correspond, but the overall weight of the elements remains about the same. In this mode, you balance large areas of gray with large areas of white, or small black areas with larger gray areas. Asymmetrical balance results in a more free-form, informal, and interesting document than symmetrical balance; however asymmetrical balance is harder to use properly and consistently (see fig. 22.10).

◀ See "Changing Paragraph Formatting," p. 88

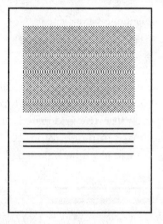
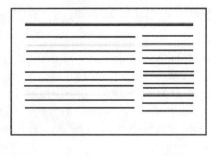

Fig. 22.10
Asymmetrical balance in either portrait (left) or landscape orientation makes the page design more interesting.

Using Modular Balance

Modular balance uses nonprinting intersecting guidelines to form boxes across the page and places text and graphics in the boxes to form an ordered systematic layout. You can begin forming the grid, or modules, by dividing the page into two or three sections. Then divide these sections into two or three more sections (see fig. 22.11).

To help divide the page, you can draw a frame that covers the page. Make the frame transparent by setting the frame properties for Pattern to none with no wraparound. You can use the Drawing feature to add vertical and horizontal lines to form the grid.

III

Professional Output

Fig. 22.11
The grid modules on the left were converted to a page using symmetrical balance.

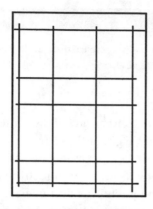
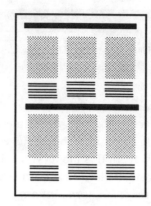

◀ See "Formatting Frames," p. 398

◀ See "Creating a Drawing," p. 426

Tip

The balance you choose needs to be consistent throughout the document. Variations, such as extra white space or more figures, can add emphasis and interest.

The modular layout can be symmetrical or asymmetrical. Figure 22.12 shows the preceding sample grid with asymmetrical balancing of text and graphics. In contrast to the example in figure 22.11, which uses the grid exactly as drawn, figure 22.12 combines two of the grid boxes into one. Word Pro's frame and grid features can help you create and use modular balance.

Fig. 22.12
The grid has been converted to an asymmetrically balanced layout.

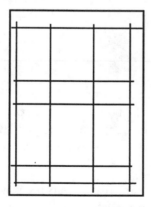

Using White Space for Contrast

To provide contrast, emphasis, and a rest for the reader's eyes, use white space with a document. A headline, text, or a graphic has far more impact when surrounded by white space. As a rule, balance white space throughout the page with text and graphics (gray space) on a 50-50 ratio. This amount of white space might seem like a lot, but multiple ways are available to apply white space.

Use generous margins in your documents as an effective way of implementing white space. Additionally, gutter space between columns, the use of left-aligned text, extra paragraph spacing, and so on enable you to add white space throughout the page. It is important to try to squeeze large areas of white space to the outside of the page instead of trapping large pockets inside the page. Such pockets prevent you from achieving balance and are obstacles to the eye. Figure 22.13 shows good use of white space in two thumbnails.

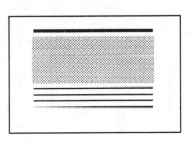 

Fig. 22.13
The width of the margins are varied to add white space to the document.

Establishing Margins

Margins are important to any document because they provide the majority of your white space, and white space contributes to the ease of reading. If you want contrast, emphasis, and the reader's attention, use wider margins; a gray page of text and crowded graphics might distract the reader.

> **Note**
>
> If you have a small amount of copy, you can make the margins one inch, two inches, or even wider. The margins don't have to be even on top, bottom, left, and right; often, a design is more effective with a large margin on one side and smaller, equal margins on the other three sides.

Figure 22.14 shows common margins for a newsletter and brochure. These layouts have three columns surrounded by margins and separated with gutter space. Figure 22.15 shows a more creative use of margins and white space for the same two documents.

III

Professional Output

Fig. 22.14
Landscape and portrait orientations using common margins for a newsletter and brochure are always a safe bet.

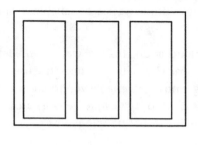
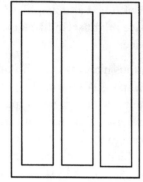

Fig. 22.15
Use columns surrounded by unequal margins to create an interesting effect.

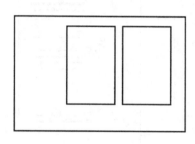
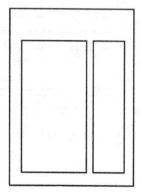

Planning Columns

Some documents might require a division of copy by *columns*. Columns help you organize the placement of text and graphics. Nonprinting vertical guides create boundaries by which you lay out the columns on the page in Word Pro.

The first point to remember when designing columns is that you read from left to right; text, therefore, should flow from the left column to the right. Because the main purpose of the document is to present information to the reader in an easy-to-understand, easy-to-follow format, don't confuse the reader by using overly creative columns.

On portrait-oriented pages, use no more than four columns per page (three is even better); on landscape-oriented pages, use no more than six (four or five columns is preferred). Too many columns clutter the page and are hard to follow. Additionally, lines of text might have to be too short to fit in narrow columns, and small graphics might be ineffective.

Columns can be of equal or uneven widths; you can even combine wide and narrow columns on the page to create interest. Figure 22.16 illustrates facing pages divided equally into six columns; whereas figure 22.17 shows uneven columns created for interest.

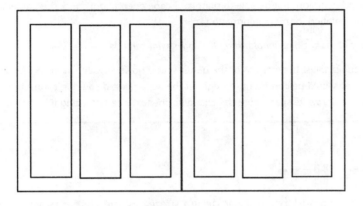

Fig. 22.16
A document divided into equal columns makes the text easy to follow.

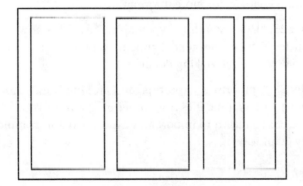

Fig. 22.17
A document divided into uneven columns is interesting to read as long as the copy fits the column widths.

When you use columns, you must consider the gutter space. A *gutter* is the white space between two columns and must be considered as another resting place for the eyes. Narrow gutters can make the text in columns hard to read by forcing a reader's eye to jump to the column to the left or to the right. On the other hand, very wide gutters tend to separate ideas or lose the reader. Limiting gutters to between 1/4 inch and 1/2 inch is a good compromise. Remember to also keep the gutters consistent throughout the document.

III

Professional Output

Troubleshooting

I changed the page orientation in Word Pro but my printer won't print the page the way I want. Is there anything I can do?

Your printer might not be able to print landscape orientation; check the printer's documentation for more information.

I can't fit the last amount of text on the page; what can I do?

You could adjust the margins or the gutter space; however, keep in mind that all changes should be consistent throughout the document. If you don't want to give up the extra white space, consider changing the text size or spacing instead.

From Here...

Now that you understand basic design strategies and elements, you can refer to the following chapters for more information:

- Chapter 23, "Understanding Typography," explains how to effectively use typefaces, type sizes, text alignment, tabs, indents, and spacing to create a professional-looking document.

- Chapter 25, "Importing, Exporting, and Linking Files," shows you how to use text and graphic files from other programs in your Word Pro documents; you learn to import and export text and graphics, and to modify graphic images.

Chapter 23

Understanding Typography

by Sue Plumley

One of the most important elements of desktop publishing and design is *typography*. Typography is the style, arrangement, or appearance of typeset matter; typography also refers to the general appearance of the printed page.

Typography is not just about the font, the size of the text, or the alignment you choose. It's also about your message, the design of your document, aesthetics, readability, and your reader. A reader judges the document by the type you choose and the way you present it. When looking at a printed page, the reader decides whether to pick up the document and read it and whether to keep the document or throw it away. The reader's decision is often primarily influenced by the strength of your design.

The purpose of any printed document is to attract and maintain a reader's attention. You can accomplish this goal through the use of certain design elements in conjunction with good typography. Just as certain rules apply to designing the page, common guidelines govern the way you format text. If followed, these guidelines guarantee an attractive, readable page.

In this chapter, you learn how to:

- Effectively use typefaces, type sizes, and text attributes
- Ensure readability with carefully chosen type
- Use text alignment as part of the page design
- Use tabs and indents to organize text

Formatting Text

◀ See "Using Design Elements," p. 455

When you format text in a document, consider the design elements and strategies. First, you should plan your use of text while considering the purpose of your document and your audience. Some typefaces, Goudy and Copperplate for example, present a sophisticated, formal look; whereas others, Hobo or Brush, exhibit an informal, unrestrained feel. Similarly, large type sizes sometimes emit an urgent or flamboyant feel, and smaller type sizes can exhibit a conservative, conventional strategy. Match the typeface and type size to your audience and your copy.

Second, consider the design elements as you format your text. Consistency, emphasis, balance, and white space can and should be applied to text formatting so the resulting document is attractive and professional-looking. Create consistency, for example, by using the same font, size, and alignment for all heads in the document. Balance the text on the page by using the largest text at the top and/or bottom and smaller text in between.

Using Typefaces

A *typeface* is a specific style or design of the actual letters of type. Arial, for example, is a typeface, as is Times Roman. These two typefaces are the most commonly used in desktop publishing programs and word processors. *Font* is often used interchangeably with typeface and is also a term used in desktop publishing.

> **Tip**
>
> Use serif type when you want the text to look dignified, legible, and classical; use sans serif when you want a more modern, contemporary look to the text.

Times Roman and Arial are examples of *serif* and *sans serif* typefaces, respectively. Serifs are the fine cross strokes across the ends of the main strokes of the characters (see fig. 23.1). Serif type has a varied *stroke* (the thickness of the lines that form the letter) that adds a horizontal flow to the text, making the letters easier to read and recognize.

◀ See "Changing Character Formatting," p. 79

Sans serif type has no serif and has a uniform stroke (refer to fig. 23.1). Many sans serif typefaces are hard to read in large quantities—such as body text— but can be used successfully in captions, headlines, forms, and so on.

In many documents, you can use a serif typeface for body text and a sans serif typeface for the heads, subheads, and captions. Using the two typefaces in this way creates variety and interest in the document.

Times Roman

Arial

Fig. 23.1
Serif type (top) has
a varied stroke,
whereas sans serif
strokes (bottom)
are a consistent
stroke.

> **Tip**
>
> Don't use more than two or three typefaces in any one document. Too many type-
> faces distract the reader and look unprofessional.

In addition, if you have Adobe Type Manager (ATM) fonts, you may want to use them with your documents. ATM contains more than 20 fonts, including Utopia Black, Symbol, Shelley Allegro Script, Brush Script, and Bodini. You can purchase ATM fonts wherever software is sold. These typefaces give you a variety of choices for your documents.

Using Type Sizes

Type size is measured in points from the top of the tallest *ascender* (b, d, t, and h are letters with ascenders) to the bottom of the lowest *descender* (g, j, and p are letters with descenders). One point equals 1/72 inch; 12 points equal a *pica*; six picas equal an inch (thus 72 points to the inch). Picas and points are standard measures in printing and typesetting.

The main portion of any document is the body text, and the common sizes for body text are 9-, 10-, 11-, and 12-point. Type smaller than 9-point is too small to read comfortably, although a great deal of advertising text today is written in sizes smaller than 9-point. Body text larger than 12-point type is difficult to read in large quantities, unless the text is geared to visually im-paired readers or meant to be read from a distance.

> **Note**
>
> If you need more space in a document to fit copy, you can reduce the type sizes of
> body text and heads; however, remember to keep the sizes consistent throughout
> the document.

Tip

Different typefaces of the same size may not measure the same; 18-point Arial, for example, is larger than 18-point Times Roman because of the style, shape, and stroke of the font.

For major heads or headings, 18-, 24-, 36-, or 48-point type serves best. Heads can be boldface, boldface italic, or if only two to four words, all uppercase. An 18-point head, for example, fits with 10-point body text well and is comfortable to read.

Use a *subhead* to categorize main topics. The subhead is more significant than the body text, yet less important than the heads. Usually boldface, italic, or all uppercase, a subhead can be 12- or 14-point, depending on the size of the body and the heads.

Display type is large type, sometimes ornamental, used sparingly in documents to grab attention. The size of display type depends on the size of the document, the length of the word or phrase, and the space the rest of the copy occupies. Display type sizes can be 48-, 60-, 72-point, or even larger.

Using Text Attributes

You use *attributes* to emphasize a word or phrase. Examples of attributes you can apply are boldface, italic, boldface italic, uppercase, condensed, or expanded type. Applying an attribute to a small amount of text is more emphatic than applying an attribute to large blocks of text. Additionally, large blocks of bold, italic, or uppercase text are difficult to read (see fig. 23.2).

Tip

A common mistake is to use uppercase letters with script type—Chancery, Bellevue, or Shelley Volante, for example; thus making the text impossible to read.

Avoid using too many different attributes in a document; a little bold and italic is fine, but using bold, italic, all uppercase, and condensed type in one document is too much. Too much variety creates chaos instead of interest.

Note

Although Word Pro does not enable you to condense fonts, you could use a condensed typeface such as Bodini Bold Condensed or Gill Sans Condensed.

YOU CAN USE UPPERCASE LETTERS FOR
HEADS OR SUBHEADS THAT ARE MADE UP OF
ONLY FOUR OR FIVE WORDS; HOWEVER, LIMIT
USING UPPERCASE FOR PHRASES OR
SENTENCES EXCEEDING FIVE WORDS.

*AVOID UPPERCASE LETTERS
WHEN USING SCRIPT FONTS IF
YOU WANT THE READER TO READ
THE TEXT.*

*Italic text is often used to emphasize a word or phrase or
to denote a book title; however, using all italic text in
more than one sentence makes the text hard to read.
Italic text has a thin stroke that makes it difficult to read
in large quantities plus the text is often lighter when it is
in italics.*

**Similarly, sentence after sentence of boldfaced type
becomes tiring to the reader's eyes. Avoid using
boldfaced type for anything but emphasizing a word,
phrase, or head. At the most, you can use the bold
attribute in one sentence when you're using that
sentence as a caption or callout.**

Fig. 23.2
It's a good idea to
avoid using any
attribute in large
blocks of text.

Underlining is one attribute that is often overused. Use underlining only in a
column of numbers as a mathematical summation line. Instead, use italic or
bold to emphasize the text. Underlined text is difficult to read and creates an
unprofessional look.

Formatting Paragraphs

Tip

A paragraph can be several sentences, several words, one word, one character, or a
blank line, as long as it has a paragraph return at the end of it.

III

Professional Output

◀ See "Changing Paragraph Formatting," p. 88

In addition to formatting typeface, type size, and the attributes of your text, you can format the paragraphs of text. Formatting paragraphs governs how the text is organized on the page and therefore, the overall look of the page. The text alignment you choose, for example, can make the page look very formal (justified text with centered heads) or relaxed (left-aligned text and heads).

Similarly, you organize the text on the page when you add tabs and indents. Tabs set text into columns or separate certain elements for easier reading; indents change the margins for one or more paragraphs of text. Line and paragraph spacing also add to the overall impression of the page and the readability of the text.

Just as with character formatting, paragraph formatting must follow some basic guidelines so that the page attracts attention, clearly presents the message, and looks professional. Use design elements—white space, consistency, emphasis, balance, and so on—to help you format the paragraphs of text on the page.

Applying Text Alignment

Alignment is a method of organizing text, paragraph by paragraph. Body text, heads, tabs, and all other text must have an alignment. If you do not choose an alignment, Word Pro's default text style is left-aligned, although the Title style uses centered text. The alignment choices are: left-aligned, right-aligned, centered, or justified (full justify). Each alignment choice offers advantages and disadvantages. Figure 23.3 illustrates each of the text alignments.

Tip

Keep alignment consistent throughout the document; changes in alignment from page to page can be frustrating and disconcerting for the reader.

Left Alignment

Left-aligned text has a flush left edge and a ragged right one. Using left-aligned text for body text has many advantages. The ragged right edge adds valuable white space that provides a rest for the reader's eyes. Of course, if your right margin is too ragged, the white space can be distracting. To avoid a too-ragged right edge, turn on hyphenation. If your right margin is still too ragged or has too many hyphens, adjust the column width.

Left-Aligned Head

Left-aligned heads, subheads, and body text provide consistency of design. The reader always knows where the next line begins. Additionally, the ragged right line endings create extra white space.

**Right-Aligned
Head**

Text that is right-aligned
should be short and
very interesting.

Center-Aligned Head

Any centered text should be
short and well-arranged.
Make sure the line length is
pleasing to the eye and easy to read.

Justified Text

Never justify a head or subhead; since the type is larger, it may space unequally to fit the line and that causes unsightly spaces between the words. Justified text looks good with either a left-aligned or center-aligned head.

Fig. 23.3
Choose text alignments carefully because the way you present the text and headings can either impress or annoy the reader.

Note

To turn on hyphenation, choose File, Document Properties, Document. In Document Properties, choose the Options tab and select Auto hyphenation.

Another advantage of left-aligned text is that equal word spacing occurs naturally and provides an even texture to the gray of the page. Left-aligned text also works well in narrow columns because the reader can easily find the beginning of the next line; flush left alignment directs the eye easily. When you use left-aligned heads and subheads, readers can find the next topic easily as well.

◀ See "Adding Lines, Borders, and Shading," p. 130

> **Tip**
>
> When using left-aligned text in multiple columns, consider using a 1/2-inch gutter space and placing a vertical line between the columns for easier reading and division between columns.

One disadvantage to left-aligned text is that you cannot fit in as much copy as you can with justified text. If you have a lot of copy and only a few pages on which to set it, left-aligned text may take up too much space; switch to justified.

Right Alignment

Right-aligned text has a flush right edge and a ragged left one. Use right-aligned text for heads, subheads, or captions but never for body text. Although right-aligned text creates interesting white space, the reader's eye has trouble finding the beginning of each new line; therefore, limit its use to no more than four or five words and no more than three or four lines of text in a row.

When using right-aligned text, use initial caps and lowercase letters instead of all uppercase so that the reader can more easily read the text. Furthermore, don't use a typeface that's difficult to read, such as a script. Make sure that when you use right-aligned text, the overall page design works with it; you might, for example, use right-aligned heads with justified body text.

Center Alignment

Centered text has ragged left and right edges. Center alignment is used most often for heads, subheads, captions, datelines, and so on. Center alignment provides visual interest to a document and works well with both left-aligned and justified body text.

Although rarely used for body text, you can center-align certain items: lists of names or dates, invitation or announcement text, and very short lines of text in a flyer, for instance. Center-aligned body text is difficult to read because the reader must search for the beginning and end of each line.

Justified Alignment

Justified text has a flush left and flush right edge and is perfectly suited for long documents, such as books, articles, and reports. Justified text also looks nice when you use two or more columns in the document. Justified text makes the page organized, quiet, and comfortable to read.

Another advantage to using justified text is that you can fit more text on a page; thus, the page looks grayer. When you use justified text, counter the gray of the page by adding extra margin space and gutter space between columns so that the eyes will have some breathing room.

> **Tip**
>
> Never use a vertical line in the gutter between columns of justified text; that just adds to the grayed page. Increase the gutters and the white space.

A disadvantage of using justified text is that it sometimes forces long words to the next line or squeezes short words to the previous line. Uneven word spacing results. You can alleviate some of the spacing problems by turning on automatic hyphenation and perhaps even adding a few *discretionary hyphens*. A discretionary hyphen is one that you place by positioning the insertion point and pressing Ctrl+hyphen. Word Pro uses the hyphen if it needs to but does not display it if the word fits all on one line.

Setting Tabs and Indents

Tabs and indents help you organize the text on the page in relation to the page margins. Indents control the width of the paragraph; you can apply an indent to the first sentence of a paragraph or to the left and/or right of an entire paragraph so that it stands out from the text. Tabs are organizational tools that enable you to line up lists of items across a line. Tabs and indents are often used to make documents look more professional and to increase readability.

Using Indents

An *indent* is the distance from the left margin to the beginning of the text or from the right margin to the end of the text. You can apply an indent to the first sentence or to all sentences other than the first. You can apply an indent to the left edge of a paragraph or to the right.

A positive measurement indents the text toward the center of a page or column. A 2-inch indent from the left, for example, indents the paragraph two inches from the left margin. A negative number used as an indent, such as –1 inch, produces an *outdent*, or *hanging indent*. Used for bullets, numbered lists, or subtitles; a hanging indent is a useful tool for text formatting (see fig. 23.4).

III

Professional Output

> **Tip**
>
> Use the Word Pro ruler to create indents and outdents so that you can see the results on-screen as you make the changes.

Fig. 23.4
Indents control how the text looks on the page.

Outdent	An outdent is where a subtitle, bullet, numbered list, and so on, hangs to the left while the rest of the paragraph indents to the right.

When using indents, you must remember a few guidelines. If you plan to indent the first sentence of the body text, indent it no more than a half inch. Additionally, do not use first line indents with extra paragraph spacing. Whether you indent the first line of text or add an extra line of space between paragraphs, you're creating paragraph divisions; use one or the other but never both. Finally, if you use any type of indent in a document, be consistent and use the same measurements for all indents in the document.

Using Tabs

Use *tabs* to organize text across a line and in columns. You can use tabs to align names, numbers, dollar amounts, or any other kind of text. A tab stop enables you to move to a specific point quickly and efficiently by pressing the Tab key; in Word Pro, default tab stops are every half inch.

A tab aligns to the left, right, center, or on a decimal point. These alignments are similar to text alignment; left tabs, for example, are always flush left and ragged right. Right tabs work well for text aligned along the right edge of the page, perhaps separated from the text on the left with a leader. A *leader* is a dotted, dashed, or solid line that separates two tabs.

> **Note**
>
> You can set tabs—alignment, location, leader, and so on—in the Set Tabs on Ruler dialog box. In the Text Properties InfoBox, choose the Misc tab.

Numeric, or decimal, tabs are perfect for aligning currency, percentages, and other numbers. The tab stop is on the decimal point, and all numbers, regardless of whether or not they have a decimal point, are aligned where the point should be.

Use center tabs for names, places, or other special items. Make sure that you allow enough space from the margin for the longest line; otherwise, the tab will not work. Figure 23.5 illustrates each tab alignment and a leader tab.

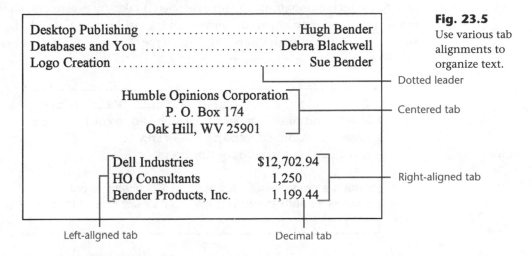

Fig. 23.5
Use various tab alignments to organize text.

Using line and paragraph spacing is an excellent way to include white space in your document. Remember, too much gray on the page fatigues a reader's eyes. Using word and letter spacing is the way you increase the readability of your text.

Setting Spacing

> **Tip**
>
> When applying spacing, be consistent so that the reader stays on track; diversions interrupt the train of thought.

When reading, the eye doesn't look closely at each word. Instead the reader uses the shape of words—the shape of ascenders (b, d, f, h, k, l, t) and descenders (g, j, p, q, y) in relation to the body of the word—to recognize what the word is. (This is one reason all uppercase letters are so hard to read.) You can use the spacing of letters, words, lines, and paragraphs to help your reader get through your material quickly and comfortably.

◀ See "Changing Paragraph Formatting," p. 88

Letter Spacing

The spacing between the letters of a word can make it easier or more difficult to read. Certain letters fit together to form instantly recognizable pairs: *th, er, sp,* and *ly* are just a few of the many familiar letter pairs. When you have too

III

Professional Output

much space between letters, recognizing these letter pairs is more difficult and thus hampers reading.

Letter spacing is the reason most typesetters rarely use monospaced fonts, such as Courier. In monospaced fonts, each letter takes up exactly the same amount of space, no matter if the letter is an *i,* an *m,* or even a period (.). Figure 23.6 illustrates both Courier and Arial type. The Arial typeface is easier to read because of the letter spacing.

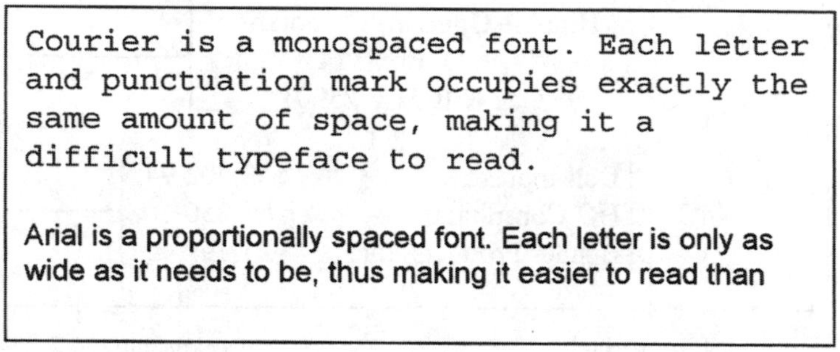

Fig. 23.6

Use monospaced fonts for only one or two words in your text; perhaps to set text off from the rest.

```
Courier is a monospaced font. Each letter
and punctuation mark occupies exactly the
same amount of space, making it a
difficult typeface to read.
```

Arial is a proportionally spaced font. Each letter is only as wide as it needs to be, thus making it easier to read than

In addition to the font choice, you can control letter spacing in Word Pro by using *kerning.* Kerning is the reduction or addition of space between certain letter pairs—such as *V, W,* and *A*—so that the characters print in an aesthetically pleasing manner. Word Pro automatically kerns letter pairs although you can adjust the kerning. Most kerning takes place in text that is 18-point or larger because the uneven letter spacing is more noticeable in the larger type sizes.

Word Spacing

Tip

Never use two spaces after a period when using proportional typefaces; two spaces can also cause "rivers" of white running through the text.

The correct spacing between words is critical to ease reading. Words too close together create a dense gray page—it's difficult to separate the words, and the reader is uncomfortable. On the other hand, words spaced too far apart create *holes* on the page. Large areas of white space between words are apparent in the overall gray of the page and sometimes form "rivers" of white space in the gray. Too little or too much spacing requires the reader to work hard to get through the message (see fig. 23.7).

> Words can be spaced too close together, thus making the gray of the page too dense and causing the reader to search for each individual word.
>
> Too much space between words can create "rivers" of white space that flow throught the page. Text that is justified   tends to   create wide word spacing   if hyphenation is   turned off.

Fig. 23.7
These examples do not make the reader want to read the message.

You can control word spacing in Word Pro. If you're using justified text, turn on the automatic hyphenation. If you still notice a problem, try adjusting the column width, indents, tabs, or margins of the page. Sometimes just a 1/4-inch adjustment can make all the difference.

Line Spacing

> **Tip**
>
> This version of Word Pro includes a special one-half-line spacing feature.

Line spacing, interline spacing, and *leading* all refer to the amount of space between two lines of text in the same paragraph. You are probably familiar with one-half-, single-, one-and-a-half-, and double-line spacing. Word Pro uses these same terms and measurements to describe line spacing.

You can measure the line spacing in points as well as in lines by choosing the Custom Line or Custom Paragraph Spacing drop-down list boxes in the Text InfoBox, Alignment tab. The Spacing Custom dialog box appears and enables you to choose the Spacing Units. As a default, Word Pro automatically spaces lines for you, increasing the space in proportion to the size of the type. Most of the time, you probably don't need to adjust the spacing.

The tallest character in a particular typeface and size is the guideline for measuring line spacing. Uppercase letters, ascenders, and descenders must all have enough space to prevent them from overlapping letters above or below them. The typical line spacing equals 20 percent of the size of the font, although many desktop publishing programs use 30 percent.

III

Professional Output

Tip

You can adjust line spacing to help fit copy to your document, but *do not* vary the line spacing throughout the document: be consistent.

Because type sizes are measured in points, you may want to learn the measurements for leading in points as well as in line spacing. For example, 12-point type often uses 14-point leading (called *12 on 14* and written 12/14). 14-point text uses 16-point leading and 18-point text uses 20- or 22-point leading. Figure 23.8 illustrates three different examples of line spacing with the same size body text.

Fig. 23.8
Adjust line spacing to make reading more comfortable.

This is 12-point Times Roman on 12-point spacing. The lines of text are too close to comfortably read. It would be better to use 11/12 if you need the extra room.

This is 12-point Times Roman on 14.4-point spacing, the Ami Pro default. This is also called Single line spacing and is comfortable for the reader to read.

This is 12-point Times Roman on 16-point spacing. Use this line spacing with a longer line length, such as seven inches or more.

Paragraph Spacing

Tip

Add no more than two lines of space between body text paragraphs; one-and-a-half lines is the preferred spacing.

After the letters, words, and lines of your document have the proper amount of space, you might want to add extra space between paragraphs. Remember this simple rule: if you indent the first line of the paragraph, don't add an extra line of space between paragraphs; if you don't indent the first sentence, add at least one line of space between each paragraph. If the reader can easily find the first sentence of a paragraph, he or she can understand the division of topics in the document more easily. Figure 23.9 shows two examples of paragraph spacing and indentation.

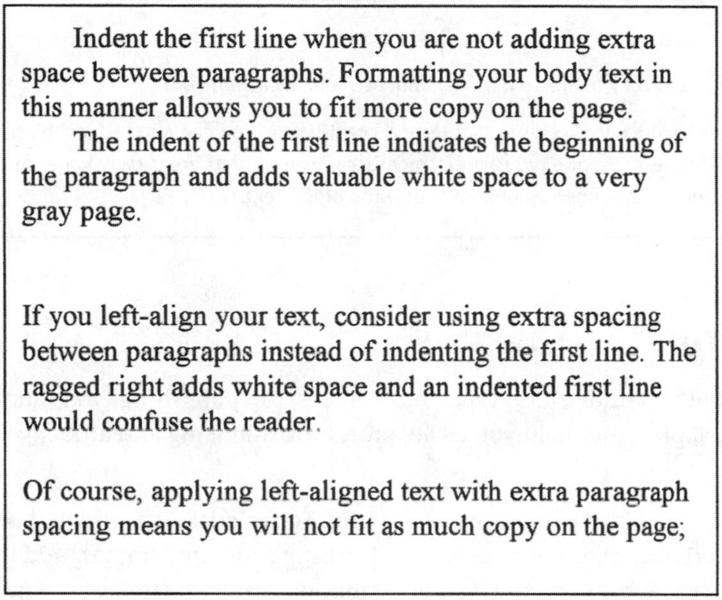

Indent the first line when you are not adding extra space between paragraphs. Formatting your body text in this manner allows you to fit more copy on the page.

The indent of the first line indicates the beginning of the paragraph and adds valuable white space to a very gray page.

If you left-align your text, consider using extra spacing between paragraphs instead of indenting the first line. The ragged right adds white space and an indented first line would confuse the reader.

Of course, applying left-aligned text with extra paragraph spacing means you will not fit as much copy on the page;

Fig. 23.9
Use either indents or paragraph spacing so that the reader can find the beginning of a new paragraph.

Troubleshooting

I spent a lot of time formatting the text and the paragraph, and now I'd like to apply that formatting to other text in the document. How do I do that?

Save the text as a style so that you can apply it to other text in the document or in other documents. To save the text as a style, select the text and choose the Style tab in the Text InfoBox. Click the Create Style button and enter a name for the new style.

I've formatted the document and now it's taking forever to print. What's happening?

When you use too many typefaces or heavy graphics, it takes longer to print the document. If you have trouble printing, you might want to cut down on the variety in the document. You can also install more RAM in your printer; consult your printer documentation for more information.

I've set tabs and indentations for the text. How can I use the same measurements on other text without having to reset them each time?

You can copy the ruler for the text that has the tab and indents set and then paste it where you want. You can also place the insertion point at the beginning or end of the text with the settings you want and press Enter. The new line of text keeps the formatting. Finally, you can create a style that includes the tab and indent settings and apply the style to any text you want.

(continues)

III

Professional Output

(continued)

I have extra copy to fit in a document but no room; what can I do?

You can reduce the leading, slightly and consistently. You can also reduce the size of the body text, change typefaces (remember sans serif fonts are usually larger than serif ones), add pages, or edit and cut some of the text.

From Here...

Now that you understand typography in desktop publishing, you can refer to other chapters that help you create professional-looking and attractive documents:

- Chapter 20, "Using Advanced Frame Techniques," shows you how to add pizzazz to your documents by using formatted frames. Add lines, borders, backgrounds to one or multiple frames to create an attractive document.

- Chapter 22, "Desktop Publishing with Word Pro," explains the design strategies you use to plan and create a successful document. Additionally, this chapter describes design elements, such as page orientation, balance, and white space.

- Chapter 25, "Importing, Exporting, and Linking Files," shows you how to bring data and graphic files to Word Pro from other applications so that your document will be effective and attractive.

Chapter 24

Making Document Revisions

by Lisa Bucki

After you create the original version of a document, there's always room for improvement. Word Pro gives you the tools you need to add notes and make changes to a document.

Word Pro enables you to add *comment notes* (also called *sticky notes*) to any document, to remind you of changes to make later or facts to double-check, for example. Comment notes appear in their own small frames on-screen when you display them. You can display, hide, and delete comment notes.

Word Pro enables you to highlight important text to call attention to it for other users. The highlighter feature lets you mark text with a yellow highlight background.

In this chapter, you learn how to:

- Mark document revisions, use the highlighter to call attention to text, and make comment notes about document text

- Protect a document in several ways using the TeamSecurity feature

- Compare documents and consolidate revisions from several people

Using the Comment Tools to Control Revisions

Revision marking lets you recognize and identify changes to a document. You can specify how you want revisions to appear so that the revisions stand out from prior versions of the text. All insertions and deletions of text, tables, frames, and graphics appear as revisions. After you finish making revisions, you can review, accept, or cancel the revisions. Accepted revisions become part of the normal text.

Word Pro consolidates the SmartIcons for these note and revision features on the Comment Tools iconbar. To display this iconbar, click an iconbar down arrow to display the iconbar pop-up menu and click Comment Tools. Or choose View, Show/Hide, Review & Comment Tools. Whichever method you use, the Comment Tools iconbar appears on-screen. Table 24.1 lists the icons that appear in the Comment Tools iconbar and explains what each of them does.

Table 24.1	SmartIcons in the Comment Tools Iconbar
SmartIcon	**Function**
	Creates a comment note
	Turns the highlighter on or off
	Highlights the selected text and lets you add a comment about it
	Opens the previous comment note in the document
	Opens the next comment note in the document
	Opens all comment notes in the document in their own frames
	Closes all comment notes in the document so that only comment-note marks appear
	Toggles the display of all comment notes in the document on or off
	Shows author initials on comment-note marks

SmartIcon	Function
	Clears highlighter marks
	Turns on revision mode
	Lets you set markup options for the current author/editor
	Displays the Revision bar
	Lets you view another version of the current document

The following sections explain how to take advantage of Word Pro's comment note, highlighter, and revision-mark features. These features can be particularly helpful if a document is created through the collaborative efforts of several people. If the revisions of one author are marked, for example, another author can easily recognize revisions from original text. The other author doesn't have to be present when the revisions are made.

Using Comment Notes

Word Pro comment notes appear at the location where you insert them, but comment notes don't affect the regular document text. You can insert a note anywhere within existing text—in the main body, in a header or footer, within the text in a frame, a table, or even within a footnote. Inserting comment notes in a document is like writing comments in the margin of a printout. Notes are especially helpful for reminding you to follow up on certain details of the text, such as researching and adding a particular statistic. You can also use notes to leave messages about the document to someone else working on the same document. Comment notes can also hold graphics, tables, sounds, or any other type of object you can create in Word Pro. Word Pro checks the Personal tab in the Word Pro Preferences dialog box to track which author is adding comments.

When comment notes are open, they appear in their own small frames on-screen. When a comment note is closed, it is depicted by a yellow comment-note mark in the document. Figure 24.1 shows a document with both an open comment note and a comment-note mark. See the section "Changing

◀ See "Setting View Preferences," p. 230

III

Professional Output

Revision Options" later in the chapter to learn how to change the color of comment-note marks that you or any other author inserts.

Fig. 24.1
Comment notes enable multiple editors to communicate or remind you to follow up on particular details.

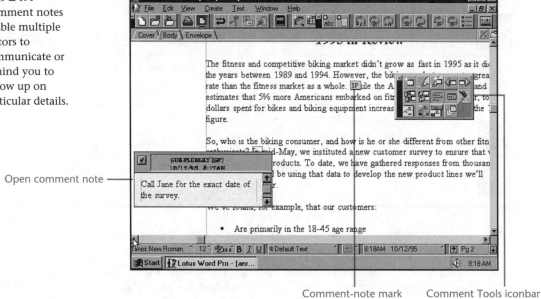

Open comment note ⎯⎯⎯

Comment-note mark   Comment Tools iconbar

Inserting and Closing Comment Notes

Inserting a comment note in a document is easy. Follow these steps:

1. Click to position the insertion point where you want the comment note to appear.

2. Choose Create, Comment Note, or click the Create a Comment SmartIcon. A blank note appears on-screen with the date and time the note is being created and the author's name across the top of the frame.

3. Click in the text area of the comment-note frame to position the insertion point there.

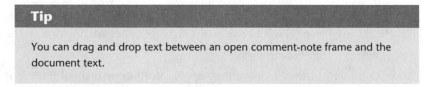

> **Tip**
>
> You can drag and drop text between an open comment-note frame and the document text.

4. Type the note, which can be any length, in the note window. You can also paste text copied from the main document (or any document) to

create a note. You can paste or create frames, graphics, tables, sounds, or any other kind of object in the note. If you type more text than the note frame can hold, a scroll bar appears at the right side of the frame to let you scroll through the comment note's text.

5. To exit the comment-note frame but leave the comment note open, click outside the comment-note frame.

You can close comment-note frames so that only the document text and the comment-note marks appear. You can use a few different techniques to accomplish this, depending on whether you want to close all the notes or only some of the notes. For example, you may want to close most of the notes but leave a particular note to a colleague open so that person will see it when he or she opens the document. Use these methods to close comment notes:

■ To close a single note, click in the comment-note frame's text area to select the comment note. Click the check mark in the upper left corner of the comment-note frame.

■ To close all open comment notes in the document, click the Close All Notes SmartIcon in the Comment Tools iconbar.

■ To use a pop-up menu to close one or more comment notes, click in a comment-note frame's text area to select the note. Click the right mouse button to display the pop-up menu (see fig. 24.2). Click Close This Comment to close the selected comment note. Click Close All Comments to close all the comment notes in the document.

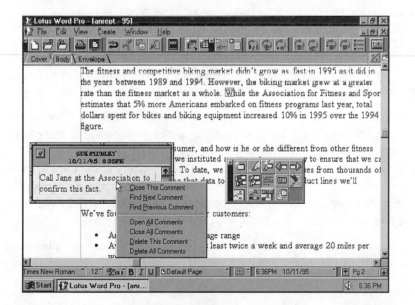

Fig. 24.2
You can use the pop-up menu to close comment notes on the comment pop-up menu.

III

Professional Output

Opening and Editing Comment Notes

The easiest way to open a comment note that appears as a comment-note mark is to double-click the comment-note mark. The comment-note frame opens and displays the comment note.

 If comment-note marks aren't visible in the document, you may have turned them off. Click the Show/Hide Notes SmartIcon on the Comment Tools iconbar to redisplay them.

  The Comment Tools iconbar offers SmartIcons for opening comment notes. You can click the Open a Previous Comment SmartIcon (it depicts a note and has a left-pointing arrow) to open the first comment note that is earlier in the document than the insertion point. You can click the Open Next Comment SmartIcon (it depicts a note and has a right-pointing arrow) to open the next comment note past the insertion point location. Finally, click the Open All Notes SmartIcon (with two small green arrows pointing up and toward the right) to open all the comment notes in the document.

> **Tip**
>
> You can choose Edit, Go To to jump to the next or preceding comment note. Using Go To is in Chapter 8, "Marking and Searching Text."

If you display a comment note's pop-up menu, you can use the menu to display additional comment notes. The pop-up menu offers the following commands, which are equivalent in function to the icons described in the preceding paragraph: Find Next Comment, Find Previous Comment, and Open All Comments.

When Word Pro displays the comment-note frame, the date and time the note was created appear at the top of the frame. The writer's name also appears.

After you display a comment note, you have to click in the text area to position the insertion point for editing. After you've positioned the insertion point within the comment-note text, you edit the text with the same editing keys, SmartIcons, and techniques you use to edit documents: Delete, Backspace, and so on. If the comment note contains more text than it can display at once, use the scroll bar at the right side of the frame to scroll to the text that you want to edit.

You can resize the comment-note frame to see more if you have a long note or a note with a large image in it. With the comment note selected, point to one of the handles along the side or at a corner of the frame border. When the mouse pointer turns to a double-headed arrow, drag the border. Release the mouse button when the comment-note frame reaches the size you want. To reposition the comment-note frame on-screen, point to an area between the handles on the frame border. When the mouse pointer turns to an open hand, press the left mouse button and then drag the comment-note frame to the new position. Release the mouse button.

Tip

To quickly move a comment note, drag to select the comment-note mark (it's hard to do without selecting the text underneath). Click the Cut SmartIcon. (Click the Undo SmartIcon if your text is cut, too.) Position the insertion point; then click the Paste SmartIcon.

◀ See "Moving Text," p. 67

To change the location of the actual comment note in the text, create a comment note at the new position, cut the text from the comment note at the current position, and paste the text into the new comment note. Then delete the old note, as described next.

Troubleshooting

I added comment notes to a document, but I can't see them when I open the document. What's wrong?

You may have turned them off in the View Preferences dialog box. Click the Show/Hide Comment Notes SmartIcon to redisplay them. The other problem may be that you are in Draft mode rather than Layout mode. Comment notes and their marks don't appear in Draft mode. Choose View, Layout to see the comment notes and marks.

Deleting Comment Notes

Word Pro provides a couple of different ways for deleting comment notes. If the comment-note frame you want to delete is not open, click the comment-note mark to place the insertion point on it. Then press the Delete key.

If the comment note you want to delete is open, click in it to select it. Right-click the comment note to display the pop-up menu, and then choose Delete This Comment.

After your document is in final form, you may want to remove all the comment notes. In this case, select a comment note and right-click to display the

III

Professional Output

pop-up menu. Choose D<u>e</u>lete All Comments. Word Pro asks you confirm the deletion. Click OK to delete all the comment notes in the document.

Adding Initials to Comment-Note Marks

If you want to display the initials of the person who created the note in every comment-note marker, click the Show Initials SmartIcon. Figure 24.3 shows a comment-note mark that includes the user.

Fig. 24.3
On the comment-note mark, you can display the initials of the person who created the note.

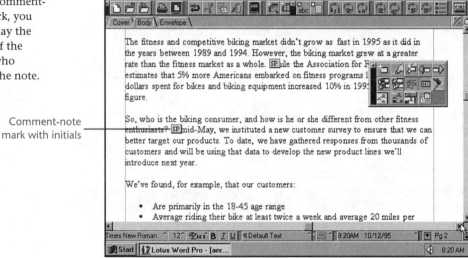

Comment-note mark with initials

◀ See "Setting Personal Information," p. 221

When you create a comment note, Word Pro checks the <u>P</u>ersonal tab of the Word Pro Preferences dialog box to track who created the note; the <u>I</u>nitials text box of this tab contains the user initials Word Pro displays in the comment-note mark.

Each editor can choose a color to use for the comment-note marks that he or she creates. For example, one editor can choose red marks and another can choose blue marks to make it easier to distinguish between comments made by different people. See "Changing Revision Options" later in this chapter to learn how to do this.

Using the Highlighter

If you've ever used a marker to highlight key words or phrases in a text book, then you already understand what the highlighter feature in Word Pro does. Basically, the highlighter lets you apply a background color to selected text to call attention to that text. The highlight appears over the text in both Draft mode and Layout mode. The highlight also appears when you print the document.

SmartIcons on the Comment Tools iconbar enable you to highlight text and remove highlighting (see fig. 24.4). To start highlighting, click the Turn On/Off Highlighter SmartIcon on the Comment Tools iconbar. The mouse pointer turns into a special highlighter pointer that looks like a marker. Press the left mouse button and drag over the text you want to highlight. The highlighter stays on until you turn it off. That means that you can drag over additional text selections to highlight them, as well. To turn off the highlighter, click the Turn On/Off Highlighter SmartIcon again. To remove all highlighting from a document, click the Clear All Highlighting SmartIcon on the Comment Tools iconbar.

> **Tip**
>
> To quickly turn off the highlighter, press the Esc key.

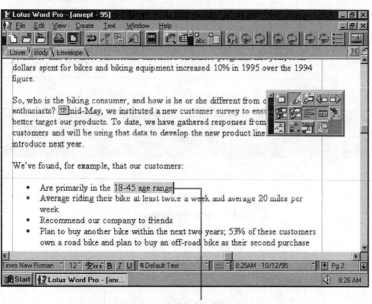

Highlighted text

Fig. 24.4
After you turn on the highlighter feature, you can drag over text to highlight it.

To make it easier to distinguish between editors of a document, each editor can choose a color to use for his or her highlighter. For example, one editor can choose yellow highlighting and another can choose pale-green highlighting. See "Changing Revision Options" later in this chapter to learn how to do this.

 Word Pro also enables you to add a comment note and highlighting to a particular chunk of text. To do this, click the Highlight & Note SmartIcon. Drag to highlight the text you want to call attention to. When you release the mouse button, Word Pro inserts a comment note at the end of the highlighted text. Click in the text area of the comment-note frame and enter the note comments. Close the comment note or click outside it when you're finished.

Marking Revisions

When you make changes to a document, you might want to compare the original text with the changes you made before finalizing the document. Or if you're editing someone else's work, you may want that person to be able to see the specific changes you've made.

Word Pro enables you to mark up your edits and revisions automatically. When you turn on revision marking, Word Pro formats deleted text with particular character formatting and formats new text with other character formatting so that you can easily see the revisions in a document (see fig. 24.5). The additions, deletions, and edits clearly stand out from the original text.

Fig. 24.5
Using revision marks in Word Pro applies special character formatting to deleted and added text to make each kind of text easy to distinguish.

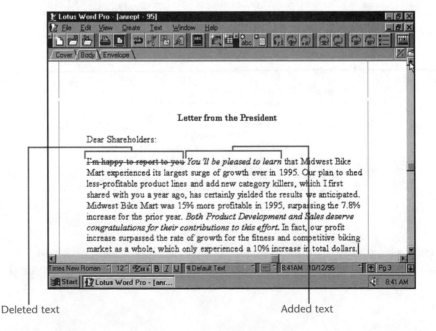

Deleted text   Added text

By default, when Word Pro is in revision mode, it formats text you insert with blue, italic characters. Word Pro formats text you delete with red strikethrough characters. (The next section describes how to change these defaults.) Revision bars appear in the left margin beside any lines that contain deletions or additions. If your document contains frames, added frames have a plus sign (+) across the text or image area of the frame, and deleted frames have an X. If you modify text by using text attributes or making style changes, those changes aren't marked with revision marks.

When you want to mark revisions, follow these steps:

1. Choose <u>E</u>dit, Mar<u>k</u>up Edits to toggle on revision marking (a check mark then appears beside the command on the menu). Alternatively, click the Revision Mode SmartIcon. Either of these actions turns on revision marking with the default settings.

2. Make the desired edits in the document. Word Pro automatically applies revision-marking character formatting and inserts revision bars in the margin.

3. When you finish making revisions and you want to return to normal editing mode, turn off revision mode by choosing Edit, Markup Edits to toggle it off, or you can click the Revision Mode SmartIcon again.

The revisions you make remain in your document until you review and remove them. When you save the document, Word Pro saves the revision marks with it. The next section, "Reviewing Revisions," explains how to deal with revision marks when you want to finalize your document.

Changing Revision Options

As mentioned earlier, Word Pro enables each person working with a document to choose custom colors for comment-note marks and highlighting. This makes it easy to tell who created particular notes and highlighting. Similarly, each person can choose what formatting to apply to deleted and inserted text in revision mode. You make the comment note, highlighting, and revision color and formatting selections in the same dialog box—the Markup Options for *User* dialog box, where *User* indicates the name of the user currently editing the document. Word Pro checks the <u>P</u>ersonal tab of the Word Pro Preferences dialog box to determine the user name.

> **Caution**
>
> Make changes to the comment-note color before you add comment notes. Word Pro cannot retroactively apply the options to additions and changes by a particular user.

Follow these steps to set the options for comment-note marks, highlighting, and revision marks:

1. Choose File, User Setup, Word Pro Preferences. Click the General tab in the dialog box and then click the Markup Options button. Alternatively, you can click the Markup Options Current Editor SmartIcon. Word Pro displays the Markup Options dialog box (see fig. 24.6).

Fig. 24.6
Use the Markup Option for *User* dialog box to choose colors for comment-note marks and highlighting, and to change the markup attributes and colors for inserted and deleted text in revision mode.

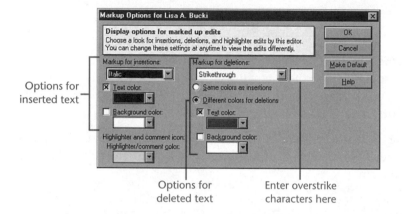

Options for inserted text

Options for deleted text

Enter overstrike characters here

2. Open the Markup for Insertions drop-down list. This list offers attribute choices for text inserted in revision mode, including Bold, Italic, Underline, Double Underline, or No Attribute (normal text). The default is Italic. Choose the formatting choice you want.

3. Mark the Text Color check box, and then click the down arrow beside the color box to display a color palette (see fig. 24.7). Choose a new color for inserted text; the palette closes automatically.

4. If you want to apply a background color to immediately surround inserted revision text, mark the Background Color check box, click the down arrow beside the color box to display the color palette, and choose the color you want.

> **Tip**
>
> If you choose to apply No Attribute as the Markup for Insertions or Markup for Deletions choices in the Markup Options dialog box, select vivid colors for inserted and deleted text so that revisions are distinct from the original text.

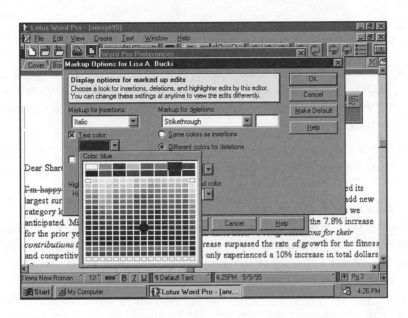

Fig. 24.7
Choose any color
from the palette to
represent inserted
text.

5. Open the Markup for Deletions drop-down list. This list offers attribute
    choices for text deleted in revision mode, including Strikethrough,
    Overstrike, Hidden, Hidden with Deleted Marker, or No Attribute (nor-
    mal text). The default is Strikethrough. Click the formatting choice you
    want. If you choose Overstrike, type the desired overstrike character in
    the blank text box to the right of the Markup for Deletions drop-down
    list. You can type any character from the keyboard or the ANSI charac-
    ter set. If you choose Hidden with Deleted Marker, Word Pro hides the
    deletions and adds an editor's deletion mark beside it; enter one or
    more overstrike characters to append your entry to the editor's deletion
    mark.

6. To assign the colors you specified for inserted text to your deletions as
    well, click the Same Colors as Insertions option button. Otherwise, use
    steps 7 and 8 to apply different colors to the deleted text and its back-
    ground.

7. With the Different Colors for Deletions option button selected, mark
    the Text Color check box, and then click the down arrow beside the
    color box to display a color palette. Choose a color.

8. If you want to apply a background color to immediately surround de-
    leted revision text, mark the Background Color check box, and then
    click the down arrow beside the color box to display the color palette.
    Choose a color.

III

Professional Output

9. To choose a different color for comment-note marks and highlighting, open the Highlighter/Comment C<u>o</u>lor palette. Choose a color.

10. If you want to use the new settings you just specified in this dialog box as the default (until you change them), click the <u>M</u>ake Default button. Then each time you start Word Pro, it uses your new Markup Options settings.

11. Click OK or press Enter to return to your document and begin applying revisions with the new colors and formatting.

Reviewing Revisions

After you make changes with revision marking, you can review the changes and choose to accept or cancel them. Word Pro offers a modeless Revision bar that you display at the top of the screen and use to work with the revisions you or another person have added to the document. It's called a *modeless* bar because you can still edit your document when the Revision bar appears on-screen, unlike when a dialog box appears. To display the Revision bar, choose <u>E</u>dit, Re<u>v</u>iew Marked Edits. Alternatively, you can click the Revision Bar SmartIcon. Word Pro displays the Revision bar at the top of the screen (see fig. 24.8).

Fig. 24.8
Use the Revision bar to find, accept, and reject edits in a document.

Revision bar

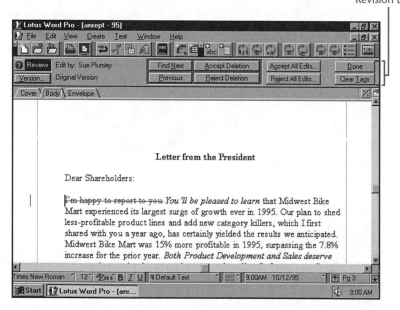

The next section explains how to work with the Revision bar after you've displayed it. Click the Done button when you no longer want to display the Revision bar on-screen.

Accepting and Rejecting Revisions

You can find, accept, or reject revisions in a document using the Revision bar. Normally, you click one of the buttons on the Revision bar to begin the process. Word Pro moves through the document and deals with each change as changes are encountered. You can review and deal with the revisions one at a time, or you can simply accept or reject all the revisions in a document. Lastly, you can simply remove all the revision markings.

If you review revisions, Word Pro starts from the first revision of the document. It finds each revision, indicating whether the revision is an insertion or a deletion and letting you accept or reject it. When you accept revisions, Word Pro inserts or deletes the revision text as called for and removes the revision marking for the accepted revision. If you choose to reject a revision, Word Pro cancels the revision by deleting revision text. If you skip revisions as you are reviewing, the skipped revisions continue to appear with the attributes and colors you specified earlier for revision marking.

To deal with revisions one at a time, follow these steps:

1. Click either the Find Next or Previous button on the Revision bar to move to the first revision Word Pro encounters, which Word Pro highlights (see fig. 24.9).

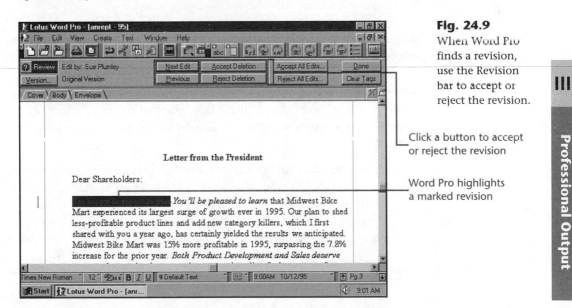

Fig. 24.9
When Word Pro finds a revision, use the Revision bar to accept or reject the revision.

Click a button to accept or reject the revision

Word Pro highlights a marked revision

III

Professional Output

2. If the found revision is a deletion, the Revision bar displays the Accept Deletion and Reject Deletion buttons. If the found revision is an addition, the Revision bar displays the Accept Insertion and Reject Insertion buttons. Choose an option:

■ To accept the edit, click the Accept Deletion or Accept Insertion button.

■ To reject the edit and return to the original text, click the Reject Deletion or Reject Insertion button.

■ To skip the edit without accepting or rejecting it (leaving the revision marks intact), click the Next Edit or Previous button.

3. Word Pro makes the change, if any, and highlights the next revision. Repeat step 3 to accept, reject, or skip the current revision and subsequent revisions as needed.

4. When you have accepted or rejected all the revisions, Word Pro displays a dialog box telling you that the Review of Markups has finished. Click OK to close the dialog box and return to your document.

> **Tip**
>
> You can review part of a document by selecting the text and then selecting the options you want on the Revision bar. However, be aware that frames and tables are skipped if you select text and proceed with the review.

If you've read the whole document with revision marks or have simply received direction from another person who has approved or rejected changes to a document, you don't need to review the revisions one by one. For example, your boss may simply send you an e-mail message telling you to go ahead with your revisions. In such a case, you can accept or reject all revisions in a document simultaneously. To do so, use one of the following methods:

■ Click the Accept All Edits button on the Revision bar to accept and put into effect all changes made while using revision marking. Word Pro displays the Accept All Edits dialog box. Choose whether to accept all the edits in the current paragraph, the current document, or a particular paragraph or document created by a certain author; then click OK.

■ Click the Reject All Edits button to revert to the original version of your text and cancel all changes made while using revision marking. Word Pro displays the Reject All Edits dialog box. Choose whether to reject all the edits in the current paragraph, the current document, or a particular paragraph or document created by a certain author; then click OK.

■ Click the Clear Tags button to delete all tags in the document. A *tag* is a duplicate paragraph with edits and the editor's initials added when you compare more than two documents.

Using TeamSecurity

When you need to share a document file with multiple people but want to control what different people can do with the document, you can use Word Pro's TeamSecurity. For example, you can use Word Pro to generate a monthly marketing report that you place in a directory on your company's network server computer. You want every salesperson to be able to open and print the document. However, you don't want anyone but you to be able to make changes to the document. In this case, you use the TeamSecurity tools to determine which users can edit the document.

Controlling who can edit a document is just one of the security controls available. You can also determine who can open a file; who can change access, editing rights, and protection for a file; how to verify user names; create different editing rights for different editors; display a greeting for document editors or ask for editing comments when the editor closes the document; assign passwords; and hide parts of documents.

You use the TeamSecurity dialog box to work with the many available tools (see fig. 24.10). To display this dialog box, choose File, TeamSecurity. The dialog box has three tabs, each of which deals with a particular set of rights. By default, the Access tab appears first when you display this dialog box. To access the options on the other tabs, click the appropriate tab. Make your choices among the options on each tab, and then click OK to close the dialog box.

The next three sections describe the TeamSecurity tools in more detail. To make it easier for you to learn about the numerous options that Word Pro offers, each section covers the options on a particular tab of the TeamSecurity dialog box.

Fig. 24.10
The TeamSecurity
dialog box, with its
first tab displayed.

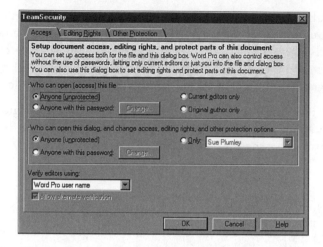

Setting Access

The first tab in the TeamSecurity dialog box is the Access tab. This tab lets
you assign a password to the document, specify who can open a document,
specify who can make changes to a document, and more.

The Who Can Open (Access) This File area offers four option buttons that let
you set document access. Select the button you want to restrict who can open
the current file; these choices are mutually exclusive, which means that you
can only select one of them at a time:

- *Anyone (Unprotected).* Leave this option selected to allow anyone to open
  the current file.

- *Anyone With This Password.* Click this option button to password-
  protect the document; then click the Change button to enter your
  password. The Enter New File Password dialog box appears. Type your
  password; asterisks appear to represent each character, keeping the password secret (see fig. 24.11). Click OK. Retype the password in the Re-
  Enter New File Password to Confirm dialog box and then click OK to
  assign the password.

Fig. 24.11
You can create a
password to
restrict access to a
document.

- *Current Editors Only.* Restricts access to only those editors who have
  editing rights to the document at the time you restrict access. The next
  section describes how to assign editing rights on the Editing Rights tab.

- *Original Author Only.* Tells Word Pro to let only you open the file.

The next area of this tab is called Who Can Open This Dialog, and Change Access, Editing Rights, and Other Protection Options. It offers three option buttons that let you set who can make TeamSecurity changes to the file. These choices are mutually exclusive, which means that you can only select one of them at a time:

- *Anyone (Unprotected).* Leave this option selected to let anyone change the TeamSecurity for the current file.

- *Anyone With This Password.* Click this option button to password-protect the document; then click the Change button to enter your password. The Enter New File Password dialog box appears. Type your password; asterisks appear to represent each character, keeping the password (refer to fig. 24.11). Click OK. Retype the password in the Re-Enter New File Password to Confirm dialog box, and then click OK to assign the password.

- *Only.* Use this drop-down list to select a person with editing rights as the person allowed to change the control options. The next section describes how to assign editing rights on the Editing Rights tab.

By default, Word Pro uses the User Name from the Personal tab of the Word Pro Preferences dialog box to verify the name of an editor trying to open a protected file. To use another verification method, open the Verify Editors Using drop-down list and choose the method you want from the list; then make sure that the Allow Alternate Verification check box is selected.

◀ See "Setting Personal Information," p. 221

Setting Editing Rights

Although the options described in the preceding section let you control who can open a document, there may be cases where you don't want to restrict access to a document, but you do want to specify who can edit it. To see the options for editing control, click the Editing Rights tab in the TeamSecurity dialog box. Figure 24.12 shows the options on this tab.

To control editing access for a particular editor, you first must select the editor's name from the Editor's Name list box. This list box contains the names of all users who have previously opened, edited, and saved the document file. To add another editor to this list, click the New Editor button. The New Editor dialog box appears; type the new editor's name. As the dialog box warns, the editor name you enter must match the user name that person entered during his or her installation of Word Pro. Click OK to finish adding the editor to the list.

Fig. 24.12
You can precisely control the edits that each person can make to a document using this tab in the TeamSecurity dialog box.

Select an editor from this list

Set options for the editor here

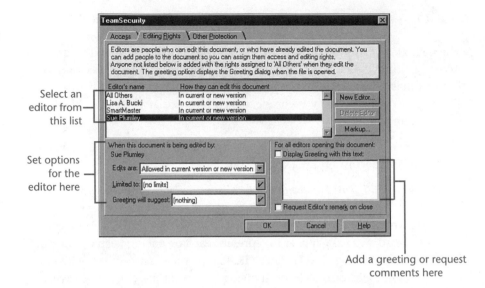

Add a greeting or request comments here

> **Note**
>
> To delete an editor's name, click the name in the Editor's Name list box and then click the Delete Editor button. When Word Pro asks you to confirm the deletion, click Yes. Note that you can't delete your own name or the All Others choice. Also, depending on other controls you've specified, you may not be able to add an editor's name back after you've deleted it, so be careful when deleting editors.

After you've added the editors you need to the list, follow these steps to complete your Editing Rights settings:

1. Click the name of the editor for which to change rights in the Editor's Name list. All Others applies to anyone whose user name is not included in the list.

2. Click the Markup button, which displays the Markup Options dialog box, to change the markup options for the selected editor. Click OK when you finish setting Markup Options to return to the Editing Rights tab of the TeamSecurity dialog box.

▶ See "Using Versions," p. 508

3. Open the Edits Are drop-down list to display its choices. Click the option you want. The options are as follows:

   ■ *Allowed in Current Version or New Version*. Lets the editor make changes to the document or any new version of the document that he or she creates.

- *Allowed in Current Version Only.* Lets the editor make changes only in the version of the document displayed when you set TeamSecurity; the editor may not make changes to versions anyone adds earlier or later.

- *Allowed in New Version Only.* Lets the editor create and edit new versions of the file but not the current version.

- *Not Allowed (Read-Only).* Prohibits the editor from changing any version of the file.

4. To limit the kinds of editing the selected editor can do, open the Limited To list. The options on this list are not mutually exclusive; you can mark as many of them as you want. The options are as follows:

   - *(No Limits).* Requires that you deselect all the other options to display this choice.

   - *All Edits Marked Up.* Means that the editor cannot turn off revision marking, so any changes that editor makes will be marked for your review.

   - *No Version Creation or Review.* Prevents the editor from creating or reviewing other versions of the file.

   - *No Editing of Named Styles.* Prevents the editor from making changes to document styles.

   - *No Copying or Saving as a New File.* Prevents the user from bypassing other controls by trying to copy or save and rename the file.

   - *No Printing.* Prevents the editor from printing the file.

5. To display a greeting with the document and make a suggestion specific to the selected editor, open the Greeting Will Suggest drop-down list. These options specify what choices are selected, by default, in the Greeting dialog box when it appears. The options on this list are not mutually exclusive; you can enable as many of them as you want. The options are as follows:

   - *(Nothing).* Requires that you deselect all the other options to display this choice.

   - *Editing in New Version.* Selects this choice in the Greeting dialog box but lets the reader also choose to edit the current version or open the document as read-only.

> ■ *Markup of Edits.* Enables the check box for revision marks in the Greeting dialog box.
>
> ■ *Review & Comment Tools.* Enables the check box for Comment Tool iconbar display in the Greeting dialog box.

6. Repeat steps 1-5 as needed to set rights for other editors.

7. To display custom text in the Greeting dialog box that greets all editors, mark the Display Greeting With This Text check box; then enter the text you want in the text box.

8. If you want to save comments from each editor with the document for your later review when you open the file again, mark the Request Editor's Remark on Close check box.

9. Click the Other Protection tab to set TeamSecurity as described in the next section, or click OK to return to your document.

Setting Other Protections

◀ See "Creating Divisions," p. 309

The Other Protection tab in the TeamSecurity dialog box provides control over what divisions in a document other editors can view and what edits they can make to a particular division. For example, you may want to show hidden text on one division of a document but not on another. In the Other Protection part of the TeamSecurity dialog box, you have the following options:

■ *Display All Division Tabs in Document.* This ensures that the editors can see all the division tabs, even if you hide the text of a particular division.

■ *Protection Settings for Division.* This drop-down list lets you select a document division. Click the down arrow to display the list. Next click the division name you want to change protection for. Then use the four check boxes below the list to set the following options for that division only; then choose another division from the list to change its settings, and so on:

Hide Entire Division. When checked, this option prohibits the editor from viewing the document text, even if you enabled display of its tab. If you're not displaying all division tabs, this option hides the division tab and text.

Honor Protection on Frames and Cells. When checked, this option ensures that your frame and table cell protection remains in force on that division.

Allow Editing of Protected Text. When checked, this option enables the editor to remove protected text on the division. Leave this option checked to ensure that no one can delete the text.

Show Hidden Text. When checked, this option controls whether Word Pro displays hidden text on the specified division.

■ *Disable Version Review*. This option prevents TeamReview revisions of the document when enabled.

■ *Disable Notes /FX of TeamSecurity Fields*. Selecting this check box turns off fields in the document that cause it to interface with Lotus Notes.

■ *Require Running of Startup Scripts*. When checked, this option prevents an editor from opening the document without running any startup scripts the document calls for.

■ *Edit Click Here Block Prompts On-Screen*. Checking this option enables other editors to adjust the prompt text for Click Here blocks.

After you set the options in this tab, either use the other tabs in the TeamSecurity dialog box, or click OK to close the dialog box and return to your document.

Troubleshooting

I set some TeamSecurity options, but they didn't work. What happened?

After you change any of the TeamSecurity options, make sure that you save your files. Otherwise, the controls you set aren't in place.

Somebody guessed my password. How can I choose a safe one?

Choosing a password that's not obvious but is still memorable to you isn't easy. Experienced computer users know the kinds of passwords beginners usually choose and can therefore guess your password and gain unwanted access to your document. So you should avoid passwords based on your name, your initials, your home phone number or work phone extension, the name of the document, your birthdate, or the name of a loved one that others might know. More secure passwords might include things like your mother's maiden name or your Social Security Number; but the best passwords are more random and include both letters and numbers. For utmost security, consider assigning random passwords, and then keep a list of document passwords in your appointment book or in a separate Word Pro file. You can also create a password by creating an acronym for a phrase. "I saw Elvis at Pizza Hut two days ago" could become the password "IsEaPH2da."

III

Professional Output

Consolidating Edits

Within most businesses, document creation has become an interactive process. You may create the initial draft of a document and then distribute copies of the document file to one or more coworkers so that they can add comments and revisions. You may even handle all this via e-mail so that you get feedback from others without even talking to them.

Handling this kind of situation used to be a nightmare. You either had to handle it all on paper—typing in the comments you want—or you had to compare many versions of the same file to enter the comments that apply.

Word Pro offers new features to facilitate team editing: TeamReview, TeamConsolidate, and document versions. Each of these features lets you more efficiently coordinate and incorporate changes from multiple editors into your important Word Pro documents. The next few sections describe how to use these important new features with your documents.

Using TeamReview

TeamReview automates the process of preparing a document for multiple reviewers. When you display the TeamReview Assistant dialog box, you see that it contains three tabs to walk you through the three-step process of setting up the file to accept edits from multiple users (editors). After you create a TeamReview document, distribute it, and receive copies of the file with changes from other editors, you can incorporate those changes into one final document using TeamConsolidate, described in the next section.

The TeamReview settings resemble the TeamSecurity settings described in the previous section of this chapter. However, TeamReview offers fewer settings that apply to the entire document and doesn't let you assign password protection or protect parts of a file. On the other hand, TeamReview offers a feature that TeamSecurity doesn't; you can automatically send or route the file you're working with via e-mail (most likely via Lotus cc:Mail for Windows or Lotus Notes on a network).

Before you distribute a document to other Team members (editors) for review, you have to set up the document for the TeamReview process. Only the person distributing the document needs to follow these steps. Other editors can simply make their changes, save the document, and return a copy of the document file to the person who originally created and distributed the document for TeamReview. To prepare a document you've previously created and saved for TeamReview, follow these steps:

1. Choose File, TeamReview. The TeamReview Assistant dialog box appears, with the Step 1: Who tab selected (see fig. 24.13). This dialog box lets you specify who can edit the document.

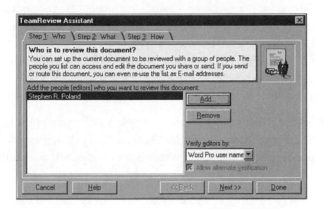

Fig. 24.13
Taking the first step in preparing your document for TeamReview.

2. Click the Add button to add an editor to the list. Type the New editor's name in the New Editor dialog box; as the dialog box warns, the editor name you enter must match the user name that person entered during their installation of Word Pro. Click Done to finish adding the editor to the list.

3. Repeat step 2 for each editor you want to add to the list.

4. Click the Next button to move to the next step of the process. The Step 2: What tab of the dialog box appears (see fig. 24.14).

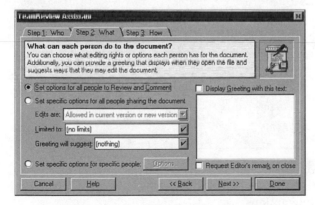

Fig. 24.14
Determining what edits particular users can make to the TeamReview document.

5. In the Step 2: What tab, choose the options you want. Here's what each option controls:

III

Professional Output

■ *Set Options for All People To Review and Comment.* Leave this option button selected to simply display the Greeting message and request comments from all editors.

■ *Set Specific Options for All People Sharing the Document.* Choose this option button if you want to limit edits to a particular version, limit the kinds of actions the editor can perform, or set up default Greeting dialog box options by using the applicable drop-down lists. These options work just the same as when you set TeamSecurity editing rights.

■ *Set Specific Options for Specific People.* Click this option button and then Options to display the TeamSecurity dialog box so that you can set rights and other options for each editor as described in the preceding section about TeamSecurity.

■ *Display Greeting With This Text.* To display custom text in the Greeting dialog box that greets all editors, mark this check box and then enter the text you want in the text box.

■ *Request Editor's Remark on Close.* If you want to save comments from each editor with the document for your later review, click this check box.

6. Click the Next button to display the Step 3: How tab (see fig. 24.15).

Fig. 24.15
Finishing up the process of creating a TeamReview document by deciding how to distribute it.

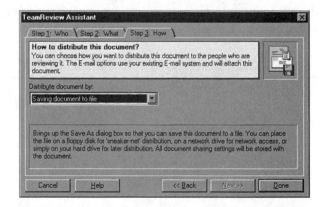

7. Open the Distribute Document By drop-down list. Select one of the following options:

■ *Saving Document to File.* Saves the TeamReview settings in a document file to distribute to others.

- *Saving Document to File on Internet.* Displays the TeamMail dialog box so you can send the file to all reviewers via the Internet.

- *Saving Document and Sending via E-Mail.* Saves the TeamReview settings in a temporary file and prepares it as an e-mail message, even letting you use the editor list as the distribution list.

- *Saving Document and Routing via E-Mail.* Saves the TeamReview settings in a temporary file and prepares it as an e-mail message to be routed from user to user, even letting you use the editor list as the distribution list.

8. Click the Done button. Depending on the option you chose in the preceding step, one of two things happens, concluding the TeamReview document creation process:

- Word Pro displays the Save As dialog box. Specify a directory and file name to save the file to and then click OK. To distribute the file, copy it to floppy disks and provide them to other editors, or place the file on a network drive that all the editors can access.

- Word Pro displays the Send dialog box. Use the Address button to adjust the e-mail addresses, if needed, and then click Send.

Using TeamConsolidate

Word Pro's document comparison feature, called TeamConsolidate, helps you keep track of changes made to multiple copies of the same document. If two or more people are editing one document on different computers, for example, ensuring that both copies of the document are updated can be difficult. In the end, you want one final updated document.

Usually, you'll use TeamConsolidate to put together the changes in different copies of a TeamReview document, which you learned to create in the preceding section. By comparing the two or more documents with Team Consolidate, you can ensure that no changes are missing in the final version of the document. The differences between the versions are marked with the same marks used in revision mode. Word Pro even identifies the editor who made each change; this ensures that if you have questions about a particular edit, you'll know who to contact to resolve the issue.

If you don't want to use the default revision marks, see the earlier section, "Changing Revision Options," for instructions on these options, such as the color of inserted text.

III

Professional Output

To compare documents, including your original and modifications from other editors, follow these steps:

1. Choose File, TeamConsolidate. The TeamConsolidate dialog box appears. As the dialog box indicates, you need to Select the Files to Compare to Your Current File. Remember, it's best to compare files you previously distributed using TeamReview.

2. Click the Add Files button to display the Browse dialog box. Select the appropriate drive, directory, and file name, and then click the Open button to add the file to the list of files you're consolidating with the open document.

3. Repeat step 3 to add as many files as you need. When you're finished, the list of files in the TeamConsolidate dialog box looks something like figure 24.16.

> **Note**
>
> Choose the Internet button to open a file from a Host server on the Internet. You can choose the server type, copy the files to a local temporary file, and connect to the Internet, all in the Open from Internet dialog box.

Fig. 24.16
Specifying which files to consolidate with the open document.

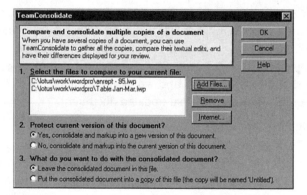

4. Under the second step of this dialog box, Protect Current Version of This Document?, choose the option button you want:

   ■ Yes, Consolidate and Markup Into a New Version of This Document creates a new document and places the markup changes there, leaving your original file intact.

■ No, Consolidate and Markup Into the Current <u>V</u>ersion of This Document enters the markup changes in the open document without creating another document.

5. Under the last step of this dialog box, What Do You Want to Do With the Consolidated Document?, choose the option button you want:

   ■ Leave the Consolidated Document in This <u>F</u>ile leaves the various versions in one file.

   ■ Put the Consolidated Document Into a <u>C</u>opy of This File creates a new file named "Untitled" to accept results of the consolidation.

6. Click OK to close the TeamConsolidate dialog box. Word Pro begins the consolidation and displays a status message at the bottom of the screen as it proceeds.

7. When the changes are consolidated, Word Pro displays a dialog box telling you that paragraphs may have been duplicated. Click OK to go to the marked up document (see fig. 24.17).

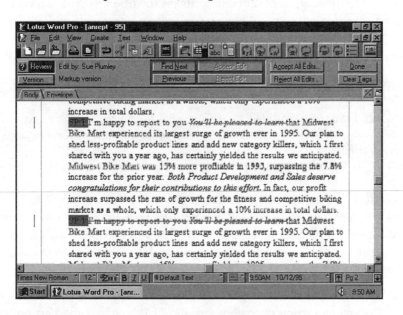

Fig. 24.17
The resulting marked up document contains all revisions; each revision is identified with the initials of the editor who created it.

8. When Word Pro displays the consolidated file, it also displays the Revision bar so that you can accept or reject revisions to create the final document. To learn how to do so, see the section called "Accepting and Rejecting Revisions" earlier in this chapter.

9. Choose File, Save or Save As to preserve the consolidated file with its revisions.

Using Versions

When you create new versions of a document, you can store different sets of changes within the same file. Each version contains a set of changes. When you save the file, it saves all the versions with it, so you can reopen the file and open the version with the changes you want. In the old days, to accomplish the same result, you would have to save multiple separate files on-disk, assigning each one a new name. This was an easy way to gobble up disk space without really trying.

Version creation is somewhat automatic. For example, when a new editor opens a file, Word Pro automatically creates a new version of the file and protects the original as a read-only version. Versions are useful if you have a complex document that you use repeatedly or need to change sequentially. For example, let's say you create a new layout for a product sales flyer, and you want to try a couple of different fonts for the title text. You can create and save the original layout. Then you can create a new version with each font you want to test. When you settle on the version you prefer, you can save it as its own file.

> **Tip**
>
> You can also display the Versions for File dialog box by clicking the Version button on the Revision bar. For more on this bar, see "Accepting and Rejecting Revisions" earlier in this chapter.

To create a version for a file, open and save the file. Then choose File, Versions. The Versions for File dialog box appears, with all the options you need for creating and managing versions (see fig. 24.18). The following list describes the key operations you can perform in this dialog box; to close the dialog box when you're finished using it, click OK.

■ To create a new version, click the Create Version button. In the Create Document Version dialog box (see fig. 24.19), change the Version Name if you want to, and enter an Editor's Remark. Click OK and Word Pro displays a reminder that you may need to later save the version in a separate file—otherwise, the changes are accessible only from within the original file. Click OK to acknowledge this warning. The new version is added to the list of versions in the document, shown in the Versions for File dialog box.

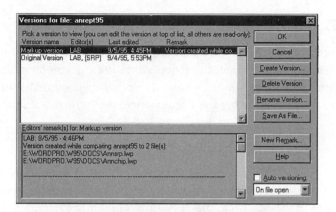

Fig. 24.18
Versions enable
you to save
multiple sets of
changes to a file,
without creating
separate files and
clogging up your
hard disk.

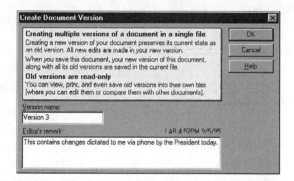

Fig. 24.19
After you choose
the Create Version
button, you use
this dialog box to
assign a name and
remarks to the new
version.

■ To remove any version from the document, click the version name in the list and then click the Delete Version button. At the dialog box asking whether you're sure you want to delete the version, click Yes.

■ To rename any version in the document, click the version name in the list and then click the Rename Version button. In the Rename Version dialog box, type a new Version Name and then click OK.

■ To save a version as a new file, click the version name in the list and then click the Save As File button. In the Browse dialog box, select a drive and directory, enter a file name, and then click OK.

■ To change the editor's remark associated with a version, click the version name in the list and then click the New Remark button. In the Editor's Remark dialog box, enter a new remark and then click OK.

■ To have Word Pro create a version automatically when you perform certain operations, mark the Auto Versioning check box and then click an option from the drop-down list.

From Here...

This chapter introduced you to Word Pro's document revision features, which offer you many capabilities for coordinating changes by multiple editors, controlling access to your documents, preparing documents for review by a team, and consolidating the team changes into a final document.

For other topics that can make you more effective in managing and refining your documents, review these chapters:

- Chapter 9, "Proofreading Documents," provides information about the tools for fine-tuning your document contents. The chapter explains how to use Spell Check, the Thesaurus, Grammar Check, and the new Format Checker.

- Chapter 11, "Customizing Word Pro," explains how to set some of the preferences that this chapter briefly discussed. The chapter explains how to control which document elements appear on-screen, how to change personal user info such as your user name and initials, how to set up the new SmartFill feature, and more.

- Chapter 16, "Managing Long Documents," introduces you to several tools for better organizing information in your documents. You learn how to create divisions and sections in a document, as well as how to control formatting within a section, set up a table of contents and index, and insert data from other applications.

Chapter 25

Importing, Exporting, and Linking Files

by Sue Plumley

You can create impressive graphics and tables in Word Pro using the program's drawing and table features. Often, however, importing a drawing or spreadsheet from another program is easier and more efficient than creating your own from scratch. You may want to use a graphic that someone else created, for example, or a spreadsheet or chart you produced in a different application. With Word Pro's improved importing and exporting features, you can save time by sharing data between applications.

In addition to importing files, you can export Word Pro files to other programs, such as Freelance Graphics or Lotus 1-2-3. You can also link files between applications. When you create a link between documents or applications, you make it possible to update data automatically in all linked documents. Linking is an excellent way to share data and save time.

In this chapter, you learn how to:

- Understand importing and exporting
- Import and export text and data files
- Import graphic files
- Modify imported images

◀ See "Saving a
Document,"
p. 72

◀ See "Closing
and Opening
Documents,"
p. 74

Word Pro's importing and exporting features are easy to use and understand. If you are familiar with the File Open and File Save As dialog boxes, you already know almost everything you need to know about importing documents into Word Pro from another word processing, database, or spreadsheet program and exporting documents from Word Pro to another application. You use the Save As dialog box to export files and the Open dialog box to import files.

The Open and Save As dialog boxes contain lists of file types (see fig. 25.1). You choose a file type to convert the file you are about to open or save.

Fig. 25.1
Use the Save as
Type drop-down
list to choose a file
type; opening a
file of a different
type is the same as
importing it.

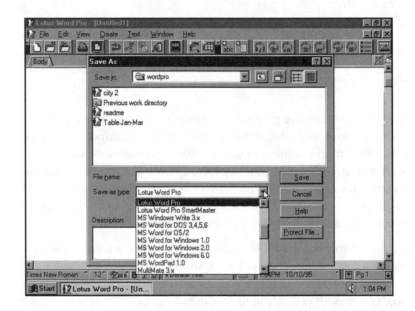

When importing or exporting files, many word processing programs (including Word Pro) use a *file filter*. The filter converts the text from its original file type to the new file type, preserving as much of the original formatting as possible.

When importing or exporting graphics files, you also specify a file filter—a graphic file filter. Most software applications can accept several different graphic file types, as explained in the section, "Importing Graphics," later in this chapter.

Importing and Exporting Text and Data Files

Importing text means converting it from another file format into Word Pro format; *exporting* text means converting it to another file format. Word Pro provides an easy method for importing and exporting files: the Import or Export dialog box (see fig. 25.2).

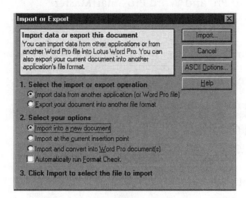

Fig. 25.2
The Import or Export dialog box leads you to the Open (import) or the Save As (export) dialog box.

Before you can import or export text or data files, you must know the file type. If, for example, you want to import a file from another word processor, you must know the name and version of the word processor so that you can identify the file type. You can enter a valid file name and its extension in the File Name text box and Word Pro imports the file for you; alternatively, you can choose the file type from a list and then select the file you want to import. Word Pro accepts the following file types:

- ANSI (Windows)
- ASCII
- dBASE (ANSI or ASCII)
- DCA/FFT
- DCA/RFT
- DIF
- DisplayWrite
- Enable 4.x
- FrameMaker (MIF)

- HTML

- Legacy 1.2

- Lotus 1-2-3 for OS/2, R3, R4, R5

- Lotus Ami Pro, Ami Pro 3.*x* Macro, Ami Pro 3.*x* Styles

- Lotus Manuscript 2.*x*, Lotus Organizer 1.*x*

- Lotus Word Pro and Word Pro SmartMaster

- MS Excel 3, 4, 5, 7

- MS Windows Write 3.*x*

- MultiMate 3.*x*, 4.*x*, and Advantage

- MS Word for Windows 1.0, 2.0, 6.0, 7.0

- MS Word for DOS 3, 4, 5, 6, and for OS/2

- MS WordPad 1.0

- ODBC Data

- OfficeWriter 4, 5, 6

- Peach Text 5000

- Professional Write 1, 2

- Q&A Write 1, 3, 4

- Rich Text Format

- SAMNA Word

- Text (E-mail)

- WordPerfect 5, 5.1, 6.*x*

- WordStar 2000 R3, 3, 4, 5, 6, 7 and for Windows 1.*x*

- XyWrite DOS/Windows

Importing Text and Data Files

You can import files by using either the Open dialog box or the Import or Export dialog box, which leads to the Open dialog box. When using the Import or Export dialog box, you can choose where you want to place the imported file and whether to run a format check on the text or data.

To import a text or data file using the Import or Export dialog box, follow these steps:

1. Choose File, Import/Export. The Import or Export dialog box appears. Alternatively, click the Import/Export SmartIcon.

2. In 1, Select the Import or Export Operation, choose Import Data From Another Application (or Word Pro file).

3. In 2, Select Your Options, choose from one of the following options:

   ■ *Import into a New Document.* Creates a new document to import the file to.

   ■ *Import at the Current Insertion Point.* Inserts the imported file at the insertion point in the current document.

   ■ *Import and Convert into Word Pro Document(s).* Imports the document and converts it into Word Pro file format.

   ◄ See "Using the Format Checker," p. 192

4. The option Automatically Run Format Check is not selected by default. Choose the option to run the Format Check on all imported files.

5. Choose the Import button. The Open dialog box appears (see fig. 25.3).

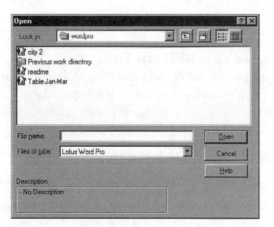

Fig. 25.3
Choose the file format from the Files of Type in the Open dialog box.

6. Choose the Drive and Directory that holds the file you want to import.

7. In Files of Type, choose the file type you want to import.

8. In File Name, choose the file name and choose Open. Word Pro imports the file to the specified location (see fig. 25.4).

III

Professional Output

Fig. 25.4
An imported Word
Pro document,
containing a
drawing, becomes
a part of the
existing document.

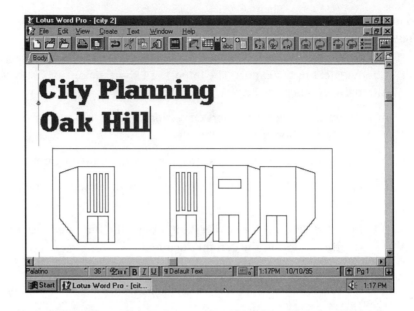

Note

You can also import text and data files to a Master Document division using the
Master Document dialog box.

Exporting Text and Data Files

You can export your Word Pro text and data files to other applications using
the Import or Export dialog box. When you export data, you choose the file
type you want to export to; these file types are the same as those listed in the
preceding section, "Importing Text and Data Files."

To export text and data files, follow these steps:

1. Choose File, Import/Export. The Import or Export dialog box appears.

2. In number 1, Select the Import or Export Operation; choose Export
   Your Document Into Another File Format. The options below number 2
   change, as shown in figure 25.5.

3. In step 2, Export to What File Format, choose the file type you want to
   export to.

4. Click the Export button. The Save As dialog box appears.

5. In File Name, enter the name of the file you want to save and then
   specify a drive and directory to save the file to.

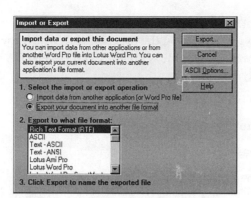

Fig. 25.5
Export a file by
choosing any of
the 25 file filters.

6. Choose OK, and Word Pro converts the file and saves it for you in the specified location. The original data remains unsaved and on-screen in Word Pro for you to save, if you want.

Troubleshooting

I tried to import a text file but got the warning File is not the correct type for the import filter.

Choose OK to close the message box and then choose File, Import/Export. In the Open dialog box, choose a different file type. If you are unsure as to which file type to use, consult the documentation of the application containing the file you want to import. You may need to go into the application and save the file to be imported using a different file filter before you can import it.

I want to import ASCII text but I have special formatting needs; the Text-ASCII file type does not convert the text the way I want.

In the Import or Export dialog box, choose the ASCII Options button when either importing or exporting. The ASCII Options dialog box appears. Specify carriage return and style options and choose OK to return to the Import or Export dialog box.

Using Graphics in Word Pro

Word Pro can import either of two kinds of graphics: *bitmap* or *vector*. Bitmap graphics, made up of pixels or small dots, import more quickly than vector graphics. Vector graphics store images as a series of lines rather than dots so the images take up less disk space. Examples of bitmap graphics include PC Paintbrush, Tagged Image File Format, and Bitmap files. Examples of Vector graphics include Hewlett-Packard Graphics Language and Windows Metafile. The type of graphic you choose depends on available disk space and the file format the graphic was stored in.

Using Graphic File Types

Graphic file types depend on the program with which the graphic was created and the way the graphic is stored. Word Pro enables you to import 9 different file types.

Following are the graphic file types you can import to Word Pro:

- Word Pro Draw (SDW)
- Equations (TEX)
- Windows Bitmap (BMP)
- PC Paintbrush (PCX)
- Tagged Image File Format (versions 5.0 and earlier) (TIF)
- Windows Metafile (WMF) (EMF)
- DrawPerfect 1.0 and 2.0 (WPG)
- Graphic Interchange Format (GIF)
- JPEG (JPG)

> **Tip**
>
> Graphics in a Word Pro document require considerable disk space, especially TIF and EPS file formats.

If you're using a scanning software or a drawing or painting program to create a graphic file, you can usually choose the file type you want to save your graphic file in. Choose a file type that Word Pro accepts.

Importing Graphics

◀ See "Understanding Tables," p. 324

◀ See "Creating a Frame," p. 385

When you import a graphic or picture to Word Pro, Word Pro creates a default frame if you do not specify a frame. If you import the graphic or picture to a table, however, Word Pro uses the table cell as a frame.

To import a picture or graphic to a frame, follow these steps:

> **Tip**
>
> Any graphic you import to a frame overwrites the frame's contents.

1. Create a frame or specify a frame by selecting it. Alternatively, select no frame and let Word Pro create the frame for you when you choose to import the picture.

2. Choose File, Import Picture; alternatively, click the Import a Picture SmartIcon. The Import Picture dialog box appears (see fig. 25.6).

3. In the Import Picture dialog box, choose the file type in the Files of Type drop-down list.

4. Select the drive and directory containing the file.

Fig. 25.6
Choose to import a graphic; you can preview the graphic first by checking the Preview option in the dialog box.

5. Select the file from the File Name list and choose Open. Word Pro imports the graphic to the selected frame or creates a frame to hold the graphic if no frame was previously indicated.

    Before choosing Open, the selected graphic appears in the preview window of the Import Picture dialog box. The Preview check box must be selected.

    You can scale and crop the imported image using the Image Properties dialog box. Only TIF, BMP, GIF, and PCX graphics can be imaged processed.

> **Note**
>
> You can also copy and paste a picture or graphic from another Windows application to Word Pro or from Word Pro to another application using the Clipboard and the Edit menu.

Working with Images

When you import an image, you may need to adjust the brightness, contrast, or other image properties. Word Pro enables you to modify images after importing them and gives you some control over printing the images as well.

◀ See "Under-
standing
Frames," p. 384

After importing a graphic, you can modify the image using the Image menu. If the Image menu does not display on-screen, double-click the picture you imported. You can change image properties and contrast, and control half-tone printing. Graphic file formats you can apply image processing to include TIF, BMP, GIF, and PCX.

> **Note**
>
> *Halftones* are images using various concentrations of small dots to form lights and darks in the picture. Halftones can be found in some clip art but are usually created by scanning a photograph or other graphic and specifying in the scanning program that you want to create a halftone.

Setting Image Properties

Image properties consist of brightness, contrast, edge enhancement, and smoothing. You can adjust the properties in the Image Properties dialog box (see fig. 25.7). Double-click the image to select it and then access the Image Properties dialog box by choosing Image, Image Properties.

To adjust any of the options in the Image Properties dialog box, enter a number from 0 to 100 in the text box or use the arrows to change the number. Alternatively, you can click the mouse on the marker and drag it to the left for less brightness, contrast, and so on or to the right to increase the bright-

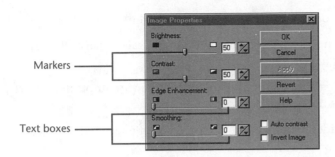

Markers

Text boxes

Fig. 25.7
By adjusting the
brightness and
contrast of an
image you can
make it stylized,
distorted, or sharp
and clear.

ness, contrast, and so on. The following list describes each option in the dialog box:

- *Brightness.* Adjusts the amount of light and dark in the image with 0 being black and 100 being white.

- *Contrast.* Adjusts the difference between blacks and whites in the image with 0 being all-over gray and 100 being black and white with no grays.

- *Edge Enhancement.* Sharpens or blurs the lines of an image with 0 being somewhat fuzzy and 100 being very sharp.

- *Smoothing.* Softens or smoothes lines with 0 being no smoothing and 100 being very smooth.

- *Auto Contrast.* Sets the Brightness and Contrast to a fixed amount that cannot be changed unless you deselect this option.

- *Invert Image.* Changes the image from positive to negative or from negative to positive.

After modifying one of the options in the Image Properties dialog box, choose Apply to view the changes on-screen. If you like the changes, choose OK to close the dialog box. If you don't like the changes, choose Revert and try again or choose Cancel to close the dialog box and cancel the changes.

Controlling Halftone Printing

You can control how halftone images are printed using the Image menu. You can choose to print the best quality image, which takes longer, or you can choose to print the images in your document faster but with poorer quality.

To access the Image menu, double-click the image. Choose Halftone Printing to display the secondary menu. Choose any of the following options from the secondary menu:

- *Fastest Printing.* Prints the selected image quickly; however, the quality of the image is sacrificed. This print option is good for proofing pages.

III

Professional Output

- *Best Quality.* Produces a fine print quality but prints more slowly.

- *Automatic.* Produces a higher quality print of a scaled image without taking as long to print.

- *Use Printer Driver.* Uses halftoning options in the current printer driver. (This option is the default.)

- *Posterize.* Provides halftones with a special poster effect and changes all grays to black or white.

Troubleshooting

I double-clicked my image but the I_mage menu did not appear.

The picture you imported is not an image that can be adjusted using Word Pro's I_mage menu. If you need to modify the image, try doing it in the program in which the image originated.

I changed the image properties of a picture and now I can't remember what the properties were before I started. I hate what I've done, but I keep making it worse. What can I do?

Select the image by double-clicking it. Choose I_mage, _Revert to change the image back to its original properties.

I just want to print a proof of my document, but the images take so long to print. What can I do?

Double-click each image and choose I_mage, _Halftone Printing, and select _Fastest Printing. Word Pro prints a proof of the image instead of a good quality image. Don't forget to choose _Best Quality from the Halftone Printing menu before printing your final copy.

Understanding Linking and Embedding

When you import a text or data file, you accept it "as is"—as the originating program created it. So although some formatting converts, you usually need to do some reformatting in Word Pro. Also, if text or data changes in the original application, those changes aren't reflected in the file in Word Pro.

In many cases, these restrictions are fine. However, sometimes you need data to be up-to-date in both applications, no matter how often you change the data. Word Pro offers linking and embedding, two methods of sharing data between applications so that you can be assured it is updated and accurate at all times.

Object linking and embedding (also called *OLE*) is a feature of many Windows applications that enables you to share text or data between two or more applications. Linking connects two documents, whereas embedding enables you to create one document within another.

When linking data, you create a connection between two documents or programs. The source program, say 1-2-3 for example, contains the original data. The destination program, Word Pro for instance, receives the linked data. When any data is changed in the source, OLE automatically updates the data in the destination program.

Just think of the time you save by linking, especially if you want to use data in several programs. You could create a spreadsheet in 1-2-3 and link it to a Word Pro business report and a Freelance Graphics presentation. To quickly update the data, simply correct the source in 1-2-3; all links are automatically updated for you.

Embedding is another feature of OLE in which you create the source object within the destination program. Say you want to create a spreadsheet in your Word Pro business report. You choose to insert the object—or spreadsheet by opening 1-2-3 within Word Pro and creating the spreadsheet there. You close 1-2-3, and the spreadsheet appears in your Word Pro document. Any time you want to update or change data in that spreadsheet, you simply double-click the spreadsheet to open 1-2-3, and you're ready to edit.

> **Note**
>
> Many Windows applications support OLE; however, check the application's documentation if you are not sure.

The main difference between linking and embedding is where the data is stored. Linked files are stored in the original, or source, document; only a copy of the data appears in the destination. Embedded data, on the other hand, is stored in the destination document as a part of that document.

Using Links

Link files together when you want to enter data only once, but use it in two or more documents and applications. Linked files can be unlinked at any time if sharing the data no longer suits your purpose. You can link files—text, data, or graphic—between any Windows applications that support OLE.

III

Professional Output

Linking Files

You can link data, text, or graphic files to a Word Pro document. The procedure is the same for all three file types.

To link files, follow these steps:

1. Open the destination application—in this case Word Pro—and the document you want to link the file to.

2. Open the source application, create the data, and save the file.

3. Select the data or text to be linked and choose Edit, Copy.

4. Switch to the Word Pro document using the taskbar.

5. Position the insertion point in Word Pro and choose Edit, Paste Special. The Paste Special dialog box appears (see fig. 25.8).

6. Choose the Paste Link to Source option.

7. From the As list, choose the type of file you want to insert if other than the type selected.

8. Choose OK. Word Pro inserts the data into the document.

Fig. 25.8
Use the Paste Special dialog box to create a link between two files.

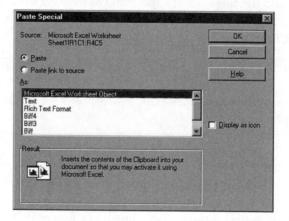

After pasting the data file into your Word Pro document and saving the document, you can change the source file at any time; the linked file automatically changes.

Managing Links

When you modify the source document of a linked file, the linked file in the destination document automatically updates. Word Pro also enables you to break links and to update links manually.

To manage linked files, follow these steps:

1. Select the data or position the insertion point anywhere in the linked file.

2. Choose Edit, Manage Links. The Manage Links dialog box appears.

3. In the Link list, choose the link you want to edit.

4. Choose from the following options in the Links dialog box:

   ■ *Update: Automatic or Manual.* Choose to update the link manually if you want the destination document to remain the same until you are ready to update.

   ■ *Update Now.* Click this button to manually update the links.

   ■ *Open Source.* Choose this command button to open the source application and document to modify the data.

   ■ *Edit Link.* Choose to reconnect broken links by first selecting the links and then entering the file name of the source document in the source text box.

   ■ *Break Link.* Choose to discontinue the link. The data in the destination document remains in its place but does not change when the source is changed.

5. Choose Cancel to close the Links dialog box.

Using Embedded Objects

Embedding objects means to insert a chart, spreadsheet, drawing, or other object from another application into a destination document. Objects embedded in Word Pro become part of the Word Pro document. You can embed a new or existing object, as long as the source application is installed in your computer. You can also easily modify, edit, and update embedded objects within the Word Pro document.

Embedding Objects

Use embedded objects when source data may occasionally need to be updated, but you only need the data in one document instead of several. You can embed text, data, or graphics into a Word Pro document.

> ### Caution
>
> Before embedding an object, make sure that the application you use to create the object is not already running in Windows. Opening the application a second time using the Insert Object dialog box uses excess system memory and may lock up your computer.

To embed an object, follow these steps:

1. In the Word Pro document, position the insertion point where you want the embedded object to go.

2. Choose <u>C</u>reate, <u>O</u>bject. The Create Object dialog box appears (see fig. 25.9).

3. Choose one of the following options:

   - Create a <u>N</u>ew Object to create an object from scratch within the Word Pro document.

   - Create an Object From a <u>F</u>ile to select an existing file in a source application.

Fig. 25.9
Insert an object from another application so that it becomes a part of the Word Pro document.

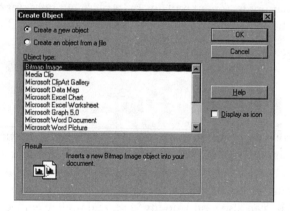

4. If you are creating a new object, choose the source application from the <u>O</u>bject Type list.

If you are creating an object from a file, the options in the dialog box change. Enter the path and file name in the File text box and choose Link to File.

5. Choose OK. The source application opens within Word Pro (see fig. 25.10).

6. Enter the data or otherwise create the object in the source application.

7. Click the mouse in Word Pro to close the source application and update the figure to your document.

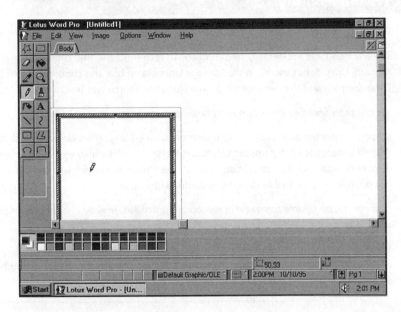

Fig. 25.10
The source application opens within Word Pro; make sure that you do not have another copy of the source application open in Windows.

Editing Embedded Objects

You can easily edit an embedded object and update the modifications to the Word Pro document. To edit an embedded object, double-click the object in Word Pro. When you double-click the object, the source application opens with the object displaying, ready to edit. Make any changes you want to the data and choose File, Update when you're done. Exit the source application, saving the copy first if you want. The changes are updated in the Word Pro document.

Note

Some objects, such as sound clips or videos, may play when you double-click them instead of enabling you to edit the object. You can also edit an object by selecting it and choosing Edit, Edit Object; the Edit Object command appears near the end of the Edit menu. There may be a secondary menu from which you choose Edit, depending on the object type.

Troubleshooting

I edited the source document, but the data did not change in the destination document.

The link may have accidentally been broken. To reconnect the link, choose Edit, Manage Links. Select the file in the Manage Links dialog box and choose Edit Link. Enter the path and the name of the source file in the Source text box.

My computer seems to slow down every time I open or update my embedded object.

Editing embedded objects takes more memory than editing linked objects. Make sure that all unnecessary programs are closed before double-clicking an embedded object. Also, make sure that the application in which the embedded object was created is not open when you double-click the embedded object.

I cannot find an Update command in my source application. How do I update the embedded object?

Some applications may not have an Update command in the File menu. Instead, choose File and either Exit or Quit. The application may display a message dialog box asking if you want to update the embedded object; choose Yes.

From Here...

You can format and modify imported and linked objects as you would other parts of a Word Pro document. For more information, refer to the following chapters:

- Chapter 16, "Managing Long Documents," explains how to create divisions and sections in a Master Document and how to import a file from another application or from Word Pro to a Master Document.

■ Chapter 20, "Using Advanced Frame Techniques," shows you how to format frames and how to scale graphics imported into the frame. Additionally, you learn to work with the image properties of imported graphic objects.

■ Chapter 21, "Using Draw," shows you how to create drawings as well as how to modify imported objects by adjusting image brightness, contrast, and so on, and managing printing halftones.

Part IV

Appendixes

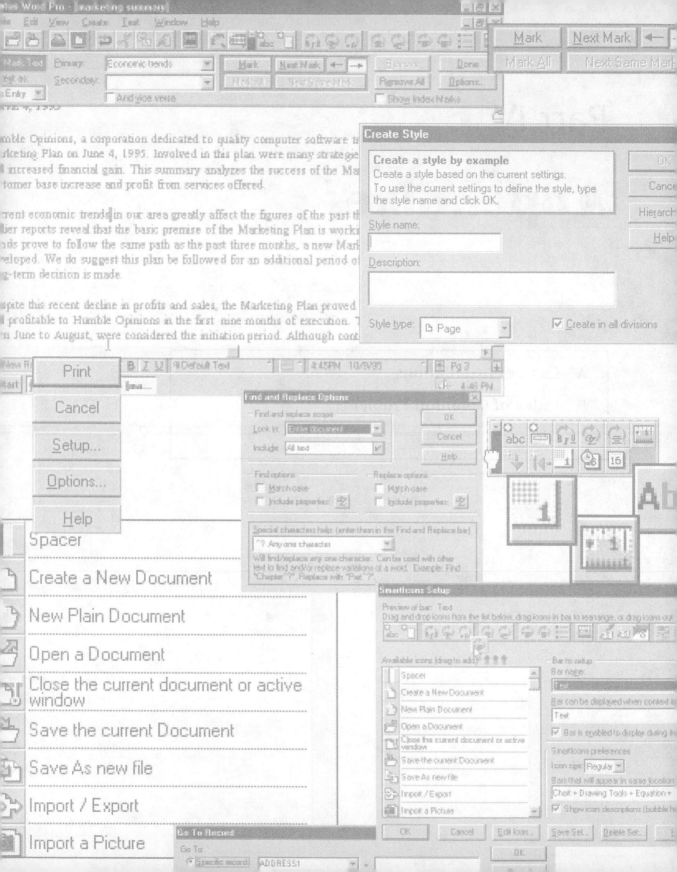

Lotus Word Pro - [marketing summary]

File Edit View Create Text Window Help

Mark Text

Primary: Economic trends
Secondary:
☐ And vice versa

Mark   Next Mark ← →   Remove   Done
HTML ?   Use Same HTML   Remove All   Options...
☐ Show Index Marks

Mark   Next Mark ←
Mark All   Next Same Mark

...mble Opinions, a corporation dedicated to quality computer software t...
...rketing Plan on June 4, 1995. Involved in this plan were many strategie...
...l increased financial gain. This summary analyzes the success of the Mar...
...tomer base increase and profit from services offered.

...rent economic trends in our area greatly affect the figures of the past th...
...lier reports reveal that the basic premise of the Marketing Plan is worki...
...nds prove to follow the same path as the past three months, a new Mark...
...veloped. We do suggest this plan be followed for an additional period of...
...g-term decision is made.

...spite this recent decline in profits and sales, the Marketing Plan proved...
...l profitable to Humble Opinions in the first nine months of execution. T...
...n June to August, were considered the initiation period. Although conti...

Create Style

Create a style by example
Create a style based on the current settings.
To use the current settings to define the style, type
the style name and click OK.

Style name:

Description:

Style type: ☐ Page

☑ Create in all divisions

OK
Cance...
Hierarch...
Help

Print
Cancel
Setup...
Options...
Help

B I U ¶Default Text   4:45PM 10/9/95   Pg 3

4:46 PM

Find and Replace Options

Find and replace scope
Look in:
Include: All text

OK
Cancel
Help

Find options
☐ Match case
☐ Include properties

Replace options
☐ Match case
☐ Include properties

Special characters help: (enter them in the Find and Replace bar)
*? Any one character
Will find/replace any one character. Can be used with other
text to find and/or replace variations of a word. Example: Find
"Chapter"?", Replaces with "Part"?".

Spacer

Create a New Document

New Plain Document

Open a Document

Close the current document or active
window

Save the current Document

Save As new file

Import / Export

Import a Picture

SmartIcons Setup

Preview of bar: Text
Drag and drop icons from the list below, drag icons in bar to rearrange, or drag icons out.

Available icons (drag to add)
Spacer
Create a New Document
New Plain Document
Open a Document
Close the current document or active
window
Save the current Document
Save As new file
Import / Export
Import a Picture

Bar to setup
Bar name:

Bar can be displayed when context is
Text
☑ Bar is enabled to display during t...

SmartIcons preferences
Icon size: Regular
Bar that will appear in same location
Chart + Drawing Tools + Equation +
☑ Show icon descriptions (bubble h...

OK   Cancel   Edit Icon...   Save Set...   Delete Set...

Go To Record

Go To:
⦿ Specific record ADDRESS1

OK

Appendix A

Custom Installations

by Lisa Bucki

Lotus Development Corporation provides an automated installation program that copies all the Word Pro 96 program files to your hard drive and sets them up to run with Windows 95. The Word Pro installation files are available on 3.5-inch floppy disks or on CD-ROM. Before you open your Word Pro software package, double-check to make sure that you've purchased the version on the media you want to install from.

> **Tip**
>
> Installing from CD-ROM requires less time and attention. You don't have to swap multiple disks in and out of the drive. If you have a CD-ROM drive, choosing the CD-ROM version of Word Pro is your best bet.

You also need to make sure that your computer system provides enough power to run Word Pro effectively. At minimum, your system should satisfy the following requirements:

- An IBM-compatible personal computer (not a Macintosh) with an 80486 or Pentium processor

- A minimum of 8MB of memory, but more is recommended

- Windows 95 installed

- A hard disk with at least 41MB of available space for installation of Word Pro, more for saving files and working in Word Pro

- A 3.5-inch floppy disk drive or CD-ROM drive, depending on the installation media you select

- An additional 10MB of free disk space for temporary files

Word Pro offers two different kinds of installations. The Default installation enables you to install <u>A</u>ll Features of the Word Pro program (41MB) or the bare <u>M</u>inimum Features version (only 17MB of files, which makes this a good choice for installing to a laptop). Beyond making limited changes such as the directory or program group to install Word Pro to, the default installation process is quite straightforward.

A Customize Features installation (Manual) enables you to select which components of Word Pro you want to install. For example, you can choose not to install the Fax SmartMasters if you won't be using Word Pro to create fax cover sheets. Choose a Manual install if you have limited hard disk space but don't want the <u>M</u>inimum features installed, or if you know you won't need certain features.

If you're installing Word Pro from 3.5-inch floppy disks, create a copy of the installation disks for safety before you begin the installation process.

A Word About Registration

Be sure to complete the registration card that comes with your software and return it to Lotus Development Corporation. Registering your software ensures that you'll have access to technical support if you need it. Registering Word Pro also enables you to get a discounted price on the next version (upgrade) of Word Pro that Lotus Development Corporation releases.

Performing a Default Installation

Most users will want to choose a default installation to eliminate the need to specify which of Word Pro's features to install. The <u>D</u>efault Features—Automatic Install choice sets up the entire Word Pro program, including all its features, on your hard drive. This installation requires that your hard drive has at least 41MB of space available. The <u>M</u>inimum Features—Default Installation choice sets up the fewest number of Word Pro features on your system; however, you aren't required to pick and choose which features to install. Because this installation requires only 17MB of disk space, it's a good option for laptop computers.

> **Tip**
>
> After you start the installation, you can abort the process at any time by clicking the E<u>x</u>it Install button.

To perform a typical install for Word Pro, follow these steps:

1. Start Windows 95 if it isn't already running. If you were already working in Windows, exit from all Windows applications that you were working in.

2. Insert Install (Disk 1) into the appropriate floppy drive, or insert the Word Pro CD-ROM into your CD-ROM drive and close the drive.

3. In Windows, click the Start button. Choose Settings, Control Panel.

4. Double-click the Add/Remove Programs icon in the control panel. The Add/Remove Programs Properties dialog box appears.

5. In the Install/Uninstall tab, choose Install. The Installation wizard box appears. Click Next, and Windows finds the disk or CD, enters the path to the EXE files, and enters the EXE file name in the Command Line text box. Click Finish to close the wizard and start the installation process.

6. Installation copies some files to your hard drive, and then displays a Welcome screen. Word Pro enters the name and company from the Windows 95 User Info box to the Word Pro Welcome dialog box (see fig. A.1). If the name is not correct, enter the new name in the Your Name text box. Press tab or click in the Company Name text box. Type your company name. Click the Next button to continue the install process.

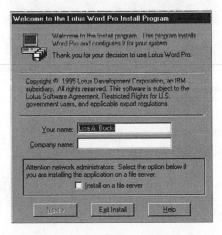

Fig. A.1
Installation gives you a warm welcome. Enter your name and your company name in this dialog box.

7. A dialog box appears asking you to confirm the names you specified. Click Yes to do so and continue installing.

8. In the Specify Main Lotus Directory dialog box, choose the <u>D</u>rive and Directory into which you want to install Word Pro. The default installation is to the C-drive and the LOTUS directory. Click <u>N</u>ext.

9. In the Install Options & Word Pro Directory dialog box (see fig. A.2), click to select one of the following options:

   Def<u>a</u>ult Features. Automatically installs default features in 39MB.

   <u>M</u>inimum Features. Automatically installs only the minimum features needed to run the application in 17MB.

   <u>C</u>ustomize Features. You manually select the features you want to install (discussed later in this appendix).

Fig. A.2
Choosing the install type and the drive and directory to hold the Word Pro program files.

Automatic install options

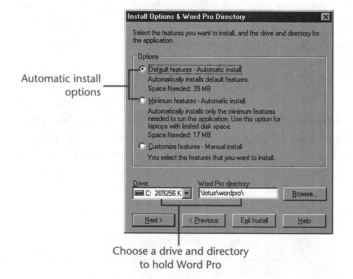

Choose a drive and directory
to hold Word Pro

10. By default, Install suggests that you install Word Pro in the \LOTUS\WORDPRO\ directory on drive C. You can change these settings at the bottom of the Install Options & Word Pro Directory dialog box. To do so, click the down arrow to display the <u>D</u>rive drop-down list; then click a drive to select it and close the list. If needed, type a new directory name in the Word Pro D<u>i</u>rectory text box. (If the specified directory doesn't exist, Install creates it.) To continue the installation, click <u>N</u>ext.

11. In the Select Program Folder dialog box (see fig. A.3), click the name of the folder where you want the Word Pro program-item icons to appear. If you want, you can accept Word Pro's Lotus SmartSuite folder as the one to install Word Pro to. Click <u>N</u>ext.

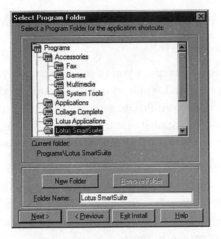

Fig. A.3
Word Pro installs
to the Lotus
SmartSuite folder;
if the folder does
not exist, Word Pro
creates it.

12. Install displays a message box saying it cannot install if any of the files
    are in use; it then tells you how to close any open files, if you have any
    that are open. This dialog box also asks whether you want to begin
    copying the Word Pro files to your hard disk. Click Yes to continue
    installation. Install begins copying files to your hard disk.

13. If you're installing from floppy disks (rather than a CD-ROM), Install
    displays a prompt asking you to insert the next disk. Each time Word
    Pro asks you for a disk, insert it in the drive and click OK to continue
    the installation. If you're installing from a CD, Word Pro transfers the
    files; during installation, Word Pro displays the Lotus Install dialog box
    that tracks the percentage of the application installed (see fig. A.4).

Fig. A.4
The Lotus Install
dialog box tells you
how much of the
application has
been installed.

14. After installation, Word Pro displays a message saying installation is
    complete. Choose OK to return to the Windows desktop. Word Pro
    adds the program's name to the Programs menu under the folder's
    name you specified during installation.

At this time, remove the last floppy disk or the install CD-ROM from the
drive, and store it (along with other floppies if applicable), in a safe, clean,
cool location.

Performing a Customize Features (Manual) Install

A Customized installation enables you to select exactly which features of Word Pro you want to install. You can use the Customized installation for the first time you install Word Pro, to reinstall selected program features, or to install a previously uninstalled feature after a default installation. The Customized installation process is similar to performing a default installation.

To perform a Customized installation, follow steps 1 through 6 of the Automatic install process described in the preceding section. In the Install Options & Word Pro Directory dialog box (refer to fig. A.2), click to select the Customize Features—Manual Install option; then click Next. Install displays the Customize dialog box, as shown in figure A.5.

Fig. A.5
The Word Pro Program tab of the Customize dialog box enables you to specify which features of the program to install.

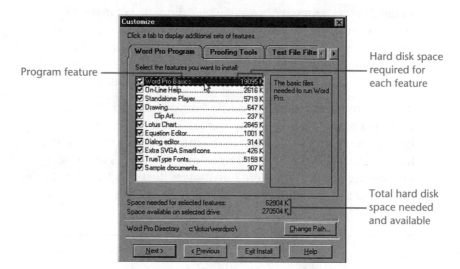

Program feature

Hard disk space required for each feature

Total hard disk space needed and available

By default, the first tab in the Customize dialog box (Word Pro Program) is selected. This dialog box offers a list of all the Word Pro features. To the right of each feature, the dialog box tells you how much hard disk space is required to install the feature. A check in the check box to the left of a feature indicates the feature will be installed. To prevent Install from installing a feature, click the feature's check box to remove the check mark.

> **Tip**
>
> Below the feature list, Install notes how much hard disk space you need to install the selected features and how much free space exists on your disk. Either continue deselecting features until the top number is less than the bottom one, or use the <u>C</u>hange Path button and install to another hard disk with more space on your system.

Here are the features you can choose not to install:

- *Word Pro Basics.* The key Word Pro program files. Deselect this option only when you're reinstalling or adding other components such as the Thesaurus; you must have these files to run the program.

- *On-Line Help.* The commands and tools that give you information for performing Word Pro operations. You may choose not to install this feature if you're a very confident user or if you'll always have this book available to guide you.

- *Tour Player.* This is needed to play the tours contained in Word Pro.

- *Drawing.* Word Pro's drawing features, including the Drawing Tools iconbar. Deselect this option if you don't want to create any graphics in Word Pro or if you prefer to use a stand-alone graphics editing program.

- *Clip Art.* Various clip art files you can use in Word Pro documents.

- *Lotus Chart.* The features that enable you to chart data. You may not need this feature if you can embed charts from a spreadsheet application such as 1-2-3 for Windows.

- *Equation Editor.* Files needed to create and edit equations.

- *Dialog Editor.* Files needed to use the Dialog editor.

- *Extra SVGA SmartIcons.* Install SmartIcons you can display if you have an SVGA video card and monitor.

- *TrueType Fonts.* Installs fonts you can use when creating documents.

- *Sample Documents.* Some sample Word Pro documents you can use or refer to.

In the Proofing Tools tab, you can install the following:

- *Thesaurus.* The tools that enable you to find synonyms for a word and insert it in your document.

- *Spell Checker.* The commands and dictionaries that enable Word Pro to check for incorrectly spelled words in your document.

- *Grammar Check.* The tools that enable Word Pro to double-check sentence structure, word choice, and sentence complexity.

After you select which features to install in the Word Pro Program and Proofing Tools tabs, you can click Next to continue the Install process, which proceeds as for an Automatic install.

You can also click one of the other tabs in the Customize dialog box to specify whether to install certain *filters* or specific *SmartMasters*. Filters are files that enable Word Pro to translate text for import and export operations and translate graphics for importing. SmartMasters enable you to easily apply predesigned formatting and styles to a document.

> **Tip**
>
> If hard disk space is at a premium and you're not sure whether you'll ever need a certain text or graphics filter, don't install it. You can perform a custom install and install only that filter later if you ever need it.

Click the Text File Filters tab to display options for importing and exporting text (see fig. A.6). The tab lists dozens of filters, with the space required to install each one to the right. To deselect a filter so that it isn't installed, click to remove the check from the check box to the left of the filter name. You can also choose Spreadsheet File Filters and DataBase File Filters from their tabs.

Fig. A.6
Use this tab to select which text file filters to install.

Click the Graphic Filters tab to display the list of filters for graphic files you may want to import (insert into a frame in a document). Figure A.7 shows the choices on this tab. To deselect a filter so that it isn't installed, click to remove the check from the check box to the left of the filter name.

Fig. A.7
Filters for graphic files you may insert into a document.

Click the SmartMasters tab to display the list of SmartMasters available to install. Figure A.8 displays the choices. Deselect a SmartMaster by clicking the check box beside it.

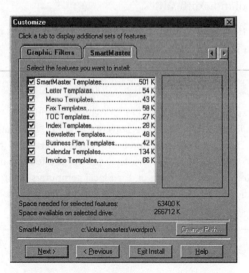

Fig. A.8
SmartMasters available to help you set up documents.

After you make your choices on any of the Filters tabs, click <u>N</u>ext to continue the installation process, which proceeds as for a default install.

Installing to a Network

Lotus enables you to install Word Pro on a network server to enable multiple users to set up and run Word Pro quickly and easily. Usually, the process works as follows:

- The network administrator installs the Word Pro files on the network server drive.

- The network administrator specifies the number of Word Pro licenses the company has purchased, to limit the number of users who have access to the Word Pro installations.

- Individual users set up their network node (local computer) by using Install to create a personal directory that holds the files needed to run Word Pro from the server.

During network installation, you have the opportunity to view and print the Network Administrator's Guide, a file named READNET.TXT that appears on the Install disk or CD-ROM. You should definitely print and read this file. It offers detailed information about installing Word Pro on different kinds of networks. In addition, it provides you with information about troubleshooting network installation difficulties.

The next two sections describe how to install Word Pro to a network server and then set up a node to access the network installation.

Note

Install also enables you to set up Word Pro for network distribution. When you use this option, Install copies compressed versions of the Word Pro installation files to the server directory. Then, when users log on to the server and run the INSTALL.EXE file from the \LOTUS\WORDPRO\ directory, they can install a full version of Word Pro from the server to the hard disk drive on their local computers. For more about network distribution, click the <u>H</u>elp button after selecting a network installation or see the readnet file on Install (Disk 1) or the Word Pro CD-ROM.

Installing to the Server

When you install Word Pro to a network file server, Install automatically creates the appropriate directories, installing the program files to one location and shared files and licensing files to other locations. The network server install process greatly resembles the default installation process described earlier in this chapter.

To set up Word Pro on a network server, follow these steps:

1. Start Windows 95 if it isn't already running. If you were already working in Windows, exit from any Windows applications that you were working in.

2. Insert Install (Disk 1) into the appropriate floppy drive or insert the Word Pro CD-ROM into your CD-ROM drive and close the drive.

3. Click the Start button, then click Settings, Control Panel.

4. In the control panel, double-click the Add/Remove Programs icon to start the Installation wizard. Click Next to enable Windows to find the CD or disk; click Finish to start the installation process.

5. Install copies some files to your hard drive, then displays a Welcome screen. If Word Pro does not include the correct name and company in the Welcome dialog box, enter your name in the Your Name text box. Press the Tab key or click in the Company Name text box. Type your company name. Click to select the Install on a File Server check box. Click Next to continue the installation process.

6. A dialog box appears asking you to confirm the names you specified. Click Yes to do so and continue installing. The File Server Install or Network Distribution dialog box appears.

7. Leave the File Server Install option selected if you want network users to run Word Pro from the server and only install minimal files to their node computer. (Choose Network Distribution to copy compressed install files on the server so that users can install a full version of Word Pro on individual computers.) Click Next.

8. Install asks if you want to open and print the Network Administrator's Guide (see fig. A.9), READNET.TXT. Click the Open button to do so. In the Notepad window that appears, click File and then click Print. Then close the window to return to Install. Click Next.

IV

Appendixes

Fig. A.9
Choose Open to view and print more detailed information from Lotus about network installation.

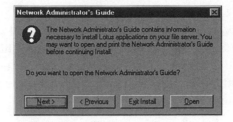

9. The Specify Main Lotus Directory dialog box appears; choose the drive and directory and then click Next.

10. In the Install Options & Directories dialog box (see fig. A.10), specify whether to install Default features or to Customize features. Then specify a Drive and directory for the Word Pro program files and shared tools. You should specify locations on the network server drive. Click Next to continue.

Fig. A.10
Tell Install where on the server to locate program files and shared tools.

11. In the Select Program Folder dialog box, click the name of the Windows program group where you want the Word Pro program-item icons to appear. If you want Install to create a new folder for Word Pro, choose New Folder. After you make your selection, click Next.

12. Install asks whether you want to begin copying the Word Pro files to your hard disk. Click Yes to continue; Install begins copying files to your hard disk.

13. If you're installing from floppy disks (rather than a CD-ROM), Install displays a prompt asking you to insert the next disk. Each time Word Pro asks you for a disk, insert it in the drive and click OK to continue.

14. After installation, Word Pro displays a message saying installation is complete. Choose OK to return to the Windows desktop. Word Pro adds the program's name to the Programs menu under the folder's name you specified during installation.

Setting Up a Network Node

Each *node* (end user computer) attached to the network has to be set up to run Word Pro from the network file server. Setting up the node involves running the INSTALL.EXE file that was copied to the server during the Word Pro server installation. INSTALL.EXE sets up a directory and copies a limited number of key files to the node to enable it to run the Word Pro program files from the server.

Working from the node computer, make sure that the Windows 95 desktop is open and that all other applications are closed. Make sure that the node can log onto the network drive. Then, click the Windows 95 Start button, select Run, and run the INSTALL.EXE file from the shared tools directory Install created on the server drive (this directory usually is named \LOTUSAPP\WORDPRO\).

After you click OK to run INSTALL.EXE from the server drive, Install displays the Personal Directory dialog box (see fig. A.11). Specify the directory on the node computer where Install will place the files needed to run Word Pro from the server. Specify the Drive and Personal Directory; then click Next. Follow the remaining dialog boxes that appear to complete the node installation.

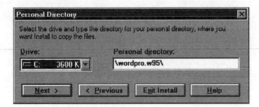

Fig. A.11
Specify the personal directory to hold files to run Word Pro from the network node.

Appendix B

Index of Common Problems

by Sue Plumley

Editing, Revisions, and Help	
If you have this problem...	**You'll find help here**
Editing: Selected text is moved accidentally	p. 62
Editing: Get error message when using Go To	p. 160
Editing: Change outline style sequences without changing original style sequences	p. 275
Editing: Find did not find words in collapsed outlines	p. 278
Revision: Comment Tools iconbar does not display	p. 480
Revision: Cannot read comment note content	p. 481
Revision: Need to exit comment note frame but leave comment note open	p. 483
Revision: Screen elements do not display	p. 235
Revision: Comment note mark does not display	p. 482
Revision: Comment note contains more text than it displays	p. 483
Revision: Comment note inserted in wrong spot in document	p. 485
Revision: Comment notes do not display in Draft mode	p. 485

(continues)

Editing, Revisions, and Help   Continued

If you have this problem...	You'll find help here
Revision: Open comment note is not deleted when pressing Del	p. 485
Revision: Final document contains comment notes, but shouldn't	p. 485
Revision: Personal information for comment note is wrong	p. 221
Revision: Revision marks are not turned on	p. 489
Revision: Revision marks are turned off, but document still contains revisions	p. 489
Revision: Previous comment note color does not change when color setting is changed	p. 490
Revision: Can't see text marked as deleted or inserted	p. 492
Revision: Modeless bar does not display on-screen	p. 492
Revision: Frames and tables were skipped during revision review	p. 494
Revision: Document cannot be modified when Document Control options are used	p. 495
Revision: Document is unprotected	p. 496
Revision: Only original author can edit document	p. 497
Revision: Verification of user name is incorrect	p. 497
Revision: Editor name does not match name on system	p. 498
Revision: Deleted editor name cannot be added to document	p. 498
Revision: Document cannot be edited (read-only)	p. 499
Revision: Named styles cannot be edited	p. 499
Revision: Document cannot be renamed or saved as new file	p. 499

If you have this problem...	You'll find help here
Revision: Document cannot be printed	p. 499
Revision: Custom text does not display in Greetings dialog box	p. 500
Revision: Cannot save comments from each editor when file is saved	p. 500
Revision: Division cannot be viewed or edited	p. 500
Revision: Division tab is hidden	p. 500
Revision: Frames and cells cannot be edited in division	p. 500
Revision: TeamReview revisions cannot be made	p. 501
Revision: Notes/FX fields are turned off	p. 501
Revision: Document does not open without running startup scripts	p. 501
Revision: Document Control options do not work	p. 501
Revision: Someone guessed my password	p. 501
Revision: TeamReview document is not automatically sent via e-mail	p. 502
Revision: Custom text cannot be viewed in a TeamReview document	p. 502
Revision: TeamConsolidate document does not show original and modified versions of document	p. 506
Revision: Original document is protected as read-only	p. 508
Help: Ask the Expert did not find an answer	p. 49
Help: Help topic prints in unwanted format	p. 52
Help: Help window disappears but was not closed	p. 52

Formatting

If you have this problem...	You'll find help here
Formatting: Characters appear in all uppercase, with initial caps slightly larger	p. 81
Formatting: Font change makes change in all styles	p. 17
Formatting: Deleted SmartCorrect entry	p. 72
Formatting: Entire page needs to be formatted	p. 105
Formatting: Font of one word needs to be changed	p. 83
Formatting: Hidden text doesn't print	p. 85
Formatting: All characters need to change to normal	p. 85
Formatting: Fast Format doesn't work with keyboard keys	p. 86
Formatting: Formatting is not automatically copied or applied to selection	p. 87
Formatting: Fast Format doesn't apply more than one type of formatting	p. 87
Formatting: Paragraph alignment needs to be removed	p. 89
Formatting: Predefined tabs are not working	p. 94
Formatting: Indentations are set too small/large	p. 97
Formatting: Line spacing needs to be decreased/increased	p. 99
Formatting: Paragraph numbering skips a paragraph	p. 100
Formatting: Need to see settings for tabs and indents	p. 97
Formatting: Need to style words, not entire paragraphs	p. 86
Formatting: Need to change outline mode	p. 275

If you have this problem...	You'll find help here
Formatting: Need to see settings for line styles and widths	p. 99
Formatting: Need to modify default for SmartMasters	p. 243
Formatting: Columns on last page are not balanced p. xx (Ch 5)	p. 114
Formatting: Columns balance as text is entered, causing text to "jump" on-screen	p. 114
Formatting: Text in one column does not line up with text in second column	p. 114
Formatting: Space does not appear between text and page number	p. 129
Formatting: Lines do not appear on all sides of page	p. 131
Formatting: Lines around page do not print	p. 131
Formatting: Design border needs to be removed	p. 132
Formatting: Need to see settings for numbering	p. 129
Formatting: Numbers are not inserted automatically	p. 128

Long Documents

If you have this problem...	You'll find help here
Footnotes: Go To cannot find footnote mark	p. 292
Footnotes: Footnote reference number and text erased accidentally	p. 292
Glossary: Need to add company names and logos to glossary	p. 293
Glossary: Need to format glossary text	p. 293
Glossary: Size limit of glossary entry name	p. 294
TOCs: Creating TOC for long documents	p. 296

(continues)

Long Documents   Continued

If you have this problem...	You'll find help here
TOCs: Changing default options of TOC	p. 293
TOCs: Creating TOC	p. 321
TOCs: I forgot what divisions and division groups are	p. 298
Index: Creating index for long documents	p. 323
Headers and footers: Do not appear on first page	p. 123
Headers and footers: Do not want same header and footer throughout document	p. 120
Headers and footers: Need to know settings for headers and footers	p. 121
Headers and footers: Need to change text attributes for headers and footers	p. 122

Tools

If you have this problem...	You'll find help here
Dictionary: User dictionary is not available	p. 179
Thesaurus: Word cannot be found in Thesaurus	p. 184
Spell Checker: Spell checker didn't work on collapsed outlines	p. 278

Printing

If you have this problem...	You'll find help here
Printing: Printer does not appear in Print Setup dialog box	p. 201
Printing: Crop marks do not print	p. 202
Printing: Printing options are wrong	p. 201
Printing: Printer does not support paper size	p. 107
Printing: Printer does not print in landscape orientation	p. 108

If you have this problem...	You'll find help here
Printing: Colored lines do not print	p. 113
Printing: Header and footer do not print	p. 123

Files

If you have this problem...	You'll find help here
Files: Cannot open files in specified directory	p. 219
Files: Saving document before moving or deleting text	p. 279
Files: File Open dialog box does not display all file types	p. 512
Files: Imported file cannot be opened	p. 515
Files: Imported file format is not supported	p. 515
Files: Format of file is not correct	p. 194
Files: Text and data files cannot be imported into Master Document division using the Import/Export dialog box	p. 516
Files: Imported text file is not correct type for import filter	p. 517
Files: Imported ASCII file does not import correctly	p. 517
Files: Graphics file cannot be opened in document	p. 518
Files: File size increases when graphic is added	p. 519
Files: Image brightness or contrast is not correct	p. 521
Files: Image prints quickly but quality is low	p. 521
Files: Document with graphic prints fine but too slowly	p. 522
Files: Links in file are broken	p. 523
Files: Links in file are not automatically updated	p. 525

(continues)

Files   Continued

If you have this problem...	You'll find help here
Files: Embedded object in document causes computer to lock up	p. 525
Files: Embedded sound file plays when double-clicked	p. 526
Files: Source application does not include an Update command	p. 528

Viewing

If you have this problem...	You'll find help here
Viewing: Turning on regular viewing	p. 235
Viewing: Turning off Clean Screen view	p. 235
Viewing: Changing to Outline mode	p. 275
Viewing: Show the page gauge on-screen	p. 314
Viewing: Takes too long to view division contents	p. 321
Viewing: Work area on-screen is not wide enough with SmartIcons displayed	p. 32
Viewing: Cannot see entire document	p. 131
Viewing: Cannot see formatting of document	p. 231
Viewing: Mouse pointer changes to frame icon	p. 36
Viewing: SmartIcons keep changing	p. 32
Viewing: Wrong SmartIcons appear on-screen	p. 222
Viewing: Functions of SmartIcons	p. 32
Viewing: Ruler does not show on-screen	p. 111
Viewing: Cannot read the document in Page Sorter view	p. 144

If you have this problem...	You'll find help here
Viewing: Layout mode is too slow to work in	p. 232
Viewing: Clean Screen hides too much of the screen	p. 235
Viewing: Page Sorter only displays one page	p. 141
Viewing: Zoom does not work in Page Sorter view	p. 144
Viewing: Layout displays horizontally across screen instead of vertically	p. 149

Styles

If you have this problem...	You'll find help here
Styles: Changing redefined style to new style	p. 247
Styles: Changing attributes back to original attributes	p. 259
Styles: Resetting styles to default styles	p. 259
Styles: Undeleting styles	p. 259
Styles: Overwriting styles using the same name	p. 263
Styles: Formatting applies only to current page	p. 106
Styles: Saving page formatting settings	p. 135
Styles: Changes affect entire document	p. 106
Styles: Need to change from portrait to landscape orientation	p. 108
Styles: Left margin not wide enough for margin notes	p. 109
Styles: Page tabs need to be changed	p. 110
Styles: New tab cannot be inserted	p. 111

(continues)

Styles Continued	
If you have this problem...	**You'll find help here**
Styles: Formatting page styles	p. 136
Styles: Need to return page style to original settings	p. 136

Frames	
If you have this problem...	**You'll find help here**
Frames: Deleting SmartMaster frames	p. 249
Frames: Frames is too small to use	p. 385
Frames: Cannot move frame	p. 387
Frames: Pointer does not change to hand over frame border	p. 389
Frames: Cannot see text in frame	p. 392
Frames: Cannot see text when frame is reduced	p. 392
Frames: Picture is resized when frame is resized	p. 394
Frames: Frame margins are not set to correct size	p. 394
Frames: Frame margins are different sizes	p. 398
Frames: Not enough room between line and text between columns	p. 401
Frames: Tab stops in frame are not at correct settings	p. 402
Frame: Headline is not centered vertically in frame	p. 403
Frame: Content of frame is not protected from modification	p. 404
Frames: Corners of frame are not rounded enough	p. 404

If you have this problem...	You'll find help here
Frames: Text in frame cannot be read	p. 405
Frames: Background pattern is only in black and white, but needs to be color	p. 406
Frames: Graphic does not fit proportionally in frame	p. 407
Frames: Image is distorted in frame	p. 407
Frames: Edges of image are not sharp enough	p. 409
Frames: Frame does not move; only graphic within frame	p. 410
Frames: New image properties are set incorrectly	p. 410
Frames: Image Properties is not a choice on Quick menu	p. 410
Frames: Text does not flow around frame	p. 410
Frames: Frame is not anchored to surrounding text	p. 413
Frames: Frame does not change positions until offset is changed	p. 413
Frames: Need to edit more than one frame at a time	p. 415
Frames: Cannot select more than one frame at a time	p. 414
Frames: Multiple frames do not align	p. 414
Frames: Multiple frames cannot be formatted all together	p. 414
Frames: Need to access a frame that is layered	p. 416
Frames: Style in frame is not correct or needs to be redefined	p. 419
Frames: Style for one frame needs to be different than other frames	p. 420

(continues)

IV

Appendixes

Frames   Continued

If you have this problem...	You'll find help here
Frames: Frames need to stretch from top margin to bottom margin	p. 420
Frames: Need alternating headers and footers	p. 123

Draw, DTP, and Typography

If you have this problem...	You'll find help here
Draw: Drawing cannot be created in text frame or in a non-draw object	p. 424
Draw: Draw objects do not move together	p. 427
Draw: Cannot see enough of object on-screen	p. 427
Draw: Overlapping objects are difficult to select	p. 428
Draw: Only one side of object resizes	p. 429
Draw: Drawing session switched to word processing session by accident	p. 430
Draw: Wrong draw object is deleted	p. 430
Draw: Fill color or pattern is wrong	p. 431
Draw: Draw object in layer is hidden	p. 432
Draw: Priority of draw objects need to be changed	p. 433
Draw: Line spacing and alignment of text in draw object cannot be set	p. 435
Draw: Text is not selected with mouse cursor when in Draw mode	p. 435
Draw: Rotation of object is in wrong direction	p. 436
Draw: Draw object needs to be rotated only a few degrees	p. 437

If you have this problem...	You'll find help here
Draw: Object is not aligned precisely	p. 438
DTP: SmartMasters need to be modified	p. 247
DTP: All of the text does not fit in the document	p. 449
DTP: Paper size and print orientation are set incorrectly	p. 107
DTP: Margins, columns, and tabs need to be reset	p. 108
DTP: Cannot print in landscape orientation	p. 462
Typography: Design elements are not balanced in document	p. 466
Typography: Document looks too crowded	p. 475
Typography: Typefaces of the same point size do not appear the same size	p. 476
Typography: Word Pro does not condense fonts	p. 475
Typography: Uppercase script type is difficult to read	p. 466
Typography: Text alignment is incorrect	p. 468
Image: Double-clicked on image does not display Image menu	p. 520
Image: Original image properties need to be shown	p. 521
Typography: Words do not hyphenate automatically at end of line	p. 468
Typography: Indent and outdent need to be resized	p. 136
Typography: Currency and percentage numbers do not line up on page	p. 110-111
Typography: Too much spacing appears between letters	p. 473

(continues)

Draw, DTP, and Typography Continued

If you have this problem...	You'll find help here
Typography: Document contains "rivers" of white space	p. 474
Typography: Text and paragraphs in document do not share formatting styles	p. 477
Typography: Formatted document takes too long to print	p. 477
Typography: Tab settings are not shared throughout document	p. 477

Tables and Merging Data

If you have this problem...	You'll find help here
Tables: Formatting long tables in frames	p. 331
Tables: Problem adding tabs in table cells	p. 331
Tables: Using cell marker to select a cell	p. 332
Tables: SmartFill does not recognize sequence	p. 333
Tables: Copying rows and columns with drag and drop instead of moving them	p. 335
Tables: Patterns or colors hide table contents	p. 339
Tables: Colors in Table Cell Properties apply only to selected cells, not entire table	p. 332
Tables: Currency format is not in Frequently Use list	p. 344
Tables: Formulas selected from @Function drop-down list do not include cell addresses	p. 346
Tables: Formula in table returns REF error	p. 346
Tables: Can't find specific symbol in list of formats	p. 346
Tables: Table is anchored to unknown text	p. 346
Charts: Existing data must be copied from Clipboard	p. 347
Merging data: Data in field is too long for field	p. 360

IV

Appendixes

If you have this problem...	You'll find help here
Merging data: Need to return to previous merge step	p. 356
Merging data: Sort type is alphanumeric, but need to sort numbers	p. 362
Merging data: Searching cannot match parts of words	p. 363
Merging data: Finding records other than first record in top tab	p. 364
Merging data: Data source is not supported	p. 367
Merging data: Delimiters in tables cannot be used	p. 357
Merging data: Tables used as data file cannot include any other contents	p. 357
Merging data: Formatting in table during data merge is ignored	p. 374
Merging data: Wrong data file is selected during merge	p. 376
Merging data: Field name needs to be used twice in document	p. 376
Merging data: Cannot undo merge field cut or deletion	p. 377
Merging data: Done button is clicked before merge is finished	p. 354
Merging data: Do not want merge for all records in data file	p. 362
Merging data: Capitalization is not matched during merge	p. 363

Appendix C

Glossary

16-bit   In Windows, this refers to the way memory is accessed. 16-bit applications access memory in 16-bit "chunks" (2-bytes). Most pre-Windows 95 applications are 16-bit (*see 32-bit*).

16550A UART   The name of the most modern chip controlling the serial port. Older chips could not support the data throughput that today's high-speed communications protocols and modems support.

32-bit   In Windows, this refers to the way memory is accessed. 32-bit applications access memory in 32-bit "chunks" (4-bytes). Large portions of Windows 95 and many of its new applications are 32-bit applications, and may run faster because it has become more efficient to access chunks of memory.

A

accelerator key   A keyboard shortcut for a command. For example, Shift-Delete is an accelerator command for the Edit Cut command.

activate   To bring a window to the front and make it active.

active printer   The printer that will be used by programs.

active window   The window that is currently being used. Active windows show the "active window color" in their title bar (settable through the control panel). Other windows are inactive. To activate an inactive window, you must click somewhere in the inactive window or use the task bar to select the window (*see taskbar*). On the taskbar, the active window looks like a pressed button; inactive windows are represented by unpressed buttons.

address book   A list of persons, phone numbers, and other information used by various Windows 95 programs, including Microsoft Fax and HyperTerminal.

Adobe Type Manager (ATM)   An Adobe program that enables you to work with Postscript fonts in Windows 95.

Advanced Program-to-Program Communications   A communications standard defined by IBM. The APPC standard is intended to allow multiple users to share the processing of programs.

alert message   A critical warning, confirmational, or informational message appearing in a dialog box.

airbrush   In "paint" and graphics programs, a tool that "sprays" dots in a randomized pattern around the point indicated by the user. In most programs, the output of the airbrush can be configured to modify the color, pattern, and density of the dot pattern.

annotate   To add notes. For example, you can add your own notes to Windows Help.

ANSI   A standard for ordering characters within a font.

anti-aliasing   A graphics technique used to hide the diagonal edges and sharp color changes ("jaggies") in a graphic or font. Because a computer screen possesses limited resolution, such changes highlight the pixels on the screen and don't look smooth. Using anti-aliasing smoothes out the changes and makes them appear more attractive.

Anti Virus   A program included with Windows 95 that helps eradicate viruses (*see virus*) from your hard drive or floppy disks.

API   *See Application Programming Interface*

APPC   *See Advanced Program-to-Program Communications*

applet   A small application unable to run by itself. When you purchase Windows 95 or another application, it may come with additional applets. For example, Word comes with applets for manipulating fonts (WordArt), drawing graphs (MS Graph), and creating graphics (MS Draw).

application   A computer program.

Application Programming Interface (API)   A set of interface functions available for applications.

archive bit   A single bit stored in a disk directory to indicate if a file has been changed since it was last backed up. Backup programs clear a file's archive bit when they back up the program. Modifying the program resets the bit and a backup program knows to make a backup the next time you do a backup.

ASCII characters   A subset of the ANSI character standard.

ASCII file   A file consisting of alphanumeric characters only. Although virtually every file can be converted to an ASCII file, all formatting (for example, bold, italics, underline, font size, and so on) will be lost in the ASCII file.

associate   Linking a document with the program that created it so that both can be opened with a single command. For example, double-clicking a DOC file opens Word for Windows and loads the selected document.

ATAPI   A specification for devices to attach to EIDE buses. This specification is almost identical to the EIDE specification.

AT command set   A set of commands, originally developed by Hayes, for modems. Its name originates from the fact that each command starts with "AT" (attention). Today, most modems support the AT command set, enabling Microsoft to supply the Unimodem driver with Windows 95.

ATM   Asynchronous Transfer Mode is a high-speed, but expensive, networking solution. ATM networks reach speeds of 155 Mb/s.

attribute   A property or characteristic.

attributes (FAT)   Settings for each file indicate if the file is used by an operating system, has read-only status, has its archive bit set, or is a hidden file.

auto arrange (Explorer)   In Explorer, auto arrange organizes the visible icons into a regular grid pattern.

B

background operation   A job performed by a program when another program is in the active window. For example, printing or creating a backup can be done by Windows 95 as a background operation.

Backup   A program that comes with Windows 95 and enables the user to back up the files from a hard disk to a floppy disk, tape drive, or another computer on a network.

backup set   The set of duplicate files and folders created by a backup program (*see Backup*). This set is stored on tapes, disks, or other storage medium that can be removed and stored safely away from your computer. *See full system backup.*

Basic Input/Output System (BIOS)   A program usually residing on a ROM-based storage device in your PC that handles instructions to and from the system bus.

batch program   A text file that instructs Window 95 to perform one or more tasks sequentially. Used for automating the loading or execution of programs. Batch files have a .BAT or .CMD extension.

Beziér   A mathematically constructed curve, such as the one used in drawing programs.

bidirectional printer port   Bidirectional Printer Communications sends print files to your printer and listens for a response. Windows quickly identifies a printer that is unable to accept a print file.

binary   A numbering system with only two values: 0 (zero) and 1 (one).

binary file   Any file containing characters other than text.

binary file transfer   A data transfer in which files aren't converted. Typically used with a modem to send programs or complex documents from computer to computer.

binary transfer protocol   When using a communications program to transmit binary files, it is very important to ensure that errors are not introduced into the data stream. Various binary transfer protocols check for matches between the data transmitted and the data received. The most common protocols are Xmodem, Ymodem, and Zmodem.

BIOS   *See Basic Input/Output System.*

bitmap   A screen page in memory. Most bitmaps represent some sort of viewable graphics. You can use a "paint" program to edit graphic bitmaps and make modifications to them. However, although objects such as rectangles and circles may appear in a graphic bitmap, these objects cannot be edited as objects. You must modify these objects one bit at a time using the paint tools in the program.

bits per second (bps)   A measurement of data transmission speed, usually over a serial data link. Roughly equivalent to baud rate. A single character requires approximately 10 bits, so a transfer rate of 9600 baud results in about 960 characters per second (cps) being transferred. This speed, however, varies depending on the make of your modem.

IV

Appendixes

boot partition   The hard-disk partition that contains the Windows 95 operating system.

bound media   In networks, this refers to traditional cabling connecting the nodes of a network together, and to a server, if any. *See also unbound media.*

bridge   In networks, a device that joins two separate LANs but restricts LAN frame traffic to either side of the bridge (unless forwarding is required). Bridges process LAN frames (not network packets) and are governed by IEEE standards. A bridge should not be confused with a router (*see router*), which uses an entirely different layer of protocol and information for forwarding packets (not frames).

browse   To search through or examine a directory tree of files, directories, disks, workstations, workgroups, or domains. Often done via a Browse button in a dialog box.

Bulletin Board System (BBS)   An electronic service that can be accessed via a modem. BBS typically includes collections of files, notes from other computer users, and many other services. Examples of commercial BBSs include CompuServe, Prodigy, Delphi, GEnie, and America Online (AOL). Information about Windows 95 and Windows 95 applications can be found on all these BBSs.

burst mode   A mode used in MCA and EISA computers and devices to facilitate greater flow of data through the bus. When bus mastering is employed, a bus master and its slave can establish a connection and send large blocks of data without CPU intervention. Without burst mode, each byte requires CPU attention to gain control of the bus, and send a byte of data.

bus   The interface between devices in a computer. PCs incorporate bus designs, including ISA, EISA, MCA, PCI, and VLB (VESA Local Bus).

bus mastering   A function used to off-load I/O processing to a processor on the interface card. Bus mastering is only truly effective when used with a bus design that can control bus master access to the computer bus, as is the case in EISA, MCA, and PCI computers. Bus mastering alone does not fully utilize the capabilities of this design unless implemented in conjunction with accessing the 32-bit burst mode and streaming data modes of EISA, MCA, and PCI computers.

bus network   One of various network topologies. A bus network is one in which all of the computers on the network are connected to the main wire of the network.

C

cache RAM A small collection of very high speed RAM. In general, modern microprocessors can process information much faster than standard dynamic RAM can even supply the information. Nevertheless, fast dynamic RAM is very expensive. Instead, a very small amount (typically 256K or 512K) of very fast "cache RAM" acts as a buffer between the CPU and the dynamic RAM. If the information needed by the CPU is in the cache, it can be processed without waiting to retrieve it from the dynamic RAM.

Calculator A program that comes with Windows 95 and enables you to perform standard or scientific calculations.

capture text In HyperTerminal, this refers to capturing and saving the text that appears in the terminal window to either a file or the printer. This is handy when reviewing the session at a later time.

Cardfile A program that comes with Windows 95 and enables you to record information cards and sort through them by using their index lines.

cascade (Windows) To arrange all the windows so that they are neatly stacked; only the title bars show behind the active window.

cascading menu A submenu that appears (usually to the left or right of the main menu item) when a menu selection is made.

CD File System (CDFS) An optimized, 32-bit, protected mode file system that significantly improves the throughput of data from a CD-ROM drive.

CD-ROM drive A CD-ROM drive uses discs (not "disks") as the storage media. These discs look much like audio CDs, but can store about 600M of data on a single disc. They can only be read by a normal CD-ROM drive (hence Read Only Memory portion of the device's name), and take special equipment to create (write) one of them. CD-ROM drives are rated in multiples of the original (1x) drives that transfer data at the same rate as audio CD Players(150kb/sec). Today, 1x drives no longer exist, and 2x drives (300-330kb/sec) are cheap. 3x (450 kbs),4x (600 kb/sec) and even 6x (900kb/sec) drives are available. 4x drives fulfill basic requirements needed to achieve decent performance when playing animations from a CD-ROM.

CD Player A program packaged withWindows 95. CD Player lets you play audio CDs from your CD drive in the background while you are working in another application. It offers many of the controls found in stand-alone audio CD players. As a result, it looks and operates in a similar fashion. In addition, it allows you to edit your playlist that corresponds to the audio CD being played. Thus, the tracks play in the order you want.

character-based   Usually used when referring to non-Windows applications. Character-based applications display information using the ASCII character set, or characters normally found on the keyboard. Also known as "text based."

character formatting   In word processing, this refers to formatting that is applied to individual characters. This type of formatting includes font, effects, size, and color.

chat room   A place on Microsoft Network where you can have a live conversation with other MSN members. They see your comments immediately.

check box   A square dialog box item that takes an off or on value. Clicking in a check box adds or removes a check mark in the box, indicating whether the setting is on (checked) or off (unchecked).

checksum   A method for creating a calculated number, frequently used as part of an error-detection protocol. Normally, a checksum is calculated against a copy of a file or other data, and compared to the checksum calculated for the original file/data. If the two numbers match, then it is very likely that the copy matches the original. Checksums are used in some forms of transmission protocols (for example, Xmodem) as well as part of the Antivirus program.

choose   A term used in many instructions in this book and in Windows books and manuals. Usually means opening a menu and clicking a command. Also can refer to dialog box items, such as in "Choose LPT1 from the drop-down list."

clear   Typically removes the check mark in an option or check box.

clicking   Quickly pressing and releasing the mouse button.

client   As opposed to *server*, a client is a workstation that connects to another computer's resources. A client also can include the server, and doesn't necessarily have to be another workstation. Basically, a client is just another application or workstation that utilizes resources from another process.

client application   In OLE context, a program that uses an object (such as a graphic) supplied by another application (the *server* application).

client/server networking   As opposed to *peer to peer* networking, an arrangement in which central computers called *servers* supply data and peripherals for use by *client* computers (workstations). Typically, a server contains a large, hard disk that supplies not only data, but also programs. It even executes programs. A server might also supply printers and modems for clients to use on the network. In other words, client/server refers to an architecture for distributed processing wherein subtasks can be distributed between services, CPUs, or even networked computers for more efficient execution.

clip art   A collection of images you can use in your documents. Clip art is often distributed on CD-ROM in large collections (thousands of clip art pieces) organized into categories. Various clip art formats are sold, and the most popular are CGM, WMF, BMP, and GIF format files.

Clipboard   A temporary storage area in all versions of Windows used for storing various types of data (for example, text, graphics, sound, and video). The Clipboard can hold one piece of information at a time for use in a program or to pass information between programs.

Clipboard Viewer   A Windows 95 program enabling you to store and save more than the single item that the Clipboard can hold.

clock   An area at the far right edge of the task bar that displays the time (and date if you leave the mouse pointer over the time). You can configure the task bar to show or hide the clock.

Close button   A button in the upper-right corner of a Window with an "x" in it. When clicked, it closes the program running in the current window.

cluster   Segment of space on a hard drive. Each file, no matter how small in actual size, takes up at least one cluster on the hard drive. As drive sizes increase, so does the cluster size. Thus, if you have a large drive and many small files, you may waste a significant amount of space on your drive. To avoid this, physically partition the drive into multiple "logical drives" of a smaller size. These smaller, logical drives also use smaller cluster sizes, wasting less space.

coaxial cable   A type of shielded cable used in wiring networks together. Although coaxial cable sufficiently shields network signals from outside electrical noise, "coax" is stiff and difficult to work with, and more difficult to run through walls and ceilings than twisted pair cable (*see twisted pair*).

codec   A technique for compressing and decompressing files, typically sound and animation files. Common codecs include Cinepak, Indeo, Video 1, MPEG (*see MPEG),* QuickTime (*see QuickTime*), and RLE.

collapse folders   To hide additional directory (folder) levels below the selected directory (folder) levels. In Explorer, you can collapse the view of a folder to hide the folders stored within by double-clicking the folder in the left pane (tree view) of Explorer. When a folder contains no additional folders, a minus sign (-) appears next to the folder.

color pattern   A color selection made up of two other colors.

color rendering intent   Provides the best ICM settings for three of the major uses of color printing, for example, presentations, photographs, and true color screen display printing.

color scheme   A selection of colors that Windows 95 uses for screen display of applications, dialog boxes, and so forth. The color scheme is set from the Control Panel.

COM   Refers to the serial port, usually to attach a mouse and/or a modem to the computer. Most computers have two serial ports, labeled COM1 and COM2. The serial port transmits data in a single-bit stream. This serial transmission of bits gives the port its name.

command   Usually an option from an application's menus. Also refers to commands typed in from a command-prompt session or from the Run dialog box from the Start menu. In essence, it's a way of telling an application or Windows 95 to perform a major chore, such as running an application or utility program.

command button   A dialog box item that causes an action when clicked.

compare files   Compares the files in a backup set to make sure they match the source files on the hard disk.

component   A portion of Windows 95. When installing Windows 95, you have the option of installing (or not) various components. For example, you might choose to not install Hyperterminal (you might have a better terminal program). Later, you can go back and add/remove components using the original install disks or CD-ROM.

complex document   *See compound document.*

compound document   A document (created using OLE) that includes multiple types of data. For example, a Word processing document that includes a Paint picture is a compound document.

compressed volume file (CVF)   A file, created by DriveSpace (*see DriveSpace*) which is treated like another "volume" (logical disk drive)— it even has a drive letter (for example, "D:") assigned to it. When you save or retrieve files compressed by DriveSpace, they are written or read from the compressed volume file. The compressed volume file exists on a hard drive (called a "host drive"), and looks like a regular file to the FAT (*see File Allocation Table*).

connection (Hyperterminal)   In Hyperterminal, a connection sets and saves all the configuration parameters for one party you wish to contact.

connection (Network)   A communication session established between a server and a workstation.

container object   An object that contains another object or several objects. For example, a Word document might be the container object that holds the Excel object. *See also compound document.*

control menu   A menu that exists in every window and enables you to modify its parameters or take global actions, such as closing or moving the window.

Control Panel   A program that comes with Windows 95 that enables you to make settings for many Windows 95 actions, such as changing network, keyboard, printer, and regional settings. Some programs (including many video card drivers) may add sections to the control panel for you to use to configure that program.

conventional memory   Memory located in the first 640K.

cover page   The page preceding a fax message. The cover page often includes such information as your name, company, telephone, and return fax number. Windows 95 includes a program (Fax Cover Page Editor) that enables you to create your own fax cover pages.

CPU   Central processing unit. Also known as a microprocessor (*see microprocessor*) or processor (*see processor*). The 80386, 80486, and Pentium are examples of CPUs built by Intel.

cross-linked file   A disk error (which can be found using ScanDisk) in which at least two files are linked to data in the same cluster.

current directory   The directory that activates if you log onto the drive at the command prompt by typing the drive letter and pressing Enter. When you switch drives, the operating system remembers the directory that was current when you switched away. It will still be the active/current directory when you switch back; it becomes the default directory. Applications will store or look for files on that drive if they're not specifically told which directory to use. This concept also works in Explorer: when you switch back to a drive, the last active directory (or *folder*) is still the active one.

current window   The window that you are using. It appears in front of all other open windows (*see active window*).

cursor   The representation of the mouse on the screen. It may take many different shapes.

Cylinder/Head/Sector (CHS)   An addressing scheme that allows IDE drives to exceed the original 512 megabyte (1/2 gigabyte) size limit. With CHS, an IDE drive can be up to 8.4 gigabytes.

D

database   A file or group of related files that are designed to hold recurring data types as if the files were lists.

data bits   The number of bits used to transmit a piece of information. Usually 7 or 8.

DCI   The Drive Control Interface is a display driver interface which allows fast, direct access to the video frame buffer in Windows. Also, it allows games and video to take advantage of special hardware support in video devices, which improves the performance and quality of video.

DDE   *See Dynamic Data Exchange.*

DEC Printer Utility   The DEC printer utility adds features to the standard Windows 95 print window and updated printer drivers. The utility includes a very detailed help file for configuring both local and network printers. Additionally, it creates an enhanced set of property menus for configuring DEC printers.

default button   The command button in a dialog box that activates when you press the Enter key. This button is indicated by a dark border.

default printer   The printer, which is established using the Printer settings, that documents will be sent to if the user doesn't specify another printer.

deferred printing   This enables people with laptop computers to print even though their laptop is not in a docking station. Once connected in a docking station, it will automatically print. This also refers to computers whose only printer access is to a network printer, and the computer is temporarily disconnected from the network. When the network connection is reestablished, the print job starts.

density   Density is a brightness control to lighten or darken a printout to more closely reflect its screen appearance and to compensate for deficiencies in toner or paper quality.

desktop   The screen area on which the windows are displayed.

desktop pattern   A bitmap decorating your desktop. You can select one of Windows 95's patterns or create one of your own.

destination document   The document into which a linked or embedded document is placed.

device driver   A program that provides the operating system with the information it needs to work with a specific device, such as a printer.

dialog box   An on-screen message box that conveys or requests information from the user.

Dial Up Networking   Dialing into a network from a remote sight using a modem.

differential backup   A differential backup backs up only those files that have changed since the time a backup was made. Normally, a backup philosophy will involve making a full system backup (which includes all files on the hard drive), and then making periodic differential backups. Windows 95 can determine which files have changed (or have been created) since the last backup by the condition of the archive bit (*see archive bit*). To restore a system that has been backed up using this philosophy, first restore using the full system backup, and then successively apply the differential backups in the same order they were made.

Disk Defragmenter   As you use your hard drive, blocks of information for a file spread across the hard drive, wherever there is room. This "fragmentation" of the information in a file can lead to a significant slowdown in file access times because the disk's read/write head must move all over the disk, looking for the various portions of a file. Disk Defragmenter arranges the blocks of information for a file into adjacent blocks on your hard drive, which may significantly improve file access times.

dither pattern   A pattern of dots used to simulate an unavailable color or gray scale in a printout or graphic. Most frequently used when specifying a printout of a color graphic on a monochrome printer or simulating more colors in a graphic than are available in the current graphics mode.

Direct Memory Access (DMA)   A PC has eight DMA channels that are used for rapidly transferring data between memory and peripherals such as a hard disks, sound cards, tape backups, scanners, and SCSI controllers. DMA is very fast because it doesn't need the computer's microprocessor to access memory.

IV

docking station   For a portable computer, an external device that provides additional resources such as speakers, CD-ROM, keyboard, empty card slots, and so on. A docking station is typically plugged into a portable computer using the port replicator connection.

document   A file created using an application. For example, you might create a text document using a word processing application (such as WordPad) or a picture document using a graphic application (such as Paint).

document formatting   In word processing, this refers to formatting that is applied to a whole document. Document formatting includes margins, headers and footers, and paper size.

document window   The window in which a document appears.

DOS   A term used to refer to any variation of the Disk Operating System (for example, MS-DOS and PC-DOS).

double-click   To press the mouse button twice in rapid succession while keeping the mouse pointer motionless between clicks.

double buffering   The process of displaying the screen currently in the frame buffer while painting the next screen in another portion of RAM. Then the new screen is quickly copied to the frame buffer. This makes video playback and animation appear much smoother.

download   Retrieving a file from a remote computer or BBS (*see upload*).

drag   To move an object on the screen from one place to another by clicking it with the mouse, holding the mouse button down, and pulling it to where you want it to be.

drag and drop   "Drag and drop" describes a particular action you can make with the mouse. Click an object, such as a folder, then hold down the mouse button as you drag the object to a new location. You drop the object by releasing the mouse button.

DriveSpace   DriveSpace is a program included with Windows 95. It enables you to compress your disks and free up more space.

DriveSpace for Windows supports drives that were compressed using DoubleSpace (which was included in MS-DOS versions 6.0 and 6.2) as well as DriveSpace for MS-DOS (which was included in MS-DOS version 6.22). You can use DriveSpace and DoubleSpace drives interchangeably. For example, you can use floppy disks that were compressed using either DoubleSpace or DriveSpace. However, such floppy disks can be used only in computers that have DriveSpace for Windows or DoubleSpace installed.

If you have drives that were compressed using either DoubleSpace or DriveSpace, you can configure them by using DriveSpace for Windows.

drop-down list   A dialog box item showing only one entry until its drop down arrow is clicked.

dual boot   The ability to reboot and enter either Windows 95 or Windows 3.1 (or whatever version of Windows you had running before installing Windows 95). This option is offered during installation, and involves not installing Windows 95 over your previous Windows installation. If you choose dual boot, you will have to reinstall your Windows programs under Windows 95.

Dynamic Data Exchange (DDE)   A feature of Windows 95 that allows programs to communicate and actively pass information and commands.

E

echoing keystrokes   In a communications program, you may type information at your terminal. If the receiving system doesn't "echo" your keystroke back to your terminal, then you can't see what you type. By setting your own system to echo keystrokes, you can see what you have typed. Systems that echo your keystrokes for you are termed "full duplex"; systems that do not echo your keystrokes are termed "half duplex."

editable fax   An editable fax is, essentially, a file transfer between computers, with the addition of a cover page optionally. Once received, the "editable fax" can be edited in the application that created it—or another application capable of reading that file type. For example, if you send a document created in Microsoft Word for Windows, which is a .DOC file, the recipient can open it in Word, WordPad, Word Pro, or WordPerfect, using import filters if necessary.

ellipsis   Three dots (...). An ellipsis after a menu item or button text indicates that selecting the menu or clicking the button will display an additional dialog box or window from which you can choose options or enter data.

embedded object   Data stored in a document that originated from another application. Differing from a linked object, this type of object doesn't have its own file on the disk. However, it runs its source application for editing when you double-click it. For example, a Paint drawing embedded in a Word document.

encapsulated PostScript (EPS) file   A file format for storing PostScript-style images that allows a PostScript printer or program capable of importing such files to print a file in the highest resolution equipped by the printer.

Enhanced Integrated Electronics (EIDE)   A design that improves on the Drive limitations of the IDE design. EIDE designs can use up to four devices (split into two pairs). For each pair of devices, one of the devices is the master; the drive electronics on the master control both the master drive and (if applicable) the secondary slave unit attached. Unlike IDE, EIDE supports devices in addition to hard drives, including CD-ROM drives and tape drives. EIDE devices can be up to 8 gigabytes in size, improving on the 524 megabyte limit of IDE devices. As with IDE, this type of drive is interfaced to a computer bus with an EIDE host adapter, not a controller. However, most newer computers include an EIDE host adapter right on the motherboard.

Enhanced Meta File (EMF)   The process of converting generic Spooling print instructions to the instruction set "understood" best by a particular printer. This conversion has the capability to create faster printouts of better quality.

Enhanced Small Device Interface (ESDI)   A drive controller type that utilizes a hard drive as a slave unit. ESDI controllers generally drive only two disk drives and have an on-board processor to translate drive geometry, manage I/O requests, and provide caching.

escape codes   A set of codes that appear in a text string on a terminal (see *terminal emulation*). Although these escape codes (which provide formatting information) aren't visible in terminal emulation, they will show up as non-text characters if you capture the text to the screen or printer. In fact, some escape codes may cause the printed output to skip pages, switch into bold mode, and other undesirable effects because they may coincide with printer command codes.

Ethernet   One of the earliest and least expensive network types. Ethernet is capable of speeds of 10MB/sec, and employs Bus and Star network types. When attempting to transmit over an Ethernet network, the transmitting workstation must "listen" to the network line to ensure that it is clear (another workstation is not currently transmitting). If the line is not clear, the workstation must wait until the line clears.

exit   When you are finished running Windows applications and Windows, you must not turn off the computer until you correctly exit Windows. Windows stores some data in memory and does not write it to your hard disk until you choose the exit command. If you turn off the computer without correctly exiting, this data may be lost.

expanded memory   Memory that conforms to the LIM 4.0 standard for memory access. Windows 95 has the capability of converting extended memory (*see extended memory*) to expanded memory (using EMM386.EXE) for programs that require it. However, most modern programs no longer use expanded memory.

expand folders   View the structure of folders that are stored inside other folders. In Explorer, you can expand the view of a folder that has a plus sign (+) next to it to see the folders stored within by double-clicking the folder in the left pane (tree view) of Explorer. When a folder does not contain any additional folders, a minus sign (-) appears next to the folder.

Explorer   A program that comes with Windows 95 that helps you view and manage your files.

Extended Industry Standard Architecture (EISA)   A computer bus and interface card design based on 32-bit bus mastering. EISA is an extension to ISA (Industry Standard Architecture) bus design and enables EISA and ISA interface cards to be used in a single type of bus interface slot in the computer.

extended memory   Memory that can be accessed by Windows 95 beyond the first megabyte of memory in your system.

external command   Unlike an internal command, a command that requires a separate file to run.

F

FDDI   Fiber Distributed Data Interchange is a network type that requires fiber optic cable (*see fiber optic*). Although expensive, it is immune to electrical interference and can achieve speeds of 100 MB/sec.

fiber optic   A type of cable which transmits information via light signals. Although both the cable and the decoders are expensive, such cabling is immune to electrical noise, and capable of much higher transmissions rates than electrical (coaxial or twisted pair) cables.

FIFO buffers   First in, first out buffers. In communications programs that use FIFO buffers, the first information added to the buffer is the also the first information transmitted when the transmission restarts.

file allocation table (FAT)   The native DOS file system that uses a table, called the file allocation table, to store information about the sizes, locations, and properties of files stored on the disk.

file converter   File converters take the file format and transform it to a format that the application can read. During a file conversion, text enhancements, font selections, and other elements are usually preserved. Sometimes, however, these elements are converted to a similar format, and then converted to ASCII format.

file name   The name that a file system or operating system gives to a file when it's stored on disk. File names in Windows 95's file system can be 256 characters long. Additionally, Windows 95 assigns a file name compatible with older DOS (eight-characters with a three-character extension) naming conventions.

file name extension   The three-character extension that you can add to a file name—either the standard eight characters of DOS and Windows 3.1, or the long file names of Windows 95. The file name extension is only visible in Explorer if you enable the appropriate option. Otherwise, the extension is hidden. Nevertheless, the extension is still part of the file name, even when you can't see it—it is this extension that Windows 95 (as well as earlier Windows) uses to associate a document with the application that created it.

file set   In the Windows 95 Backup program, a collection of files to back up and the destination to back them up to. By saving a file set in Backup, you won't have to reselect the files to back up the next time.

file utility   A program that can directly manipulate the information available on the disk that defines where files are found, sized, and other attributes. It is important to NOT use file utilities that were designed for earlier versions of Windows, as Windows 95 stores some file information in different places—and earlier file utilities could scramble the file information, destroying the file.

fixed space font   Fonts that have a fixed amount of space between the characters in the font.

font   A description of how to display a set of characters. The description includes the shape of the characters, spacing between characters, effects (for example, bold, italics, and underline) and the size of the characters.

folder window   A window in Explorer that displays the contents of a folder.

folder   Folders represent directories on your drives. Folders can contain files, programs, and even other folders.

foreground operation   The program in the active window.

forum   On Microsoft Network, a folder with a collection of related documents and subfolders.

frame   A unit of data that is exchanged on a LAN. Frame formatting implements an access protocol for the purpose of enabling communications between nodes on a LAN (Ethernet, Token Ring, and so on). A frame should not be confused with a packet, which is encapsulated within a frame for transport across the LAN.

full system backup   A backup set (*see backup set*) that contains all the files on your hard drive, including Windows 95 system files, the registry, and all other files necessary to completely restore your system configuration on a new hard drive.

G

grid   A background pattern that defines regular intervals—for example, a 1/4" grid displays dots in the background every quarter inch on in a rectangular pattern. Many graphics programs make a grid available. Even when turned on, a grid won't print. When you "snap to grid," your graphic endpoints are constrained to fall on a grid point.

H

handshake   A protocol used between two devices to establish communications. For example, a portable computer and a PC card "handshake" to set up the communications between the devices.

header information   Data sent to a printer to define aspects of the printout and prepare the printer prior to printing. PostScript documents include header information.

heap   An area of memory (also known as the "System Resources area") that Windows uses to store system information (such as menus) about running applications. If the "heap" fills up, you may get an "out of memory" error, despite the fact that you have plenty of regular memory (RAM) available. In Windows 95, you have a much less chance of getting an "out of memory" error. Although Windows 95 still uses a 64KB heap to store systems information for 16-bit applications, a lot of the information that was stored in this area by older versions of Windows is now stored elsewhere. As a result, there is much less chance of your application failing due to this error.

Hearts   A card game included with Windows 95 for up to four players. The winner is the player who has the fewest points.

At the end of each round (each player has played all 13 cards), the following points are given:

1 point for each Heart you collected.

13 points for the Queen of Spades.

If one player wins all the Hearts and the Queen of Spades (called Shooting the Moon), then that player gets zero while all other players are penalized 26 points.

Help   A program that gives you information about how to run Windows 95 and its programs, including how to use the Help program.

hexadecimal   A base-16 numbering scheme with values ranging from 0 to 9, and A to F. Used in many programming languages. Not particularly relevant to users, except that memory address areas are frequently stated in hexadecimal. Hex is used whenever the actual internals of the computer are being revealed as in memory addresses and I/O ports.

hidden file   A characteristic of a file that indicates that the file is not visible in Explorer under normal circumstances. However, by selecting the View Option to view all files, hidden files will still be visible.

hierarchical   A way of displaying text or graphics in a structure. In a hierarchical structure, items closer to the top of the structure are considered "parents" of items connected to them, but which are lower down in the structure. The tree structure of Windows Explorer is an example of a hierarchical structure.

Home Page   A document on the World Wide Web dedicated to a particular subject. From a Home Page, you can use hyperlinks to jump to other Home Pages to gain more information.

host drive   The physical hard drive upon which a DriveSpace compressed volume file exists (*see compressed volume file*). You can choose to either show or hide the host drive when working with Explorer.

hot docking   For a portable computer, "hot docking" refers to the ability to insert the computer into a docking station (which may provide additional resources such as a CD-ROM, speakers, hard drive, and so on) and have the computer recognize that the new resources of the docking station are now available.

hot swapping   For a portable computer, or any other computer that uses PC cards, "hot swapping" refers to the ability to remove a PC card and/or insert a new card, and have the computer recognize the change.

HP JetAdmin   The HP JetAdmin Utility is a tool that can be used to install and configure networked Hewlett-Packard printers using the HP JetDirect network interface. The HP JetAdmin utility appears as a substitute for the Windows standard Printer window. This utility can also be used to interface printers connected to a NetWare LAN.

hub   A wiring concentrator or multiport repeater (*see repeater and wiring concentrator*). Hubs may be active or passive.

hue   The numerical representation of the colors of a color wheel. It is almost always seen with saturation and brightness.

hyperlink   A link in a document that, when activated (often by clicking it), links—or jumps to—another document or graphic.

HyperTerminal   HyperTerminal is a program included with Windows 95, which enables you to easily connect to a remote computer, a bulletin board, or an online service. It replaces Terminal from Windows version 3.1.

Hypertext Markup Language (HTML)   A hypertext language used to create the hypertext documents that make up the World Wide Web.

I

I-beam   The shape the cursor takes in the area of a window where text can be entered.

icon   A small graphic symbol used to represent a folder, program, shortcut, resource, or document.

image color matching (ICM)   Image Color Matching (ICM), a technology developed by Kodak, creates an image environment that treats color from the screen to the printed page. Microsoft licensed ICM from Kodak to be able to repeatedly and consistently reproduce color-matched images from source to destination.

import   An OLE term. In Object Packager, you can import a file into a package and later embed it into a destination document.

inactive   An open window that is not currently in use. On the task bar, the active window looks like a pressed button, inactive windows are represented by unpressed buttons.

Inbox   Inbox holds incoming and outgoing messages and faxes that are sent or received over Microsoft Exchange.

incremental backup   *See differential backup.*

Industry Standard Architecture (ISA)   This term describes the design of the 8/16-bit AT bus (sometimes called the "classic bus") developed by IBM in the original IBM PC.

in-place editing   A feature of OLE 2. With in-place editing, you may edit an embedded or linked object without that object being placed into an additional window (the way it was in OLE 1.0). Instead of creating an additional window, the tools for the object you want to edit appear in the toolbar for the container object (*see container object*). Also, the menus for the object you want to edit replace the menus of the container object. In-place editing is less disruptive; it is much simpler to ensure that the changes you make to an embedded or linked object are updated to the original complex document.

insertion point   A flashing vertical line showing where text will be inserted.

Integrated Drive Electronics (IDE)   A more recent drive design that incorporates an embedded controller on a smaller (3 1/2 inch) disk drive. IDE drives can be connected together, but the second drive must be a slave to the first, using the primary disk controller and not its own embedded controller. This type of drive is interfaced to a computer bus with an IDE host adapter, not a controller.

Integrated Services Digital Network (ISDN)   A special phone line that supports modem speeds up to 64Kbps. However, these phone lines can be quite expensive to acquire. Many ISDN adapters support two-channel access.

interface   The visible layer enabling a user to communicate with a computer. In DOS, the interface consisted largely of typed commands and character-based feedback; Windows 95 is an entirely graphical interface, using a mouse, menus, windows, and icons to allow the user to communicate his instructions and requirements to the computer.

internal command   A command embedded in CMD.EXE, the command interpreter for Windows 95, or in COMMAND.EXE, the MS-DOS equivalent. Internal commands don't require additional support files.

Internet   The Internet is a "network of networks," a global linkage of millions of computers, containing vast amounts of information, much of it available to anyone with a modem and the right software... for free. The Internet is an aggregation of high speed networks, supported by the NSF (National Science Foundation) and almost 6,000 federal, state, and local systems, as well as university and commercial networks. There are links to networks in Canada, South America, Europe, Australia, and Asia, and more than 30 million users.

Internet Explorer A web browser bundled with the Windows 95 Plus kit. It takes advantage of features in Windows 95, such as shortcuts and long file names.

Internet Protocol (IP) A network protocol that provides routing services across multiple LANs and WANs that is used in the TCP/IP protocol stack. IP packet format is used to address packets of data from ultimate source and destination nodes (host) located on any LAN or WAN networked with TCP/IP protocol. IP provides routing services in conjunction with IP routers, which are incorporated into many computer systems and most versions of UNIX. IP Packet format is supported in NetWare 3.11 and 4.0 operating systems, and is used throughout the Department of Defense Internet—a network of thousands of computers internetworked worldwide.

interoperability Compatibility, or the capability for equipment to work together. Industry standards are agreed upon or used by vendors to make their equipment work with other vendors' equipment.

interrupt request line (IRQ) A line (conductor) on the internal bus of the computer (typically on the motherboard) over which a device such as a port, disk controller, or modem can get the attention of the CPU to process some data.

interframe compression A technique that achieves compression of a video file by eliminating redundant data between successive compressed frames.

intraframe compression A technique that compresses the video by removing redundancy from individual video images.

I/O address Input/Output address. Many I/O devices, such as COM ports, network cards, printer ports, and modem cards, are mapped to an I/O address. This address allows the computer and operating system to locate the device, and thus send and receive data. Such I/O addresses don't tie up system memory RAM space. However, there are a limited number of I/O addresses. You can access an I/O port in one of two ways: either map it into the 64KB I/O address space, or map it as a memory-mapped device in the system's RAM space.

IPX Internetwork Packet Exchange (IPX) is a network protocol developed by Novell to address packets of data from ultimate source and destination nodes located on any LAN networked with NetWare. IPX also provides routing services in conjunction with NetWare and third-party routers. An IPX packet has information fields that identify the network address, node address, and socket address of both the source and destination, and provides the same functionality of the of the OSI Network layer in the OSI model.

J

jumpers   jumpers are small devices that complete a circuit between two pins of a multi-pin header, specifying various aspects about a card—for example, which IRQ, base memory address, or I/O port address to use. Jumpers are not normally used on a card that is compliant with Plug and Play, but were common on "legacy" (pre-Plug and Play) cards.

K

kernel   The core of an operating system, usually responsible for basic I/O and process execution.

kernel driver   A driver with direct access to hardware. A hardware driver.

keyboard buffer   Memory set aside to store keystrokes as they're entered from the keyboard. Once it's stored, the keystroke data waits for the CPU to pick up the data and respond accordingly.

keyboard equivalent   *See keyboard shortcut.*

keyboard shortcut   A combination of keystrokes that initiates a menu command without dropping the menu down, or activates a button in a dialog box without clicking the button.

kiosk   In the Microsoft Network, a download-and-run document that contains additional information about a forum. Kiosks are usually found in forums.

L

legacy   Refers to pre-Windows 95 software or hardware. Legacy cards don't support Plug and Play, and legacy software is older software (although you may have just purchased it!) typically designed for Windows 3.1 or Windows for Workgroups 3.11.

license   Refers to the agreement you are assumed to have acceded to when you purchase Windows 95. As with much other computer software, you don't own your copy of Windows 95, but instead, just license the use of it. As such, there is a long list of legalese-type things you supposedly agree to when you open the envelope containing your copy of Windows 95. These legal agreements are part of the *license*.

line by line   When using terminal emulation (see *terminal emulation*), some primitive terminals only allowed you to edit text on the single line on which you were working. Once you pressed Enter to move to the next line, you couldn't go back and change something on the previous line(s)—because those lines had already been sent to the host computer that the PC emulates a terminal of. In line by line editing, there is a line length limit as well, so you can't simply type an entire paragraph before pressing Enter.

linked object   In OLE terminology, data stored in a document that originated from another application. Unlike an embedded object, this type of object has its own file on the disk. The source application is run for editing when you double-click it. For example, a Paint drawing linked to a Word document. Linking saves space over embedding when a particular object must be included in more than one other document, since the data does not have to be stored multiple times. Additionally, you can directly edit a linked file, and all the documents that link to the file update automatically.

list box   A dialog box item that shows all available options.

local area network (LAN)   A limited-distance, multi-point physical connectivity medium consisting of network interface cards, media, and repeating devices designed to transport frames of data between host computers at high speeds with low error rates. A LAN is a subsystem that is part of a network.

local printer   A printer connected directly to your computer.

local reboot   The ability of Windows 95 to close down a single misbehaving application. When you use the Alt+Ctrl+Delete key sequence, Windows 95 queries you for the application to shut down. In this way, you can close down only the application you want, without affecting other running applications.

logical block addressing (lba)   A type of addressing scheme for IDE disk drives that allows the drive to exceed the original 512 megabyte (1/2 gigabyte) IDE size limit. With logical block addressing, an IDE drive can hold up to 8.4 gigabytes.

logical drive   A drive that isn't a physical drive, as in the floppy drive A or B. Instead, a logical drive is a drive created on a subpartition of an extended partition and given an arbitrary letter such as C, D, or E.

long file name   A reference to Windows 95's ability to use file names up to 256 characters long.

lossy compression   Compression techniques that lose some of the data when compressing the file. Although lossy compression isn't acceptable for compressing application file and certain types of data files (for example, database, word processing), it is often acceptable to have a low degree of loss when compressing video or graphic files, since you likely won't notice the missing data. Also, lossy compression can gain considerably higher compression ratios than "lossless" compression. However, when using lossy compression, you don't want to decompress the file, then use the result to recompress, as the loss of data gets worse with each cycle.

LPT   The parallel port (used for printing). Most computers have a single parallel port (labeled LPT1), but some may have two. The parallel port transmits data one byte (eight bits) at a time. This parallel transmission of all eight bits gives the port its name.

luminosity   When working with colors, indicates the brightness of the color.

M

macro   A sequence of keyboard strokes and mouse actions that can be recorded so that their playback can be activated by a single keystroke, keystroke combination, or mouse click. Unlike Windows 3.1 and Windows for Workgroups, Windows 95 does not come with a Macro Recorder.

Mailing List (Internet)   An e-mail discussion group focused on one or more topics. The Mailing List is made up of members who subscribe to that mailing list.

map network drive   The act of associating a network drive makes the drive available in My Computer. Windows 95 uses the next available drive letter, and you can access the network drive just like any other hard drive.

maximize button   A button in the upper right corner of a Window with a square in it. When clicked, it enlarges the window to its maximum size. When the window is already at its maximum size, the maximize button switches to the restore button, which returns the window to its previous size.

media control interface (MCI)   A standard interface for all multimedia devices, devised by the MPC counsel, that allows multimedia applications to control any number of MPC-compliant devices, from sound cards to MIDI-based lighting controllers.

menu   A list of available command options.

menu bar   Located under the title bar, the menu bar displays the names of all available menu lists.

menu command   A word or phrase in a menu that, when selected, enables you to view all the commands.

Micro-Channel Architecture (MCA)   A proprietary 32-bit computer and bus architecture designed by IBM to improve bus bandwidth and facilitate bus mastering. MCA is not backward-compatible with ISA and requires exclusive use of MCA devices.

microprocessor   A miniaturized processor. Previous processors were built in integrated circuit boards with many large components. Most processors today use high-tech, silicon-based technology that improves performance, reduces heat generation, and increases efficiency.

Microsoft Client for Netware Networks   Windows 95 Microsoft Client for NetWare Networks allows users to connect to new or existing NetWare servers. It permits you to browse and queue print jobs using either the Windows 95 network user interface or existing Novell NetWare utilities. The Microsoft Client for NetWare interfaces equally well with both NetWare 3.x and 4.x servers.

Microsoft Exchange   Microsoft Exchange provides a universal Inbox that you can use to send and receive electronic mail (e-mail). In addition, you can use the Inbox to organize, access, and share all types of information, including faxes and items from online services.

Microsoft Fax   Microsoft Fax is a program included with Windows 95 that enables you to send and receive faxes directly within Windows 95.

Microsoft Network (MSN)   Access to The Microsoft Network, a new online service, is a feature of Windows 95.

With The Microsoft Network, you can exchange messages with people around the world; read the latest news, sports, weather, and financial information; find answers to your technical questions; download from thousands of useful programs; and connect to the Internet.

MIDI   Musical Instrument Digital Interface. Originally a means of connecting electronic instruments (synthesizers) and letting them communicate with one another. Computers then came into the MIDI landscape and were used to control the synthesizers. Windows 95 can play MIDI files.

Minesweeper   A game of chance and skill included with Windows 95. When playing Minesweeper, you are presented with a mine field, and your objective is to locate all the mines as quickly as possible. To do this, uncover the squares on the game board that do not contain mines, and mark the squares that contain mines. The trick is determining which squares are which.

If you uncover all the squares without mines, you win; if you uncover a mine instead of marking it, you lose the game. The faster you play, the lower your score. You can use the counters at the top of the playing area to keep track of your progress.

minimize button   The button in the upper right corner of the window that has a line in it. When clicked, it reduces the window to display the task bar only.

mission-critical application   An application program considered indispensable to the operation of a business, government, or other operation. Often, these applications are transaction-based, such as for point-of-sale, reservations, or real-time stock, security, or money trading.

modem   A device, usually attached to a computer through a serial port or present as an internal card. A modem makes it possible to use ordinary phone lines to transfer computer data. In addition to a modem, a communications program is required. "Modem" is short for "modulator/demodulator"—the processes whereby a digital stream of data is converted to sound for transmission through a phone system originally designed only for sound (modulator) and the conversion of received sound signals back into digital data (demodulator).

Motion JPEG   Developed by the Joint Photographic Experts Group, motion JPEG is a compression /decompression scheme (codec) for video files. It is a variation on JPEG, this group's codec for compressing still pictures. It uses only intraframe lossy compression (*see intraframe compression, lossy compression*), but offers a tradeoff between compression ratio and quality.

mounting a compressed drive   When you are working with removable storage media— such as disks— that are compressed, you must mount the compressed drive if it wasn't present when the computer was started. Mounting a drive links a drive letter with a compressed volume file (CVF). This enables your computer to access the files on the compressed volume files. Mounting a compressed drive is done using DriveSpace.

mouse pointer   The symbol that displays where your next mouse click will occur. The mouse pointer symbol changes according to the context of the window or the dialog box in which it appears.

MPEG   Created by the Motion Picture Experts Group, MPEG is a specification for compressing and decompressing (*see codec*) animation or "movie" files, which are typically very large. Although extremely efficient at reducing the size of such a file, MPEG is also very processor-intensive.

MS-DOS-based application An application that normally runs on a DOS machine and doesn't require Windows 95. Many MS-DOS-based applications will run in Windows 95's DOS box, but some will not.

multimedia A combination of various types of media, including (but not necessarily limited to) sound, animation, and graphics. Due to the generally large size of "multimedia" files, a CD-ROM is usually necessary to store files. Of course, a sound card and speakers are also necessary.

multitasking The capability of an operating system to handle multiple processing tasks, apparently, at the same time.

multithreading A process allowing a multitasking operating system to, in essence, multitask subportions (threads) of an application smoothly. Applications must be written to take advantage of multithreading. Windows 95 supports multithreading.

my computer An icon present on the Windows 95 desktop that enables you to view drives, folders, and files.

my briefcase An icon present on the Windows 95 desktop. My Briefcase is the way that portable computer users can take data with them as they travel. When they return to the office, Windows examines the files in My Briefcase and updates the contents of their desktop computer.

N

NetBIOS An IBM protocol (and packet structure) that provides several networking functions. NetBIOS was developed by IBM and Sytek to supplement and work with BIOS in PC-DOS-based, peer-to-peer networks. NetBIOS protocol provides transport, session, and presentation layer function equivalent to layers 4, 5, and 6 of the OSI model. The NetBIOS software that is used to implement this protocol is the NetBIOS interface.

NetWare A trademarked brand name for the networking operating systems and other networking products developed and sold by Novell.

NetWare Core Protocol (NCP) A NetWare protocol that provides transport, session, and presentation layer functions equivalent to layers 4, 5, and 6 of the OSI model.

Net Watcher A tool included with the Windows 95. Net Watcher allows you to monitor and manage network connections, as well as create, add, and delete shared resources.

network   A group of computers connected by a communications link that enables any device to interact with any other on the network. The "network" is derived from the term "network architecture" to describe an entire system of hosts, workstations, terminals, and other devices.

Network Interface card (NIC)   Also called a network adapter, an NIC is an interface card placed in the bus of a computer (or other LAN device) to interface to a LAN. Each NIC represents a node, which is a source and destination for LAN frames, which in turn carries data between the NICs on the LAN.

network neighborhood   An icon which Windows 95 displays only if you are connected to a network and Windows has been installed for a network. Double-clicking the Network Neighborhood icon displays all the resources available on any network to which you are connected.

non-volatile RAM   RAM memory on a card that is not erased when power is cut off. Cards that don't use jumpers often store their resource requirements (IRQ, I/O Base address, I/O port, DMA channel, etc.) in non-volatile RAM. Non-volatile RAM is not normally used on a card that is compliant with Plug and Play, but was common on "legacy" (pre-Plug and Play) cards.

non Windows program   A program not designed to be used specifically in Windows. Most non-Windows applications or programs are character-based in nature (for example, DOS programs).

Notepad   A program that comes with Windows 95 and enables you to view and edit text files.

null modem cable   A serial cable link between computers. Standard modem software is often used to transmit information, but because there are no actual modems in the connection, very high transfer rates with good accuracy are possible. The cable must be different from a regular serial cable, however, because several of the wires in the cable must be cross-connected to simulate the modem's role in acknowledging a transmission.

object   Any item that is or can be linked into another Windows application, such as a sound, graphics, piece of text, or portion of a spreadsheet. Must be from an application that supports Object Linking and Embedding (OLE).

object linking and embedding   *see OLE.*

OEM Fonts   OEM fonts are provided to support older installed products. The Term OEM refers to Original Equipment Manufacturers. This font family includes a character set designed to be compatible with older equipment and software applications

offline   A device that is not ready to accept input. For example, if your printer is off-line, it will not accept data from the computer, and attempting to print will generate an error.

OLE   A data sharing scheme that allows dissimilar applications to create single, complex documents by cooperating in the creation of the document. The documents consist of material that a single application couldn't have created on its own. In OLE version 1, double-clicking an embedded or linked object (see *embedded object*, and *linked object*) launches the application that created the object in a separate window. In OLE version 2, double-clicking an embedded or linked object makes the menus and tools of the creating application available in the middle of the parent document. The destination document (which contains the linked or embedded object) must be created by an application which is an OLE client, and the linked or embedded object must be created in an application that is an OLE server.

OLE automation   Refers to the capability of a server application to make available (this is known as expose) its own objects for use in another application's macro language.

online   Indicates that a system is working and connected. For example, if your printer is online, it is ready to accept information to turn into a printed output.

Open Data Link Interface (ODI)   A Novell specification that separates the implementation of a protocol and the implementation of the NIC hardware driver. Novell's MLID specification enables NIC drivers to interface through Link Support Layer with IPX ODI and multiple ODI-onforming packet drivers.

option button   A dialog box item that enables you to choose only one of a group of choices.

orientation   For printer paper, indicates whether the document is to be printed normally (for example, in "portrait" mode) or sideways (in "landscape" mode).

OSI Model   Opens Systems Interconnect seven-layer Model is a model developed by the International Standards Organization to establish a standardized set of protocols for interoperability between networked computer hosts. Each layer of the model consists of specifications and/or protocols that fulfill specific functions in a networking architecture. Novell's UNA was patterned against the OSI model. The OSI model consists of specific protocols that are nonproprietary and offered in the hope of unifying networking protocols used in competing vendors' systems.

P

packet   A limited-length unit of data formed by the network, transport, presentation, or application layer (layers 3-7 of the OSI Model) in a net-worked computer system. Data is transported over the network, and larger amounts of data are broken into shorter units and placed into packets. Higher-layer packets are encapsulated into lower-layer packets for encapsulation into LAN frames for delivery to the ultimate host destination.

Paint   A program that comes with Windows 95 and enables you to view and edit various formats of bitmaps.

palette   A collection of tools. For example, in Paint, there is a color palette that displays the 48 colors available for use in creating a graphic.

pane   Some windows, such as the window for Explorer, show two or more distinct "areas" (Explorer's window shows two such areas). These areas are referred to as "panes."

Panose   Panose refers to a Windows internal description that represents a font by assigning each font a PANOSE ID number. Windows uses several internal descriptions to categorize fonts. The PANOSE information registers a font class and determines similarity between fonts.

paragraph formatting   In a word processing program, this refers to formatting that can be applied to an entire paragraph, including alignment (left, center, right), indentation, and spacing before and after the paragraph.

parallel port   A port (usually used for printing) that transmits data eight bits at a time. This parallel transmission of eight bits at a time gives the port its name.

parity   An additional portion of data added to each byte of stored or transmitted data. Used to ensure that the data isn't lost or corrupted. In HyperTerminal, parity is used to ensure that the data is transmitted and received properly. Parity is also used in RAM chips to determine if RAM errors have occurred.

partial backup   *See differential backup.*

partition   A portion of a physical hard drive that behaves as a separate disk (logical drive), even though it isn't.

path   The location of a file in the directory tree.

PC Cards   Formerly called PCMCIA cards, these are small (usually only slightly larger than a credit card) cards that plug into special slots provided in notebook computers. PC Cards can provide functionality for additional memory, modems, sound, networking, hard drives, and so on. PC Cards normally identify themselves to the computer, making configuring them quite simple.

PCMCIA   The old name for PC Cards (see PC Cards).

peer-to-peer   A type of networking in which no workstation has more control over the network than any other. Each station may share its resources, but no station is the sole resource sharer or file server. Typically less expensive than client/server networks, peer-to-peer networks are also more difficult to administer and less secure because there is no central repository of data.

personal information store   The Personal Information Store is Exchange's term for the file that contains the structure of folders that make up your In box, Out box, sent files, deleted files, and any other personal folders you may choose to create.

phone dialer   Phone Dialer is a program that is included with Windows 95 that enables you to place telephone calls from your computer by using a modem or another Windows telephony device. You can store a list of phone numbers you use frequently, and dial the number quickly from your computer.

picon   Picons are small bitmapped images of the first frame of your video clip. They can be used to represent the in and out source of your video segments.

PIF   A file that provides Windows 95 with the information it needs to know in order to run a non-Windows program. Unlike earlier versions of Windows, there is no PIF editor in Windows 95. Instead, you set up a PIF file from the properties for the file. Access the file properties by right-clicking the file from My Computer.

Ping   A network utility that determines if TCP/IP is working properly. Simply executing the Ping command (from a DOS prompt) and specifying the IP address should produce a response (the response will depend on how the remote machine has been programmed to respond to a Ping), but virtually any response that references the remote machine's identity indicates that the Ping was successful and TCP/IP is working correctly.

Play List   In CD Player, a list of tracks from an audio CD that you want to play.

plug and play   An industry-wide specification supported by Windows 95 that makes it easy to install new hardware. Plug and Play enables the computer to correctly identify hardware components (including plug-in cards) and ensures that different cards don't conflict in their requirements for IRQs, I/O addresses, DMA channels, and memory addresses. In order to fully implement plug and play, you need an operating system that supports it (as stated, Windows 95 does), a BIOS that supports it (most computers manufactured since early 1995 do) and cards that identify themselves to the system (information from these cards stored in the Windows Registry). If you have hardware, such as modems that aren't Plug-n-Play (so called "legacy hardware"), then Windows 95 will prompt you for the information necessary for setup, and store such information in the Registry.

pointer   The on-screen symbol controlled by the mouse. As you move the mouse on the desk, the pointer moves on-screen. The pointer changes shape to indicate the current status and the type of functions and selections available.

polygon   A multisided shape, in which each side is a straight line.

port   A connection or socket for connecting devices to a computer (*see I/O address*).

port replicator   On portable computers, a bus connection that makes all bus lines available externally. The port replicator can be used to plug in devices which, in a desktop computer, would be handled as cards. Port replicators are also the connection used to connect a portable computer to its docking station.

Postoffice   This machine will be the place in which all mail messages are stored for the workgroup.

Postproduction editing   The steps of adding special effects, animated overlays,and more to a production video.

Postscript   A special description language, invented by Adobe. This language is used to accurately describe fonts and graphics. Printers which can directly read this language and print the results are termed "postscript printers."

preemptive processing   In a multitasking operating system, multiple tasks (threads) are generally controlled by a scheduler that preempts or interrupts each process, granting processor time in the form of a time slice. This enables multiple tasks to apparently run at the same time. However, each task runs for a time slice and is then preempted by the next process, which in turn is preempted—rotating processor time among active threads. In preemptive multitasking, the operating system is empowered to override (or preempt) an application that is using too much CPU time, as opposed to cooperative multitasking, where the application is responsible for relinquishing the CPU on a regular basis.

primary partition   A portion of the hard disk that can be used by the operating system and that can't be subpartitioned like an extended partition can. Only primary partitions are bootable.

printer driver   A Windows 95 program that tells programs how to format data for a particular type of printer.

printer fonts   Fonts stored in the printer's ROM.

printer settings   A window that displays all the printers for which there are drivers present. You can select the default printer from the installed printers, as well as configure each printer using the shortcut menu and the options dialog box.

printer window   For each installed printer, you can view the printer window. The printer window displays the status of each print job in the queue, and enables you to pause, restart, and delete the print job.

processor   The controlling device in a computer that interprets and executes instructions and performs computations, and otherwise controls the major functions of the computer. This book discusses Intel 80x86-series processors, which are miniaturized single-chip "microprocessors" containing thousands to millions of transistors in a silicon-based, multilayered integrated circuit design.

program file   A program that runs an application directly (not via an association) when you click it.

program window   A window that contains a program and its documents.

property sheet   A dialog box that displays (and sometimes enables you to change) the properties of an object in Windows 95. To access a property sheet, right click the object to view the shortcut menu, and select Properties from the shortcut menu. Property sheets vary considerably between different objects.

proportional-spaced fonts   Proportional-spaced fonts adjust the inter-character space based on the shape of the individual characters. An example of a proportional-spaced font is Arial. The width of a character is varied based on its shape. Adjusting inter-character spacing is really a function of kerning, which is a similar but not exactly the same. For instance, the letter 'A' and the letter 'V' are typically stored in each font as a kerning pair where they will be spaced differently when appearing next to each other. In a monospace font versus a proportional font you will see a difference in the width of the letter 'i.'

protected mode   A memory addressing mode of Intel processors that allows direct "flat memory" addressing (linear addressing) rather than using the awkward "segmented" scheme required by real mode, which was pioneered on the Intel 8088 and 8086 processors. Protected mode derives its name from the fact that sections of memory owned by a particular process can be protected from rogue programs trying to access those addresses.

protocol   Rules of communication. In networks, several layers of protocols exist. Each layer of protocol only needs to physically hand off or receive data from the immediate layer above and beneath it, whereas virtual communications occur with the corresponding layer on another host computer.

Q

QIC   A formatting standard for tapes used by various tape backup devices. The amount of information that can be stored on a tape varies by the QIC number. The Windows 95 Backup program supports QIC 40, 80, 3010, and 3020 formats. It also supports QIC 113 compression format.

queue   Documents lined up and waiting to be printed, or commands lined up and waiting to be serviced. Use the Printer window to view the print queue for a printer.

quick format   A quick way to format a floppy disk, quick format doesn't actually wipe the whole disk, nor does it test the media for bad sectors. It just erases the FAT.

QuickTime   Developed by Apple, QuickTime is a compression and decompression (codec) scheme for animation files. It is unique in that versions are available for both Windows and Macintosh, enabling software designers to provide their data in a format compatible for both platforms.

Quick View   A program included with Windows 95 that enables you to view files stored in 30 different file formats without needing to open the application that created the file. Quick View is available from the File menu of Explorer if a viewer is available for the selected file type.

R

RAM   Random Access Memory. Physical memory chips located in the computer. Typically, Windows 95 machines have 16 million bytes (16MB) of RAM or more. However, Windows 95 will run on machines with 8MB of RAM.

raster font   A font in which characters are stored as pixels.

read-only   Characteristic of a file indicating that the file can be read from, but not written to, by an application. Note however, that a "read-only" file can be deleted in Explorer, although you will get a warning (beyond the normal "are you sure" you normally get when you try to delete a file) if the file is read-only.

real mode   As opposed to *protected mode*, real mode is a mode in which Intel x86 processors can run. Memory addressing in real mode is nonlinear, requiring a program to stipulate a segment and memory offset address in order to access a location in memory. It originally appeared on the Intel 8086 CPU and has been the bane of PC programmers ever since. Although subsequent CPU chips supported protected-mode linear addressing, backward compatibility with the thousands of real-mode applications slows the evolution of operating systems. Note that all Intel CPUs boot in real mode and require specific software support to switch into protected mode.

recycle bin   An icon that appears on the Windows 95 desktop. To discard a file, you drag the file from Explorer, My Computer, or any other file handler to the Recycle Bin. This action hides the file—but doesn't actually erase it from the disk. You can "undelete" the file by dragging it from the recycle bin back to a folder. To actually delete the file, select the recycle bin menu selection to empty the recycle bin.

registering a program   The act of linking a document with the program that created it so that both can be opened with a single command. For example, double-clicking a DOC file opens Word for Windows and loads the selected document.

registry   A database of configuration information central to Window 95 operations. This file contains program settings, associations between file types and the applications that created them, as well as information about the types of OLE objects a program can create and hardware detail information.

registry editor   The Registry Editor ships with Windows 95. Using this tool you can fine tune Windows 95 performance by adjusting or adding settings to key system information. Since Windows 95 has placed WIN.INI and SYSTEM.INI file settings in the registry, the ability to remotely edit these parameters is an extremely powerful tool. Warning: you can totally destroy a workstation using this tool!

repeater   A device that repeats or amplifies bits of data received at one port and sends each bit to another port. A repeater is a simple bus network device that connects two cabling segments and isolates electrical problems to either side. When used in a LAN, most repeaters take a role in reconstituting the digital signal that passing through them to extend distances a signal can travel, and reduce problems that occur over lengths of cable, such as attenuation.

resize button   A button located in the lower left corner of a non-maximized window. When the mouse pointer is over this button, it turns into a two-headed arrow. You can click and drag to resize the window horizontally and vertically.

resource (card)   When installing a card, certain "resources" are needed: these often include a DMA channel, I/O Base address, and IRQ. Although these are detected and set automatically with Plug and Play compliant cards, you will have to set them using jumpers or the setup program to store the resource values in non-volatile RAM when installing a "legacy" (pre-Plug and Play) card.

restore button   A button in the upper right corner of a Window that has two squares in it. When clicked, it returns the window to its previous size. When the window is at its previous size, the restore button switches to the maximize button, which returns the window to its maximum size

restore files   Copies one or more files from your backup set to the hard disk or to another floppy.

rich text format (RTF)   RTF (Rich Text Format) is compatible with several word processors and includes fonts, tabs, and character formatting.

ring network   One of a variety of network topologies. Ring networks connect computers by using an In and an Out port for data. Each computer sends information to the next computer down the wire. Data flows from one computer's Out port to the next computer's In port.

ROM   Read-Only Memory. A type of chip capable of permanently storing data without the aid of an electric current source to maintain it, as in RAM. The data in ROM chips is sometimes called firmware. Without special equipment, it is not possible to alter the contents of read-only memory chips, thus the name. ROMs are found in many types of computer add-in boards, as well as on motherboards. CPUs often have an internal section of ROM as well.

routable protocol   A network protocol that can work with non-proprietary routers. Traditional routers use the network packet header fields to identify network addresses (network numbers)/node addresses for ultimate source and destination nodes (or hosts) for packets of data. This scheme for routing packets across internetworks is used in OSI, NetWare (IPX), TCP/IP, and AppleTalk network protocols.

router   In a network, a device that reads network layer packet headers and receives or forwards each packet accordingly. Routers connect LANs and WANs into internetworks, but must be able to process the network packets for specific types of network protocol. Many routers process various packet types and therefore are termed multiprotocol routers.

S

safe mode   A special mode for starting Windows 95 that uses simple, default settings so that you can at least get into Windows and fix a problem that makes it impossible to work with Windows otherwise. The default settings use a generic VGA monitor driver, no network settings, the standard Microsoft mouse driver, and the minimum device drivers necessary to start Windows.

safe recovery   An installation option provided by Windows 95 to recover from a faulty or damaged installation of Windows 95.

saturation   When working with colors, saturation indicates the purity of a color; lower values of saturation have more gray in them.

ScanDisk   A program used to check for, diagnose, and repair damage on a hard disk or disk. Part of your routine hard disk maintenance, (along with defragmenting your hard disk) should include a periodic run of ScanDisk to keep your hard disk in good repair. In its standard test, ScanDisk checks the files and folders on a disk or disk for *logical* errors, and if you ask it to, automatically corrects any errors it finds. ScanDisk checks for *crosslinked* files, which occur when two or more files have data stored in the same *cluster* (a storage unit on a disk). The data in the cluster is likely to be correct for only one of the files, and may not be correct for any of them. ScanDisk also checks for *lost file fragments*, which are pieces of data that have become disassociated with their files.

screen fonts   Font files used to show type styles on the screen. These are different from the files used by Windows to print the fonts. The screen fonts must match the printer fonts in order for Windows to give an accurate screen portrayal of the final printed output.

screen resolution   The number of picture elements (or "pixels") that can be displayed on the screen. Screen resolution is a function of the monitor and graphics card. Higher resolutions display more information at a smaller size, and also may slow screen performance. Screen resolution is expressed in the number of pixels across the screen by the number of pixels down the screen. Standard VGA has a resolution of 640 by 480, although most modern monitors can display 1024 by 768, and even higher (larger monitors can usually display a higher resolution than smaller ones).

screen saver   A varying pattern or graphic that appears on the screen when the mouse and keyboard have been idle for a user-definable period of time. Originally used to prevent a static background from being "burned into" the screen phosphors, this is rarely a problem with modern monitors. Many screen savers (including those that come with Windows 95) can be used with a password—you must enter the correct password to turn off the screen saver and return to the screen. However, someone could simply reboot the machine, so a screen saver password is not very sophisticated protection.

scroll arrow   Located at either end of a scroll bar, it can be clicked to scroll up or down (vertical scroll bar) or left or right (horizontal scroll bar). Clicking the scroll arrow will move your window in that direction.

scroll bar   Scroll bars allow you to select a value within a range, such as what part of a document to see, or what value to set the Red, Green, and Blue components of a color to.

scroll box   A small box located in the scroll bar that shows where the visible window is located in relation to the entire document, menu, or list. You can click and drag the scroll box to make other portions of the document, menu, or list visible.

select   To specify a section of text or graphics for initiating an action. To select also can be to choose an option in a dialog box.

selection handles   Small black boxes indicating that a graphic object has been selected. With some Windows applications, you can click and drag a selection handle to resize the selected object.

serial port   *See COM.*

Serif Fonts   Serif Fonts have projections (serifs) that extend the upper and lower strokes of the set's characters beyond their normal boundaries; for example, Courier. San-Serif Fonts do not have these projections; for example, Arial.

server   A centrally-administered network computer, which contains resources that are shared with "client" machines on the network.

server application   In OLE terminology, an application that supplies an object, (such as a drawing), to a client application, (such as a word processing program), for inclusion in a complex document.

shareware   A method of distributing software, often including downloading the software from a BBS or the Microsoft Network. With shareware, you get to use the software before deciding to pay for it. By paying for the software and registering it, you usually receive a manual; perhaps the most up-to-date version (which may include additional functionality). Shareware versions of software often include intrusive reminders to register—the registered versions do not include these reminders.

shortcut   A pointer to a file, document or printer in Windows 95. A shortcut is represented by an icon in Explorer, on the desktop, or as an entry in the Start menu. Selecting the program shortcut icon or menu entry runs the program to which the shortcut "points". Selecting a document shortcut runs the application that created the document (provided the document type is associated with a program). Dragging and dropping a document onto a printer shortcut prints the document. Note that a shortcut does NOT create a copy of the program or document itself.

shortcut keys   A keystroke or key combination that enables you to activate a command without having to enter a menu or click a button.

shortcut menu   A popup menu that appears when you right click an object for which a menu is appropriate. The shortcut menu displays only those options which make sense for the object you select and current conditions.

Small Computer System Interface (SCSI)   An ANSI standard bus design. SCSI host adapters are used to adapt an ISA, EISA, MCI, PCI, or VLB (VESA Local Bus) bus to an SCSI bus so that SCSI devices (such as disk drives, CD-ROMs, tape backups, and other devices) can be interfaced. An SCSI bus accommodates up to eight devices, however, the bus adapter is considered one device, thereby enabling seven usable devices to be interfaced to each SCSI adapter. SCSI devices are intelligent devices. SCSI disk drives have embedded controllers and interface to an SCSI bus adapter. An SCSI interface card is therefore a bus adapter, not a controller.

IV

Small Computer System Interface-2 (SCSI-2)   An ANSI standard that improves on SCSI-1 standards for disk and other device interfaces. SCSI-2 bandwidth is 10 MB/sec, whereas SCSI-1 is 5 MB/sec. SCSI-2 also permits command-tag queuing, which enables up to 256 requests to be queued without waiting for the first request. Another SCSI-2 feature is the bus' capability to communicate with more than one type of device at the same time, where a single SCSI-1 host adapter only supported one type of device to communicate on the bus.

SCSI Configured Automagically (SCAM)   The specification for Plug and Play or SCSI buses. This specification makes it unnecessary to set an SCSI Id, as the configuration software negotiates and sets the id for each connected SCSI device (that is Plug and Play-compliant!).

soft fonts   Depending on your printing hardware, soft fonts may be downloaded to your printer. Downloading fonts reduces the time taken by the printer to process printouts. Although downloading soft fonts is done only once (per session), benefits are realized through subsequent printing.

Solitaire   A card game included with Windows 95 for a single player. The object of solitaire is to turn all the cards in the seven face-down stacks face-up on top of each of the four aces for each of the four suites.

Soundblaster   An extremely popular family of sound boards, developed and marketed by Creative Labs. Because of the popularity and large market share of this product family, most sound boards advertise themselves as "soundblaster compatible," meaning that drivers provided in Windows, Windows 95, and programs such as games will work with these boards. However, some boards' compatibility is not perfect.

source document   In OLE, the document that contains the information you want to link into (to appear in) another document (the destination document).

spool   A temporary holding area for the data you want to print. When printing a document, it can take some time (depending on the length of the document and the speed of your printer) for the document to come off your printer. By spooling the data, you may continue using your computer while the document is printing, because the computer "feeds" the spool contents to the printer as fast as the printer can handle it. When the print job is completed, the spool file is automatically deleted.

star network   One of a variety of network topologies. Star networks connect computers through a central hub. The central hub distributes the signals to all of the cables which are connected.

Start menu   A menu located at the left end of the task bar. Clicking the button marked Start opens a popup menu that makes Help, the Run command, settings, find, shutdown, a list of programs (actually, program shortcuts), and a list of recently accessed documents available for you to run with a single click. For some items (such as the Documents item), a submenu opens to the side of the main item to display the list of choices. You can configure the Start menu to specify which programs are available to run from it.

Startup Folder   A folder that contains any programs that you want Windows 95 to run whenever you start up. You can drag and drop program shortcuts into the Startup Folder to add them to the list of programs to run.

static object   In OLE, where objects have a "hot link" to their original application, static objects are simply pasted into a destination document using the Clipboard. These objects are not updated if the original object is updated. This is the simple "pasting" that most Windows users use on a daily basis.

stroke font   A font that can have its size greatly altered without distorting the font.

stop bits   In a communications program, the number of bits used to indicate the "break" between pieces of information (*see data bits*). Usually 1 or 2.

submenu   A related set of options that appear when you select a menu item (*see cascading menus*).

swap file   A file that gives Windows 95 the ability to use a portion of hard drive as memory. With the use of a swap file, you can load and run more programs in Windows 95 than you actually have RAM memory for. A swap file allows Windows 95 to "swap" chunks of memory containing currently unused information to disk, making room in RAM memory for information you need to run the currently selected program. Using a swap file is slower than holding everything in RAM memory, however.

system disk   The disk containing the operating system, or at least enough of it to start the system and then look on another disk for the support files.

system fonts   System fonts are used by Windows to draw menus, controls, and utilize specialized control text in Windows. System fonts are proportional fonts that can be sized and manipulated quickly.

System monitor   A program that enables you to monitor the resources on your computer. You can see information displayed for the 32-bit file system, network clients and servers, and the virtual memory manager, among other things. Most of this information is highly technical in nature and most useful to advanced users. You can display the information in either bar or line charts, or as a numeric value.

system policies Policies, established by a system administrator, which override Registry settings on individual machines. By setting up policies, a system Administrator can restrict a user from changing hardware settings using Control Panel, customize parts of the Desktop like the Network Neighborhood or the Programs folder, and maintain centrally located network settings, such as network client customizations or the ability to install file & printer services. This program can also control access to a computer, enable user profiles, and maintain password control.

System Resources *See heap.*

T

tab (dialog boxes) In dialog boxes, there may be multiple panels of information. Each panel has an extension at the top that names the panel. This small extension is called a tab.

TAPI Telephony Applications Programming Interface, or TAPI, provides a method for programs to work with modems, independent of dealing directly with the modem hardware. All the information you give Windows during the modem configuration is used for TAPI to set up its interface. Communications programs that are written specifically for Windows 95 will talk to TAPI, which will then issue appropriate commands to the modem. This is called device independence.

taskbar An area that runs across the bottom of the Windows 95 desktop. The Start button (*see Start menu*) is at the left end of the taskbar, and the clock can be displayed at the right end of the taskbar. Running applications are represented as buttons on the taskbar, the current window is shown as a depressed button, and all other applications are displayed as raised buttons. Clicking the button for an inactive application activates that application and displays its window as the current window.

task list A list of currently running applications. You can switch tasks by clicking an item in the task list. The task list is accessed by pressing Alt+Tab on the keyboard.

TCP/IP Transmission Control Protocol/Internet Protocol is a set of networking protocols developed in the 1970s. TCP/IP includes Transport Control Protocol, which is a connection-oriented transport protocol that includes transport, session, and presentation layer protocol functions, which is equivalent to layers 4,5, and 6 of the OSI Model and Internet Protocol, and a widely used routable network protocol that corresponds to layer 3 of the OSI model. User Datagram Protocol (UDP) can be substituted in cases where connectionless datagram service is desired. TCP/IP is an entire protocol stack that includes protocols for file transfers (FTP), termination emulation services (Telnet), electronic mail (SMTP), address resolution (ARP and RARP), and error control and notification (ICMP and SNMP). TCP/IP is used extensively in many computer systems because it is nonproprietary—free from royalties. Its use was mandated by Congress for use in computer systems for many government agencies and contract situations. TCP/IP is also used in the Internet, a huge government and research internetwork spanning North America and much of the world. TCP/IP is the most commonly used set of network protocols.

terminal emulation   In the old days of computing, a "terminal" was an input/output device that was a slave of a CPU, such as a terminal for a mini-computer or mainframe. Generally, terminals had no computing power of their own, but simply provided an interface to a remote host computer. Terminal emulation refers to a mode (character-based) in which a PC emulates one of these terminals to communicate with a remote host—typically a BBS computer or a corporate mainframe that only "knows" how to talk to a terminal.

text based   *See character based.*

text box   A space in the dialog box where text or numbers can be entered so that a command can be carried out.

text file   A file containing only text characters.

thumbnail   A miniature rendition of a graphic file. A thumbnail gives an idea of what the full-size graphic looks like, and is usually used as a gateway to view the full-size graphic.

thread (program execution)   A "thread" is a chunk of a program. In a multi-threading environment such as Windows 95, multiple threads (multiple portions of a program) can execute at the same time—provided the program has been programmed to take advantage of this feature.

thread (BBS/Communications)   A set of messages pertaining to one general idea.

tile   To reduce and move windows so that they can all be seen at once.

time slice   A brief time period in which a process is given access to the processor. Each second is divided into 18.3 time slices; multiple tasks can be scheduled for processing in these slices, yet outwardly appear to be occurring simultaneously.

time-out   A time period after which a device or driver might signal the operating system and cease trying to perform its duty. If a printer is turned off, for example, when you try to print, the driver waits for a predetermined period of time, then issues an error message. In computer terminology, the driver has *timed out.*

title bar   The bar at the top of a program or document window that shows you what its title is. The control menu, maximize, minimize, restore, and task bar buttons can be accessed in the title bar.

token ring   A network type developed by IBM. It is more expensive than Ethernet to implement, but can run at 16 Mb/s. Unlike Ethernet, where the workstations must listen for a clear line before transmitting, workstations on a token ring take turns sending data—passing the "token"—from station to station to indicate whose turn it is.

toolbar   A collection of buttons that typically make the more common tools for an application easily accessible. Although often grouped in a line under the menus, a toolbar can be located on the left or right side of the working area—or even be relocatable to any area of the screen the user wishes. In some applications (for example, MS Office applications such as Word), the toolbar is user-configurable—the user can display different toolbars, and add or remove tool buttons from the bar.

topology   The layout or design of cabling on a network.

TrueType fonts   A font technology developed by Microsoft in response to Adobe's success in the scaleable font business with its own Type 1 and Type 3 PostScript fonts. Used as a simple means for all Windows applications to have access to a wide selection of fonts for screen and printer output. TrueType fonts greatly simplify using fonts on a Windows computer. The same fonts can be used on Windows 3.1, Windows NT, Windows 95, and other Windows products, such as Windows for Workgroups. Consisting of two files (one for screen and one for printer), hundreds of TrueType fonts are available from a variety of manufacturers. Depending on your printer, the TrueType font manager internal to Windows, in conjunction with the printer driver, generates either bitmapped or downloadable soft fonts.

twisted pair   Cabling that consists of lightly insulated copper wire, twisted into pairs and bundled into sets of pairs. The twists enhance the wire's capability to resist "crosstalk" (bleeding of signal from one wire to the next). This cabling is used extensively in phone systems and LANs, although even moderate distances in a LAN require "repeaters" (*see repeaters*).

U

unbound media   In a network, this refers to connections that are not implemented using traditional cabling. Instead, unbound media is wireless—implemented through use of various portions of the radio wave spectrum.

Unimodem driver   A universal modem driver supplied by Microsoft as part of Windows 95. The modem driver assumes that the modem supports the Hayes AT command set (most do).

uninstalling applications   When you install an application in Windows 95, it places the necessary files in many different places on your hard drive. You can't remove all of a program by simply erasing the contents of its main subdirectory. To uninstall the application—and remove all the files it placed on your hard drive—you must run a special program that should have been included with the application. Many applications do not include the "uninstaller" program, although, to be certified under Windows 95, the uninstaller program must be included.

Universal Naming Convention (UNC)   With UNC, you can view, copy or run files on another machine without assigning it a drive letter on your own. It also means if you are running short of logical drive letters, you can get to servers that you use only intermittently with a simple command from the MS-DOS prompt.

unprintable area   The area, usually around the extreme edges of the paper, in which the printer is incapable of printing. For example, a laser printer cannot print in the 1/4" at the left and right edges of the paper. It is important to know the unprintable area, since graphics or text you place in this area will be cut off when printed.

Upload   The act of sending a file to a remote computer (*see download*).

V

Vcache   Windows 95 uses a new 32-bit VCACHE which replaces the older SmartDrive that ran under DOS and previous versions of Windows. VCACHE uses more intelligent caching algorithms to improve the apparent speed of your hard-drive as well as your CD-ROM and 32-bit network redirectors. Unlike SmartDrive, VCACHE dynamically allocates itself. Based on the amount of free system memory, VCACHE allocates or deallocates memory used by the cache.

vector fonts   A set of lines that connect points to form characters.

video for windows   A set of utilities and protocols for implementing full-motion video in Windows 95.

virtual machine   A "logical" computer that exists inside a PC. Multiple virtual machines can be running in a PC. Applications that run on one virtual machine are unlikely to affect the applications running on a different virtual machine. 16-bit applications (for example, Windows 3.1 applications) all run on the same virtual machine in Windows 95, thus, if one crashes, it is likely to make the rest of the 16-bit applications unusable as well. However, such an occurrence will likely not affect 32-bit applications that are running simultaneously.

virtual memory   The use of permanent media (for example, hard drive) to simulate additional RAM (*see swap file*). This allows large applications to run in less physical RAM than they normally would require. When RAM runs low, the operating system uses a virtual memory manager program to temporarily store data on the hard disk like it was in RAM, which makes RAM free for data manipulation. When needed, the data is read back from the disk and reloaded into RAM.

virus   A virus is a computer program written to interrupt or destroy your work. A virus may do something as innocuous as display a message, or something as destructive as reformatting your hard drive—or almost anything in between. Your computer can "catch" a virus from a floppy disk, or even from a file downloaded from a remote source, such as a BBS. Once your computer has become "infected", the virus may spread via connections on a network or floppy disks you share with others. A variety of virus-detecting software exists, (including one packaged with Windows 95).

ViSCA   A protocol for daisy chaining up to seven video devices together and connecting them to a single serial port.

volume   Disk partition(s) formatted and available for use by the operating system.

volume label   The identifier for a volume (*see volume*) or disk. This is specified when formatting the volume or disk.

W

wallpaper   A backdrop for the Windows desktop, made up of a graphics file. The graphics can be either *centered*, appearing only once in the center of the desktop, or *tiled*, repeating as many times as the graphic will fit.

WAV files Named for a three-character extension .WAV (for sound wave) these files have, a WAV file is a file containing a digitized sound. Depending on the sampling rate and resolution, the sound recorded in the WAV file seems realistic (provided you have the sound card and speakers to hear it). These files can be quite large, running into the multi-megabyte range for high-quality recordings.

Web browser A software program that enables you to view Home pages and retrieve information from the Internet.

What's This? A new feature of Windows 95 Help. In a dialog box, click the small button with a question mark (?) on it. Then, click where you want help. A small description should pop up to explain what the item is and how to use it. Click in the description popup to remove it.

Winpopup Winpopup is an applet that is included in the Accessories group when you install the network component of Windows 95. This tool normally sends short messages from one computer on the workgroup to another (or from a shared printer to a workstation). It is designed so that when a message is received, the program will pop up over anything else on the screen and show the message.

wiring concentrator In a network, a multiple port repeating device used in Ethernet LANs to connect multiple cable segments into one LAN. Sometimes called a "hub" (*see hub*) or "multiport repeater" (see repeater), this device isolates cabling problems by separating each workstation connection on an isolated cabling segment.

wizard Microsoft's name for a step-by-step set of instructions that guide you through a particular task. For example, there are many wizards included with Windows 95 for installing new hardware, configuring the Start menu, and changing other aspects of the environment.

World Wide Web (WWW) The fastest growing part of the Internet, the "Web," or WWW, is a collection of hypertext documents. It provides access to images and sounds from thousands of different Web sites, via a special programming language called **H**yper**T**ext **M**arkup **L**anguage, or **HTML**. This language is used to create "hypertext" documents, which include embedded commands.

WordPad A program included with Windows 95 that enables you to do basic word processing and save the results in plain text format, Word 6 format, or Rich Text Format.

word wrap   In word processing, this refers to words that cannot be completed on one line automatically "wrapping" to the beginning of the next line. Most word processors use word wrap automatically—an exception is Notepad, where you must turn on word wrap.

workgroup   A collection of networked PCs grouped to facilitate work that users of the computers tend to do together. The machines are not necessarily in the same room or office.

WYSIWYG   Short for "What you see is what you get," this term refers to the ability of an application to display an accurate representation of the printed output on the screen.

X

x coordinate   The position of an item relative to the left side of the screen. Values increase as you move to the right.

Xmodem   An error-correction protocol (*see binary transfer protocol*) used by the DOS application XMODEM and many other communications programs. Xmodem using CRC (cyclical redundancy check), a means of detecting errors in transmissions between modems or across wired serial links.

Y

y coordinate   The position of an item relative to the bottom of the screen. Values increase as you move down the screen.

Ymodem   Another form of Xmodem that allows batch transfers of files and (in Ymodem G) hardware error control.

Z

Zmodem   ZModem is a full functional streaming protocol where XModem is a send and acknowledge protocol which causes delays in the transfer equal to twice the modem lag on a connection. ZModem is the preferred was of exchanging data since it is reliable, quick, and relatively easy to implement.

Index

Symbols

^ (caret) wild card character, 166
* (asterisk) wild card character, 166
+ (plus sign) wild card character, 166
< (less than sign) merge operator, 377
<= (less than or equal to) merge operator, 377
= (equal to) merge operator, 377
> (greater than sign) merge operator, 377
>= (greater than or equal to sign) merge operator, 377
? (question mark) wild card character, 166
| (vertical bar) delimiter, 356
~ (tilde) delimiter, 356
¶ (paragraph mark), displaying/hiding, 88
... (ellipsis), defined, 576
16-bit applications, 563
16550A UART chip, 563
32-bit applications, 563

A

accelerator keys, 563
activating, defined, 563

active
  printer, 563
  windows, 563
Add SmartCorrect Entry dialog box, 71
address books, 564
addresses on envelopes, changing, 207
Adobe Type Manager (ATM)
  defined, 564
  fonts, 465
Advanced Program-to-Program Communications (APPC), defined, 564
Advanced Technology Attachment Packet Interface (ATAPI), defined, 565
airbrush, defined, 564
alert messages, defined, 564
Align command (Draw menu), 438
alignment
  CycleKey, 93
  desktop publishing, 468
    center alignment, 470
    justified text, 470-471
    left alignment, 468-470
    right alignment, 470
  drawings
    text in, 435
    objects, 438-439

frames, 389, 403, 414, 420
keyboard shortcuts, 40, 93
paragraphs, 90-94
tables, 340-341
Alignment command (Frame menu), 389
American National Standards Institute (ANSI), defined, 564
anchoring
  frames, 411-414
  tables, 340-341
    troubleshooting, 346
annotating, defined, 564
  see also comment notes; revisions
ANSI (American National Standards Institute), defined, 564
Anti Virus program, 564
anti-aliasing, defined, 564
antonyms, see Thesaurus
API (Application Programming Interface), defined, 564
APPC (Advanced Program-to-Program Communications), defined, 564
applets
  defined, 564
  Winpopup, 610
  see also Draw program

D

G

games
Hearts, 580
Minesweeper, 588
Solitaire, 603
General tab, customizing
default settings, 213-216
generating indexes,
301-303, 323
GIF (Graphic Interchange
Format) files, importing,
518
glossaries, 27, 292-295
entries, 294-295
paths, customizing
default settings, 218
Glossary command (Edit
menu), 294
Go To command (Edit
menu), 63, 127, 156-157,
291
Go To command (Help
menu), 53
Go To dialog box, 63, 157,
292
Go To feature, 157-160
troubleshooting
problems, 160
Go To Record dialog box,
363
Grammar Check bar, 185
Grammar Check
command (Edit menu),
186, 190
Grammar Check
SmartIcon, 186
Grammar Checker, 18,
185-186
defined, 171
installing, 540
option settings, 186-188
rules, 188-190
running, 190-192
see also Format Checker;
Spell Checker;
Thesaurus
Graphic Interchange
Format (GIF) files,
importing, 518

graphics
anti-aliasing, defined, 564
Bezler curve, 566
bitmap
defined, 517, 566
picons, 594
brightness, 408
clip art, defined, 570
contrast, 408
cropping, 394
data in tables, 330-331
displaying, hierarchical
structure, 581
dither pattern, 574
edge enhancement, 408
files
filters, 512
thumbnails, 606
types, 518
frames, 392-394
image properties, 406,
408-410
moving, 410
resizing, 394
scaling, 406-408
halftone, 406, 520
printing, 521-522
imported, 519-520
brightness, 520-521
contrast, 520-521
edge enhancement,
520-521
smoothing, 520-521
tables, 330-331
printing
dpi (dots per inch),
200
troubleshooting, 522
screened, 406
smoothing, 408
text in, finding, 162
troubleshooting, 522
vector, defined, 517
see also Draw program
graphs, *see* charts
greater than or equal to
sign (>=), merge operator,
377
greater than sign (>),
merge operator, 377

Grid command (Draw
menu), 439
gridlines
defined, 580
displaying/hiding
drawings, 439
table, 326
Group command (Frame
menu), 415
grouping
drawings, 432
frames, 415
gutters (columns), 400

H

half duplex systems, 576
halftone graphics, 406, 520
printing, 521-522
Halftone Printing
command (Image menu),
522
hand pointer shape, 37
handles (selection
handles), 601
handshake protocol, 580
hard returns, finding, 167
hardware
drivers, kernel drivers,
585
fonts, 80
see also components
headers
defined, 120
deleting, 124
finding (Go To feature),
157-160
information, 580
inserting, 120-124
margin settings, 122
newsletters, 453
outlines, *see* sections
printing,
troubleshooting, 123
tables
columns, 232
displaying/hiding, 326
rows, 232
heap (memory), 580
Hearts (game), 580

X-Y-Z

Complete and Return this Card
for a *FREE* Computer Book Catalog

Thank you for purchasing this book! You have purchased a superior computer book written expressly for your needs. To continue to provide the kind of up-to-date, pertinent coverage you've come to expect from us, we need to hear from you. Please take a minute to complete and return this self-addressed, postage-paid form. In return, we'll send you a free catalog of all our computer books on topics ranging from word processing to programming and the internet.

Mr. ☐   Mrs. ☐   Ms. ☐   Dr. ☐

Name (first) ☐☐☐☐☐☐☐☐☐ (M.I.) ☐ (last) ☐☐☐☐☐☐☐☐☐☐☐☐☐☐☐☐☐

Address ☐☐☐☐☐☐☐☐☐☐☐☐☐☐☐☐☐☐☐☐☐☐☐☐☐☐☐☐☐☐☐☐☐

☐☐☐☐☐☐☐☐☐☐☐☐☐☐☐☐☐☐☐☐☐☐☐☐☐☐☐☐☐☐☐☐☐

City ☐☐☐☐☐☐☐☐☐☐☐ State ☐☐ Zip ☐☐☐☐☐ ☐☐☐☐

Phone ☐☐☐ ☐☐☐☐☐☐ Fax ☐☐☐ ☐☐☐☐☐☐

Company Name ☐☐☐☐☐☐☐☐☐☐☐☐☐☐☐☐☐☐☐☐☐☐☐☐☐☐☐☐

E-mail address ☐☐☐☐☐☐☐☐☐☐☐☐☐☐☐☐☐☐☐☐☐☐☐☐☐☐☐

1. Please check at least (3) influencing factors for purchasing this book.

Front or back cover information on book .... ☐
Special approach to the content .... ☐
Completeness of content .... ☐
Author's reputation .... ☐
Publisher's reputation .... ☐
Book cover design or layout .... ☐
Index or table of contents of book .... ☐
Price of book .... ☐
Special effects, graphics, illustrations .... ☐
Other (Please specify): _____ ☐

2. How did you first learn about this book?

Saw in Macmillan Computer Publishing catalog .... ☐
Recommended by store personnel .... ☐
Saw the book on bookshelf at store .... ☐
Recommended by a friend .... ☐
Received advertisement in the mail .... ☐
Saw an advertisement in: _____ ☐
Read book review in: _____ ☐
Other (Please specify): _____ ☐

3. How many computer books have you purchased in the last six months?

This book only .... ☐   3 to 5 books .... ☐
2 books .... ☐   More than 5 .... ☐

4. Where did you purchase this book?

Bookstore .... ☐
Computer Store .... ☐
Consumer Electronics Store .... ☐
Department Store .... ☐
Office Club .... ☐
Warehouse Club .... ☐
Mail Order .... ☐
Direct from Publisher .... ☐
Internet site .... ☐
Other (Please specify): _____ ☐

5. How long have you been using a computer?

☐ Less than 6 months   ☐ 6 months to a year
☐ 1 to 3 years   ☐ More than 3 years

6. What is your level of experience with personal computers and with the subject of this book?

	With PCs	With subject of book
New	☐	☐
Casual	☐	☐
Accomplished	☐	☐
Expert	☐	☐

Source Code ISBN: 0-7897-0149-9

7. Which of the following best describes your job title?

Administrative Assistant ☐
Coordinator ☐
Manager/Supervisor ☐
Director ☐
Vice President ☐
President/CEO/COO ☐
Lawyer/Doctor/Medical Professional ☐
Teacher/Educator/Trainer ☐
Engineer/Technician ☐
Consultant ☐
Not employed/Student/Retired ☐
Other (Please specify): _____ ☐

8. Which of the following best describes the area of the company your job title falls under?

Accounting ☐
Engineering ☐
Manufacturing ☐
Operations ☐
Marketing ☐
Sales ☐
Other (Please specify): _____ ☐

9. What is your age?

Under 20 ☐
21-29 ☐
30-39 ☐
40-49 ☐
50-59 ☐
60-over ☐

10. Are you:

Male ☐
Female ☐

11. Which computer publications do you read regularly? (Please list)

_____
_____
_____
_____
_____
_____
_____
_____
_____
_____

Comments: _____
_____
_____

Fold here and scotch-tape to mail.